Translated Texts for Historians
Volume 49

NEMESIUS
On the Nature of Man

Translated with an introduction and notes by
R. W. SHARPLES and P. J. VAN DER EIJK

Liverpool
University
Press

First published 2008
Liverpool University Press
4 Cambridge Street
Liverpool, L69 7ZU

Copyright © 2008 R. W. Sharples and P. J. van der Eijk

The right of R. W. Sharples and P. J. van der Eijk to be identified
as the authors of this work has been asserted by them in accordance
with the Copyright, Designs and Patents Act, 1988

All rights reserved. No part of this book may be reproduced
stored in a retrieval system, or transmitted, in any form or
by any means, electronic, mechanical, photocopying, recording,
or otherwise, without the prior written permission of the publisher.

British Library Cataloguing-in-Publication Data
A British Library CIP Record is available.

ISBN 978-1-84631-132-1 limp

Set in Times by
Koinonia, Manchester
Printed in the European Union by
Bell and Bain Ltd, Glasgow

Translated Texts for Historians

This series is designed to meet the needs of students of ancient and medieval history and others who wish to broaden their study by reading source material, but whose knowledge of Latin or Greek is not sufficient to allow them to do so in the original language. Many important Late Imperial and Dark Age texts are currently unavailable in translation and it is hoped that TTH will help to fill this gap and to complement the secondary literature in English which already exists. The series relates principally to the period 300–800 AD and includes Late Imperial, Greek, Byzantine and Syriac texts as well as source books illustrating a particular period or theme. Each volume is a self-contained scholarly translation with an introductory essay on the text and its author and notes on the text indicating major problems of interpretation, including textual difficulties.

Editorial Committee
Sebastian Brock, Oriental Institute, University of Oxford
Averil Cameron, Keble College, Oxford
Henry Chadwick, Oxford
John Davies, University of Liverpool
Carlotta Dionisotti, King's College, London
Peter Heather, King's College, London
Robert Hoyland, University of St Andrews
William E. Klingshirn, The Catholic University of America
Michael Lapidge, Clare College, Cambridge
Robert Markus, University of Nottingham
John Matthews, Yale University
Claudia Rapp, University of California, Los Angeles
Raymond Van Dam, University of Michigan
Michael Whitby, University of Warwick
Ian Wood, University of Leeds

General Editors
Gillian Clark, University of Bristol
Mark Humphries, Swansea University
Mary Whitby, University of Liverpool

A full list of published titles in the Translated Texts for Historians series is available on request. The most recently published are shown below.

Avitus of Vienne: Letters and Selected Prose
Translated with introduction and notes by DANUTA SHANZER and IAN WOOD
Volume 38: 472pp., 2002, ISBN 0-85323-588-0

Constantine and Christendom: The Oration to the Saints, The Greek and Latin Accounts of the Discovery of the Cross, The Edict of Constantine to Pope Silvester
Translated with introduction and notes by MARK EDWARDS
Volume 39: 192pp., 2003, ISBN 0-85323-648-8

Lactantius: Divine Institutes
Translated with introduction and notes by ANTHONY BOWEN and PETER GARNSEY
Volume 40: 488pp., 2003, ISBN 0-85323-988-6

Selected Letters of Libanius from the Age of Constantius and Julian
Translated with introduction and notes by SCOT BRADBURY
Volume 41: 308pp., 2004, ISBN 0-85323-509-0

Cassiodorus: Institutions of Divine and Secular Learning and On the Soul
Translated and notes by JAMES W. HALPORN; Introduction by MARK VESSEY
Volume 42: 316 pp., 2004, ISBN 0-85323-998-3

Ambrose of Milan: Political Letters and Speeches
Translated with an introduction and notes by J. H. W. G. LIEBESCHUETZ and CAROLE HILL
Volume 43: 432pp., 2005, ISBN 0-85323-829-4

The Chronicle of Ireland
Translated with an introduction and notes by T. M. CHARLES-EDWARDS
Volume 44: 2 vols., 349pp. + 186pp., 2006, ISBN 0-85323-959-2

The Acts of the Council of Chalcedon
Translated with an introduction and notes by RICHARD PRICE and MICHAEL GADDIS
Volume 45: 3 vols., 365pp. + 312pp. + 312pp., 2005, ISBN 0-85323-039-0

Bede: On Ezra and Nehemiah
Translated with an introduction and notes by SCOTT DEGREGORIO
Volume 47: 304pp, 2006, ISBN 978-1-84631-001-0

For full details of Translated Texts for Historians, including prices and ordering information, please write to the following:
All countries, except the USA and Canada: Liverpool University Press, 4 Cambridge Street, Liverpool, L69 7ZU, UK (*Tel* +44-[0]151-794 2233, *Fax* +44-[0]151-794 2235, Email J.M. Smith@liv.ac.uk, http://www.liverpool-unipress.co.uk). **USA and Canada:** University of Chicago Press, 1427 E. 60th Street, Chicago, IL, 60637, US (*Tel* 773-702-7700, *Fax* 773-702-9756, www.press.uchicago.edu)

CONTENTS

Preface	vii
Abbreviations	ix
Introduction	1
1 The importance of Nemesius	1
2 Nemesius and the scope of his treatise	2
3 Nemesius' Christianity	5
4 Nemesius' views	7
5 Nemesius' sources	18
Nemesius, *On the Nature of Man*	
1 On the nature of man	35
2 On the soul	51
3 On the union of soul and body	78
4 On the body	87
5 On the elements	91
6 On imagination	100
7 On sight	104
8 On touch	109
9 On taste	114
10 On hearing	116
11 On smell	116
12 On thought	117
13 On memory	118
14 On immanent and expressed reason	123
15 Another division of the soul	125
16 On the non-rational part or kind of the soul, which is also called the affective and appetitive	127
17 On the desirous part	132
18 On pleasures	134
19 On distress	140

20	On anger	141
21	On fear	142
22	On the non-rational element that is not capable of obeying reason	145
23	On the nutritive faculty	145
24	On pulsation	150
25	On the generative or seminal faculty	153
26	Another division of the powers controlling living beings	157
27	On movement according to impulse or choice, which belongs to the appetitive part	158
28	On respiration	161
29	On the intentional and unintentional	168
30	On the unintentional	169
31	On the unintentional through ignorance	172
32	On the intentional	174
33	On choice	176
34	About what things do we deliberate?	180
35	On fate	184
36	On what is fated through the stars	186
37	On those who say that choice of actions is up to us	188
38	On Plato's account of fate	190
39	On what is up to us, or on autonomy	194
40	Concerning what things are up to us	197
41	For what reason were we born autonomous?	200
42	On providence	204
43	About what matters there is providence	209

Bibliography	222
Index of passages cited	235
General index	255

PREFACE

This translation is a substantially revised version of one initially prepared (but never published) by J. O. Urmson. In addition to Urmson's own draft, we have also had the benefit of Gillian Clark's comments on the earlier part of it. The revision of the translation, and the writing of the notes and sections of the Introduction that relate to sections 1–3 and 29–43, were initially undertaken by RWS, that relating to sections 4–28 by PJvdE, but we have each revised the other's work so that the result is throughout a joint production. Some of the notes are taken over from Urmson's draft. Parts of the Introduction derive from a paper given by RWS in London in March 2005 and in Leiden in May 2005, and from presentations given by PJvdE in London in November 2005, in Freiburg in July 2006, in Princeton in October 2006, in Toronto and Philadelphia in November 2006, in Budapest and Rostock in June 2007, and in Hamburg in July 2007, and we acknowledge contributions made in discussion there, as well as comments on draft translation and notes, in particular by Han Baltussen, Chris Carey, Gillian Clark, Patricia Crone, Erik Eliasson, Bill Fortenbaugh, Emma Gannagé, Jim Hankinson, Jean-Michel Hulls, David Langslow, Gert-Jan Lokhorst, Vivian Nutton, Raffaele Passarella, Peter Pormann, David Runia, Mark Schiefsky, Heinrich von Staden and Mary Whitby. PJvdE would like to acknowledge the technical support of Sarah Francis and the financial support of his contribution to this publication by the Wellcome Trust and by the Institute for Advanced Study in Princeton, where his part of the work was completed.

The translation is based on Morani's 1987 Teubner text; variations from this are noted. (We share the view of Mansfeld and Runia (1996) 292 n.4 that Morani was too ready to delete material because it is not reflected in the Armenian translation.) The apparatus of parallels in Morani (1987) and that in Verbeke and Moncho (1975) has been of very considerable assistance to us in preparing the notes, as have the translation and the comments in Telfer (1955) and the discussion in Streck (2005). Telfer's notes were written from the perspective of a specialist in patristics. Neither of us is an expert in this field; our specialisms are in pagan Greek philosophy and, in the case of PJvdE, in ancient Greek medicine. Given Nemesius' extensive dependence on pagan philosophical and medical sources, these areas of expertise do not seem inappropriate for commenting on his work. However, those whose interest in Nemesius' treatise is primarily in his place in the history of Christian theology and in his views – explicit or implied – on matters of Christian doctrine should also consult Telfer and other relevant literature in our Bibliography.

In giving translations of passages from other ancient authors cited in the notes we have been guided by several more or less pragmatic considerations; the importance of full quotation for the point being made, the amount of text that would need to be quoted, and the accessibility of the text in translation. For the last-mentioned reason full quotations are given of some medical texts in particular. We have not, except where it seemed particularly important to do so, quoted in full those parallel texts which are accessible in the Loeb Classical Library or in the Ancient Commentators on Aristotle series edited by Richard Sorabji; nor have we quoted passages which are included in standard sourcebooks such as Long and Sedley, *The Hellenistic Philosophers* (LS – see our Abbreviations and Bibliography) or Sorabji, *The Philosophy of the Commentators* (2004), to which we have instead given references.

The summaries in italics at the start of individual chapters or connected groups of chapters are our own; they are not part of the original text.

PJvdE, RWS
Newcastle and London,
April 2007

ABBREVIATIONS

ACO Acta Conciliorum Oecumenicorum, 1.1, ed. E. Schwartz, Berlin: De Gruyter, 1928
CAG Commentaria in Aristotelem Graeca, Berlin: Reimer, 1882–1907
DK H. Diels, ed. W. Kranz, Die Fragmente der Vorsokratiker, 10th ed., Berlin 1952
GCS Die griechischen Christlichen Schriftsteller der ersten Jahrhunderte, Berlin 1897–
K (in references to Galen) Galeni Opera Omnia, ed. C.G. Kühn, Leipzig: Knobloch, 1821–1833
L (in references to Hippocrates) Hippocrates, Oeuvres complètes, ed. É. Littré, Paris: Baillière, 1839–1861
LS A.A. Long and D.N. Sedley, The Hellenistic Philosophers, Cambridge 1987.
PG Migne, Patrologia Graeca
PL Migne, Patrologia Latina
RE Pauly-Wissowa, Real-Encyklopädie der Altertumswissenschaft
RUSCH Rutgers University Studies in Classical Humanities
SVF H. von Arnim, Stoicorum Veterum Fragmenta, Leipzig, Teubner, 1903–1924

INTRODUCTION

1. THE IMPORTANCE OF NEMESIUS

Nemesius' treatise *On the Nature of Man* is an important text for historians of ancient thought, not only as a much-quarried source of evidence for earlier works now lost, but also as an indication of intellectual life in the late fourth century AD. The author was a Christian bishop; the subject is the nature of human beings and their place in the scheme of created things, and this topic is interpreted in the broadest possible way to include everything from detailed physiological functioning to the question of divine providential concern for mankind. The medical works of Galen and the philosophical writings of Plato, Aristotle and the Neoplatonist Porphyry are all major influences on Nemesius, directly or indirectly; so too the controversial Christian Origen. Both for Platonists and Aristotelians and for Christians human beings are made up of a body and a soul; the relation between the two is therefore a key theme running through Nemesius' discussion.

Nemesius advances his views in a Christian context, and engages in debate with other Christians; but he explicitly designs the work to appeal to pagans as well as to Christians, and draws examples and arguments both from Greek traditions and from Biblical texts. He makes extensive use of pagan philosophical sources in such a way that his text is not only evidence for pagan debates but also a contribution to them in its own right. On some issues, such as the origin of the human soul and the limitations of human agency, his relation to orthodox Christian thought has seemed questionable, at least with hindsight; and the question arises how far this is to be connected with the influence of his pagan sources – or better, with the influence of pagan thought on the intellectual framework within which he develops his views; for Nemesius is not a mere scissors-and-paste compiler of earlier material, and indeed shows a concern to be up-to-date in matters of medicine, philosophy and theology alike. More than most other prose writings from later antiquity, Nemesius' work sits on the borderline between pagan and Christian cultures, and thus has a part to play in raising questions about the relation between them. It was itself used as a source by medieval writers, influenced in part by misattributions of all or part of the work to Gregory of Nyssa, and translated into Syriac, Arabic, Armenian, Georgian and Latin.

2. NEMESIUS AND THE SCOPE OF HIS TREATISE

The author of the treatise was bishop of Emesa in Syria.[1] It seems to have been written towards the end of the fourth century CE. References to the Christian writers Apollinaris, Eunomius and Theodore of Mopsuestia all suggest a late fourth century date;[2] there is no reference to the condemnation of Origen, in 399 in Alexandria, 400 in Rome,[3] and his writings are apparently used as a source (below, Introduction 5.a.1); on the other hand his views are also criticised, which may be a tacit reaction to the condemnation.[4] A Nemesius was governor of Cappadocia 383–389, was interested in philosophy and discussed Christianity with Gregory of Nazianzus;[5] it has been suggested that he may have been identical with our author and that he may have converted to Christianity late in life,[6] but it would be rash to couple this with our author's evident interest in pagan philosophical literature and argue from it that his Christianity was therefore superficial, attractive though

---

1 So the heading in the majority of the principal MSS.

2 Quasten (1975) 353–54; see the Index for references to these authors. Apollinaris was bishop of Laodicea from 362 and died in 392; Eunomius died c. 393; Theodore of Mopsuestia died in 428 (Skard [1940] 562). (All dates in the present book are CE unless otherwise indicated.)

3 Telfer (1955) 206.

4 Telfer (1955) 303 n.7. This, however, seems to be the only argument for dating the treatise as late as 400, which Quasten (see n.2 above) regards as the latest possible date on the grounds that there is no explicit reference to the condemnation of Origen. He also points out that Eunomius and Apollinaris, apparently referred to as contemporaries, both died in the early 390s. A later date still has been suggested on the basis both of a supposed reference to Nestorius (see below, n.414) and of the occurrence of the formula, employed at the Council of Chalcedon in 451, 'without being confounded' (below, n.372); but the arguments in both cases are weak. Ferro (1925, 227–28) argues that the lack of references to fifth-century heresies is a strong argument against a mid-fifth-century date, and suggests (238, cf. 228) that Nemesius may have transferred from pagan psychology to Christian theology the formula that was later used at Chalcedon. Zeller (1903, 509 n.1) used the argument from the Chalcedonian formula, but he did so in order to argue for a mid-fifth-century date as opposed to an even later *sixth*-century one.

5 Gregory of Nazianzus, *Letters* 198–201 Gallay; *Poems to Other Persons* 7, *PG* 37 1551–1577.

6 Telfer (1955) 208–09.

we may find Telfer's suggestion that he had not had time to develop a taste for theological hatred.[7] Our author's medical knowledge has been judged to be that of an educated layman, not of a former practitioner.[8]

Nemesius begins his treatise with a discussion of man's place in the hierarchical order of beings in the universe (section 1). He then considers the human soul and its relation to the body in general terms (sections 2–3), followed by issues relating to physiology, psychology and the emotions (sections 4–28). This leads to a discussion of voluntary action, and thence to fate, providence and God's government of the universe (sections 29–43). The presence of these last topics may seem surprising, but they mark a return to the consideration of the universe as a whole which was also the background to the first section, and there is an interesting parallel in the consideration of fate and responsibility at the end of a collection of originally separate texts, composed around two centuries before Nemesius, which has been arranged in a way that broadly reflects the structure of Aristotle's treatise *On the Soul*, namely Alexander's *Supplement* or *Mantissa*.[9] In the Greco-Roman world, to consider man without reference to his place in the whole scheme of things would have seemed artificial;[10] and the discussion of voluntary action is explicitly presented as a development of the account of psychological functions.[11]

Is the work complete? Section 42 promises an account of creation, and section 43 refers to further discussion of Democritus, Heraclitus and Epicurus; neither of these appears in the treatise as we have it, and it ends with a series of arguments on how wicked deeds can serve a providential purpose, with no apparent attempt at any summing-up or rhetorical conclusion. In section 13, 69.15–16, an explanation of the Platonic Forms is promised but never appears; this, however, is double-edged, for it suggests

7 Telfer (1955) 210.
8 Telfer (1955) 206–08.
9 We need not therefore suppose, with Telfer (1955, 211) that the discussion of fate and providence was a later addition to the original plan reflecting Nemesius' conversion to Christianity. Koch (1921, 23) argues that the structure of sections 15–25 is basically Aristotelian.
10 Verbeke and Moncho (1975, lxii-lxiii) connect Nemesius' discussion of these topics with the fact that he is writing for pagans and wishes to demonstrate his command of pagan learning, and draw a contrast with Gregory of Nyssa's *On the Creation of Man* for which the agenda is set by the treatment in Genesis. The latter point seems correct even if the former is debatable (see below, 3.a). They also note that, compared to Aristotle in his *On the Soul*, Nemesius concentrates on freedom, fate and providence rather than on epistemology, and connect this with the prominence of these topics in Nemesius' time.
11 Below, n. 869.

that we are dealing not with a treatise missing its intended conclusion but rather with one containing various loose ends.

The second and third sections, on the nature of the soul in general and its relation to the body, also exist in the form of a separate treatise attributed to Gregory of Nyssa;[12] the work as a whole is sometimes attributed to him in the MSS.[13] It is not our intention, here or in our notes, to give a full account of the later influence of Nemesius' treatise,[14] but, to assist readers who may encounter references to the following works elsewhere, we note the following. Nemesius' treatise was extensively excerpted by John of Damascus (c.660–750) in his *On the Orthodox Faith*[15] and by Meletius (*On the Nature of Man,* 7th–9th century),[16] and also by Anastasius of Sinai (7th century),[17] Maximus Confessor (7th century),[18] Nilus Doxopatres (11th century)[19] and Michael Glycas (12th century).[20] It was translated into Armenian (c. 717),[21] Syriac (surviving only in later excerpts), Arabic (attributed to Gregory of Nyssa)[22] and Georgian,[23] and into Latin by Alfanus (11th century),[24] Burgundio of Pisa (1165),[25] Giorgio Valla (15th century: published at Lyons in 1538), Iohannes Cono (Strasbourg, 1512) and Nicasius Ellebodius (Antwerp, 1565).[26]

---

12 *PG* 45 128–221.
13 Cf. Morani (1991) vi–vii (MSS A and K); so too in the Armenian and Arabic versions. Streck (2005, 183–92) compares and contrasts the views of Nemesius and the genuine Gregory.
14 See the various studies by Dobler (e.g. 1950, 2001 and 2002) on the influence of Nemesius on Thomas Aquinas.
15 See Morani (1981) 104–14.
16 Morani (1981) 132–50.
17 *Questions and Answers,* in *PG* 89. Morani (1981) 121–25.
18 *Minor works, to Marinus* and *Book of Questionable Points,* in *PG* 91. Morani (1981) 101–04.
19 See Morani (1981) 127–32.
20 *Annals,* in *PG* 128. Morani (1981) 125–26.
21 Attributed to Gregory of Nyssa (Morani [1981] 68).
22 Nemesius' treatise was also summarised in the Arabic [Apollonius of Tyana], *Book on the Secrets of Nature and the Hidden Causes of Things,* ed. Weisser (1979).
23 See Morani (1981) 88.
24 Edited in Burkhard (1917).
25 Edited in Verbeke and Moncho (1975).
26 See Verbeke and Moncho (1975) lxxxvi–c.

3. NEMESIUS' CHRISTIANITY

3.a. Paganism and Christianity

Nemesius makes it clear that he is preaching not only to Christians, but also to the unconverted, who will be persuaded by philosophical argument rather than by Biblical authority.[27] He draws heavily on pagan philosophical sources, sometimes identified and sometimes not. But he also cites Christian writers, supports his arguments by Biblical quotations, and in discussions of specific issues tends to move from a review of pagan opinions to a discussion of what he regards as the proper Christian position. Some of his points would not be comprehensible to pagans who did not have at least some knowledge of the New Testament.[28] At the end of section 2 he appeals to scripture for the immortality of the soul, referring to the difficulty of Plato's arguments; one may perhaps here suspect a degree of weariness at the end of what is already a very long discussion of the nature of the soul. In section 3 he puts forward an account of how an incorporeal soul can be present in, and affect, a physical body that depends upon a favourite Neoplatonist analogy, that of light, and concludes by arguing that the combination of divine and human in Christ can be explained in the same way. Telfer notes that, whereas most Christian writers use discussion of the relation between soul and body in every human being to support their account of the Incarnation, in Nemesius the Incarnation is cited to support the general argument about body and soul.[29] While this may be formally true, it is surely also deliberate that the structure of his discussion enables Nemesius to build up to the Incarnation as the climax of the first three sections of his treatise.[30] One remarkable feature in a Christian writer is the reference to 'the first God' at 18, 79.16; this may have slipped in from a pagan source, or Nemesius may intend his readers to understand that he is still reporting the Aristotelian view in Aristotelian terms, but if the latter is the case he has hardly made the point clear.

As we will see in part 4 of this Introduction, Nemesius' allegiance, in terms of pagan thought, is above all to Platonism, which is to be expected both in view of his date and in view of his Christianity; there is considerable dependence on Aristotle, especially in the more technical discussions of soul functions, and on Galen in the more medical and physiological parts of the

---

27 2, 38.7–9, 42, 120.21–23 Morani.
28 Cf. 43, 134.8–12.
29 Below, n.406.
30 See, however, Streck (2005, 35 n.84), emphasising the anthropological rather than the Christological aspect.

work. More controversial is how Nemesius' Platonism is to be classified; he refers to Neoplatonists such as Porphyry and Iamblichus, but much of his Platonism shows strong affinities with the so-called 'Middle Platonism' of the period before Plotinus. The situation is made more complicated by the facts that the boundaries between Middle Platonism and Neoplatonism are not hard and fast ones, and that the position of Porphyry in particular in this regard is a complicated one. See further below, Introduction §5.

3.b. Christian doctrine

Nemesius engages in controversy with a number of his Christian predecessors and contemporaries. Although he makes use of Origen's works, he rejects Origen's view that even Satan may be pardoned; man alone, for Nemesius, is capable of repentance (1, 9.22–10.21). He also rejects Origen's account of the destiny of the soul (3, 44.19–21). He accepts (2, 30.18–32.19) – though without mentioning him by name – Origen's view that souls exist before bodies, rather than the alternatives that they are created by God at the same time as bodies (Eunomius) or inherited from parents (Apollinaris); however, he does so not because he shares Origen's view that souls descend into bodies as punishments, but rather to preserve the imperishability of the soul.[31] His use of the concept of relation in a Christological context (3, 41.14–42.11) is shared with Theodore of Mopsuestia and, later, Nestorius; the doctrine was attacked by Cyril of Alexandria.[32] On the other hand Nemesius rejects Theodore's view that the unification of soul and body in Christ was due to divine consent (3, 44.15–16). He rejects Apollinaris' view that man is tripartite, made up of body, soul and spirit,[33] and argues against the Manichaean view that individual souls are all parts of a single universal soul (2, 32.20–33.19).

Nemesius engages in polemic against *Christians* (presumably) who had appealed to the Old Testament in an argument against human autonomy.[34]

---

31 Verbeke and Moncho (1975, xlvii and nn.65–68), contrasting Nemesius' view with that of Gregory of Nyssa (*On the Creation of Man* 38, PG 44 229bc, 235b) that the body and soul of each individual are created at the same time but that human beings pre-exist in divine providence. In the sixteenth century Ellebodius identified the pre-existence of the soul as the one point on which Nemesius diverged from orthodoxy; Verbeke and Moncho (1975) xcviii.
32 Below, n.401.
33 See n.185; also n.373.
34 40, 115.17–21.

His insistence on human autonomy has led to suspicions of Pelagianism.[35] He does not mention divine grace as necessary for salvation,[36] but equally does not mention salvation by works either.[37] The absence of a clear position on the Pelagian controversy is to be explained by the fact that his interests in this work lie elsewhere, and in particular that he is writing for pagans as well as for Christians[38] – though this is not to say that his insistence on human autonomy does not create other philosophical and theological problems.[39] His emphasis is on human responsibility for practical action, with little reference to asceticism;[40] nor, as Streck notes, does he relate the individual to the common life of the Church.[41]

Verbeke (1971) asks whether Nemesius' Platonism compromises his Christianity. In addition to the issues already mentioned, concerning human autonomy and the pre-existence of the soul, it may be argued that his treatment of the body as inferior to the soul is a Platonising distortion of original Christian thought – but one in which Nemesius is far from alone, both in antiquity and in more recent times.[42]

4. NEMESIUS' VIEWS

4.a. The soul

4.a.1. Its nature in general

In section 1 Nemesius argues for the view that man is composed of body and soul, against the more complex analyses of Plotinus and Apollinaris. The

---

35 See Domański (1900) 161–63 n.1; Koch (1921) 44; Siclari (1974) 241–43; Streck (2005) 9–17, 117–19, 189, 196–97.

36 Except in passing at 1, 7.8–9 (cf. 10.11, and Streck [2005] 110 n.351).

37 Unless implicitly at 1, 6.6–10 and 18–20? But it is one thing to describe salvation, as Nemesius here does, as involving human beings' choice and progress, another to say explicitly either that these are entirely their responsibility or that they are only possible for fallen human souls through divine grace; and Nemesius does not do either of the latter. Streck (2005, 183–92) emphasises Nemesius' and Gregory of Nyssa's *optimistic* view of mankind.

38 Cf. Domański (1900) and Siclari (1974); Telfer (1955) 215–16; Streck (2005) 117–19. Koch (1921) takes a different view, arguing that Theodore of Mopsuestia held Pelagian views and that Nemesius may have shared them; but against the interpretation of Theodore as a Pelagian see Quasten (1975) 419.

39 Below, Introduction 4.c.

40 Streck (2005) 39, 187. See below, n.979.

41 Streck (2005) 191.

42 Cf. the (deliberately provocative?) discussion in Findlay (1982) and the comments of Sharples (1984) citing *inter alia* Robinson (1977, 39–53). Nemesius' remarks on the contemplative's being unmoved by worldly affairs may also, as Gillian Clark points out to us, owe more to the pagan philosophical tradition than to Christianity; see below, nn. 701 and 979.

soul is superior to the body and uses it as an instrument, a view for which Nemesius cites Plato. In the hierarchy of beings man is on the boundary between the mortal and the immortal;[43] he can prefer either aspect of his nature, as happened in the Fall and as can happen even now, for man alone is capable of repenting and being pardoned. With the exception of the reference to the Biblical Fall, there is little here that would not be equally acceptable to at least some pagan Platonists; true, Plato himself and some of his followers accepted transmigration of human souls into animals, which complicates the picture, but Nemesius at the end of section 2 cites the pagan Neoplatonist Iamblichus as rejecting this. In this context Nemesius observes how animal, as opposed to human, behaviour is as we might say 'hard-wired'.[44] As Verbeke and Moncho observe (1975, liv) it is remarkable that, while rejecting transmigration into animals, Nemesius says nothing in explicit rejection of transmigration of souls from one human body into another.

In section 2 Nemesius rejects pagan philosophical views both of the soul as corporeal, and of it as incorporeal but non-substantial; the latter include the harmony theory criticised in Plato's *Phaedo* and the Galenic theory that soul is a mixture of the bodily elements.[45] Again, his discussion draws heavily on Platonist sources, and his basic position is one that would be equally acceptable to pagan Platonists. With Plato, against Aristotle, he argues for soul being self-moving;[46] and, as already mentioned, in section 3 he follows the Neoplatonists in using the notion of relation and the parallel with light to explain how an immaterial soul can be united with, but not affected by, an immaterial body. The related Neoplatonist (and earlier) idea that the sun is not polluted by the objects on which it shines is also used by Nemesius in controversy over divine providence in section 43.[47] In the context of Christian doctrine, Nemesius' rejection both of the view that souls are created by God at the same time as bodies and of the view that they are inherited from parents (above, 3b) reflects an insistence that the soul, even though not in the strict sense eternal, has existed from the beginning of the world and will exist for ever.[48] This does not, however, imply acceptance

43 See below, n.214.
44 See n.363.
45 Verbeke and Moncho (1975, l–li) point out that some Christians – including Tertullian and Arnobius – regarded the human soul as corporeal.
46 Aristotle allows that soul is self-moving only accidentally, soul being moved along with the body: *Physics* 8.6 259b16–20.
47 43, 131.12–16.
48 2, 30.22, 32.12. Verbeke and Moncho (1975, xlv n.55; cf. xlvii) connect this with Nemesius' adherence to the principle that what is generated will also perish; it would be more accurate to say that he insists that to be imperishable souls must be part of the initial generation

INTRODUCTION 9

of Origen's view of the descent of the soul.[49]

Nemesius' view of the soul is essentially Platonist. He insists on the distinction between soul and body, the superiority of the former to the latter, and its ability to exist without it; but he also requires an explanation of the connection between soul and body.[50]

4.a.2. Its faculties

Having dealt with the soul and its relationship to the body, and having defined the body as the soul's 'instrument' (*organon*), Nemesius turns to a discussion of the specific 'powers' or 'faculties' (*dunameis*) of the soul and the relevant bodily parts that serve as their 'instruments' (*organa*). The latter are consistently regarded from the viewpoint of their suitability to the unimpeded exercise of the psychic functions for which they are intended;[51] and thus a teleological perspective on bodily parts, similar to Aristotle's *On the Parts of Animals* and Galen's *On the Usefulness of the Parts*, is maintained throughout, which complements the discussion of soul functions.

As to the latter, Nemesius is aware of the diversity of opinions among earlier thinkers on the division and classification of faculties of the soul. He mentions several different methods of classification without stating which ones are superior or inferior, the only exception being his preference for Panaetius' division of faculties 'of the soul' and faculties of 'nature' over Zeno's classification into eight different faculties;[52] for the rest, he seems to treat these divisions as broadly complementary. He begins in section 6 with a threefold division between 'imagination' (*phantastikon*), 'reason' (*dianoêtikon*, 12) and 'memory' (*mnêmoneutikon*, 13), with reason being presented as superior to sensation, imagination and a fourth faculty, 'movement according to impulse'.[53] He discusses the five senses – vision, touch, taste,

---

of the world – which is indeed the implication of Plato, *Timaeus* 41ab; and cf. Nemesius' insistence against Eunomius that divine creation all took place at the *beginning* of the world (2 31.26). See Streck (2005) 31–32 and n.68.

49 3, 44.19–21; Streck (2005) 32.

50 Verbeke and Moncho (1975) xii; cf. Streck (2005) 34–35. At lvi–lvii Verbeke and Moncho represent Nemesius as occupying, with the aid of the Neoplatonist account, a middle position between Platonic dualism and the Aristotelian immanence of the soul. But this may be to represent Plato's own dualism in too extreme a fashion; the Neoplatonists certainly thought they were interpreting Plato, and it is not clear that their interpretation was a misrepresentation of his position on this issue.

51 5, 55.1.

52 15, 72.7–9.

53 6, 57.8–10; 'movement according to impulse' is discussed more extensively later on in section 27; see also note 803.

hearing and smell – as subordinate to imagination (7–11). In each case, he explicitly considers the physical location and bodily 'instruments' involved in the exercise of the respective functions: for imagination and sensation, these are the front cavities of the brain, the 'psychic pneuma' that these contain, the relevant nerves growing out of these cavities and the sense-organs themselves;[54] in the case of thought, it is the central cavity of the brain and the psychic pneuma contained there;[55] and in the case of memory, it is the posterior cavity of the brain and the psychic pneuma residing there.[56]

This division is clearly concerned with the cognitive functions of the soul only and is broadly Aristotelian in its psychological and Galenic in its physiological detail. But in section 14 Nemesius introduces a new division within the rational part of the soul using the Stoic distinction between 'immanent' and 'expressed' reason and their respective organs; and in 15 he considers yet another division of soul functions, presented as a combination of Stoic (Panaetius) and Aristotelian thinking, according to 'nutritive and affective', 'sensitive' and 'reasoning' functions and thus accommodating also the non-cognitive aspects of the soul.[57] Interestingly, Nemesius shows himself aware here of a problem that still bothers students of Aristotelian psychology,[58] viz. the differences in divisions of soul functions between Aristotle's works on natural philosophy (including *On the Soul* and *Parva Naturalia*), which distinguish between the nutritive, sensitive, locomotive, appetitive and rational parts of the soul, and the *Ethics*, which distinguishes (1.13) between rational (*logon ekhon*) and non-rational (*alogon*) parts of the soul. Nemesius adopts this distinction but goes further in subdividing the latter into two constituent parts, a part that is capable of being controlled by reason and a part that is not (15, 72.19–20), with the part that is capable of being controlled by reason being further subdivided by Nemesius into two, viz. 'spirit' (*thumos*) and 'desire' (*epithumia*: 17, 75.9).The latter subdivision goes beyond what is found in Aristotle himself and is, fundamentally, a rearrangement of the Platonic tripartition of the soul that was also adopted by Galen in his work *On the Doctrines of Hippocrates and Plato*, possibly following Posidonius.[59]

---

54 6, 56.2–4; 7, 59.7–10; 8, 65.24; 9, 66,7; 10, 67.7. On the concept of 'psychic pneuma' see note 505; on the location of cognitive functions in the brain see note 544.
55 12, 68.11–13.
56 13, 69.18–20.
57 15, 72.9–17.
58 15, 72.17–18.
59 See Vander Waerdt (1985).

In the subsequent discussion (16–21), Nemesius dwells at length on what we would regard as the 'emotive' part of the human psyche, the area of the 'affections' (*pathê*), pleasures and forms of distress, anger and fear. The framework is again broadly Aristotelian/Peripatetic, with Stoic distinctions inserted. The medical, Galenic strand of thinking becomes dominant in the subsequent discussion of functions related to the non-rational part of the soul which is not subject to reason such as nutrition, pulsation and reproduction (23–25). And in the course of this discussion, some of these faculties turn out to be not functions of soul (*psukhê*) but rather of nature (*phusis*),[60] for Nemesius follows the division between psychic, natural and vital functions[61] – a distinction that, again, is found in Galen but that has antecedents in Hellenistic philosophy (esp. Stoicism) and medicine (especially Erasistratus). The discussion is concluded by an account of 'movement according to impulse' and of respiration, both of which present examples of what Nemesius, again following Galen, calls 'combined' (*sumpeplegmena*) functions of soul and nature,[62] since they operate partly independently of rational control, partly as a result of conscious will power. As such, Nemesius' physiological treatment of soul functions prepares the ground for the discussion of free will in the next part of the treatise.

4.b. The body and medicine

Nemesius devotes a remarkable amount of attention to the human body, especially to what we would now call physiology, i.e. the key functions and activities of the body and its parts, such as nutrition, digestion, reproduction, pulsation and respiration. (By contrast, the work is less elaborate on anatomical detail.) This is in accordance with what the title of the work suggests, for 'On the Nature of Man' was, ever since the Hippocratic treatise with that name, the standard heading for discussions of the structure, constitution and workings of the human body. The title is attested also for Democritus, Diogenes of Apollonia, Prodicus, Strato, Zeno the Stoic and for late antique authors such as Vindicianus; and Nemesius' 'programme' roughly corresponds to what we find in the Hippocratic works *On Fleshes, On Places in Man*, Aristotle's *On the Soul* and *Parva Naturalia*, and book 4 of Lucretius' *On the Nature of Things*. Following a systematic order of topics developed by Galen, Nemesius discusses in ascending order the physical structure

60 This distinction had been anticipated in 6, 57.7–15.
61 22, 82.21–22.
62 27, 88,25; 28, 90.12.

and constitution of the body, its elements and elementary qualities, the four humours, the homogeneous and heterogeneous parts, the 'mixtures' and the various psycho-physical faculties. This is in accordance with the purpose of the work as stated in the first sentence, viz. to show that the connection between soul and body in the human species is as good as it possibly can be and that the bodily parts are all carefully designed for the 'psychic' purposes they are meant to serve.

In dealing with this material, Nemesius makes extensive use of medical ideas, especially (though not exclusively) those of Galen. This is not to say, of course, that he had medical experience of his own, for it was quite possible throughout antiquity, and especially in late antiquity, for a layman to possess extensive medical knowledge, as is witnessed by authors such as Plutarch, Lucian, Philostratus and others. And certainly other early Christian authors such as Clement of Alexandria, Origen, Eusebius, Basil, Gregory of Nyssa, Ambrose, Philoponus and Augustine all reflect, to varying degrees, sometimes remarkably detailed medical knowledge.[63] Yet the question of how Nemesius compares to other Christian authors seems to be more than just a matter of degree. For no other Christian author earlier than the fifth century can be shown to follow Galen so closely, often verbatim, and to possess such detailed knowledge – whether directly or indirectly – of a considerable number of Galen's works. Nemesius mentions Galen's name six times – once calling him 'the marvellous physician'[64] – and he refers explicitly to Galen's works *On Mixtures*,[65] *On Simple Medicines*,[66] *On the Usefulness of the Parts*[67] and *On the Doctrines of Hippocrates and Plato*, the latter being referred to by him as 'the Agreement' i.e. between Hippocrates and Plato.[68] In addition, Nemesius refers to and cites from a work by Galen which we no longer have, the treatise *On Demonstration*,[69] and he seems well aware – without mentioning the treatises by name – of the contents of Galen's *That the Faculties of the Soul follow the Mixtures of the Body*,[70] *On*

---

63 See von Harnack (1892); Gossel (1908); Leven (1987); Wallace-Hadrill (1968); Schulze and Ihm (2002); Boudon-Millot and Pouderon (2005); van der Eijk (2005a) 4–5.
64 2, 37.10. For this expression cf. Oribasius, *To Eunapius*, pr 1.5.
65 2, 24.15.
66 2, 24.20–21.
67 2, 37.12: the reference is to 'the first book'.
68 7, 58.15: the reference is to 'the seventh book'.
69 2, 23.25; 21, 82.7.
70 2, 24.1ff.

the *Elements according to Hippocrates*,[71] *On the Affected Parts*,[72] *On the Natural Faculties*,[73] *On Semen*,[74] *On the Movement of the Muscles*[75] and *On the Usefulness of Respiration*.[76] While some of the ideas mentioned in these works are also reflected in other authors – e.g. the long criticism of Galen's theory of soul as a mixture (*krasis*) is also attested elsewhere (e.g. in Philoponus' commentary on Aristotle's *On the Soul* 1) and may well go back to a Middle or Neoplatonist criticism of Galenic psychology – the overall impression one gets is that Nemesius knew his Galen well and used him extensively, perhaps more than some other Christian authors would have tolerated.[77] The attraction of Galen's work was obvious: it offered a teleological account of the structure and workings of the human body and its parts, showing in great detail its purposeful design and referring, in language very similar to the Christian accounts of the creation, to the craft and skill of 'the Craftsman' (*ho dêmiourgos*). Behind this is, of course, Plato's *Timaeus* – another work that had a profound influence on Christian accounts of the creation of the universe – and Galen himself makes no secret of the fact that he, too, regards himself as working within a profoundly Platonic framework. But for a Christian writer like Nemesius, Galen had the advantage of taking on board both Platonic and Aristotelian teleology while displaying much more detailed and up-to-date anatomical and physiological knowledge. That Nemesius cared about being up to date is clear enough, not only in matters of

71 Throughout sections 4 and 5 (see notes).
72 13, 70.13ff.
73 Throughout section 23 (see notes).
74 25, esp. 86.22ff.
75 Throughout section 27 (see notes).
76 Throughout section 27 (see notes).
77 In this regard, it is worth mentioning that Eusebius, himself no stranger to medical ideas (see Leven 1987), refers to a Christian group led by a certain Theodotus of Byzantium (early 3rd century CE) who were taken to task by other Christians for following Galen too closely – indeed for 'worshipping' him (*proskuneisthai*). This group, condemned as heretic for their 'Adoptionist' views on the divinity of Christ, antedates Nemesius by presumably at least a century, and we are not suggesting any historical connection between the two; but the reference serves as a good example of the enthusiastic reception Galenic ideas could enjoy in early Christian circles. For discussions of the evidence see Walzer (1947) 75–86; Spanneut (1957) 197; von Harnack (1892) 5–7. Gossel (1908, 14–29) offers a detailed examination of Ambrose's use (in his exegesis of the Biblical narrative of the creation of the world) of Galen's *On the Usefulness of the Parts*, a work also alluded to by Philoponus in his commentary *On Aristotle on the Soul* 274.8–10; there is even evidence that Philoponus wrote a commentary on this Galenic work; see van der Eijk (2005a) 134 n.371, with further references to discussions of the surviving evidence.

theological doctrine (as witnessed by his references to Eunomius and Apollinaris) but also in medical matters (see below); and for all his dependence on Galen, his attitude to the physician of Pergamon is by no means uncritical, as witnessed by his independent stance in section 2, where he criticises Galen's view of the soul as a 'mixture' with a range of arguments.

4.c. Fate and the voluntary

Nemesius insists on human autonomy and on our responsibility for our actions. His conception of what is involved in human autonomy derives ultimately from Aristotle, and is the conception of the ability to do a thing or not to do it, or to do a thing or its opposite, which Susanne Bobzien has argued is characteristic of the thought of the second century CE in particular.[78] Given that the first formulation is found in Aristotle himself,[79] the significant issue is whether the ability in question is to be understood as absolute or qualified; does autonomy involve the categorical claim 'I could have done otherwise', or only the counterfactual claim 'I could have done otherwise *if* ...' ('if I had been a different sort of person', for example).[80] Interpreters have tended to interpret Aristotle on this point in the light of their own views on whether or not responsibility is compatible with determinism. However, it is clear that by the time of Nemesius a categorical notion of autonomy had been advanced by Alexander of Aphrodisias,[81] and it seems natural to interpret Nemesius' notion of autonomy as equally non-deterministic. However that may be, two points are important for our understanding of Nemesius. First, his notion of autonomy is not that found in Neoplatonism

78 Bobzien (1998b). See below, nn. 959, 971.
79 Aristotle, *Nicomachean Ethics* 3.5 1113b7–8; cf. *Eudemian Ethics* 2.6 1223a2–9.
80 Cf. Austin (1956). In the ancient context the question is whether the issue is seen in terms of freedom from determination by external factors alone, or from that by internal factors as well (cf. Bobzien [1998a] 290; [1998b] 143), or how far internal factors are seen as something different from the choosing self (Brennan [2001] and [2005] 264–67 and 297–98). Aristotle's formulation is interpreted in terms of qualified possibility only, leading to a position in which responsibility is compatible with determinism, by (for example) Fine (1981) 578; Meyer (1993) and (1998); and Bobzien herself (1998b) 144.
81 Though even this is controversial. See Frede (1984) and the reply at Sharples (1987b). Boys-Stones (2007) interprets the Middle-Platonist doctrine of conditional fate (below, at n.100) as compatible with determinism; but Nemesius quotes the conditional-fate theory rather than endorsing it himself, and, given that he objects both in this and in other contexts that a necessitating fate in effect removes *God's* autonomy (below, Introduction 4.d.) it is hardly likely that he would accept a view of human responsibility that made it compatible with determinism.

INTRODUCTION 15

and in some Christian authors which, rather than the ability to do otherwise, emphasises rather the need to rise above the constraints of the body and fate.[82] Secondly, from a historical perspective it is hardly surprising that he adopts the notion of the ability to do otherwise that Bobzien has traced to precisely those Middle-Platonist discussions of contingency, drawing on Aristotelian materials, that Nemesius himself reflects.[83]

Martin Streck has laid considerable emphasis on the notion of a 'power of choice', *dunamis prohaeretikê*, which Nemesius uses at 41, 119.4ff., noting that this particular formulation is found neither in Aristotle nor in the anonymous commentator on the *Nicomachean Ethics*, and first occurs in Clement of Alexandria.[84] From one point of view the difference may seem slight, for Nemesius can go on to link vice with choice and habit (*hexis*) as opposed to power or potentiality, just as Aristotle and the anonymous commentator do;[85] he thus preserves the basic Aristotelian structure of a potentiality which it is up to us to develop in one of a number of different possible ways, on the one hand, and of habit or disposition which develops through and is intrinsically connected with choice, on the other. From another point of view, however, the notion of a power *of* choice, rather than of our choosing how to develop our powers, provides in Christian Greek thought something akin to the notion of the human will found in Latin writers and above all in Augustine, and it is this perspective that Streck emphasises.[86] Nevertheless, Streck acknowledges that Nemesius does not recognise the will as a distinct and

---

82 Cf. e.g. Plotinus 3.1 [3] 9.5, 3.1 [3] 10.4 (cf. 3.2 [47] 10); Augustine, *City of God* 22.30; Proclus, *On Providence and Fate and What Depends on Us* II.3.13–19 and II.4.10–19, pp. 29–30 in Isaac (1979) (and on this Steel [2005] 292–93); Boethius, *Consolation of Philosophy* 4.6.15–17, 5.2.9–10; and for our being above fate Tatian, *Oration to the Greeks* 9 p.10.7–10 Schwartz, cited by Polites (1979) 124 and n.13. A similar concept (but without the notion of transcending fate) is at home in Stoicism: Seneca, *On the happy life* 15.7, 'to obey god is freedom'. The ultimate source is the Socratic paradox 'no-one does wrong willingly'; freedom, from this perspective, is freedom from *error*. Streck (2005, 115) well argues that the Aristotelian, as opposed to Platonist, elements in section 41 are introduced precisely to block any suggestion that man is not responsible for his wrong-doing.
83 Bobzien (1998a) 397–98; (1998b) 146–57; below, n.162; section 34 and n.916.
84 Clement of Alexandria, *Miscellanies* 6.16.4 (GCS 2[52] p. 500.20f. Stählin). Streck (2001) 561; (2005) 5, 106–08, 188.
85 Nemesius 41, 119.16–17; Anonymous, *On the Nicomachean Ethics* 199.17–23. See below, n.987, and Streck (2005) 108, rightly noting that the difference is between speaking of a power of choice in general and of a choice (or 'policy') which has developed in a particular direction and so is no longer morally indifferent.
86 Indeed the phrase *dunamis prohairetikê* provided the title of the doctoral thesis on which Streck (2005) is based; Streck (2005) 5.

independent faculty of the soul; choice is still explained in terms of *other* faculties, appetitive and cognitive, and it is the latter that is decisive.[87]

A recurrent theme in Nemesius' discussion of fate is his opposition to any doctrine that makes God subject to necessity.[88] He dismisses the Stoic (and Pythagorean) doctrine of the eternal recurrence of events,[89] and objects to the Platonist view that once we have made our choices the consequences of our actions are inevitable, on the grounds that this restricts divine providence.[90] But he also rejects, as compromising the notion of fate, the idea of an astrological determinism that can be overruled by higher divine powers in answer to prayer.[91] Nevertheless, his view is that fate is produced by God and so can be over-ruled by him.[92]

How human autonomy is to be reconciled with divine providence Nemesius does not say,[93] except for his insistence that providence can prevent our actions having what would otherwise be their natural consequences[94] and that wrong-doers are responsible for their actions even when providence uses them for its own ends, as in punishing the wicked.[95] At 41, 118.4–8 Nemesius argues that to blame God for making us autonomous is to blame him for making us rational; he does not, however, explicitly argue that if we were not capable of vice we would not be capable of virtue either.[96]

4.d. Divine providence

In section 1 Nemesius insists that the physical world, including animals, has been created for man's sake, an idea with resonances both in the Old Testament and in pagan philosophy, above all in Stoicism. In section 41 he argues for the existence of divine providence on the basis both of biblical stories and of the maintenance of the order of the universe, and in section 43 he

---

87 Streck (2005) 73–74, 84 and 185; see also nn.365 and 971.
88 38, 110.21–111.13; 43, 126.17–21. Cf. Verbeke and Moncho (1975) lxx.
89 38, 111.14–112.6.
90 38, 110.13–111.13; cf. 37, 108.13–18 and 40, 116.3–6.
91 Section 36. Astrological determinism admitting of no exceptions is rejected too; 35, 104.13–105.5.
92 38, 110.21–111.13.
93 Cf. Verbeke and Moncho (1975) lxx–lxxi: 'wanting at all costs to save the freedom of human action, he saw no other solution than to remove human choice from the agency of divine providence'.
94 Below, Introduction 4.d.
95 43, 136.9–16.
96 See also Streck (2005) 116.

insists on divine providence for individuals, which pagan authors from the first century BCE onwards had tended to qualify in various ways.[97]

Discussion of divine providence in pagan philosophy had tended to emphasise the role of divinity in maintaining the order of the cosmos, which does not fit well with the idea that God intervenes in the course of events in answer to our prayers.[98] That a doctrine of providence worthy of the name should allow divine concern for the fortunes of individuals had indeed been urged in polemical contexts, notably in Atticus' attacks on Aristotelianism;[99] but it is one thing to make this point in criticising others, another to build it into a coherent positive doctrine. The Middle Platonists taught that, once we have made our free choices, their consequences follow inexorably;[100] and in this Plato's followers were being true to their master. After all, in *Laws* 10, a text that was fundamental for all later ancient discussions of the issue, Plato opposes three types of 'atheism' – the belief that the gods do not exist, the belief that they are not concerned with human affairs, *and the belief that they can be influenced by prayers and sacrifices* – the latter attacked also in *Republic* 2 364.

Nemesius, on the other hand, insists that necessity and providence are incompatible,[101] and that one role of providence is precisely to decide whether in any given instance our actions should be followed by certain consequences or not. But it is not clear how this is to be reconciled with the idea of providence maintaining order that he takes over from pagan (and, indeed, Old Testament) sources; that is not to say that a reconciliation is not possible,[102] along the lines of divine foreknowledge having anticipated special cases where a given outcome is appropriate, only that Nemesius does not explicitly address the issue. Nor is it clear how he proposes to combine human autonomy with divine omnipotence. Nevertheless, the very fact that this part of Nemesius' work is a compilation, to which he has contributed his own views even if we cannot be sure how much of the compilation of the views of others is his own work rather than that of his sources, makes it all the more interesting both as an indication of the tensions between different views and as a source for the history of ideas in later antiquity.

97 With exceptions, notably Epictetus and the Platonist Atticus; Bergjan (2002) 248. See Sharples (2003).
98 See on this Sharples (2002) 12–14.
99 Atticus, fr.3.7–10 Des Places.
100 See below, n.934.
101 Above, nn.88, 90.
102 The two aspects are indeed put in explicit juxtaposition at 41, 120.25–121.9; cf. 43, 128.8–11, on providence and nature.

5. NEMESIUS' SOURCES

5.a. On the soul

5.a.1. Origen

There are parallels between Nemesius' first section and Philo of Alexandria, especially the work of the latter *On the Creation of the World*.[103] Nemesius twice refers to the view of 'the Hebrews';[104] Telfer argues that 'the Hebrews' is Origen's way of referring to Philo, taken over by Nemesius, and suggests, following Jaeger and Skard, that Nemesius' source is Origen's lost commentary on *Genesis*.[105] On Nemesius' relation to Origen see further above, 3.b.

5.a.2. Porphyry

As already mentioned,[106] in section 3 Nemesius puts forward an account of how an incorporeal soul can be present in, and affect, a physical body. His account depends upon a favourite Neoplatonist analogy, that of light.[107] Nemesius himself attributes it to Ammonius – presumably Ammonius Saccas, the teacher of Plotinus and of the two Origens, pagan and Christian. Nemesius also cites 'Ammonius the teacher of Plotinus' in section 2, along with Numenius the second-century CE Neopythagorean, against the view that soul is corporeal.[108] In the course of the discussion in section 3 (42.22ff.) Nemesius mentions the *Miscellaneous Investigations* of Porphyry, Plotinus' pupil, biographer and editor. The natural conclusion, developed most fully by Dörrie, is that it is Porphyry who is Nemesius' source for the views of Ammonius Saccas, and that Nemesius' discussion in section 3 is based on Porphyry, since much of the material appears, often in abbreviated form but in the same sequence, also in Priscian of Lydia, *Answers to Chosroes*, who himself earlier cites Porphyry's *Miscellaneous Investigations* as a source.[109] However, in section 2 (25.6–7) Nemesius explicitly approves the view

---

103 See nn.193, 207, 214. 246.

104 1, 6.5, 11.15. See also 12, 68.11 and our note 589 there; and below, n. 214.

105 Telfer (1955) 238 n.1; Skard (1936), developing a rather cursory suggestion by Jaeger (1914, 143) that Nemesius used a commentary on Genesis that incorporated material from the *Timaeus*, and that this commentary is to be identified as Origen's. Zambon (2002, 182 n.6) notes Waszink's view that Calcidius (e.g. *On Plato's Timaeus* 219 and 300) and Nemesius (with specific reference to 12, 68.11) derive their knowledge of Philo from Porphyry who in turn got it from Numenius, but suggests that Porphyry may also know Philo through Origen.

106 Above, Introduction 3.a and 4.a.1.

107 Below, n.391. See also Galen, *On the Affected Parts* 1.7 (8.67 K.).

108 2, 17.17. Von Arnim (1887) 278–79; Siclari (1974) 76 n.36.

109 See below, n.372.

INTRODUCTION 19

of Iamblichus that transmigration of human souls into animals is impossible, and contrasts this with the view of Porphyry. So – unless Porphyry himself reported the view of Iamblichus, and Nemesius then preferred it to Porphyry's own – Nemesius is not here dependent solely or directly on Porphyry.[110]

5.a.3. Middle Platonism
Section 2 begins with a doxography of the views of pagan Greek philosophers on the soul which is closely parallel to that in book 4 chs. 2–3 of Aëtius, the writer whose work Diels reconstructed from pseudo-Plutarch, *Epitome of Physical Opinions*, and from Stobaeus, along with various other sources including, notably, Theodoret's *Remedy for Greek Attitudes*. Nemesius includes material that is present in Theodoret but neither in pseudo-Plutarch nor in Stobaeus.[111] It seems likely that Nemesius was dependent, directly or indirectly, on Aëtius' own work. Theodoret[112] gives *his* sources as Plutarch, Porphyry and Aëtius; which raises the question whether the Aëtius material reached Nemesius from Porphyry,[113] or from a Middle-Platonist source, as Dörrie argues,[114] or *both* – i.e. via a Middle-Platonist source used in turn by Porphyry, as Mansfeld suggests.[115]

Nemesius – or his source – has arranged his Aëtian material, as Dörrie points out,[116] in a way that structures the subsequent argument. He proceeds to criticise, first, views that make the soul itself something bodily, and then those that make it some quality or property of the body – among the supporters of which he includes, tendentiously, Aristotle.[117] Then he argues

---

110 Dörrie (1959) 147–51 argues that Nemesius is here citing Porphyry through Iamblichus; see also nn.189, 360.
111 See n.354.
112 Theodoret, *Remedy for Greek Attitudes* 5.18.
113 Krause (1904, 16) derives the *whole* of ch.2 as far as 20.17 from Porphyry. Jaeger (1914, 61ff., 68) argues that Porphyry, along with Galen, was Nemesius' source on soul. See also Emilsson (1994) 5347–48.
114 Dörrie (1959, 121–27) argues that Nemesius' source in section 2 is in general *Middle Platonist*, because of the nature of Nemesius' arguments against the views he rejects, but holds that Nemesius has added material from Porphyry, notably (i) in the refutation of the Manichaeans (32.20–33.19) and (ii) where his main source, being concerned to combat the Stoic view that soul is a body, did not sufficiently emphasise the substantiality of the soul.
115 Mansfeld (1990) 3076 n.70
116 Dörrie (1959) 111–17; cf, 119, observing the same strategy in Plotinus 4.7 [2] and comparing Cicero, *Tusculan Disputations* 1.18–22. See also Mansfeld and Runia (1996) 297–98.
117 The interpretation of Aristotle as making soul non-substantial reflects discussions originating in the first century BCE; see below, n.263.

in defence of the view that the soul is an incorporeal substance in its own right and separable from the body, a view that he has already in section 1 identified as the Platonist view and has himself endorsed. In Aëtius, on the other hand, the views that make the soul bodily come *after* those that do not. Nemesius is not simply copying out material from reference works; he is structuring it and using it in a way that fits into an overall design.[118]

In the course of the argument in section 2 against the view that soul is itself a body, Nemesius cites and attacks three Stoic arguments, attributing the first and second to Cleanthes and the third to Chrysippus. The same three Stoic arguments occur in the Latin treatise *On the Soul* of the early third-century CE Church Father Tertullian, and in Greek in the third section of the *Mantissa* or *Supplement to On the Soul* of Alexander of Aphrodisias. Dörrie suggested that Nemesius took the sequence of arguments and counter-arguments from a Middle-Platonist source; Krause that Nemesius' source was Porphyry; Waszink that Tertullian and Nemesius derived it from the physician Soranus (early 2nd century CE); Mansfeld that the source might be Arius Didymus' *On the Sects*.[119] There are various ways in which more than one of these possibilities might be combined.

5.a.4. Galen

In section 2 (35.11–37.9) Nemesius gives a series of arguments against transmigration of human souls into animals.[120] At the end of this series Nemesius cites, explicitly and verbatim, two passages from Galen's *On the Usefulness of the Parts*.[121] Skard argued that the preceding arguments, as opposed to the references to Porphyry and Iamblichus at the beginning of the discussion of transmigration, were taken over by Nemesius from the same lost work by Galen that he supposed had been the source for some passages in section 1.[122] Nemesius himself, according to Skard (1942, 48),

---

118 A similar sequence to that in Nemesius is also found in Calcidius, *On Plato's Timaeus* 214–35, but differs in that it cites fewer views than either Aëtius or Nemesius, and combines discussion of the nature of the soul with that of the location of the ruling principle. See Mansfeld (1990) 3112–17; Polito (2006) 291–92 and 300; Reydams-Schils (2006) 178 and 181. Calcidius, *On Plato's Timaeus* 219, cites as the view of 'the Hebrews' a view which appears to be that of Philo of Alexandria; see above, Introduction 5.a.1, and also Calcidius 276 with Reydams-Schils (2002) 205.

119 Below, n.277.

120 See above, Introduction 4.a.1.

121 1.1 p.1.10–16 and 1.22 p.1.59.4–6 Helmreich, cited by Nemesius at 2, 37.12–16 and 2, 37.17–19 respectively.

122 Skard (1942) especially 43 and 48; (1937) 11. Skard (1937) derived 1, 2.13–4.24 and

added the argument at 37.4–9 that transmigration into animals cannot be a punishment for sinning humans, since according to Genesis animals were created before humans, and then proceeded to quote *On the Usefulness of the Parts*, citing Galen explicitly where previously he had, in Skard's view, used him anonymously. A further question is whether Nemesius is using Galen directly or not. Earlier in section 2, at 23.24ff., Nemesius reports and criticises Galen's view that character depends on bodily temperament, and it seems possible that he was citing Galen, *That the Faculties of the Soul follow the Mixtures of the Body* from memory but with the intention of looking up the actual text subsequently.[123]

5.a.5. Posidonius

Jaeger (1914) argued for the extensive influence on Nemesius of the first-century BCE Stoic philosopher and polymath Posidonius. The claims made in the earlier part of the twentieth century for Posidonius' influence on all subsequent ancient philosophy provoked a counter-reaction, exemplified in the determination of Edelstein and Kidd[124] to include in their collection of the fragments of Posidonius only material that could be securely connected with him.[125] Jaeger used a comparison between the eulogies of man at the end of Nemesius' section 1 and Cicero, *On the Nature of the Gods* 2 to argue for Posidonius as a common source;[126] but he exaggerated the similarities, and even if they were as great as he claimed the identification of Posidonius as the source would still be conjectural. Jaeger's view that the notion in section 1 (5.4–8) of man as uniting the intelligible and the visible derives ultimately from Posidonius has been criticised by Verbeke.[127]

Pohlenz (1941, 6) argued that some of the material in the arguments against transmigration in section 2 derives from Posidonius; but that, even if true, does not itself answer the question how it reached Nemesius. Telfer (1955, 230–32 and 235) suggested that Nemesius in section 1 is dependent on Posidonius, sometimes via Philo and Origen, and sometimes via Galen.

7.12–9.22, as well as some other details in section 1, from Galen. See notes 206, 226, 233, 367. At 1, 9.2–3 Nemesius takes the phrases 'ill-balance of the qualities' and 'loosening of bodily coherence' from Galen, *Method of Healing* 13.1 (10.874.2–4 K.), without explicit citation.

123 See n.301.
124 Edelstein and Kidd (1988–1989) (and already in the first edition of their vol.1 in 1972).
125 See Bobzien (1998a) 323.
126 Below, n.250.
127 Verbeke (1971); cf. Verbeke and Moncho (1975) xxxvi n.5, saying that the doctrine is *Neo*platonist. For another example of undue readiness to find Posidonian influence see n.202.

That each of these may be the case in *some* passages cannot be ruled out. But the view that it is systematically so seems both unprovable and odd; would it be simply coincidence that led Nemesius back through different proximate sources to a common remote source, or is it rather that the assumption of Posidonius' influence on a range of authors itself leads to his identification as the common lost source behind different extant ones?

Ironically, Jaeger failed to notice a strong indication of possible Posidonian influence in one place at least. At section 1, 13.12, Nemesius refers to man's upright posture – by implication only, indeed, for what he actually mentions is the non-upright posture of other animals. That man alone stands upright was a commonplace. It was made popular by Plato, *Timaeus* 90a, 91e–92a, but it is also mentioned by, among others, Xenophon, Aristotle, Cicero, Sallust, Ovid, Seneca, Gregory of Nyssa, Basil of Caesarea, Theodoret and Boethius.[128] (Jaeger, unsurprisingly, uses the mention in Sallust as evidence that the doctrine was put forward by Posidonius.)[129] In section 6, 57.8, Nemesius uses the image of the senses as bodyguards for reason. Jaeger pointed out that Plato in the *Timaeus* uses both the image of the head as an acropolis and that of the senses as bodyguards, and argues that the occurrence of these two images is a sign of the influence of Posidonius' discussion of the *Timaeus*.[130] Nemesius does not explicitly use the image of the acropolis at all, and refers to upright posture and to bodyguards in two different sections. Moreover, the overlap between the authors who use the two images is only partial. That of the acropolis occurs in Cicero, Philo of Alexandria, Galen and Calcidius;[131] that of the bodyguards in Philo, Alcinous, Galen, Gregory of Nyssa and Nemesius.[132] What Jaeger does *not*,

128 Below, n.238.
129 Jaeger (1914) 130–31.
130 Jaeger (1914) 21–22.
131 *Timaeus* 70a; Cicero, *On the Nature of the Gods* 2.140, *Tusculan Disputations* 1.20; Galen, *On the Doctrines of Hippocrates and Plato* 2.4.17, p.120.1–4 de Lacy = vol.5 230.10–14 K; Philo, *On the Special Laws* 4.92, *On Dreams* 1.32; Calcidius, *On Plato's Timaeus* 231 (p.245.3 Waszink). Cf. Dörrie (1959) 118 n.4. The image also occurs in [Galen], *On Remedies that are Easily Obtained* 14 313.11K, in connection with the custom of structuring medical discussions by proceeding 'from the head to the heels', and in similar listings in (Hippocrates), *Letter* 23, 9.934.9 Littré, and Anonymus Parisinus, *On Acute Diseases* 1, p.2.16–17 Garofalo; see van der Eijk (2000–2001) vol.2 147–48.
132 *Timaeus* 70b, Galen, *On the Doctrines of Hippocrates and Plato* 2.4.17, p.120.1–4 de Lacy = vol.5 230.10–14 K and *On the Usefulness of the Parts* 8.2.3 p.614.12 K, Philo, *On the Special Laws* 3.111, 4.93, 4.123, Alcinous, *Instruction Manual (Didascalicus)* 17.4, Gregory of Nyssa, *On the Creation of Man* PG 44 156c, Nemesius 6 57.8. Cicero has rather the image of the senses as messengers and servants: *On the Laws* 1.26 (*satellites ... ac nuntios*), *On the*

INTRODUCTION 23

however, emphasise, though Philip de Lacy commenting on Galen does do so,[133] is that whereas the later texts that use the image of bodyguards all apply it to the *senses*, in the *Timaeus* itself it is applied to the *heart*, as the seat of a lower part of the soul. This alone justifies, and *does* justify, the suggestion that there is a common source of the later references which is *not* the *Timaeus* itself. We know that Posidonius was interested in the *Timaeus* and *may* even have written a commentary on it.[134] That he must be the source is still far from proven, but here perhaps Jaeger's case was stronger than he himself made it.

5.b. On medicine and the body

For medicine, too, there has been considerable discussion about the question of Nemesius' knowledge and use of medical ideas and the sources on which he drew.[135] While earlier contributions to this discussion are still useful, the debate was for a long time coloured by underlying presuppositions typical of the kind of *Quellenforschung* that was popular throughout late nineteenth- and early twentieth-century classical scholarship. One such presupposition was that, once a text was deemed 'eclectic', all elements in that text were believed ultimately to be derived from previous (often lost) sources without the author being able in any way to develop, add, select or vary the material according to his own judgement or literary and rhetorical purposes, audience etc. Related to this was the tendency of some classical scholars to speak with greater confidence about texts that are lost than about texts that have been preserved.[136]

Be that as it may, some scholars have argued for Nemesius' almost complete dependence, in medical matters, on Galen – and on Aristotle and

---

Nature of the Gods 2.140 (*nuntios*). Nemesius indeed has both bodyguards and servants.

133 De Lacy (1984) 628.

134 Edelstein and Kidd (1988–89) vol.2.1 338–40 are agnostic on the question of an actual commentary, but have no doubts about Posidonius' interest in the dialogue.

135 See Evangelides (1892); Domański (1900); Jaeger (1914); Skard (1937–1939).

136 A telling example of these two attitudes can be found in Skard (1939) 53, who argues that Nemesius, in ch. 28, cannot have used Galen's *On the Usefulness of the Parts*, for then he would have had to gather his material from different books of that treatise and the result would have been chaotic; but since Nemesius' account is well structured, he must have used a lost treatise by Galen ('Freilich – der Schrift *De usu partium* kann dies alles nicht entlehnt sein. Dann hätte ja nämlich Nemesius sein Material aus verschiedenen Büchern sammeln müssen und es wäre gewiss eine traurige Unordnung entstanden. Aber Kap. 28 ist wohl geordnet, die Disposition ist tadellos. Nemesios hat sie aus einer verlorenen Schrift des Galen übernommen.')

Hippocrates only *through* Galen – and denied him any originality.[137] In more recent times, this view has been critically reviewed by Telfer (1955) and especially by Kallis (1978), who argues that, however close the resemblances between Nemesius and a specific Galenic text often are, they do not prove beyond doubt that the Galenic text in question was Nemesius' direct source ('Vorlage'). That may be true in principle, although it is in our view equally rash to argue, as Kallis does on a number of occasions, that certain variations in Nemesius' usage of Galenic ideas and phrases *prove* that a specific Galenic text cannot have been Nemesius' direct source. There may of course have been intermediaries, e.g. compendia or summaries of the type of Oribasius' *Medical Collections* or Porphyry's *Miscellaneous Investigations* which Nemesius may have used.[138] But for medicine, apart from Oribasius, none of this material is extant – and even of Oribasius' work only parts survive – and we have been unable to find examples where it is clear that Nemesius was using Oribasius rather than Galen.[139] By contrast, the parallels between Nemesius and Galen's extant works are often so close that one could hardly wish for stronger evidence of dependence – much stronger at any rate than hypothetical parallels with lost works such as Posidonius' commentary on the *Timaeus* or Galen's work *On Demonstration* – although the fact that Galen often repeats himself in different works,[140] and the fact that many works of Galen are lost, makes it virtually impossible to be certain as to the *exact* work Nemesius may have been drawing on.

Notwithstanding this, several scholars have argued for a relative independence, on Nemesius' part, of Galen and have pointed to what they perceive as examples of Nemesius' departure from Galenic doctrines. Thus Lammert (1941) has argued that on a number of specific medical issues (pulse lore, pneuma theory, theory of reproduction), Nemesius reflects the views of the Hellenistic medical writer Erasistratus (which Galen rejected),[141] a point taken over by Telfer and Wallace-Hadrill.[142] Furthermore, there are cases

---

137 See Evangelides (1892); Skard (1937–1939). A parallel is Gossel (1908), who has argued for direct dependence of Ambrose on Galen's *On the Usefulness of the Parts*.
138 The latter was argued for by Krause (1904) 37–45. See above, 5.a.2.
139 See notes on section 14.
140 Examples are given in the footnotes to the relevant sections of the translation. It is, for example, quite possible that on topics such as nutrition, reproduction and respiration, Nemesius has used Galen's summary account as given in *On the Usefulness of the Parts* rather than his more specialised or polemical accounts in *On the Natural Faculties*, *On Semen* and *On the Usefulness of Respiration*.
141 Lammert (1941) 129. See, however, our reservations in n.766.
142 Telfer (1955) 366; Wallace-Hadrill (1968) 43–44: 'Nemesius did not follow Galen in

where it has been argued that Nemesius reflects knowledge of post-Galenic medical ideas. The best-known example is his localisation of the psychic faculties of imagination, thought and memory in the anterior, middle and posterior cerebral cavities in section 13 – a view not found in Galen (at least not in the extant works of Galen) but first attested for the presumably late fourth-century medical writer Posidonius of Byzantium.[143]

Although not all examples of Nemesius' alleged independence with regard to Galen are in our view equally persuasive,[144] we see no reason to rule out the possibility that Nemesius, like other learned writers of late antiquity who drew on a variety of traditions, (i) ensured that his sources were up to date and (ii) made selective and creative use of the material he found in them by rewording, rearrangement, abbreviation, variation, etc. Examples of this practice on the medical side can be found in other late antique authors such as Oribasius and Aëtius, whose direct dependence on Galen for many parts of their work is not in doubt but who sometimes modify their material considerably and who also use sources other than Galen. Even if, in medical matters, Nemesius was perhaps not an independent thinker, he certainly stands out, compared to these medical writers, as a more creative writer with an agenda and a voice of his own.

Whether Nemesius had direct access to the authors and works he mentions is, as said, not always possible to determine; and just as it is very likely that he knew certain works and views of Aristotle and Plato at least also, if not predominantly, through intermediaries (such as commentaries or compendia), this may also be the case with regard to his references to medical literature. We have in the notes commented on specific passages where pronouncement on the sources seems possible. On the whole, however, for the reasons mentioned above, our citing of parallels lays no claim to a considered view on the *exact* sources of Nemesius' ideas, although we have where possible tried to select those parallels which we believe are most likely to have been part of Nemesius' cultural baggage.

---

believing that arteries distribute blood as well as pneuma, but was aware of the presence of blood in the arteries, and is probably relying upon the older authority of Erasistratus in saying that the heart's beat distends and contracts arteries, causing them to suck a certain amount of refined blood from neighbouring veins'.

143 See n.607.
144 See nn. 543–44, 607, 766, 776. By contrast, at 25, 86.9–10 Nemesius seems to ignore or be unaware of Galen's rejection of the Hippocratic view that the cutting of the vessels behind the ears impairs fertility.

5.c. On fate and the voluntary

Nemesius' discussion of voluntary action and choice in sections 30–34 is ultimately dependent on book 3 of Aristotle's *Nicomachean Ethics*.[145] However, it appears that Nemesius is dependent not, or not only, on Aristotle directly, but on a commentary; if he was using the text of Aristotle, and elaborating it himself, there is a remarkable similarity between the way in which he did so and the way in which commentators did so.[146]

There are four extant commentaries, or quasi-commentaries, on this part of the *Nicomachean Ethics* that are relevant. One is the commentary by Aspasius, from the first half of the second century CE.[147] The second is the anonymous commentary on books 2 to 5 that forms part of the Byzantine composite commentary. The date of the commentary on books 2 to 5 is uncertain. It appears to incorporate material from Adrastus of Aphrodisias, who in the first half of the second century CE wrote a work explaining the historical and literary background to references in Aristotle and Theophrastus, but this does not in itself help us to date the commentary in which the material from Adrastus is embedded, though Moraux argued for a date late in the second century CE.[148] Thirdly, several of the *Ethical Problems* attributed to Alexander of Aphrodisias discuss passages from this section of the *Nicomachean Ethics*;[149] whether Alexander also wrote a full-scale commentary on the *Ethics* is controversial.[150] In some details Nemesius' account seems closer to the anonymous commentary than it does either to Aspasius

---

145 Amand (1973) 559 says this not only of sections 30–34 but also of sections 39–41. The latter do not, however, follow the course of Aristotle's exposition in all its details in the same way as do the former; see below, at n. 174. Domański (1900, 165) observes the absence of explicit references to Aristotle in 30–34, suggesting that this was because Aristotle had become associated with the views of Arius and Eunomius; but Aristotle is referred to explicitly in 39 (below, at n.160).

146 Whether his knowledge of Aristotle's own text derived *entirely* from this source is less clear; if it did the commentary was clearly one which included a considerable amount of paraphrase of the original text. Verbeke and Moncho (1975, lxxiv f. n.51) argue that 'it appears undeniable' that Nemesius knew the *Nicomachean Ethics* at first hand; Amand (1973, 559–60) suggests rather that he did not.

147 *CAG* 19.1; see Alberti and Sharples (1999).

148 Atticus (the Platonist), whose *floruit* was placed by Eusebius in 176–80, is referred to as a contemporary. Moraux (1984) 327 (cf. 324 n.115); Anon., *On Aristotle's Nicomachean Ethics* 248.25–26. On the origin and date of the anonymous commentary (in *CAG* 20) see Mercken (1990) 419–29; Streck (2005) 48 n.142 and references there.

149 Alexander, *Ethical Problems* 9, 11, 12 and 29. See Sharples (1990).

150 Cf. Abbamonte (1995) 250 n.4; Sharples (2001a) 593–95.

or to Alexander's *Ethical Problems*.¹⁵¹ Finally, similarities have also been detected between Nemesius and the commentary on the *Nicomachean Ethics* printed in *CAG* 19.2 and variously attributed to Andronicus, Olympiodorus and a probably fictitious Heliodorus.¹⁵² Since the date of this commentary is quite uncertain, it is difficult to be sure whether Nemesius is influenced by it or vice versa; and, as always, there is the possibility of a common source.¹⁵³

Nemesius states what he considers to be Plato's doctrine both on fate (section 38) and on providence (section 43).¹⁵⁴ He presents as Platonic a view that fate is conditional: actions are up to us, but fate decrees that from certain actions certain consequences will follow. This has its basis in the myth of *Republic* 10, and is found in a number of the authors customarily labelled 'Middle Platonist'.¹⁵⁵ Nemesius also attributes to Plato a doctrine of three levels of divine providence which derives ultimately from Plato's *Timaeus* 42de; this, too, is paralleled in a smaller group of Middle-Platonist authors.¹⁵⁶ One work in which both doctrines are found is the treatise *On Fate* attributed to Plutarch; the treatment of possibility in Nemesius' section 34, 103.10ff., too, is closely parallel to that in the treatise attributed to Plutarch. However, it appears that the treatise and Nemesius share a common source or tradition, directly or indirectly, rather than the former being the source

---

151 See below, nn. 645–46, 669, 702, 704, 720, 872–74, 876–77, 886–87, 894–95, 903, 909, 911, 949, 957, 981, 985. Koch (1921) suggests (33) that Nemesius was following a common source used by both the anonymous commentary and Aspasius, and (36) that Nemesius' source was a *Christian* commentary on Aristotle; at 26 he notes that the stories of Zeno and Anaxarchus cited by Nemesius in section 30 were also referred to by Clement of Alexandria. See Streck (2005) 52 n.156, and nn.871, 874, 882. Koch (1921, 34) notes the reference to God at section 34, 102.12, but, as he remarks, this is shared with the anonymous commentary, which seems unlikely to be Christian in its entirety. Nemesius could have added other Christian colouring himself (so Amand [1973] 560 n.1, arguing against Koch that Nemesius should not be treated as a mere compiler), as he seems to have done in the discussion of providence later in the work. See also Siclari (1974) 232 and n.18; Streck (2005) 76–77 and n.252, 82. Telfer (1955, 436) argued from the interest in terminology that the commentary used by Nemesius was from Nemesius' own period; the source certainly shows signs of scholastic elaboration and schematisation, but this could be true of the second century as well as the fourth.
152 See Nicol (1968).
153 See nn.877, 886.
154 We are here dealing with the doctrines that later Platonists constructed on the basis of remarks in Plato's dialogues, not with clearly formulated doctrines that Plato himself puts forward – if he ever does.
155 See below, n.934.
156 See below, n.1004. Nemesius' version has some strange features: cf. n.1005.

of the latter.¹⁵⁷ The question also remains how much, if any, of the material that intervenes between the three passages with parallels in the Plutarchan treatise also comes from that same source. The idea that choices are up to us, but consequences follow, in fact appears *twice* in Nemesius' account, in section 38 attributed to Plato as in the Plutarchan treatise but in section 37 attributed to 'the wisest of the Greeks'. Some of the criticism advanced against this theory by Nemesius in section 37 could come from a Platonist source attacking the Stoics, but some is probably Nemesius' own.¹⁵⁸ Nemesius' account of chance in section 39 shows distinctively Platonist, as opposed to Peripatetic, features, even though the ultimate source is Aristotle.¹⁵⁹ On the other hand, Aristotle on the moral virtues is cited (by name) at 39, 113.17.¹⁶⁰

The question presents itself whether and how the source Nemesius used for sections 30 to 34a might be related to the source of the material in sections 34b to 39. One possibility is that Nemesius was using, directly or indirectly, a Platonist source that had *already* incorporated material from an *Ethics* commentary,¹⁶¹ or indeed vice versa.¹⁶² But it may be that Nemesius simply

---

157 The general definition of power that introduces the discussion of power and possibility at Nemesius 34, 103.11–12, taken from Plato, *Republic* 5 477c, does not appear in pseudo-Plutarch. See in general Dillon (1996) 338.

158 See below, nn.932–33.

159 Below, n.952.

160 As Streck (2005) 195 and n.9 notes, this is the only place where Nemesius breaks the rule of citing Aristotle by name only when disagreeing with him. To name sources when rejecting their views, but not when taking them over, was common practice among ancient writers. Authorities can indeed be named when their reputation enhances the status of the views expressed, but Aristotle did not have such a reputation in late antiquity, especially not among Christian writers: cf. Streck (2005) 21.

161 Domański (1900, 165) noted the more Platonist character of Nemesius' discussion from the middle of section 34 onwards. Siclari (1974, 226) regards Nemesius' attitude to freedom as Peripatetic rather than Neoplatonist; but it may rather be *Middle* Platonist; see above, n.83. Platonist parallels are present in the discussion of astrological determinism in section 36; see n.924.

162 So Amand (1973) 559–60, suggesting that the commentary was also the source for sections 39–41 and that it incorporated an excursus attacking deterministic theories, reflected in Nemesius' sections 35–38. (Koch [1921, 37] had suggested that the presence of such material shows Nemesius' *independence* from the commentary.) Bobzien (1998b, 147) notes that the discussion of chance, contingency and what depends on us in pseudo-Plutarch, Calcidius and Nemesius itself differs from the other material that they share in that it is Aristotelian rather than Platonist in character, apart from some of the examples of chance in pseudo-Plutarch (7 572bc) only. So we may be dealing with a Peripatetic commentary incorporating a Platonist excursus that itself drew on Peripatetic material. Indeed, as Bobzien says (1998b, 148) the

started drawing on a different authority from the second part of section 34 onwards. The fact that the unintentional actions discussed in sections 30–34 are different in type from the involuntary bodily functions discussed in sections 23–25 suggests that, although there is a general thematic connection, Nemesius starts using a different source in section 30.[163]

In section 35 Nemesius preserves a distinctive Stoic argument claiming to reconcile determinism and responsibility, which we also find in Alexander, *On Fate* 13. Nemesius attributes the argument to Chrysippus – the third head of the Stoic school, in the third century BCE, and its most prolific author – and to Philopator, referred to by Galen[164] as the teacher of one of his own teachers. Alexander does not name the source at all. This is in line with his general policy in *On Fate*; but it shows that *this* work of Alexander's, at least, cannot be Nemesius' sole source.[165]

Another author who gives the same account of the Platonist view of fate that we find in Nemesius section 38 is Calcidius, who wrote a commentary on the *Timaeus* in Latin during the fourth century.[166] Waszink argued that Porphyry was the source for both Calcidius' and Nemesius' material on fate, and in particular the route by which material from Alexander was transmitted to them[167] – though many of Waszink's parallels between Alexander and Calcidius are of a rather general nature.[168] There are similarities on the question of divine foreknowledge between Calcidius, Porphyry as recorded

---

distinction between Platonists and Peripatetics may be artificial in the context of the second century CE.

163 See below, n.871.
164 *On the Diagnosis of the Affections of the Soul*, vol.5 p.41 K.
165 It is on the basis of the correspondence between these two passages that Bobzien (1998a) 370ff. uses 'PHILOPATOR' as a label for the originator of the innovations in the discussion of determinism and responsibility that she detects in this period.
166 See Waszink (1962).
167 Waszink (1962) lxiii and n.1. Krause (1904, 44) argues that Porphyry is the source of section 38, on the basis of the references to fate at 2, 34.15–17; see nn.345, 353.
168 See Sharples (1978) 265 and n.225. Den Boeft (1970, 98) sees the absence of the 'doctrine of three providences' from Calcidius, *On Plato's Timaeus* 176, as a difficulty for Waszink's view that Nemesius and Calcidius are alike dependent on Porphyry. But it is possible that Calcidius' use of Porphyry was more selective than Nemesius'; so Dillon (1996, 323), implying that Calcidius showed sound judgement in omitting the doctrine of three providences as 'another elaborate flourish which does not succeed in resolving any substantive problems' (see n.913). Dillon is too harsh; the question of providential concern for individuals, and the relation between providence and fate, especially astrological fate linked with the heavens, were both live philosophical issues.

by Proclus, and Alexander.[169] Rather more than a century after Nemesius, Boethius and Ammonius the son of Hermias, discussing the paradox of truth about the future in Aristotle's *On Interpretation* 9, both make this the occasion to discuss wider issues relating to fate and responsibility.[170] Porphyry's commentary on that chapter of Aristotle is lost, as is Alexander's. But the way seems open to suggest that points of contact between Alexander's treatise *On Fate*, Calcidius and Nemesius might be explained by supposing that Alexander's commentary on *On Interpretation* 9 contained excursuses on fate and responsibility, and that Alexander named opponents such as Philopator in the commentary where he did not do so in the treatise *On Fate*.[171] Porphyry might then have taken over Alexander's discussion in his own commentary, adding some points and omitting others, and drawing on Middle-Platonist sources as well as on Alexander; Porphyry's commentary may then have been used by Calcidius and Nemesius.[172] Another possibility is that Alexander discussed non-Peripatetic views on fate in his commentary on the *Nicomachean Ethics* – if he ever wrote one.[173] But these are only possibilities; the similarities between the various texts may be explained in other ways.

A further question is how the source or sources of 39–41 might be related to the source of 30–34a. It has already been noted that the account of chance in 39 has specific affinities to the Platonist material that is reflected in 34b and 38. Sections 39–41 as a whole draw on material from the part of Aristotle's discussion (*Nicomachean Ethics* 3.4–5 in the standard English numbering) that follows that which is the ultimate source of 30–34a. They do so, however, in a much more independent way than in 30–34a; in 39–41 Nemesius, or a source, is shaping the discussion himself and drawing on Aristotelian ideas among others in doing so, rather than making Aristotle's discussion (perhaps as mediated through a commentary) the basis of the structure of his own. This very fact makes it more difficult to be sure that

---

169 See Sharples (1978) 261–62.
170 Boethius, *On Aristotle's On Interpretation, second version* 193.23–198.3, 217.17–218.25, 223.15–226.25; Ammonius, *On Aristotle's On Interpretation*, CAG 4.5 130.27–128.10 Busse (cf. Seel [2000]).
171 Alexander adopts a deliberate policy of not naming his determinist opponents in *On Fate*. See Sharples (2001) 517. For Alexander's possible use of the same material both in commentaries and in independent treatises cf. the recognition by Accattino and Donini (1996, vii–xi) of his treatise *On the Soul* as a less technical version of his commentary on Aristotle's *On the Soul*.
172 On parallels between Boethius and *Alexander* see Sharples (1978) 254, 256–58.
173 Above, n.150.

INTRODUCTION   31

Nemesius is not in 39–41 using the same source as in 30–34a, and possibly in 34b–38 as well; but if he is doing so he is using it in a different way.[174]

5.d. On providence

Nemesius' discussion of providence in sections 42–43 includes, as already indicated (5.c.), material deriving from the Middle-Platonist tradition shared with pseudo-Plutarch and Apuleius. It also includes arguments that, like much of the whole history of discussion on this topic in pagan philosophy, go back ultimately to Plato, *Laws* 10;[175] and some aspects of Nemesius' reporting of non-Platonist pagan views suggest Platonist perspectives.[176] It seems likely, here as elsewhere, that Nemesius is using a Platonist source, though adding a considerable amount of material of his own, especially in the defence of divine providence which concludes his discussion and draws heavily on scriptural sources.

Nemesius rejects the view that providence is concerned with universals rather than with particulars. This was advanced, notably, by Alexander of Aphrodisias,[177] though he was drawing on a tradition widespread in pagan discussion of limiting providence, in more or less specifically formulated ways;[178] and some of the points made in connection with the view that providence is limited seem particularly appropriate in discussing a Peripatetic such as Alexander.[179] How far Nemesius, or his source, is drawing on Alexander's discussion specifically is uncertain, but some connection, direct or indirect, seems likely.

Nemesius refers to a tripartition of rejected possibilities – God does not know that he should exercise providence, or is not willing, or is not able –

---

174 Streck (2005, 41–42 and 195) argues against 30–34a and 39–41 being parts of a single composition either by Nemesius or by a predecessor, and raises the possibility that the differences *might* be explained by Nemesius' following an earlier source in one passage and contributing more of his own composition in the other. He nevertheless suggests (2005, 104–06) that the Aristotelian material used in section 41, as well as that in 30–34a, was mediated through the commentary tradition, even if Nemesius is here using that tradition in a different way (cf. Streck [2005] 114–15, 195). See also n.893.
175 See below, n.1037.
176 See below, nn.1027, 1032.
177 Below, nn.1030, 1038. It was only in the second half of the twentieth century that Alexander's doctrine was recovered from the Arabic version of his treatise *On Providence*; the Greek text is lost except for a few quotations by Cyril of Alexandria. For the text see Fazzo and Zonta (1998).
178 Cf. Sharples (2003).
179 See below, nn.1038–39.

variations on which are used by Alexander in the course of his dialectical discussion. But the possibilities are commonplaces of the tradition, deriving ultimately from Plato, *Laws* 10.[180] Moreover, Alexander's and Nemesius' use of the point actually reflect different branches of this tradition of discussion.[181] Nemesius' list, which is closer to Plato's own text, occurs also in Simplicius and Maimonides,[182] while Alexander gives us permutations of two of the possibilities (unwilling, unable, *or both*), which we also find in various forms in Cicero, Sextus, Theodoret and Calcidius.[183] The apparent parallel, in other words, indicates a *difference* between the allegedly similar texts, not a connection.

5.e. Conclusion

Whatever hypotheses we may form concerning Nemesius' sources, and concerning the extent to which material from several remoter sources had already been combined in immediate sources, the important point, in the end, is that he takes his material and structures it in a certain way. It is no accident that the doxographical account of earlier views of the soul at the start of section 2 has been rearranged in a way that gives a specific structure to the subsequent discussion; it is no accident that the discussion of the relation between soul and body in section 3 should culminate in discussion of the doctrine of the Incarnation; it is no accident that the work should end with discussion of divine providence. Nemesius is far from a passive transmitter of material he finds in his sources.

---

180 Below, n.1037. The tripartition is indeed *still* present in modern arguments that there cannot be a God who is both omniscient and omnipotent and benevolent – which simply shows how natural the tripartition is in this context.
181 *Pace* Koch (1921, 48), who sees a similarity between the list of reasons why providence might not be exercised that we find in Nemesius, and passages in Theodoret (*On Providence* 2.581) and Calcidius (*On Plato's Timaeus* 173).
182 Below, n.1037.
183 Alexander, *On Providence* 6.22 and 24.15; Cicero, *On the Nature of the Gods* fr.8 Pease, citing Epicurus; Sextus, *Outlines of Pyrrhonism* 3.10ff.; Theodoret, *On Providence* 2.581 and Calcidius, *On Plato's Timaeus* 173. Sharples (2003) 119–21.

ON THE NATURE OF MAN

Nemesius, Bishop of Emesa

[SECTION 1]

The place of human beings in the scheme of things, on the boundary between the perceptible and the intelligible, between the rational and the non-rational; man's superiority to the non-rational animals.

It has been the opinion of many good men that man is eminently constructed of an intellectual soul and a body, indeed so well that he could not have (5) come to be, nor be composed, well in any other way. But the statement that the soul is intellectual is ambivalent – for it can either mean that the intellect came to the soul as one thing to another and thus made it intellective, or that the soul possesses intellect of itself and from its own nature, and that this is its best part, like the eye in the body. So some, Plotinus among them,[184] have held the doctrine that the soul is one (10) thing and the intellect another, and maintain that man is composed of three things, body, soul and intellect. Apollinaris also, who became bishop of Laodicea,[185] followed them. For he laid this down as the foundation of his own opinion and built on the rest in accordance with his own doctrine.

But some did not set the intellect apart from the soul, but believe that

---

184 Plotinus the Neoplatonist (205–270). On the debate in Neoplatonism over this issue see Sorabji (2004) vol.1 118–19, who notes that Iamblichus (c.245–c.325) may have accused Porphyry (234–c.305, Iamblichus' teacher and Plotinus' pupil and biographer) of failing to distinguish between Soul and Intellect. Plotinus' view is not as clear-cut as Nemesius here implies: at *Enneads* 4.7 [2] 1.5–6 and 1.1 [53] 3.1–3 he speaks of human beings as made up of body and soul, simply. Cf. 1.1 [53] 8; Raven (1923) 190–91, and Sorabji (2004) vol.1 118–19.

185 Apollinaris (315–392; on the spelling see below), bishop of Laodicea in Syria, held that man was composed of body, soul and intellect or spirit (cf. Gregory of Nyssa, *Controversy (Antirrheticus) against Apollinarius* 209.1, 211.26, 213.7 Mueller; Dräseke [1886] 27, [1892] 194; Domański [1900] 50 n.1) and that Christ's body and soul were human but his intellect or spirit divine (Telfer [1955] 226; cf. Gregory *Controversy (Antirrheticus) against Apollinarius* 213.21–25, 214.19–21). Apollinaris' doctrine was condemned at Rome in 376, anonymously, and by name at the first Council of Constantinople in 381. See also Lietzmann (1904) 152, and Verbeke and Moncho (1975) xl n.23; our text is Apollinaris fr.169 Lietzmann, p.269.17–22. On Apollinaris generally see Raven (1923) and Quasten (1975) 377–83; on the specific issue here Raven (1923) 169–76 and Kallis (1978) 127–28. Kallis compares the discussion of the relation between soul and spirit at Didymus Caecus, *On Psalm* 30.5–6, 139.1–13 Gronewald. See also below, n.373. We adopt the spelling 'Apollinaris', used by Quasten; Nemesius' text here has 'Apolinarius', and 'Apollinarius' is also found.

(15) the intellect is the ruling part of its being.[186] Aristotle is of the opinion that while the potential intellect is part of the composition of man, intellect that is in actuality comes to us from outside, not as something that makes man's being and existence complete, but as contributing to the advancement of knowledge of natural things and of contemplation.[187] At any rate he affirms that few men and only those [2] who have philosophised possess intellect that is in actuality at all.[188] But Plato does not seem to say that man is the composite, i.e. soul and body, but a soul that uses a body of a particular sort, having a more worthy impression of the human [condition].[189] And immediately [thereby] he turns us away from body to the divinity (5) of the soul alone and its care, so that, trusting it to be the soul that is our <true>

---

186 Presumably the Stoics are meant; but in their view reason, as the ruling or commanding faculty of the soul, performs more functions than others would ascribe to intellect, since all the perceptions and impulses of human beings involve reason and take place in this faculty. See Aëtius 4.21.1 = *SVF* 2.836 = LS 53H.

187 Aristotle, *Generation of Animals* 2.3 736b27: 'it remains that the intellect comes from outside and is alone divine. For bodily activity is in no way associated with it.' The distinction between potential intellect and another type is, however, based rather on Aristotle, *On the Soul* 3.5, where the second type is called 'productive' intellect, and was problematic from the time of Theophrastus onwards; the two passages were linked in discussion from at least the second century CE onwards. See Sharples (2007a), and the next note. Telfer (1955, 225 n.5) suggests that Nemesius' concern here is to use Aristotle to refute the Neoplatonist, and more specifically Apollinarian, view that human beings are essentially tripartite, composed of intellect, soul and body, by emphasising that for Aristotle potential intellect is personal to the individual, and therefore part of the soul, even if 'the intellect from outside' is not. See below, n.318.

188 On the history of interpretations of Aristotle's 'intellect from outside' and of its relation to the 'productive' (often translated as 'active') intellect of Aristotle, *On the Soul* 3.5, see Sorabji (2004) vol.1 102–18; Sharples (2007a). Nemesius' account here of Aristotle's view, discussed by Kallis (1978) 129–30, is unusual in implying that 'intellect from outside' acts on only a few individuals. Alexander of Aphrodisias, *On the Soul* 81.13–83.2, says that the intellectual capacity is not fully developed in all human beings (cf. Aristotle, *On the Soul* 1.2 404b6), but leaves it unclear whether this means that 'intellect from outside' has no effect at all in the case of those whose capacity does not develop fully. And it is far from clear that Aristotle would deny that intellect that is in actuality 'makes man's being and existence complete'. (Is his suggestion at *Nicomachean Ethics* 10.7 1177b26 that the life of theoretical philosophising is *super*human in the background here?) See also Verbeke and Moncho (1975) xl and n.24.

189 Plato, *Alcibiades* I, 129E; man is what uses the body, i.e. the soul (cf. Wyller [1969]) 131–33 and 143, comparing Julian, *Or.* 6 183b). See also *Republic* 5 469d (the body of a slain warrior is not himself but only that with which he fought); *Phaedo* 62b (while in the body we are on duty in a guard-post) and 115ce (Socrates points out that it is not himself that his friends will be burying, but his body); *Axiochus* 365e (Wyller [1969]). Wyller notes that the reference to a body 'of a certain sort' is in origin Aristotelian (below, 17.5) rather than Platonic, and suggests (140) that it derives from Iamblichus' commentary on *Alcibiades I*, noting Iamblichus' insistence that certain souls go with certain bodies (below, 35.7).

self, we should pursue only the goods of the soul, virtues and piety, and should not be content with the desires of the body, for they do not belong to man qua man, but primarily to animals and consequently to man, since man is also an animal.

The soul is in any case agreed by all men (10) to be superior to the body; for the body is moved as a tool by the soul. Death clearly shows this: for when the soul is separated [from it] the body remains altogether immobile and inactive, as tools remain immobile when the craftsman is separated from them.[190]

It is well known that man[191] has something in common even with inanimate things, that he has a share in the life of non-rational animals, and that he participates in (15) the thinking of rational beings. He is associated with inanimate things in virtue of the body and the mixture of the four elements, with plants both in virtue of these things and in virtue of the power of growth and generation, and with non-rational beings both in virtue of these things and, for good measure, in virtue of movement by impulse, desire, spirit,[192] and the power of sensation and breathing. (20) For all these are common to men and to non-rational animals, even if not all to all.

But man is linked by rationality to the incorporeal and intellectual natures, in reasoning and apprehending and judging each matter, pursuing the virtues and cherishing piety, the coping stone of the virtues. So he is, as it were, also on the boundary between intelligible and perceptual being.[193]

[3] He is joined together with non-rational and inanimate beings in virtue of the body and bodily powers, and to incorporeal beings in virtue of reason, as was said earlier. For the Creator appears to link together the different natures by small differences,[194] so that the whole creation is one and (5) akin, by

190 Wyller (1969, 134) suggests that this comparison too derives from a commentary on *Alcibiades I*.

191 Or: 'the human soul'; cf. 5.9. Cf. Galen, *Exhortation to Study the Arts* 9 (vol.1 p.21.4–6 K), 'Children, the human race has something in common both with gods and with the irrational animals, the former in so far as it is rational, the latter in so far as it is mortal'; Gregory the Great, *Homilies on the Gospels* 29, PL 76 1214C, 'man has something of every created thing. For he shares being with stones, life with trees, sensation with animals, understanding with the angels.'

192 That is, *thumos*, the middle part, between reason and desire, of Plato's tripartite soul; 'spirit' in the sense of anger and excited emotion.

193 Cf. Philo of Alexandria, *On the Creation of the World* 135: 'for this reason one might properly say that man is the *boundary* between mortal and immortal nature, sharing in each to the extent that is necessary, and that he has been made mortal and immortal together, mortal in his body, immortal in his reason'.

194 The doctrine that 'nature does not make jumps', *natura non facit saltum*; derived, as

which it is particularly evident that the Creator of all things is one. For He not only unified the existence of each individual thing,[195] but He also linked them together with each other fittingly.

For as in each of the animals He unified the insensitive with the sensitive, bone, fat, hair and other insensitive parts with the sensitive nerves,[196] and made (10) the animal a composite of the sensitive and insensitive, and displayed it as not only a composite but a unity, so He did in each of the other kinds of created things, linking them together by their graduated affinity and the variation of their nature. So as a result beings that are altogether inanimate are not widely separated from plants that have the power of nourishment, nor these in turn from non-rational (15) sensitive animals: nor are non-rational animals, indeed, wholly foreign to those that are rational, separated without any inborn and natural bond. For, true, one stone differs from the other in some capacity, but the magnetic stone[197] seems to have exceeded the nature and power of other stones, in that it visibly draws iron to it and holds on to it, as if (20) it wished to make it its food.[198] It does not do this only with one piece of iron, but holds on to another through one by sharing its own power with all that adjoin it. For iron holds on to iron, when it is held by a magnet.

Then again, subsequently, the Creator, as He moved on from plants to animals, did not at once proceed to a nature that changes its place and is sensitive, (25) but took care to proceed gradually and carefully in this direction. He constructed the bivalves and the corals[199] like sensitive trees, for He rooted them in the sea like plants and put shells around them like wood,[200]

Morani points out, from Aristotle, *History of Animals* 8.1 588b4ff. See Lovejoy (1936) 58–65, and below, n.241.

195 The idea of 'unification' here is Stoic; cf. Simplicius, *On Aristotle's Categories* 214.24 = *SVF* 2.391 = LS 28M.

196 The contrast between parts that have sensation and those that do not is Stoic, if we can rely on Philo of Alexandria, *Allegory of the Laws* 2.22–23 = *SVF* 2.458 = LS 47P, though there bones are said to be lifeless and hair to be plant-like.

197 Magnetite, the lodestone or naturally occurring magnet.

198 The attraction of the iron to the magnet is explained in terms of desire for food also in Alexander of Aphrodisias, *Quaestio* 2.23; but there, oddly, it is the iron that desires something that it lacks but the magnet possesses, even though the magnet is said to be iron that has lost its moisture.

199 So Telfer (1955) 233 n.4, following a suggestion by H.B. Cott. *akalêphê*, the Greek term here, '(sea-)nettles', is applied to jellyfish and sea-anemones. But neither of these have shells. See d'Arcy Thompson (1947) 5–6.

200 The Greek indicates that the shells themselves are compared to wood, rather than the shells being said to surround the animals as bark surrounds wood.

ON THE NATURE OF MAN

and made them stationary like plants; but He endowed them with the sense of touch, **[4]** the sense common to all animals, so that they are associated with plants by having roots and being stationary, with animals by the sense of touch. The sponge, at any rate, Aristotle tells us, although growing on rocks, both contracts and defends itself when it senses something approaching.[201] For such reasons (5) the wise men of old were accustomed to call all such things zoophytes.[202] Again, He linked to bivalves and the like the generation of animals that change their place but are incapable of going far, but move to and from the same place. Most of the animals with shells and worms[203] are like this. Then in the same way he gradually added more senses to some, to others (10) mobility over great distances, and progressed to the more complete of the non-rational animals. I call more complete those that have all the senses and can travel a long way.

Again, when moving from the non-rational animals to the rational animal, man, He did not construct this all at once, but first He endowed the other animals also with certain natural forms of understanding, devices and (15) resources for their preservation, so that they appear near to the rational animals,[204] and thus He projected the truly rational animal, man. In the same way, too, if you also investigate voice you will also find a gradual progress from the simple and undifferentiated vocalisation of horses and cattle to the varied and differentiated[205] voice of crows and imitative birds, until He finished (20) with the articulated and perfect voice of man. Again, He linked

201 Aristotle, *History of Animals* 1.1 487b10, 5.16 548b10, 549a8; 8.1 588b20 takes a different view, saying that the sponge is like a plant. See Balme (1991) vol.3 64 note (b) ad loc.

202 As Telfer 233 n.5 points out, the term 'zoophyte' is not actually found before the second century CE. Telfer claims, citing Jaeger (1914) 104 n.2 and 116, that this passage reflects Galen, *On the Doctrines of Hippocrates and Plato* 5.6.38 (*CMG* 5.4.1.2 334.4-8 De Lacy = vol.5 476.14–477.2 K), 'as many animals as move with difficulty and grow attached *like plants* to rocks or other such things, these [Posidonius] says are ruled by desire alone; the other irrational animals employ both faculties, that of desire and the spirited faculty; man alone employs all three, for he has gained the principle of reason in addition'. But there is no trace of Posidonius' allusion to the Platonic tripartite soul in our Nemesius passage, and the parallellism identified by Jaeger between the text in Galen and that in Nemesius extends only to the expression 'like plants' (*dikên phutôn*). Edelstein–Kidd (1988–9, vol.2.1 p.165) express agnosticism on whether this discussion of non-mobile animals in Nemesius derives from Posidonius.

203 Literally 'so-called "earth's guts"': Aristotle, *History of Animals* 6.16 570a15, *Generation of Animals* 3.11 762b26, in both cases in connection with the belief that eels originate in a certain type of worm.

204 Cf. Pohlenz (1941) and below, 2 36.16–21.

205 Cf. Porphyry, *On Abstinence* 3.4.2: 'the *variation* and *differentiation* of [animals'] utterance shows that it gives indications'.

articulate speech to thought and reasoning, making it a messenger of the movements of the intellect. Thus He joined everything to everything harmoniously, and bound them together and collected into one things intelligible and things visible, by the medium of the generation of man'.[206]

So also Moses, in his exposition of the creation, **[5]** correctly said that man came to be last,[207] not only because, since everything came to be on his account, it followed that things for his use should he prepared first and then he who was to use them should be added, but also because when intelligible reality and also visible reality had come to be, something needed to come to be (5) to bind them both together, so that everything should be one and in sympathy with itself and not foreign itself to itself. So man, the animal that binds both natures together, came to be.[208] Such is a concise account of the works of the wisdom of the creator.

Therefore man was assigned a place on the boundary between the non-rational and the rational nature. (10) If he inclines towards the body[209] and loves more the things of the body, then he embraces the life of the non-rational beings and he will be reckoned among them, and he will be called 'earthy', as by Paul,[210] and will be told 'For you are earth, and to earth you will return'[211] and 'he was compared to the foolish cattle and made like unto them'.[212] But, if he moves towards the rational and despises all the bodily pleasures, (15) he will enter into the divine life that is most dear to God and pre-eminently human, and he will be like a heavenly being, in accordance with the saying 'As is the earthy, such are they also that are earthy, and as is the heavenly, such are they also that are heavenly.'[213] But the summit of the rational nature is to flee from and turn away from evils, but to pursue and choose things that are good.

206 Skard (1937, 18–22) argues that 2.13–4.24 derive from a lost work by Galen. See below, n.226. Jaeger (1914, 104) sees Posidonian influence in the notion of 'binding together', and compares, ultimately, Plato, *Timaeus* 31c. But the connection is a remote one.

207 Genesis 1:26. Telfer (1955, 235 n.1) notes that the issue was discussed by Philo of Alexandria in *On the Creation of the World* 77ff., and suggests Philo is Nemesius' source, via Origen. Cf. Gregory of Nyssa, *On the Creation of Man* 2, *PG* 44.132–33.

208 In uniting the sensible and intelligible Nemesius gives to the creation of man the role that Plato in the *Timaeus* gives to the creation of the world-soul. See Introduction, 5.a.5.

209 Telfer (1955, 236 n.3) notes that Origen uses this expression (*inclinet*) in his *First Homily on Genesis* (15, *GCS* 6.1 [29] p. 19.18). For the general theme Verbeke and Moncho (1975) xxxviii n.11 compare Plotinus 3.4 [15], 3.

210 1 Corinthians 15:47–49.
211 Genesis 3:19.
212 Psalm 49(48):13=20.
213 1 Corinthians 15:48.

Of things (20) good, some involve the co-operation of soul and body: but these also have reference to the soul, since the soul is making use of the body. Such are the virtues. But some involve the soul alone by itself, having no need of the body as well: such is piety and the contemplation of realities. Now such as choose to live a human life as that of a human and not just the life of a mere animal **[6]** pursue the virtues and piety. But what belongs to virtue and what belongs to piety will be distinguished in what follows when we give an account of soul and body. For, as long as we do not yet know what our soul essentially is, it is out of sequence to go through its activities.

(5) The Hebrews say that man came into existence in the beginning as neither incontestably mortal nor immortal, but at the boundary of each nature,[214] so that, if he should pursue bodily affections, he would be subjected also to bodily changes, while, if he should estimate more highly the goods of the soul, he might be thought worthy (10) of immortality. For if God had made him mortal from the beginning He would not have condemned him to death when he had sinned: for nobody condemns the mortal to mortality. If, however, He had rather made him immortal, He would not have made him in need of food, since nothing immortal needs bodily food. Nor would He have so easily changed his mind and at once made mortal what was born immortal. For (15) He has evidently not done so in the case of the angels who sinned,[215] but they continued immortal as in their original nature and received a different punishment for their sins, but not death.

So it is better to consider the matter before us either in that way, or else [to suppose] that [man] was created mortal, but capable of becoming immortal if perfected by progress:[216] in other words, potentially (20) immortal. But since it was not expedient for him prior to being perfected to know his own nature, [God] forbade him to eat from the tree of knowledge. For there were,

---

214 See Philo of Alexandria, *On the Creation of the World* 135, quoted in n.193 above; Theophilus, *Against Autolycus* 2.27, '[God] did not create [man] either immortal or mortal, but ... admitting of both, in order that, if he inclines to the things that are of immortality, observing God's command, he may receive immortality as reward from him and become a god, but if he turns to the things that are of death, disobeying god, he may be the cause of his own death'. Nemesius' interpretation of man's intermediate state agrees with Theophilus', against Philo's (and possibly Origen's) view that man's body is mortal, his mind immortal (Telfer [1955] 238 n.1). Telfer further argues that 'the Hebrews' is Origen's way of referring to Philo, taken over by Nemesius, and suggests, following Jaeger (1914) 141 and Skard (1936), that Nemesius' source is Origen's lost commentary on Genesis 2:7. The expression 'the Hebrews' occurs also below in 11.15; 53.7; 68.11; 121.10.
215 2 Peter 2:4: 'God did not spare the angels who sinned'.
216 Cf. Philo of Alexandria, *On the Creation of the World* 77 p.23.23ff.

or rather, still are now, very great powers in plants; but then, it being the beginning of creation, these powers were intact and had their activity at its strongest. So even a taste of some fruit was sufficient to instil a knowledge (25) of [man's] own nature. But God did not want him to know his own nature prior to being made perfect, **[7]** so that he might not recognise himself to be lacking in many things and attend to his bodily needs, while abandoning the care for his soul. For this reason He stopped him from partaking of the fruit of knowledge. But when man did not heed and came to know himself, he fell away from perfection (5) and became subject to bodily needs. At any rate he immediately sought covering: for Moses says 'he knew that he was naked'.[217] Previously He had made him unselfconscious and unaware of himself. So when he fell away from perfection he fell away also from immortality, which he will later regain by the grace of his Maker.

After the fall he was permitted also the enjoyment of meats: (10) for beforehand [God] had commanded him to be satisfied with the fruits of the earth, for these were in the garden. But when perfection was lost he was subsequently allowed luxuries at his fall.[218] But since man is composed of body, and every body is constituted by the four elements, he inevitably became subject to the same changes as the (15) elements are, to division and change and flux, which happen only to body: to change qualitatively, to flux through emptying. For an animal is always being emptied both through the obvious channels and through the obscure, about which we will speak later.[219] Now it is necessary that either equal amounts should be brought in to things that are being emptied or the animal disintegrates through lack of the things it takes in. Since it is dry things, (20) liquids and breath that are evacuated, an animal inevitably needs dry and liquid food and breath. Our food and drink **[8]** are through the elements from which we are also constituted. For each thing is fed by what is akin to and like it, but is treated medically by what is opposite. Of the elements we receive some directly, some also through certain intermediaries, as water sometimes neat and sometimes

217 Genesis 3:7.
218 For meat-eating as a mark of the Fall cf. Sorabji (1993) 198. There are verbal parallels between the present passage and Basil, *On the Origin of Man* 2.7 p.244.14–20 (Jaeger [1914] 141–42) though Basil refers to eating of meat after the *Flood:* 'when man changed his way of life and went beyond the boundaries that had been given to him, after the Flood the Lord saw that men were neglectful [of his commands] and *permitted* them the *enjoyment* of everything'. (The page reference is to Smets and Esbroeck [1970]. Jaeger cites the work as Basil, *On the Structure of Man* 2.3, *PG* 30 45a; it is identical to Gregory of Nyssa, *Oration 2 on the words "Let us make man"*, *PG* 44 284b. *PG* 30 treats the attribution to Basil as doubtful, but Smets and Esbroeck endorse it.)
219 Below, section 23. For the general point cf. Plato, *Timaeus* 43ab.

through the intermediary of wine, oil and (5) all of what are called liquid produce. For wine is nothing other than water endowed with the qualities of the vine. Similarly we sometimes partake of fire immediately when we are warmed by it, sometimes through the medium of what we eat and drink. For a greater or lesser portion of fire is disseminated in everything. The case is the same with air: we (10) take it in immediately by breathing and by having it lying all about us and by drawing it in as we eat and drink, and through the medium of all the other things with which we are brought in contact. We never take in earth immediately, but through certain media: for earth becomes food and we eat food. For while larks and pigeons often eat earth, and so do partridges,[220] man does so only through the media of seeds, (15) tree-fruits and flesh.

Not merely for comeliness, but also on account of sensitivity of touch, in which man surpasses all other animals, [God] did not clothe us in a thick skin, like oxen and the other thick-skinned animals, nor in long thick hair like goats, sheep and hares, nor in scales like snakes and (20) fish, nor in shells like tortoises and oysters, nor in a pliable shell like beetles, nor in wings like birds.[221] As a result, we inevitably needed clothing, as a supplement to us of what nature gave to other species. For these reasons we need food and clothing, and we need housing **[9]** both for these reasons and especially as refuges from wild beasts. Because of the ill-balance of the qualities[222] and the loosening of our bodily coherence we became in need of physicians and medical care. When qualitative change occurred it was necessary (5) to restore the bodily constitution to equilibrium by the opposing quality. For the task of physicians is not, as some think, to make a heated body cold but to restore it to a balance; for if it be chilled the condition is converted into the opposite illness.[223]

---

220 Telfer (1955, 241 n.4) plausibly suggests that the birds were actually eating ants or grubs in the soil. Skard (1937, 13) points out that Nemesius omits to mention the Serpent's being cursed to eat earth (Genesis 3:14); Kallis (1978, 71 n.3) responds that to do so would not suit the context, concerned as it is with human beings taking in earth by eating intermediaries. For we do not eat serpents.

221 For the general thought compare Gregory of Nyssa, *On the Creation of Man* 7 141a, and Theodoret of Cyrrha, *On Providence* 4 p.613.

222 The elementary qualities hot, cold, dry and wet which, in Galen's medical thinking, are fundamental to human bodily health; see e.g. Galen, *On the Elements according to Hippocrates*, *On Mixtures*, and section 5 below. 'Ill-balance' and 'loosening of coherence' are coupled at Galen, *Method of Healing* 13.1 (10.874.1–4 K): 'It has already been shown how two kinds of diseases may be cured in a methodical way; one, ill balance (*duskrasia*), has an ancient name, the other has been given a name by us, the loosening of coherence'.

223 Galen, *Method of Healing* 9.15 (10.650.7–9 K): 'healing is nothing other than bringing

So man has a need of food and drink because of evacuation and dispersal, (10) of clothing because he has no natural strong covering, of a house because of the lack of proportion with regard to the environment and because of wild beasts, of medical care because of the change of qualities and the sensitivity with which the body has been endowed. For if we had no sensation, we would not suffer pain, and without suffering pain we would not ask for medical treatment, and we would be destroyed, since in our ignorance of the evil we would (15) not be cured of the affection.[224]

On account of the crafts and the sciences and the useful things that arise from these we have need of each other. Because we have need of each other we come together in numbers and share what is useful for life in our co-operative activities; this coming and living together they called a city. This was so that we should enjoy the benefit of each other from near and not from afar. (20) For man was naturally born to flock together and to be a creature living in a social community:[225] for no one man is self-sufficient in all things. So it is clear that cities were formed for co-operative activities and for learning.[226]

Man received these two special privileges: he alone receives pardon on repentance, and his is the only body, though mortal, to be made immortal; he receives (25) the bodily privilege because of the soul and that of the soul because of the body.[227] For man alone of rational beings was thought worthy [10] of pardon on repentance. For neither demons nor angels are thought worthy of pardon on repentance, and in this especially God is shown and declared to be both just and merciful. For the angels have no compulsion that leads them to sin, but they are free by nature (5) from bodily affections, needs and pleasures, and reasonably there is no pardon given to them on

the present disposition in the body to a natural condition'.

224 So Galen, *On the Usefulness of the Parts* 5.10, vol. 3 p.380.9–14 K = p.278.16–22 Helmreich, explaining why animals have sensation in their digestive tract: 'Since [the organs of nutrition] have no sense-organ or organ of movement, it was necessary that they should all be equipped with small nerves for the third use only, to discern what would cause pain. For if they did not possess even this, and had no sensation of the troubles in them, nothing would have prevented animals from perishing in a very short time.'

225 Aristotle, *Politics* 1.1 1253a2, 7; Basil, *Homilies on the Psalms* 14.6, *PG* 29.261C: 'man is an animal that *lives in a social community* and *flocks together*'.

226 Skard (1937, 9–18) argues that 7.12–9.22 derive from a lost work by Galen, which at his (1938) 41 he suggests might have been either the *Timaeus* commentary or *On Demonstration*. On 8.15–9.22 cf. Kallis (1978) 72–78.

227 As the end of the paragraph makes clear, the second part of the sentence reverses the order of the first part; the 'bodily privilege' is being made immortal, the 'privilege of the soul' is receiving pardon.

repentance; but man is not only rational, but also an animal, and animal needs and other affections often pervert his reason. So when he becomes sober and flees from such things, and pursues the virtues, he receives the just mercy of pardon. As the power of laughter is a special (10) property of his being, since it is present in him alone, in all and always,[228] so in the matters of grace it is special to man among the whole rational creation to throw off through repentance the blame for sins committed. For man alone was given this gift, every one and for ever throughout his life in this world, but no longer after death.[229] Thus some (15) hold that the angels, too, after the Fall[230] no longer receive the pardon that arises from repentance; for to them, the Fall is their death. Yet prior to the Fall, parallel with the life of men, they also were thought worthy of pardon, but since they did not do this [i.e. repent], afterwards they suffer the fitting justice of a punishment that admits of no repentance and is eternal. From these considerations (20) it is clear that those who do not accept repentance reject this exclusive gift which is special to man.

It is also peculiar to him and exclusive that alone among the other animals his body rises after death and proceeds to immortality; this he receives because of the immortality of the soul, **[11]** as he receives the other because of the weakness and many afflictions of the body.

Understanding of the skills and sciences is also peculiar to man, as are his activities in accordance with these. That is why they[231] also define man as a rational animal, mortal and receptive of intellect and knowledge. An animal, because man too is (5) an animate, sensitive being: for this is the definition of an animal. 'Rational', in order to separate him from non-rational animals. 'Mortal', in order to separate him from rational immortals. 'Receptive of intellect and knowledge', because it is by learning that we acquire skills and

---

228 Aristotle, *Parts of Animals* 3.10 673a8; Porphyry, *Introduction (Isagôgê)* 20.11–12, 19–22.

229 This is, as Streck (2005, 191) notes, a rather negative and one-sided attitude to death in a Christian writer; the doctrine in itself is not in itself unorthodox, but Nemesius' concentration on human action here leads him away from reference to salvation and the hope of eternal life.

230 The Greek could mean 'their fall'. But Telfer (1955, 245–46 n.2) notes that Gregory of Nyssa, *Catchetical Oration* 6 attributes the fall of Satan to his envy of man; in prompting the Fall of man, and not repenting of doing so, Satan irrevocably sealed his own fate (though most writers took the view that Satan's repentance was not excluded until after the Incarnation). Nemesius does not follow Origen, for whom, notoriously, even Satan still has the possibility of repentance.

231 This definition verbatim at [Galen], *Medical Definitions* 27 (19 p.355.7–8 K) and at David, *Preliminaries (Prolegomena), CAG* 18.2 15.17–18.

the sciences; for we have a capability to receive both intellect and skills, but the actual possession of these is the result of learning. (10) They say that this was added later to the definition: for the definition is sound also without it. But since some introduce both nymphs and other kinds of demons that are long-lasting, but not in fact immortal, they added 'being receptive of intellect and knowledge' in order to set man apart from these. For none of them learns, but what they know they know naturally.[232]

(15) It is a doctrine of the Hebrews that this universe came to be because of man[233] – immediately for his sake such things as beasts of burden and oxen used for farming, and fodder for their sake. For of things that came to be some did so for their own sake, some for other ends; for their own sake all rational beings, for the sake of others non-rational animals and the inanimate. But if these came to be for the sake of other things, let us consider for what sort of other things. Was it for the sake of the (20) angels? But nobody in his senses would say that these things came to be for the sake of the angels; for what comes to be for the sake of other things does so for their formation, preservation and recreation, for it does so for the renewal of the kind, or for food or shelter or cure or business and recreation. But an angel needs none of these. For there is no renewal of its race, nor does it need bodily food (25) nor shelter nor the rest. And, if not angels, it is clear that it is not any other nature superior to angels; for the more superior it is, so much more is it without needs. So we must look for some nature that is rational, **[12]** but in need of the things mentioned. But what other such a nature will appear if we omit man? So the conclusion follows that it was for his sake that non-rational animals and the inanimate came to be.

Thus since, as was shown, it was for him, for that reason he was also established as their ruler.[234] But it is the task of the ruler to use the ruled (5)

---

232 'Receptive of knowledge' is a *proprium* (peculiar characteristic) of man at Aristotle, *Topics* 5.2 130b8. Alexander, *On Aristotle's Topics* 43.26–28, on 1.5 102a1, says that this is because gods do not *acquire* knowledge. But he does not say that the phrase is to be included in the actual definition, and the contrast with *gods* does not indeed make this necessary; for gods, unlike nymphs in the continuation to our passage (and in David), are not mortal. Telfer (1955, 246 n.3) regards the extended definition as from a Neoplatonist source. See also Kallis (1978) 81 and nn.

233 Cf. Origen, *Against Celsus* 4.74 and *Homily on Genesis* 1.12 (*GCS* vol. 6.1 [29] p.14.5–6): 'that great creation of God, man, on account of whom the entire world was created'. Skard (1937, 23–25), while arguing that Origen is the principal source in what follows, suggests that specific biological details derive from Galen. For 'the Hebrews' as a way of referring to Philo see above, n.214.

234 Genesis 1:26. Origen, *Homily on Genesis* 1.12 (*GCS* vol. 6.1 [29] p.13.24–14.7) uses man's dominion over the animals as an allegory for the soul ruling over the body.

according to the measure of need, not to exploit them for pleasure without restraint, nor to behave towards the ruled with overbearing disregard. So those who do not treat non-rational animals well commit sin: for they do not perform the function of a ruler nor of a righteous man according to the scripture 'the righteous man regardeth the life of his beasts'.[235]

But perhaps somebody will say that nothing came to be for the sake of something else, (10) but everything for its own sake. So let us first separate the animate from the inanimate, and see if the inanimate can come to be for their own sake. For if these do so for their own sake, how and whence shall animals be fed?[236] For we see that nature provides for animals food from the fruits and crops of the earth, except for a very few carnivores, while the carnivores themselves feed on the animals that crop the earth, as wolves and lions eat sheep, goats, (15) pigs and deer, eagles eat partridges, doves, hares and the like, which feed on the fruits of the earth. Moreover, though the nature of fish is to eat each other, the flesh-eating does not extend to them all, but terminates with those that feed on seaweed and other aquatic plants. For if (20) all the kinds of fish had been carnivorous, and there was none that escaped from the eating of flesh, there would not have been enough for even a short time, but they would have been destroyed, some by each other, some by lack of food. In order that this should not come about some fishes were constituted to abstain from flesh but rather, as one might say, to graze the pastures of the sea, so that the others too might be preserved (25) through them. For their food is seaweed, and they are the food of other fishes, and these of yet others, so that from the food of those at the end of the chain, provided inexhaustibly from the earthy seabed, the **[13]** existence of the others too is preserved.

So the argument has shown that plants do not come to be for their own sake, but have come to be as food and maintenance for man and the other animals. But if these are for the sake of men and animals it is clear that the causes of the growth and birth of these things must also be (5) for the sake of these. So the motions of the stars, the heavens, the seasons, rain and all such things come to be for their sake, in order that, since the food chain is a continual circle, the nature of what produces the crops should also continue

---

235 Proverbs 12:10.
236 The argument appears to assume that a thing cannot come to be both for its own sake and for the sake of something else; and indeed, in the case of plants eaten by animals the interests of the plants and of the animals on the face of it conflict (though in fact the tempting fruits of many plants persuade animals to benefit the plants by conveying their seeds). The treatment of plants as inanimate is distinctively Stoic, in opposition to the Aristotelian view.

inexhaustible, so that these are found to be for the sake of the crops, and the crops for animals and man.[237]

It remains to consider (10) whether the nature of the non-rational animals also came to be for its own sake, or for the sake of man. But perhaps it is absurd that things which have no share in wisdom, and live only by natural impulse, that are bent down towards the earth and display their servitude in their form,[238] should be said to have been brought to be for their own sake. Much could be said on this topic, and it almost needs a separate monograph (15) through its volume. But the present enterprise does not run to lengthy discussion, so it is best to have recourse to what is brief but relevant.

If we should see matters external to him reflected in man as in an image, we should be constructing our proofs from the very being of the things under investigation. For we see in our soul the non-rational and its parts (20) (I refer to appetite and spirit)[239] devoted to the service of the rational part, the latter ruling, the former ruled, the latter commanding, the former being commanded and under orders and serving whatever needs reason indicates, when man preserves his nature. If the rational part in us rules the non-rational parts in us, how is it not reasonable that it should also have mastery over the non-rational things external [to us] and that they (25) should have been given to serve its needs? For it is the natural role of the non-rational to serve the rational, as was shown with regard to ourselves.

The conformation of most animals **[14]** also shows this, since it is suitable for the service of man – cattle and all beasts of burden for farming

---

237 As Koch (1921, 46–47) and Telfer (1955, 250 n.3) note, this is given as a Stoic view by Origen, *Against Celsus* 4.74–78, and in Cicero, *On the Nature of the Gods* 2.133. From a parallel in Gregory of Nyssa, *On the Creation of Man* 8, *PG* 44 144D, 'perhaps we learn from this not only what can readily be understood, that crops seemed useful to the Creator for the sake of animals, and grazing animals on account of man' (see also the next note). Telfer suggests that Nemesius' source is Origen's commentary on Genesis; cf. Verbeke and Moncho (1975) xxxix n.19. Koch suggests that the parallels between Nemesius and Theodoret, *On Providence* may indicate that Nemesius transferred to this first part of his treatise material on providence that he found in his source for sections 41–43 below; but it seems equally possible that the material had already been linked with the creation of mankind in his source.

238 This contrast between upright human posture and that of the animals is a commonplace; it was made popular by Plato, *Timaeus* 90a, 91e–92a, but cf. also Xenophon, *Memorabilia* 1.4.11; Aristotle, *Parts of Animals* 4.10 686a27; Cicero, *On the Nature of the Gods* 2.140; Sallust, *Catiline* 1; Ovid, *Metamorphoses* 1.84–6; Seneca, *Letter* 92.30, 94.56; Gregory of Nyssa, *On the Creation of Man* 8, *PG* 44 144B Basil, *On the Six Days (of Creation)* 9.2, *PG* 29 192A; Theodoret of Cyrrha, *On Providence* 3 p.597; Boethius, *Consolation* 5 metr.5 9–11. Koch (1921) 10, 46–47; Telfer (1955) 251 n.1; Gruber (1978) 406–07; Sharples (1991) 227.

239 Above, n.192.

and load-carrying, the majority of birds, whether of water or of land, to produce enjoyment, imitative ones[240] for pleasure and recreation. If they do not all serve (5) such needs, but some even harm man, one must know that while it is those that are for service that come to be in a primary way, all the others that were possible were also constituted, so that nothing should be lacking to creation that could possibly come to be.[241] But not even these altogether escaped being of advantage to man, but reason harvests even the harmful ones for its own need. (10) For it makes use of them to cure the harm which is caused by them themselves and for the cure of other indispositions. Of this sort are the so-called poisonous preparations which reason has discovered in order to conquer them by means of themselves,[242] and so to be helped as by vanquished enemies. Man has thousands of such ways of counteracting these that have been provided (15) by the Creator, capable of containing, warding off and correcting their attacks. Different ones are fitted for different needs, but in general all are of a nature to contribute to the medical treatment of mankind, even those things that are not serviceable for other needs.

Let so much be said regarding the present condition of our life, since of old none of the other animals dared (20) harm man, but all were servants, subordinate and obedient, so long as he controlled his own emotions and the irrationality within him. But when he did not master his own emotions but was mastered by them, he was also mastered by the wild beasts external to him, as might be expected. For together with sin came harm from these.[243] That this is true is clear from **[15]** those who have followed the best life. For they were seen to be unconquerably masters over the attacks of wild beasts, as Daniel of lions[244] and Paul of the bite of the viper.[245]

Who, then, could rightly be surprised at the nobility of such an animal that binds together in himself mortal and immortal elements, and (5) joins the rational with the non-rational; who carries in his own nature the image

---

240 The Greek suggests, but does not require, that the reference is still to birds, as at 4.19 above. Telfer (1955, 252 n.1) suggests rather that the reference is to monkeys.
241 The doctrine that 'nature does not make jumps', above n.194; here an expression of the 'principle of plenitude', for which cf. Lovejoy (1936) 64–65.
242 The reference is to small doses of poison conferring immunity from larger amounts, as famously in the story told of Mithradates VI Eupator (Appian, *Mithridatica* 537).
243 Genesis 3:15.
244 Daniel 6:19–24; cf. Theodoret, *On Providence* 5.641; Koch (1921) 48.
245 Acts 28:3–6; cf. Theodoret, *On Providence* 5.641. Skard (1936, 35–40) argues that 13.10–15.3 derive from Origen.

of the whole creation, for which reason he was also called a microcosm;[246] who was thought worthy of so great divine providence; for whom is every thing that is now and is to be, and for whom indeed God became man; who ends in incorruption and escapes mortality? He is king over the heavens; being born in the image (10) and likeness of God,[247] he communes with Christ, is a child of God, and surpasses all principalities and powers. Who could express the advantages of this living thing? He crosses the seas, in contemplation he enters into the heavens, he recognises the motions of the stars, their intervals and their dimensions, he crops the earth and the sea, he thinks nothing of wild beasts and sea-monsters, he controls every science, craft (15) and procedure, he converses by writing with those with whom he wishes to do so beyond the horizon, impeded in no way by the body,[248] he forecasts the future; he rules all things, controls all things and enjoys all things, he converses with angels and with God, he gives orders to the whole creation, instructs spirits, discovers the nature of things, concerns himself with God and becomes the house and temple of God.[249] All (20) this is the fruit of virtue and piety.[250]

But lest we seem to some to be writing a vulgar encomium of man and not merely setting forth his nature, which was our project, let us leave the account at this point, even if in stating the greatest advantages of his

---

246 Democritus fr. 68B34 DK, 'man, who is a microcosm according to Democritus'; Galen, *On the Usefulness of the Parts* 3.10 vol.3 p.241.15–16 K = p.177.10 Helmreich, 'men of old who were competent about nature say that a living creature is like a microcosm'; *Life of Pythagoras* quoted by Photius, *Library* 249 440a33, 'man is said to be a microcosm'. Cf. Jaeger (1914) 135–36, who compares, significantly, the description of man as a 'little (*brakhus*) cosmos' at Philo, *On the Creation of the World* 82; Kallis (1978) 90–93.

247 Genesis 1:26–27.

248 It is debatable whether 'impeded in no way by the body' should be taken with what precedes it, as our punctuation implies, or with the following reference to prophecy. Matthaei and Morani take the latter view, but Burgundio of Pisa (at least as punctuated by Verbeke and Moncho [1975]) and Telfer (1955, 255 n.4) take the former, arguing that ch.12 below shows that Nemesius did not regard prophecy through dreams as the only form. That claim is in fact debatable; but Telfer's punctuation is favoured both by the rhythm of the sentence and by the fact that a reader who came across the clause would have no way of knowing that it was not to be taken with what preceded it.

249 The expression is found in Origen: *On John* 10.51 (*GCS* vol. 4 [10] p.219.6), *Homily on Exodus* 8.4 (*GCS* vol. 6.1 [29] p.226.1–2). Verbeke and Moncho (1975) 22.

250 Jaeger (1914, 134) compares 15.11–24 with Cicero, *On the Nature of the Gods* 2.152–53 (and, at 132–33, more generally 13.10–15.3 with 2.148–59); but the correspondences are in fact slight. Telfer (1955, 256) is right to note that what Nemesius says here is 'a series of rhetorical commonplaces'; and the account in Cicero develops from a specific point about the advantage to man of having hands, absent from Nemesius.

nature we describe this very nature. So, if we know in what noble birth we share and that **[16]** we are heaven-born,[251] let us not dishonour our nature, nor show ourselves unworthy of such gifts, nor deprive ourselves of such power, such glory and such blessedness; let us not for short-lasting and brief pleasure abandon the enjoyment of all eternal things, but let us preserve our nobility by good deeds, by abstaining from what is low, by a right aim, to which especially (5) the divine is accustomed to give aid, and by prayers.

So much is sufficient on these matters. But since what is generally said lays it down that man consists in soul and body, let us separate them and first analyse the soul, leaving aside those questions that are too subtle, (10) too difficult and too hard for most men to understand.

SECTION 2

ON THE SOUL

Review of opinions about the soul; it is an incorporeal substance, unique to each individual and created at the beginning of the world.

Nearly all the ancients disagree in their account of the soul.[252] For Democritus and Epicurus and the whole college of Stoic philosophers declare that the soul is a body; and these same people who declare (15) the soul to be a body differ about its essence. For the Stoics say that it is hot and fiery breath,[253]

---

251 For 'heaven-born' cf. Plato, *Timaeus* 90a; Clement of Alexandria, *Protreptic* 10.100 p.72.28; Basil, *On the Six Days (of Creation)* 9.2 192A, and (ironically, citing Plato) Palladas, *Anth. Pal.* 10.45

252 The doxography of the views of pagan Greek philosophers on the soul that follows is closely parallel to that in book 4 chs. 2–3 of Aëtius, the writer whose work Diels reconstructed from pseudo-Plutarch, *Epitome of Physical Opinions*, and Stobaeus, along with various other sources including, notably, Theodoret's *Remedy for Greek Attitudes*. See Mansfeld (1990) 3076–82, Mansfeld and Runia (1996) 293–94, 296–97, and our Introduction, 5.a.3. The criticisms of Eunomius and Apollinaris (30.18–32.19) are Nemesius' own contribution.

253 Aëtius 4.3.3 gives the Stoic view as 'hot breath' ('intelligent and hot breath' in Stobaeus); Theodoret, *Remedy* 5.18 as 'breath with a great portion of heat'. On the Stoic doctrine of breath and soul see LS 47 and 53.

Critias that it is blood,[254] the philosopher Hippo that it is water,[255] Democritus that it is fire – for when atoms of spherical shape are mixed together, being fire and air, they result in a soul.[256] Heraclitus says that the soul of the universe is a rising vapour from moist things, (20) while that in animals is from both the rising vapour from outside and that within themselves, and is of the same kind.[257]

Again, there are countless disagreements among those who say that the soul is incorporeal. Some say that it is a substance and **[17]** immortal, others that it is incorporeal but neither a substance nor immortal. For Thales first said that the soul was eternally in motion and self-moving;[258] Pythagoras that it was a self-moving number;[259] Plato that it was an intelligible substance, self-changing according to an harmonic number;[260] Aristotle that it was the

---

254 The reference to Critias (for which see Aristotle, *On the Soul* 1.2 405b5: Mansfeld [1990] 3077 and n.74) is absent from our two main sources for Aëtius, the pseudo-Plutarch *Tenets* and Stobaeus, but is present in Theodoret, *Remedy for Greek Attitudes*; Mansfeld points out that this shows that Nemesius is not dependent on pseudo-Plutarch (see below, nn.257–58). It does not, however, as Mansfeld (1990, 3077 n.74) rightly notes (cf. Mansfeld and Runia [1996] 294), show that Nemesius is not dependent on *Aëtius*, as was wrongly claimed by Dörrie (1959, 117), followed by Siclari (1974, 72 n.24). Philoponus, *On Aristotle's On the Soul* 9.3–10.9 has an account which includes Critias (9.19); but, as Mansfeld (1990) 3209–12 shows, Philoponus' account has a structure in the account of theories which make the soul corporeal, a systematic sequence of simple elements followed by compounds, which Mansfeld suggests goes back to Aristotle himself, and which is different from the less systematic sequence in Nemesius. It therefore seems likely that the presence of Critias in both Philoponus and Nemesius is to be explained by Aristotle as the common source, rather than Philoponus as well as Nemesius depending on a text of Aëtius which was fuller than in pseudo-Plutarch or Stobaeus. Philoponus' account of Democritus is different from those in Aëtius and Nemesius, not mentioning either fire or air.

255 Aëtius 4.3.9 (Stobaeus only).

256 Aëtius 4.3.5; Aristotle, *On the Soul* 1.2 403b31–404a2, 405a8-13. See KRS p.427. Only Nemesius, however, mentions air as well as fire; Domański (1900, 16 n.5) therefore proposed deleting the reference to air.

257 ~ Aëtius 4.3.12 (pseudo-Plutarch only). (We use '~' here and in what follows to indicate correspondence in wording as well as in content). See Mansfeld (1990) 3066–67 and n.18; KRS pp.203–05.

258 ~ Aëtius 4.2.1. The sequence from Thales to 'Deinarchus' (see below) corresponds to that in pseudo-Plutarch (but see above n.254); Stobaeus has Thales, Alcmaeon, Pythagoras, Xenocrates (omitted here by Nemesius, but see below n.328 and Mansfeld [1990] 3078 n.75), Aristotle and Dicaearchus, omitting Plato.

259 ~ Aëtius 4.2.3. See below, n.327.

260 ~ Aëtius 4.2.5. That soul is intelligible rather than apprehended by the senses is implied at Plato, *Phaedo* 79b–80b; that it is self-changing or self-moving (the Greek term can mean either; see below, nn.323–24) at *Phaedrus* 245e; that it is *constructed* according to a harmonic number at *Timaeus* 35b–36b. For soul being a substance see below, n.263.

ON THE NATURE OF MAN 53

first actuality of an organic (5) natural body which potentially has life;[261] Deinarchus[262] that it was an attunement of the four elements, equivalent to the mixture and agreement of the elements – for he does not mean the attunement consisting of sounds but the attuned mixture and agreement of the hot and cold, moist and dry, in the body. It is clear that of these the rest say that the soul (10) is a substance, but Aristotle and Deinarchus that it is not substance.[263] Furthermore in addition to these some have thought that the soul of all things was one and the same, divided up among individuals and again returning to itself, as do the Manichaeans[264] and certain others, some that they are many and different in kind, some that there are both one and many. So it is very necessary to make a lengthy (15) rebuttal of this multitude of opinions.

261 ~ Aëtius 4.2.6, who adds: '"actuality" (*entelekheia*) should be understood as "activity"' (*energeia*; 'form and activity' in Stobaeus). Aristotle, *On the Soul* 2.1. 412a27.

262 Normally emended to 'Dicaearchus', but Mansfeld (1990, 3078) has argued that 'Deinarchus' is what Nemesius wrote and should therefore be printed, even if Nemesius was wrong; Aëtius 4.2.7 has 'Dicaearchus'. There was indeed an early Pythagorean named Deinarchus (Iamblichus, *Life of Pythagoras* 36.267 p.145.15 Dübner; Goulet [1994] vol.2 617) but it seems most likely that Nemesius has made a simple mistake. Cf. Mansfeld (1990) 3072; Caston (1997) 340–41; Sharples (2001b) 145–46 n.10. The Greek word here translated as 'attunement' is *harmonia*. It is sometimes translated as 'harmony', rather unfortunately. The word has a basic meaning in carpentry and similar crafts of the joining together of the component parts: in music it refers to the tuning of the strings. It does not mean a vertical relation between sounds as does 'harmony' in modern music.

263 This is an incorrect judgement as far as Aristotle is concerned; for soul is form for Aristotle, and form is substance (*Metaphysics* H1 1042a28). But Nemesius' agenda – or that of his Platonist source; cf. Telfer (1955) 269 n.1 – is to argue for the view that soul is incorporeal substance separable from the body, and the form of an enmattered body will not satisfy this requirement. See below, 37.23. Here as elsewhere Nemesius' discussion reflects the debates of the 1st century BCE and the first two centuries CE; the 1st-century BCE Peripatetic Boethus suggested that form was quality (Simplicius, *On Aristotle's Categories* 78.4ff.; see also Iamblichus ap. Stobaeus 1.49.32, p.363.20 Wachsmuth); for the contrary argument that soul is not in a substrate (as a quality would be) see Alexander, *Supplement to On the Soul* (*mantissa*) §3, with Sharples (2004) 61–72 and references there, Alexander *Quaest.* 1.8, 1.17, 1.26, and Philoponus, *On Aristotle's On the Soul* 52.26–53.8. Cf. Siclari (1974) 72 n.24; Mansfeld (1990) 3078–81; Ellis (1994); Caston (1997); Rashed (2004) 45–47 and n.82. However, Nemesius' objection does not simply reflect this controversy; his fundamental objection is, along with the Platonists, to the inseparability of soul and body implied by soul being the form, in the Aristotelian sense, of body, whether soul is analysed as quality or substance. See Verbeke and Moncho (1975) xliv n.47. Some Neoplatonists, arguing for the agreement of Aristotle and Plato, do indeed emphasise Aristotle's distinction between intellect as separable from the body and the rest of the soul as being inseparable; cf. Philoponus, *On Aristotle's On the Soul* 10.9–11, against Alexander's interpretation of Aristotle; above, n.188.

264 Mansfeld (1990, 3081 n.89) argues that the reference to the Manichaeans was added by Nemesius to his source. See below, n.345.

What Ammonius,[265] the teacher of Plotinus, and Numenius the Pythagorean said is satisfactory in reply to all those together who say that the soul is a body. It is as follows: bodies by their own nature are mutable, dispersable and throughout infinitely divisible, with nothing in them remaining [18] unchangeable; so they need something to bind them together, hold them together and, as it were, to chain and force them together, which is what we call the soul.[266] Now if the soul is a body of whatever sort, even with the most minute parts, what is there to preserve it in its turn? For it was shown that every body needs something to hold it together, and (5) so to infinity, until we arrive at the incorporeal.

If they were to say, as the Stoics do,[267] that it is a certain elastic motion surrounding bodies, which moves at once inwards and outwards, the motion outwards being productive of quantities and qualities, the inward of unity and substance, they must be asked, since every motion results from some power, what (10) this power is and in what substance it resides. So if this power is some sort of matter, we shall continue to repeat the same arguments; if it is not matter, but something enmattered (for what is enmattered is different from matter: for what partakes of matter is said to be enmattered), what then is this that partakes of matter? Is it also matter itself or is it immaterial? If it is matter, how can it be enmattered and not be matter? But if it is not matter it is immaterial, (15) and if immaterial not a body; for every body is

265 I.e. Ammonius Saccas. 17.16–19.16 = Numenius fr.4b des Places. Domański (1900, 19), followed by Dörrie (1959, 129–31) (who identifies Porphyry as the source; see below, n.372) and by Siclari (1974, 76 n.36), argues that the report of Ammonius and Numenius extends to 19.5, against Thedinga who extended it to 22.17 and Vacherot who held that it ended at 18.5. See also Schroeder (1987) 515–17; Emilsson (1994) 5348–49; Steel (2002) 85–86. Nemesius' Greek literally translates as 'the things said by …'; the preposition for 'by' is *para*, which Schroeder (1987, 516) argues may refer to a 'tradition deriving from' Ammonius and Numenius, rather than to explicit statements by them, comparing the titles at Alexander of Aphrodisias, *Supplement to On the Soul (mantissa)* 17 150.19, 22 169.33 and 23 172.16.

266 Cf. Numenius, *On the Good* quoted by Eusebius, *Preparation for the Gospel* 15.17 = Numenius, fr.4a des Places; 'since bodies are by nature dead and corpses and in motion and not remaining in the same place, is there not a need of something that will hold [or 'restrain'] them? … What then is it that will hold them? If this too were a body, it seems to me that it would need Zeus the Saviour [to restore it] if it itself were undone and scattered; if however it must itself be free from what body undergoes, so that it may be able to ward off destruction from those things too when they are thrown into confusion and may hold them, it seems to me that it is nothing other than only what is incorporeal.' For soul holding body together cf. Aristotle, *On the Soul* 1.5 410b10–15, and Alexander, *Supplement to On the Soul (mantissa)* 3 114.24ff. For *pneuma* (of which soul is constituted according to the Stoics) holding itself and other bodies together see *SVF* 2.444, and LS vol.1 pp. 282, 287. Steel (2002); Sharples (2004) 46–47 and nn.

267 Alexander, *On Mixture* 10 224.14 = *SVF* 2.442 = LS 47I.

material.[268]

If they were to say[269] that bodies are three-dimensional and the soul which penetrates the whole body is three-dimensional and therefore must be a body, we shall say that while every body is three-dimensional, not everything three-dimensional is body. For both quantity and quality are incorporeal in themselves but are incidentally (20) quantified in a bulk. So in the same way the soul as such has no dimensions, but incidentally is viewed together with the three-dimensional thing in which it is, and is itself three-dimensional.

Again, every body is moved either from within or from without; but if from without it is not ensouled, if from within it is ensouled. But if the soul is a body, it is not ensouled if it be moved from without, but if **[19]** from within it is ensouled. But it is absurd both to call the soul not ensouled and to call it ensouled; so the soul is not a body.[270]

Again, the soul, if it is nourished, is nourished by the incorporeal; for it is studies that nourish it. But nothing corporeal is fed by the incorporeal; so the soul is not a body. That is the conclusion of Xenocrates.[271] But if the soul (5) is not nourished, but every body of an animal is nourished, the soul is not a body.

The above is directed to all those in common who say that the soul is a body. Specifically in reply to those of the opinion that the soul is blood or breath, since when breath or blood leaves it the living creature becomes a corpse, we must not therefore say what certain of those who think they are

---

268 One may compare the regress arguments of Alexander, *Supplement to On the Soul (mantissa)* 3 114.25ff., and Philoponus, *On Aristotle's On the Soul* 12.26–30; but these are in terms of body, not matter. The present argument begins by distinguishing what partakes of matter (the 'material') from matter, but then shows that this 'material' must either be the same as matter or, paradoxically, be immaterial.

269 Attributed to the Stoic Apollodorus by Diogenes Laertius 7.135 = LS 45E. But the full Stoic definition was that body was the three-dimensional *with resistance*; cf. LS vol.1 p.273. Porphyry describes the world-soul as three-dimensional at *On Abstinence* 2.37 166.7; Theiler (1966) 107.

270 Cf. Calcidius, *On Plato's Timaeus* 227, 243.6–10 Waszink; Tertullian, *On the Soul* 6.1 p.7.2–8 Waszink. Alexander, *Supplement to On the Soul (mantissa)* 3 114.7ff. criticises an attempt to escape from this dilemma by saying that soul is a *tertium quid* outside the division into what has soul and what does not. Krause (1904) 26.

271 'That is the conclusion of Xenocrates' is deleted by Morani on the grounds that the Armenian version here has a different text. Our text is Xenocrates fr. 203 Isnardi-Parente; Tertullian, *On the Soul* 6.6 p.8.2–5 Waszink, which gives the same argument but without naming its originator, is Xenocrates fr. 204 Isnardi-Parente (both texts together constituting Xenocrates fr.66 Heinze).

of some importance have written, saying: (10) 'Then surely a portion of the soul must flow away when a portion of blood flows away'. For such talk is empty. For in the case of homogeneous things even a remainder is the same as the whole. A lot of water and a little are the same thing, as of silver and gold and everything whose parts are not different from each other in essence. So in the same way, the remaining blood also, (15) whatever its quantity, is soul, if blood is soul. Rather one should say this,[272] that, if the soul is that on the removal of which the animal dies, then both phlegm is soul and also both kinds of bile.[273] For if any of these gives out it brings an end to life. Also the liver, the brain, the heart, the stomach, the kidneys and the intestines and many other things. For when (20) one of these is removed will not the animal die? Apart from that, there are many things that are bloodless but animate,[274] like the cartilaginous fishes and the soft such as cuttlefish, squid and *smyli*[275] and all the hard shelled and soft shelled, such as crayfish, crabs and lobsters. If they are animate but bloodless, it is clear that the soul is not blood.

In reply to those who say that the soul is water because water (25) seems to be life-giving for all things and it is impossible to live without **[20]** water, many things tell against this. For it is also impossible to live without food; so against them it must be said that also all foods in turn are soul. Again, there are many animals that do not drink, as is related of some eagles, and the partridge can live without drinking. And why is water (5) soul rather than air? For it is possible to abstain from water even for a long time, but not even for the shortest time from breathing air. But air is also not soul: for there are many living things that do not breathe air, like all insects, such as bees, wasps and ants, also the bloodless animals, most sea creatures, and all things that have no lungs. For nothing that has no (10) lungs breathes air, and conversely nothing that does not breathe air has lungs.[276]

---

272 With the objection cf. Alexander, *Supplement to On the Soul (mantissa)* 3 117.32ff. (against the identification of soul with breath, not blood). Zeno's argument for the identification of soul and breath is reported by Calcidius, *On Plato's Timaeus* 220, 232.13–16 Waszink. Krause (1904) 26; Gourinat (2005) 565.

273 That is, yellow bile and black bile, standardly counted as two of the four humours.

274 Cf. Philoponus, *On Aristotle's On the Soul* 89.18–20 (with different examples; insects rather than sea-creatures), explicitly against the view of Critias (above, n.254).

275 Unidentified. Mentioned (in the form *smylai*) along with crabs, lobsters and cuttlefish by Alexander of Tralles, *Therapeutics* vol.2 p.525.24 Puschmann; not mentioned in d'Arcy Thompson (1947).

276 Cf. Aristotle, *Parts of Animals* 3.6 669a3–7.

ON THE NATURE OF MAN 57

But since arguments of Cleanthes the Stoic[277] and Chrysippus are handed down which are not easily dismissed, one must set out the refutations of these also, in the way that the Platonists did. Cleanthes contrives an argument of this sort; he says that (15) we are born not only like our parents physically but also psychologically in our feelings, habits and dispositions; but similarity and dissimilarity are of bodies, not of the incorporeal. Therefore the soul is a body.[278] – But, first, a universal proposition is not derived from particulars;[279]

---

277 Cleanthes (331–232 BCE) was the second head of the Stoic school, Chrysippus (c.280–c.206 BCE) the third. The sequence of three arguments, the first two attributed to Cleanthes and the third to Chrysippus, which appears at 20.13–21.6, 21.6–22.3 and 22.3–17 also appears, with the same attributions but without the refutations, at Tertullian, *On the Soul* 5.4 p.6.16–20, 5.5 p.6.20–25 and 5.6 p.6.26–7.1 Waszink, and also in Alexander of Aphrodisias, *Supplement to On the Soul* (*mantissa*) 3 117.1–9, 9–21 and 21–30, without any attributions and with some different, specifically Peripatetic counter-arguments, which Nemesius – or the Platonist source which he explicitly indicates he is following – would not have been happy to accept: for example that the separation of soul from body is different from that of body from body because the former involves the perishing of the soul. Dörrie (1959, 131–40) argues that Nemesius has derived this sequence of arguments from a Middle-Platonist source (cf. 20.14 here) which was preoccupied with the question of whether (as the Stoics argued) qualities are bodies, rather than with the question whether the soul is a substance. (Verbeke and Moncho [1975, xlix n.80] argue that the source of *all three* authors is *Neo*platonist, but that is difficult chronologically in the case of Alexander, if the *Supplement* is his own work, or even that of his immediate followers.) Krause (1904, 17) (see also 26–27 and 32) argued that Nemesius' Platonist source was Porphyry (cf. Siclari [1974] 80 n.47, and above, Introduction 5.a.2–3). Waszink suggests (128, cf. 33*) that Tertullian and Nemesius derived the sequence of three arguments from the physician Soranus (early 2nd century CE); that Soranus was Tertullian's source was argued, on the basis of the reference at Tertullian, *On the Soul* 6.6 p.8.5 Waszink, by Diels (1879) 207. Mansfeld (1990, 3135 n.373) suggests that the sequence of arguments, and that attributed to Zeno which precedes them in Tertullian, may derive from Arius Didymus, *On the Sects*. Gourinat (2005, 563–66) has drawn attention to features in the presentation of the arguments which suggest that Alexander preserves more arguments from the original source, some which are not in Nemesius also being parallelled in Calcidius (*On Plato's Timaeus* 220 232.13–19); he further argues that Alexander follows the original source more closely than do Nemesius and Tertullian, that the latter derive from a common intermediate source, and that it was Chrysippus himself who quoted his predecessors' arguments and then added his own.

278 On this argument cf. Dörrie (1959) 132–34. Dörrie (1959, 132 n.3), followed by Morani (ad loc.) and by Mansfeld (1990, 3134 and 3135 n.373), compares the argument from the resemblance of children to their parents attributed to Panaetius at Cicero, *Tusculan Disputations* 1.79 and to Chrysippus at Plutarch, *On Stoic Self-Contradictions* 41 1053d = *SVF* 2.806. But that argument claims that the resemblance of children to parents shows that the soul does not pre-exist the body, which is a quite different point from the logical, or ontological, claim that similarity applies only to bodies.

279 Telfer (1955, 266 n.2) suggests that Nemesius' objection here is that the fact that some people are similar to their parents in some respects, and others in others, does not mean that

in addition, 'not of the incorporeal' is false. For we say that numbers are (20) similar if their factors are in the same ratio, such as 6 and 24. For the factors of 6 are 2 and 3, of 24, 4 and 6. But 2 is in the same ratio to 4 as is 3 to 6, for they are seen in the relationship of being double; for 4 is twice 2 **[21]** and 6 is twice 3. But numbers are incorporeal. Also figures are similar to figures, if they have equal angles and the sides adjoining the equal angles are in proportion. But [the Stoics] themselves admit that figure is incorporeal.[280] Further, as it is a property of quantity to be equal or unequal, so being like and unlike (5) is a property of quality.[281] But quality is incorporeal. Therefore the incorporeal is like the incorporeal.

[Cleanthes] also says that nothing incorporeal shares affections with a body, nor any body with the incorporeal. Now the soul is affected with the body when the body is ill or cut, and body is affected with the soul, for when the soul is ashamed the body becomes red, and pale when it is afraid. Therefore the soul is a body.[282] But first, one of the assumptions (10) is false and too inclusive, the one that says 'nothing incorporeal shares affections with a body'. For what if the soul alone does so? It is as if one were to say: no animal moves the upper jaw; but the crocodile moves the upper jaw; so the crocodile is not an animal. For the premiss is false, here too, through being too inclusive, [namely] the one which says 'no animal moves the upper jaw'. (15) For look, the crocodile both is an animal and moves the upper jaw.[283] It is the same also when [Cleanthes] says that nothing incorporeal is affected together with body; for he includes the very point at issue in what he denies. But if someone were to suppose that it is true that nothing incorporeal is affected together with the body, still the induction that the soul is affected together with the body when it is diseased or cut is not something agreed.

---

childrens' souls are similar to their parents', full stop. This first objection is not a good one; if similarity is a feature only of bodies – which Nemesius will deny – even the fact that a child's soul *may* be similar to its parent's in *some* respect will be enough to show that the soul is a body.

280 Dörrie (1959, 133 n.3) argues that the early Stoics regarded surfaces or shapes as corporeal, but that Posidonius, as reported by Diogenes Laertius 7.135, allowed that they existed both in reality and in thought. For the early Stoic view he cites *SVF* 2.382ff. *SVF* 3.282 is from [Galen], *On Incorporeal Qualities*; its context in anti-Stoic debate may make it dubious evidence for the actual Stoic position. *SVF* 2.383 (Simplicius, *in Cat.* 271.21 = LS 28K) says that the Stoics make shapes bodies *like the other qualities*, and may be drawing an inference from the latter to the former. Edelstein and Kidd (1988–89, vol. 2.1 126), on the other hand, argue from *SVF* 2.482, 485, 487 and 488 that the orthodox early Stoic view was that points, lines and surfaces are simply concepts, and that Posidonius' innovation was to grant them real existence.

281 Aristotle, *Categories* 8 11a15–19.
282 On this argument see Dörrie (1959) 134–36.
283 Herodotus, 2.68.3; Aristotle, *History of Animals* 1.11 492b23.

(20) For it is debated whether the body alone is in pain when it receives the sensation from the soul, while the soul remains unaffected, or whether [the soul] is in pain together with the body. The former view prevails among the more highly reputed;[284] but one should not base arguments on disputed propositions, but on what is agreed. It is superabundantly shown that also certain incorporeal things are affected together with [22] bodies. Qualities, at least, which are incorporeal, are affected together with affected bodies, being altered together with the body in coming to be and ceasing to be.

But Chrysippus says that death is the separation of soul from body; now nothing incorporeal is separated from body; for neither is there anything incorporeal (5) attached to body; now the soul is both attached to body and separated from it; therefore the soul is not incorporeal.[285] Of these propositions it is true that death is the separation of soul from body, but it is false as a universal proposition that the incorporeal is not attached to body, though true of the soul. It is false, on the one hand, since a line is incorporeal but is attached to and separated (10) from a body, as is also whiteness. But it is true of the soul; for the soul is not attached to the body; if it is attached it clearly lies alongside it; but if so it does not lie alongside the whole of it, since it is impossible for the whole of one body to lie alongside the whole of another, and thus the whole of the animal will not be animate.[286] So if the soul is attached the soul will be a body, but the whole animal (15) will not be animate; but if the whole animal is animate the soul is neither attached nor a body. But the whole animal is animate; so the soul is neither attached nor a body, and it is separated as being incorporeal.[287]

So it is clear from what has been said that the soul is not a body: it follows next to say that it is not insubstantial.[288] Since Deinarchus defined

---

284 Dörrie (1959, 135) interprets this as a reference to Porphyry. Cf. Plotinus 3.6 [26] 1–4; also the discussion at Philoponus, *On Aristotle's On the Soul* 50.16–55.5.

285 22.3-6 = *SVF* 2.790.

286 Cf. Alexander, *Supplement to On the Soul* (*mantissa*) 3 115.33–34, 'nor [does body possess soul] by juxtaposition; for neither in this way will the whole body be animate'; Priscian, *Answers to Chosroes* 44.17–20, 'the soul is either juxtaposed to the animal it animates, or mixed with it, or has grown together with it. But if it is juxtaposed like something touching, the whole animal will presumably not be animate, for it is impossible for a whole body to be juxtaposed to a whole body; but the whole animal is animate; so the soul is not juxtaposed, and by this argument is not a body', and below, n.377. Dörrie (1959) 30–35 and 138.

287 On this argument see Dörrie (1959) 136–39.

288 Steel (1978, 23 n.3) compares Nemesius' division of his argument here to Iamblichus fr.4 Dillon (1973) = Olympiodorus, *On Plato's Phaedo* 78.15ff. Norvin. Iamblichus argued that the affinity argument in the *Phaedo* (78b ff.) is a self-contained and complete proof of the immortality of the soul, citing Plotinus for the view that everything that perishes is either

the soul as an attunement,[289] and also Simmias, (20) in reply to Socrates, said that the soul was an attunement,[290] saying that the soul was like an attunement and the body like a lyre, we must set out the refutations of this to be found in Plato's *Phaedo*. One of these is based on what he had already proved: for he had already proved that acts of learning are acts of recollection. Taking this as agreed he constructs his argument (25) as follows:[291] if acts of learning are acts of recollection our soul existed before [23] being in human form; but if it is an attunement it did not exist before, but came to be afterwards when the body had been attuned. For no composition differs in its condition from the things out of which it is composed. For a composition is a union of the things put together, and an attunement, and this is not prevented by its not (5) preceding the things out of which it is composed but rather following them. Now the soul's being an attunement is in conflict with acts of learning being acts of recollection: but the thesis concerning recollection is true, so it is false that the soul is an attunement.

Further, the soul both opposes the body and imposes the word of command, as being its ruler; but an attunement neither leads nor opposes; (10) so the soul is not an attunement.[292] Further, one attunement is greater or less than another attunement, by the strings being slackened or tightened, not through the ratio of the attunement – for it is impossible for a ratio [itself] to be greater or less[293] – but through its adjustment. For if a high and low note are blended, and then the strings are slackened, they preserve the same ratio in the magnitude of the sounds, but the attunement is (15) altered through the adjustment as the strings are more or less tightened. But one soul is not more or less such than another soul: so the soul is not an attunement.[294] Also a soul admits goodness and badness, but attunement does not admit attunement and discord; so the soul is not an attunement.[295] Further the soul by admitting opposites in turn is a substance and a substrate,[296] while (20) an

---

a composite or in a substrate (and therefore not a substance) (Olympiodorus 78.20–24 Norvin = 175.10–13 Westerink), and arguing that the soul's ruling over the body (*Phaedo* 80a) shows that it is not present in it as in a substrate (78.27 Norvin = 175.16 Westerink). The Plotinus references are identified by Dillon (1973) 243 as 4.7 [2] 12,12-13 and 17-19 respectively.

289 Above, n.262.
290 Plato, *Phaedo* 86b. On 'attunement' see above, n.262.
291 Plato, *Phaedo* 91e–92e; Philoponus, *On Aristotle's On the Soul* 142.6–15.
292 Plato, *Phaedo* 92e–93a, 94be; Philoponus, *On Aristotle's On the Soul* 142.15–22.
293 The ratio 3:1 is greater than the ratio 2:1; but a given ratio, e.g. 2:1, cannot vary.
294 Plato, *Phaedo* 93ae; Philoponus, *On Aristotle's On the Soul* 142.22–26.
295 Plato, *Phaedo* 93e–94a; Philoponus, *On Aristotle's On the Soul* 142.26–33.
296 Admitting opposites is characteristic of substance: Aristotle, *Categories* 5 4a10–11.

attunement is a quality and in a substrate; but substance is other than quality; so the soul is also other than attunement.[297] But that the soul *participates* in attunement is nothing absurd, yet it is not on that account [itself] an attunement; for the soul is not goodness because it admits of goodness, either.

Galen has nothing to say on this point,[298] and he bears witness in his works on (25) demonstration that he had made no declaration about the soul.[299] But, from what he says, he seems on the whole to consider that the soul is a mixture, since from this **[24]** follows difference in character:[300] his argument is based on those of Hippocrates. If this is so, he clearly also thinks that the soul is mortal, not all of it, but in man only the non-rational soul. About the rational soul he is in two minds, saying <I see that this is in accordance with Plato's doctrine concerning the soul, but I have no proof to give of it, because I do not know what the substance of the soul is like>.[301] But it is clear from the following that the (5) bodily mixture cannot be soul: every body, animate and inanimate, is a mixture of the four elements;

297 This argument does not appear in the *Phaedo*; the contrast between substance and quality, and the notion of a substrate admitting opposites, are Aristotelian. Aristotle himself in the (lost) *Eudemus* made the different point that soul itself has no opposite (Philoponus, *On Aristotle's On the Soul* 144.22–25; Aristotle fr.45 Rose³). Krause (1904, 21) derives this argument from Porphyry, but the parallel with Priscian, *Answers to Chosroes* 46.4ff. on which he bases his argument is tenuous. Philoponus, *On Aristotle's On the Soul* 142.33–143.1 has as his fifth argument, in the sequence which has up till then been parallel to Nemesius', that if soul does not admit disharmony all souls will be good.

298 For Galen's reluctance to express judgement on the status of the soul see *That the Faculties of the Soul follow the Mixtures of the Body (Quod animi mores)* 3, p.773 K = 36.12–16 Müller, 'That, of these kinds and parts of the whole soul, the rational [part] is immortal – of this Plato seems to be persuaded, but I am not able to maintain either that it is or, against him, that it is not'; *On my own Opinions* 15.2, p.116.20–118.5 Nutton, 'As for the soul, whether it is immortal and governs living creatures being mixed with the bodily substances, this is something I do not claim to know for sure, just as [I do not claim to know] either whether the soul in itself has no being at all. But what is clearly apparent to me is that, even if it [only] makes its home in bodies, it is enslaved to their natures, which, as I said, come to be of a certain sort as a result of a certain sort of blending of the elements.' Moraux (1984) 784.

299 Domański (1900, 9 n.1), followed by Telfer (1955, 271 n.2), suggests that this is not Galen's work *On Demonstration*, which partly survives in Arabic, but a mistake for, or a misleading way of referring to, *That the Faculties of the Soul follow the Mixtures of the Body* (see the previous note). Cf. below on 22 82.7.

300 The theory advanced by Galen in *That the Faculties of the Soul follow the Mixtures of the Body*. See Boudon-Millot (2005) 74–75.

301 There is a lacuna in the text here. Telfer (1955, 273 n.5), whom we have followed, supplies the missing text from Galen, *That the Faculties of the Soul follow the Mixtures of the Body* 3, vol.4 775.18–776.3 K =38.18–21 Müller, suggesting that Nemesius himself left a gap, intending to look up and insert Galen's actual words as a quotation.

for their mixture makes up bodies. If, then, the bodily mixture is the soul, nothing will be inanimate. The argument is formulated as follows: if bodily mixture is soul, and every body contains a mixture, then every body has a soul; but if every body (10) has a soul no body is inanimate. So neither a stone nor wood nor iron nor anything else will be inanimate.

But if he were to say that not every bodily mixture is universally a soul, but only that of a certain sort, one must ask him what sort of mixture it is that makes an animal and provides the formula for a soul. For, whatever mixture he says, we shall find that among the inanimate also. For there are nine (15) mixtures, as he himself showed in his work on mixture,[302] eight being bad mixtures and one a good mixture, and he says that man's mixture is the good one (not of every man but of him who has the mean mixture), while the other animals have the other bad mixtures according to their species, which involves a greater or less slackening and tension. But the nine mixtures are found also (20) in the inanimate, involving the greater and less, as he himself once again proved in his work on simples.[303]

Further, if the soul is a mixture, while mixtures change according to age, seasons and way of life, the soul alters, and if it alters we do not have the same soul but, according to the mixture, sometimes a lion's, sometimes a sheep's, sometimes that of something else, which is absurd.

(25) Further, the mixture does not oppose the bodily desires, but even [25] works with them: for it stimulates, while the soul opposes.[304] So the soul is not a mixture.

Further, if the soul is a mixture, and mixture is a quality, while a quality comes and goes without the destruction of the substrate, then the soul will be separated without the destruction of its substrate; (5) but this is not true. So

---

302 Galen, *On Mixtures* 1.8, vol.1 559.4–9 K = 31.28–32.4 Helmreich: 'there are nine differences of mixture in all, one the well-mixed, eight those that are not well mixed: four simple, moist and dry and cold and hot, and four others that are compound, moist together with hot and dry together with hot and cold together with moist and cold together with dry'.

303 Jim Hankinson suggests to us that this is a reference to Galen's general pharmacological theory in *On Simple Medicines*, since drugs are themselves inanimate even if derived from living creatures; and drugs can also be derived from metals (*On Simple Medicines* 6.1 [11.791.17 K], and book 9 [12.160 K] onwards). Cf. Harig (1974), especially 50 n.68 and 84-85, and compare, perhaps, the connection between man and lifeless things in section 1, 2.13ff. above.

304 Streck (2005, 38 and nn.107–08) notes that, to be consistent with what he said at 1 13.19–21 above, Nemesius should here have referred to reason rather than to the soul. But he is presumably influenced here by a way of seeing the issue going back to Plato, *Phaedo* 94bc; see n.292 above.

the soul is neither a mixture nor a quality. For they surely will not say that one of the contraries is naturally present in an animal, as heat is in fire; for this is unalterable, but mixtures can be seen to alter. And it is these men[305] more than any who alter mixtures through their medical skill.

Further, the qualities of every body are (10) perceptible. But the soul is not perceptible, but intelligible. So the soul is not a quality of a body.[306]

Further, the right mixture of body and breath, with the arrangement of flesh, sinews and the rest, is strength, and the right mixture of the warm, cold, dry and moist [elements] is health, and the symmetry of the limbs with a good complexion constitutes the beauty of the body.[307] If, then, the (15) combination[308] of health, strength and beauty were the soul, it would be necessary for a man who is alive not to be diseased nor weak nor ill-shaped: but it often happens that not only one but all three right mixtures together are destroyed and the man lives; for it happens that the same man is ill-shaped, weak and diseased all together. So the soul is not (20) the good mixture of the body.

305 Nemesius seems to have moved from considering Galen in particular to doctors in general.
306 Dörrie (1959, 140–42) argues that 25.5–9 may derive from Porphyry and that 25.9–11 definitely do.
307 Cf. Aristotle, *Topics* 3.1 116b18–22, 'that which is in better or prior or more honourable things is better, for example health than strength or beauty; for [health] is in what is moist and dry and warm and cold, in short those things out of which the living creature is primarily constituted, but the others are in what is posterior; for strength is in sinews and bones, while beauty is thought to be a certain proportion of the limbs'; Chrysippus, reported by Galen, *On the Doctrines of Hippocrates and Plato* 5.2.33 = *SVF* 3.471, 'the proportion or disproportion that has come to be in what is warm and cold and moist and dry is health or disease, the proportion or disproportion in the sinews is strength or weakness and fitness or unfitness, the proportion or disproportion in the limbs is beauty or ugliness'; Alexander, *Supplement to On the Soul (mantissa)* 20 162.10–14, 'the goods of the soul are health, which comes about by the right mixture of the primary bodies in which [the body] has its being, strength, which is in the right tension of the secondary bodies and those composed from them, and beauty, which is in the good shape and proportion of the tertiary and non-uniform bodies, which we call the proximate parts of the body'; Alexander, *On Aristotle's Topics* 236.10–16, 'health is in the proportion of the primary bodily powers, which are heat, coldness, moistness, dryness ... strength is in the proportion of the uniform [parts], sinews and bones and lung, beauty in the proportion of the non-uniform parts in us, face, neck, hands, the other parts'; Philoponus, *On Aristotle's On the Soul* 145.1–5, 'The disharmony of an animate body is disease and weakness and ugliness; of these disease is disproportion of the elements, weakness of the uniform [parts], ugliness of the organic [parts]. If then the disharmony is disease and weakness and ugliness, the harmony will be health and strength and beauty.' Alexander and Philoponus employ Aristotelian technical terminology which is absent from Nemesius' account. See Sharples (2004) 182 n.614.
308 Literally *harmonia*, 'attunement': above, n.262.

How, then, do certain natural faults and excellences come upon men? Truly it happens because of the bodily mixture. For as men are naturally healthy and diseased because of the mixture, so some who naturally have bitter bile are ill-tempered, others are cowards, others lewd. But some men conquer and overcome: clearly they conquer their mixture. (25) But it is one thing that conquers, another that is conquered: so mixture and soul are different things. For the body is an instrument of the soul: if it is suitably constituted, it works with it and is itself in a suitable condition. But if it [26] is in an unsuitable condition it impedes the soul, and then the soul has a need of resources to fight against the unsuitability of the instrument and, unless thoroughly self-controlled, it will be perverted together with it, just as a musician will go wrong together with the distortion of his lyre, unless he first brings it into good condition. So there is also (5) a need for the soul to take care of the body in order to make it an instrument fitting for itself. This it does through reason and [formation of] character, as in attunement slackening this and tightening that, in order to make it attuned to itself and so to have a fitting instrument for itself, unless the soul is itself perverted together with it. For this happens also.[309]

(10) Aristotle, who says that the soul is an actuality,[310] none the less agrees with those who say that it is a quality.[311] Let us first make clear what actuality he means. He uses 'being' in three senses: one is substrate as matter, which in itself is nothing but has potentiality of coming to be [something]: another is shape and form, according to which the matter is given a form; a third is the combination (15) which has come to be from matter and form and which is already ensouled.[312] So matter is potentiality, form actuality, and that in two ways,[313] one is as knowledge, the other is as contemplation of what is known: in other words, the former is a disposition, the latter is active. Knowledge, because while a soul exists there is both sleep and waking: being awake is analogous to (20) contemplation, sleep to having but not activating. Knowledge is prior to its activation; that is why he calls form the first actuality, its activation the second. Similarly the eye

309 For the whole argument cf. Philoponus, *On Aristotle's on the Soul* 1.1, 50.25–52.3 and 1.5, 183.30–34 with the notes in van der Eijk (2005b) 133–35.
310 Above, n.261.
311 The identification of Aristotelian form with quality is questionable. See above, n.263.
312 Aristotle, *On the Soul* 2.1 412a6–11, 17–19, 2.2 414a14–19.
313 Aristotle, *On the Soul* 2.1 412a22–28. Nemesius' expression is misleading in implying that *form* is actuality in two ways; as he indeed indicates in what follows, form or soul is for Aristotle the *first* actuality, analogous to the possession of knowledge rather than to its exercise in contemplation.

consists of a substrate and form: its **[27]** substrate is that which receives sight, that is the matter of the eye,[314] and this also is ambiguously called the eye; the form, i.e. the first actuality, of the eye is sight itself, which gives it its capability of seeing; the second actuality of the eye is the activity by which it sees. So, as the newly born (5) whelp has neither actuality, but the capacity to receive the actuality, so one must take it to be in the case of the soul. For as in the illustration sight, when it has come to be, perfects the eye, so here, when the soul has come to be in the body, it perfects the animal. So soul never exists without body, nor body apart from soul.[315] For soul is not body but belongs to body, and therefore (10) it exists in a body and a body of a certain sort, but it does not exist on its own.[316]

But, first, he calls the life-giving[317] part of the soul the soul, separating off from it the rational part.[318] But the whole of the soul of man should have been taken, and a declaration about the whole should not have been made on the basis of a part, and that the weakest.[319] Next, he says that the body has life potentially even (15) before the soul comes to be. For he says that the body potentially has life within itself. But the body which potentially has life must actually be a body first. But it cannot be a body in actuality before

---

314 Morani follows Evangelides in deleting this phrase. Aristotle says that the eye is the matter of sight (*On the Soul* 2.1 412b20). For what is said in general about the eye here cf. Aristotle, *On the Soul* 2.1 412b18–21, 412b27–413a3.

315 'Body' here must clearly be intended in the sense of 'a natural body potentially possessing life' (Aristotle, *On the Soul* 2.1 412a20–21, 27–28), i.e. an animal or plant body; *inanimate* bodies can exist without souls.

316 Aristotle, *On the Soul* 2.1 413a3–7, 2.2 414a20–21 (though the former passage allows that *some* part of the soul may be separable from the body; see below, n.318).

317 Some MSS have 'the part of the soul that can be affected'.

318 Aristotle, *On the Soul* 2.2 413b24–27. Being rational is, in the case of man, simply a further complexity of soul which distinguishes him from other animals. He is defined as a rational animal. But Aristotle wishes to separate off theoretical, intuitive intellect from reason in general. While reason in general uses imagination and imagination relies on sensation and is thus linked to bodily functions and sense-organs, he believes that pure reason is a divine element which is imperishable. It is a different kind of thing from soul, being separable from body; but views differed and differ as to whether Aristotle intends it to be a part of each individual or something distinct from each individual. Aristotle appears to have held this view of reason at least partly because he thought that pure reason required no bodily activity, partly because he thought that this was the activity of the divine itself. See above, section 1 n.187.

319 That is to say: Aristotle denies the immortality of the soul, because he – wrongly, in Nemesius' view – identifies the soul with the part that is linked to the body and can be affected. (So Domański [1900] 3 n.1.) For similar criticism of Aristotle by Atticus (the Middle Platonist) and Numenius compare Karamanolis (2006) 147 and 172.

it receives its form, for it is matter without qualities and not a body.[320] For it is impossible for what does not exist in actuality to have the potentiality for something to come from it. Even if it is body potentially, how can the (20) potential body potentially have life in itself? Moreover, while it is possible in other cases to have something but not use it, as it is to have sight but not use it, this is impossible in the case of the soul. Even he who sleeps is not without activity of the soul; for he is nourished and grows and imagines and breathes, which is the supreme evidence of life. From this [28] it is evident that nothing can have [only] the capacity of being alive, but everything has it actively. Primarily, what gives the soul its form is nothing other than life: for life is present to soul naturally, but to body by [its] participation [in soul]. But he who says that health is analogous to life[321] does not refer to the life of the soul but to that of the body, and thus produces a sophism. For (5) bodily being is receptive of opposites in turn, but that of the form is not so in any way. For if some differentia of form be changed, then the animal changes into something different, so that formal being is not receptive of opposites, but only being as substrate, i.e. bodily being. Therefore the (10) soul cannot be the actuality of the body in any way, but is an incorporeal being complete in itself. For it is receptive of opposites in turn, badness and goodness, which form could not accept.

Again, [Aristotle] says[322] that the soul, which is an actuality, is unmoved in itself, but moves incidentally. There is nothing implausible in its moving us while being unmoved; for (15) beauty, which is unmoved, causes motion in us.[323] But, if that is also the case here, it initiates motion while being unmoved, but it moves what is of a nature to be moved, and not what is unmoved. If, therefore, body also had been self-moving, there would have been nothing absurd in its being moved by something unmoved: but, as it

---

320 Nemesius is noting the apparent implications of Aristotle's definition of soul as 'the first actuality of an organic natural body which potentially has life' (*On the Soul* 2.1 412a20–21; see also 2.1 412b15–17, and above n.261). This is the problem that has become known in modern discussions as 'Ackrill's paradox', from Ackrill (1972–1973). It is discussed in Alexander, *Quaest.* 2.8. See e.g. Cohen (1992), Whiting (1992), Shields (1993). Kallis (1978, 143 n.90) notes that Nemesius disregards the solution given by Alexander of Aphrodisias, *Supplement to On the Soul (mantissa)* 1 104.11–17.

321 Alexander, *Supplement to On the Soul (mantissa)* 102.32–103.2; Themistius, *On Aristotle's On the Soul* 46.12.

322 Aristotle, *On the Soul* 1.3 405b31–406a2, 1.4 408a30–34; Aëtius 4.6.2.

323 The term translated in this passage by 'movement' can refer more generally to change; but the reference here is probably to beauty's power to move us by attracting us.

is, it is impossible for what is unmoved to be moved by what is unmoved.[324] So whence comes motion in bodies if not from the soul? For the body is not (20) self-moving. So when Aristotle wished to exhibit what was the first beginning of motion he did not exhibit primary but secondary motion. For if what is not moved caused motion it would have produced primary motion: but if what is self-moving also causes other movements, he is giving an account of secondary motion. Whence, then, is the primary source of motion in the body? For it is false to say that the elements are self-moving,[325] some being (25) light by nature, some heavy; for if lightness and heaviness are motion, the light and heavy will never remain stationary, whereas they remain stationary **[29]** when they come to their own place. So heaviness and lightness are not the causes of primary motion, but qualities of the elements.

But, even if this point be conceded, how can reasoning and opinion and judgment be the products of lightness and heaviness? But if not of these, nor are they of the elements; if (5) not of the elements, nor of bodies.

Further, if the soul is moved incidentally, but the body of itself, the body will move of itself even if the soul does not exist; but, if that is so, there will be a living being even without a soul. All this is absurd; so it is absurd right from the start.

But it is also not true to say that everything that is moved naturally is also moved forcibly, and that everything that is moved forcibly (10) is moved naturally. For the heavens move naturally but are not moved forcibly. Nor, indeed, if something is moved naturally, does that thing also naturally remain unmoved; for the heavens, the sun and the moon move naturally,

---

324 The argument rather requires 'it is impossible for what *has no power of moving itself* to be moved by the unmoved'. An object of desire which is itself unmoved can cause movement in a soul that *moves itself* towards the object of desire; but body has no power of motion of its own, and so cannot be moved by what is itself unmoved. Nemesius, or his source, is arguing for the Platonic notion of self-moving soul (*Phaedrus* 245e), to be contrasted with Aristotle's view that a self-mover is, strictly speaking, impossible (*Physics* 8.5). Porphyry, cited by Eusebius, *Preparation for the Gospel* 15.11.1, criticises the doctrine of an unmoved soul on the ground that it does not allow for those activities that are (it is claimed) activities of the soul alone; his argument is thus *different* from Nemesius' here. Similarly Porphyry ap. Themistius, *On Aristotle's On the Soul* 16.19ff. Atticus, fr.7.42–53 des Places, criticises Aristotle for making the soul unmoved, and sees this view as logically implying Dicaearchus' alleged elimination of the soul altogether (below, n.369). On Nemesius' argument here cf. Kallis (1978) 146–47.

325 Aristotle argues that the elements have natural motions (*On the Heaven* 3.2 300a20), but he seems reluctant to say that they are actually self-movers (*Physics* 8.4 255a5ff.); Alexander is less hesitant (cf. Sharples [1987a] 1215 and n.156, and references there).

but they cannot remain naturally at rest.[326] In the same way the soul is also ever-moving by nature, and as it moves naturally it cannot remain unmoved. For remaining unmoved is the (15) passing away of the soul and of everything that always is moving. In addition to all this the problem we started with remains unsolved, how the body is held together, being of a nature to fragment.

The above arguments are sufficient, among many, to prove that the soul is neither an actuality, nor unmoved, nor brought into existence in the body.

Pythagoras was always accustomed to liken symbolically God and everything else to (20) numbers, and he defined the soul too as a self-moving number,[327] and Xenocrates followed him,[328] not because the soul is a number but because it is among things that can be numbered and among things that are multiple, and because it is the soul that distinguishes things by assigning to each of them a shape and character. For it is the soul that separates forms from forms and declares them [30] to be different, through both the difference of the forms and the plurality of numbers, and thereby makes things numerable. For this reason things are not altogether divorced from kinship with numbers. He[329] also gave testimony of the soul's being self-changing.

But that the soul is not a number is clear from the following: (5) number is a quantity, but the soul is not a quantity but a substance: so the soul is not a number, even if they especially wish to claim that number is a substance amongst things intelligible, as we shall say in what follows.[330] Further, the soul is continuous: but numbers are not continuous; so the soul is not a number. Further, a number is either even or odd; but the soul is neither even nor odd; so the soul is not a number.[331] Further, number increases by addition; but the soul is (10) not increased by addition. Further, the soul is self-changing, but a definite number is unchanging. Further, since a number remains one and the same in its nature, it cannot alter any quality present

---

326 For the arguments rejected in the first part of this paragraph see Aristotle, *On the Soul* 1.3 406a22–25. The objections brought by Nemesius are not among those, apparently from Porphyry, recorded by Themistius, *On Aristotle's On the Soul* 16.19ff.; cf. Todd (1996) 160 n.8.

327 Above, n.259.

328 Aëtius 4.2.4 (Stobaeus only); Theodoret, *Remedy for Greek Attitudes* 5.17 p.126.24. See above, n.258. The view is mentioned, without its proponent being named, at Aristotle, *On the Soul* 1.4 408b32.

329 It is not clear whether the reference is to Pythagoras or to Xenocrates.

330 Telfer (1955, 285) notes that this promise is not taken up, and suggests that it has been taken over from Nemesius' source rather than being a commitment by Nemesius himself.

331 Aristotle, *Topics* 3.6 120b3–6.

ON THE NATURE OF MAN 69

in numbers; but the soul, while remaining one and the same in substance, changes its qualities, (15) passing from ignorance to knowledge, and from badness to goodness; so the soul is not a number.

Such, then, are the opinions of the ancients concerning the soul.

Eunomius[332] defined the soul as an incorporeal substance created in a body, agreeing with both Plato and Aristotle.[333] He took 'an incorporeal (20) substance' from truth, but 'created in a body' from the teaching of Aristotle: he did not notice, though acute, that he is trying to join incompatibles into the same thing. For everything that has a bodily, and thus temporal, origin is perishable and mortal. With this the words of Moses agree: for in sketching the creation of things visible, he did not explicitly (25) assert that the nature of things intelligible, too, came to be in this creation. But some conjecturally [31] believe this, though not all agree with them. If someone were to believe that the soul came to be after the body, because the soul was inserted after the formation of the body,[334] he errs from the truth. For neither does Moses say that it was created then when it was inserted in the body, nor is that (5) in accordance with reason. So either let it be said that it is mortal, as Aristotle said[335] asserting it to come to be in the body, and as the Stoics also said, or let one say that it is an incorporeal substance and decline to say that it was created in the body, in order that we may not acquire the notion of a soul that is mortal and totally non-rational.[336]

Also, according to Eunomius, the universe is not yet complete, but it is even now half-finished and always in need of supplement. (10) At any rate,

---

332 Bishop of Cyzicus; banished in 383 for his extreme version of the Arian heresy. Telfer (1955, 282 n.6) explains that Eunomius thought that souls were created by God at the origin of the world, but that their creation was only *completed* when they were born in bodies.

333 The last clause is deleted by Morani; a different text appears in the Armenian version. The words make sense, however, provided it is understood that the agreement in each case is partial, as is shown by the sequel – where, significantly, Plato's view and truth are implicitly identified. (Burgundio's Latin version actually has 'Plato' rather than 'truth'.) Cf. Verbeke and Moncho (1975) xlv. Ferro (1925, 233) draws attention to Nemesius' formulation in what follows, 'everything that has a bodily, and thus temporal, origin is perishable and mortal', *not* just 'everything that has a temporal origin is perishable and mortal'; souls are both everlasting and created, but not created in bodies.

334 Genesis 2:7.

335 Above, n.319.

336 Nemesius adopts Origen's view, that souls exist before bodies, rather than the alternatives that they are created by God at the same time as bodies (Eunomius) or inherited from parents (Apollinaris). See Dräseke (1892) 195–96; Koch (1921) 16; Raven (1923) 171; Telfer (1955) 282 n.8. Streck (2005, 32 and n.70) compares in this connection the use made of Plato's argument from recollection, implying the pre-existence of the soul, at 22.24–23.8 above.

fifty thousand new intellectual beings at least are added to it every day and, what is hardest to accept, when the universe is completed it will then be dissolved according to him, since the last men will complete the number of souls required for the resurrection. Can anything be more irrational than this, to say that the universe will be destroyed then when it has been completed? For that is simply the behaviour of (15) children, who knock down what they have made playing in the sand as soon as it is completed.[337] For to say that souls now come to be by reason of providence, and not of creation, shows ignorance of the difference between creation and providence. For providence introduces no new existence other than what there is, but protects what there is. For it is the function of providence (20) to preserve[338] by successive birth the existence of animals that perish.[339] (I speak of those that are not born from putrefaction, since the succession of these is preserved by further putrefaction.) But the supreme function of creation is to make from what was not. So, if souls come into existence by birth from each other, they come to be by reason of providence and are perishable, just as other things do that come to be (25) by racial succession. But if souls come to be from what is not, what happens is creation, and the statement of Moses that God 'rested from all the works that he had made'[340] is not true. But both are absurd. So souls do not come to be *now*.[341] For **[32]** even [Eunomius] believes that 'my father works hitherto'[342] was said with reference not to creation but to providence.

But Apollinaris[343] believes that souls are born from souls, as bodies are born from bodies. For, he holds, soul progresses by transmission from the (5) first man into all his progeny, just like bodily transmission. For souls are [in his view] neither stored up nor now created; for those who say this make

---

337 Cf. Philo, *On the Eternity of the World* 42 p.86.1, '(If a new world is created like the old one), the craftsman labours in vain, in no way at all different from foolish children, who often playing on the beach set up hills of sand and then remove them and throw them down again with their hands', where Colson notes the origin of the image in Homer, *Iliad* 15.362ff.

338 This is the required sense, but the word used, *pleistêriazesthai*, means 'make expensive'.

339 This is Alexander's theory of providence: *On Providence* 33.1–8, 87.5–91.4 (page and line numbers of Ruland [1976] reproduced in Fazzo and Zonta [1998]), *Quaest.* 1.25 41.11–19, 2.19 63.18–28. See also below, 43 126.4–7, 130.18–20, and n.1038.

340 Genesis 2:2.
341 For the translation see Domański (1900) 44 n.1.
342 John 5:17.
343 See above 1.12 with n.185. Dräseke (1886) 28–31, (1892) 195–96; fr.170, p.269.23–28 Lietzmann (1904).

God an accomplice of adulterers, since children are begotten by them also. And 'God rested from all the works' that he had begun to make is false since he is still now making souls. – (10) But if all things that are born successively from each other have been shown to be mortal – which is why they beget and are born, so that the race of mortals may persist – then this man also must either say that the soul is mortal, being born from reproduction, or that souls are not born successively from others. For let us leave what is born from adultery to the decision of providence, (15) which is unknown to us. But if we must make some conjecture about providence, in any case it knows that what is born will be useful either to life or to itself, and therefore allows the ensoulment. We find sufficient testimony of this in the case of Solomon, born of the wife of Uriah and of David.[344]

(20) Next let us examine also the belief that the Manichaeans have about the soul.[345] They say that it is immortal and incorporeal, but that there is only one, the soul of the universe, which is chopped up and divided into particular bodies, both inanimate and animate, and that the latter have a greater, the former a lesser share. The animate have more, the inanimate [33] have less; heavenly beings have much more. So the souls of particular things are parts of the universal soul. If they said that this is shared out without being divided,[346] as a voice is to those who hear it, the harm would have been moderate; but as it is they say that the very substance of the soul is shared out, and, (5) most difficult of all, because they claim that it is properly in the elements, it is divided out with them in the birth of bodies, and comes together again when bodies decay, like water which is divided out and collected again and mixed. They say that pure souls turn towards light, being themselves light, but those tainted by matter go into the elements (10)

---

344 The union of David with Bathsheba, Solomon's mother, was not only, it is implied, adulterous, but David had facilitated Uriah's death: 2 Samuel 11–12. Telfer (1955) 285 n.14 argues that Nemesius disregards 2 Samuel 12:15–25; David *married* Bathsheba after Uriah's death, the first child born to David and Bathsheba died, David repented, and Solomon was conceived subsequently. Whether this alters the moral, as opposed to legal, situation depends on whether the death of the first child is regarded as expiating the crime.

345 Dörrie (1959, 142–44), followed by Sorabji (2004, vol. 3 345) argues that 32.20–33.19 on the Manichaeans derive from Porphyry. Cf. also Augustine, *On the Two Souls* 12.16, '[the Manichaeans] say that there are two kinds of soul: one good, which is from God in such a way that it was not made by him from some matter or from not-being, but a certain part of it is actually said to have gone forth from his very substance', and O'Daly (1987) 31–34 and 60–61; and (on the general issue, but without explicit reference to the Manichaeans) Plotinus 4.3 [27] 1–8, cited by Sorabji (2004) vol. 3 345. On Nemesius' criticism of the Manichaeans and agreement with Plotinus see Kallis (1978) 98–110.

346 Plotinus 4.1 [2] 1.32, 62.

and again from the elements into plants and animals. They thus divide up the soul's substance, and depict it as corporeal, and subject it to being affected, but say that it is immortal. But they also fall into contradictions. For while saying that tainted souls revert to elements and are mixed together with each other, they still say that they are punished in (15) reincarnations according to the greatness of their sins, unifying them and again separating them in their existence. For they say that shadows are separate in the light, but are unified when it becomes dark, which could not happen in the case of an intelligible nature. For shadows are also among perceptible things, even if one were to allow that they are separated and again united.

(20) Plato[347] declares that souls are both one and many; for the soul of the universe is one, but there are also others of particular things. So the universe is ensouled on its own by the soul of the universe, and each particular thing also on its own by its own particular soul. He says at least that the soul of the universe spreads out from the centre of the earth to the extremes of the heavens,[348] (25) not meaning that it spreads out in place, but intelligibly. It is this soul, he says, that turns the universe in its orbit and holds it together, and [34] binds together the corporeal cosmos. For it was shown in what preceded that bodies need something to hold them together,[349] and that this is what the soul that gives form does. For, he says, each thing that there is lives its own life and suffers its own decay; so long as the body is held together and bound together it is said (5) to exist, but when dissolved it perishes. Also he says that everything is alive, but not everything is an animal. For they distinguish plants from the inanimate by their growth and nourishment, that is to say by their nutritive and vegetative power, non-rational animals from plants by sensation, the rational from the non-rational by reason. Thus, while saying that all are alive, they distinguish the nature of each. (10) So they say that even altogether inanimate things live a life of endurance,[350] in which they are sustained by the soul of the universe so as merely to exist and not be

---

347 Plato, *Timaeus* 34B ff. Dörrie (1959, 144–47) derives 33.20–23 from Porphyry; Krause (1904, 23) the whole of 33.20–34.17. See Mansfeld (1990) 3081.
348 Plato, *Timaeus* 34B, 36E.
349 Above, n.266.
350 That is to say, they have a state or condition (*hexis*) that holds them together. The idea that inanimate things have a *hexis* is Stoic; the idea that the universe as a whole, of which inanimate things are a part, is alive is both Stoic and Platonic. But to regard having a *hexis* as having a sort of *life* is Neoplatonist rather than Stoic: cf. Plotinus 3.2 [47] 4.11, 4.3 [27] 24.11–13, and, on the growth of stones, 4.4 [28] 27.9–11, 6.7 [38] 11.24–30. Domański (1900) 38 n.1; Armstrong (1966–1988) vol. 4 p.54 n.1; Sharples (1998) 182 n.529. Dörrie (1959, 146) suggests that the doctrine reflects a Middle Platonist substitution of soul for Stoic *pneuma*.

dissolved. This, they say, is the soul that governs the universe and sends out the particular souls which were previously produced by the Demiurge,[351] since clearly the Demiurge himself has both given to the soul laws in accordance with which it must control (15) this universe, which [Plato] also calls fate,[352] and the Demiurge also provides a sufficient power to watch over us. These matters will also be discussed in the treatment of fate.[353]

All the Greeks in common who declare the soul to be immortal hold the dogma of transmigration. But they differ about the species of souls. (20) For some say there is one species, the rational, and that this passes over into the bodies of plants and non-rational animals. Some say that it is at certain stated periods of time, some that it happens randomly. But some say that there is not only one species of soul, but two, the rational and the non-rational; some say that there are many species, as many as there are species of living creatures. The followers of Plato particularly disagreed with this view. For Plato (25) said[354] that fierce and proud and greedy souls take in exchange the bodies of wolves and lions, those that were given to **[35]** self-indulgence assume the bodies of asses and the like; and some understood this literally to mean lions and asses, while others discerned that he had spoken metaphorically, as obliquely referring to habits via beasts. For Cronius[355] in his work on palingenesis, which is what he calls transmigration, (5) claims that all souls are rational. Similarly the Platonist Theodorus[356] in his *That the Soul is the Totality of Forms*, and Porphyry likewise.[357] Iamblichus takes the opposite

---

351 Plato, *Timaeus* 41–43 describes the Demiurge as creating the immortal part of human souls, and the secondary gods as creating mortal bodies (see below, section 43). But he does not there say that it is the *world-soul* that sends souls into bodies.

352 Plato, *Timaeus* 41E.

353 Below, section 38. (Burgundio's Latin version renders this wrongly: 'these things have also been discussed in the book *On Fortune*'.) Krause (1904, 44) uses this reference to argue that Porphyry is Nemesius' source not only here (above, n.345) but also in section 38.

354 Plato, *Phaedo* 81E–82A, *Republic* 620A. Krause (1904, 37) notes that while lions are not mentioned in the former passage, nor wolves in the latter, both are mentioned together by Porphyry cited by Stobaeus 1.49, p.447.19 Wachsmuth.

355 An associate of Numenius. See Dillon (1996) 379–80. The present text is Cronius fr.12 in Leemans (1937).

356 Theodorus of Asine, Neoplatonist philosopher (3rd–4th century CE).

357 On Nemesius' presentation of the contrast between Porphyry and Iamblichus over whether animal souls are rational, see Sorabji (1993) 192–93; (2004) vol. 1 213–16; above, Introduction, 5.a.2. Sorabji (1993, 191; cf. his [2004] vol. 1 213) notes that Augustine, *City of God* 10.30 and Aeneas of Gaza, *Theophrastus* 12.11–25 deny that Porphyry allowed transmigration of human souls into animals, and suggests that Porphyry's position might have been ambivalent, like Plotinus' at 1.1 [53] 11.8–15. See also Kallis (1978) 113–21; Beatrice (2005) 255–60.

course to them;[358] he says that there is a species of soul for each species of animal, i.e. a different species [of soul]; at any rate he wrote a monograph *That transmigrations do not occur from men into irrational animals nor from irrational* (10) *animals into men but from animals to animals and from men to men*.[359] He seems to me for this reason to have divined better not only Plato's judgment but also the truth itself,[360] as can be established on many other grounds, especially the following: non-rational animals do not exhibit (15) any rational behaviour; for they possess neither skills nor learning nor plans nor virtues nor anything else that involves thought. From this it is clear that they have no share in rational soul. For it is also absurd to say that the non-rational are rational. For even if, when children are extremely young, they exhibit only non-rational behaviour, we still say that they have a rational soul, since, as they grow, (20) they exhibit rational activity. But a non-rational animal at no age exhibits rationality and would have a rational soul superfluously, since rational ability was going to be absolutely useless. For everyone is agreed with one voice that nothing was brought to be by God that was superfluous. If that is so, a rational soul that would never be able to exhibit its function (25) would have been inserted into domestic and wild animals superfluously, and it would have been a reproach to him who **[36]** provided an unsuitable soul for the body. For that is not the work of a craftsman nor one who understands order or attunement.

But if someone were to say that in disposition animals behave rationally, but their formation does not allow skilled activity, basing their argument on humans – for if the fingers (5) of their hands alone are taken away, nearly all skills are destroyed with them – this does not solve the problem. For the same absurdity remains, that God fitted the body with a soul that was not suitable, but superfluous, useless and ineffective, since it is prevented throughout their whole life from carrying out its characteristic activities.

In addition they also construct their argument from unclear and (10)

---

358 Neoplatonist philosopher, c.245–c.325, who taught in Syria.

359 Sorabji (2004, vol.1 213) suggests that one motive for denying transmigration into animals was to maintain the practice of animal sacrifice.

360 Telfer (1955, 289 n.6) suggests that this judgement on Iamblichus is that of Nemesius' Platonist source, rather than Nemesius' own. But unless we assume totally mechanical copying, Nemesius makes it clear that he endorses the judgement. The question then arises whether he is endorsing the view that there is transmigration of souls from human to human, or just the claim that human souls and animal souls are intrinsically different. Ferro (1925, 235) argues against the former on the basis of the dismissal of Origen at the end of section 3 below – but the possibility remains that Nemesius might have changed his position in the course of composition in the light of the controversies over Origen.

controversial premises; for whence comes the premise that in disposition animals behave rationally? So it is better to believe that a suitable soul is fitted to each body, and that animals have no disposition beyond the natural simplicity which they exhibit in their doings. For each species of non-rational animals behaves in accordance with its natural drive, for which need and activity it (15) originally came to be, and for these it also received its appropriate formation. For the Craftsman did not leave them utterly without resource, but endowed each with its natural understanding, though not of a rational sort,[361] and He implanted in some a resourcefulness as a sort of image of skill and a shadow of reason for the sake of two things:[362] so that that they might turn away from their immediate aims and take steps to guard (20) those in the future, and in order to join together the whole creation to itself, as was said before. That they do not act in this way rationally is clear from the fact that each animal of a species does the same things in the same way and that their activities do not vary in number, except in degree.[363] But still the whole species is stirred to action by a single impulse. For each hare is cunning in the same way, each wolf plays its tricks in the same way, and each ape mimics in the same way, which is not (25) the case with man.[364] For men's actions take thousands of different routes.

361 Aristotle, *History of Animals* 8.1 588a23, 9.1 608a17. See Fortenbaugh (1971); Sorabji (1993) 12–16, and above 1 4.12–16.
362 'for the sake of two things' is omitted by the Armenian and the earliest Latin versions, and is consequently deleted by Morani.
363 Literally, 'except by the more and less'. I.e., one member of a species may perform certain activities more often than another member of the same species; but it does not perform more *types* of activity. On this contrast between animals and men see, at much greater length, Bardesanes ap. Eusebius, *Preparation for the Gospel* 6.10.1–10 (GCS 8.1 [43.1] 335.1–337.3 Mras) and Origen, *Against Celsus* 4.87, 'if it was reason that discovered [remedies used by animals], it would not be this [remedy] alone that was discovered among snakes, in a fixed way, or even a second or a third, nor something else in the case of the eagle and so in the other animals, but there would be as many as in the case of man. But as it is it is clear, from the fact that each animal naturally inclines in a fixed way to certain remedies, that it is not wisdom or reason that is present in them, but rather a certain natural constitution directed towards such things for the sake of the preservation of the animals, one that has been brought about by [the divine] reason'; Domański (1900) 50–51 n.2; Pohlenz (1941) 6; Kallis (1978) 121–24; Sorabji (1993) 86 and n.62. Pohlenz attributed the point to Posidonius; Kidd, in Edelstein and Kidd (1988–1989) vol 2.2 572–73, argues that the interest in human skill might derive from Posidonius, but that the general point would have been acceptable to all Stoics and that the examples are standard ones. The idea that the activities of humans are more varied than those of other animals is already present in Aristotle, *On the Heaven* 2.12 292b3–8.
364 Boudon-Millot (2005) lists numerous parallels for the notion there that apes are inferior imitators of human beings. In the present passage, however (as she notes: 85), Nemesius

For reason [37] is something free and self-governed,[365] which is why the work of man is not one and the same for all men, as it is for each species of non-rational animal. For they are moved only by their nature, and what is natural is the same for all. But rational actions are different for different people, and they are not the same for all by necessity.

If people were to say that (5) the soul of those who had sinned before in their human life was degraded into such bodies for punishment, they are basing their proof on later events. For why were rational souls cast into the first bodies of animals that came to be? Presumably not as having sinned in human bodies prior to coming into a human body![366]

Galen also, the marvellous physician, (10) seems to share this opinion and to believe that for each species of animal there is a different species of soul. For right at the beginning of the first book of his work *On the Usefulness of [Bodily] Parts*, he speaks as follows: 'If this is so, animals will have many parts, some bigger, some smaller, some altogether impossible to divide off into another form. The soul has a use for all of them; for the body is (15) the instrument of the soul, and therefore the parts of animals differ greatly from each other, since their souls do also.'[367] Further, as he goes on in the same book he adds this also about the ape: 'Moreover, O wisest of accusers, Nature would answer you that it was proper to give a ludicrous bodily constitution to an animal with a ludicrous soul'.[368] Thus he knows that different sorts of soul (20) are present in different species of bodies.

So much on these matters. If we have proved that the soul is neither a body nor an attunement nor a mixture nor any other quality, it is clear from this that the soul is some incorporeal substance. For that it exists is agreed by all.[369] If it is neither body nor accident, it is clear that it is an incorporeal

---

emphasises rather the similarity between apes and other non-human animals, in that all by contrast with human beings are limited to specific activities.

365 For the link between reason and freedom Streck (2005, 185 n.27) compares 41 117.7–8 below. See the Introduction, 4.c.

366 In the Genesis account animals were created before there were any human beings: Telfer (1955) 291 n.2.

367 Galen, *On the Usefulness of the Parts* 1.1 vol.3 2.3–9 K = 1.10-16 Helmreich. Skard (1942) argues, against Pohlenz (1941, 7 n.1), that 35.14–37.9, as well as the sequel, derives from Galen. See our Introduction, at n.122, and n.226; also Boudon-Millot (2005) 75–76, who notes the contrast between this and the critical treatment of Galen earlier at 23.24ff.

368 Galen, *On the Usefulness of the Parts* 1.22 vol.3 80.13–15 K = 59.4–6 Helmreich.

369 However, Cicero, *Tusculan Disputations* 1.21 and a number of later sources say that Dicaearchus (on whom see above, n.262) denied the existence of the soul altogether. This *may* be a tendentious representation of his denial that it was a separate substance. See Sharples (2001b) 148–51.

(25) substance and none of those things that have their being in something else. For these come and go without the destruction of their substrate. But when the soul is separated from it the body is altogether destroyed. It is possible to prove that the soul is immortal using the same facts. For if it is neither a body, which **[38]** was shown to be naturally able to be dispersed and perishable,[370] nor a quality nor quantity nor anything else perishable, it is clear that it is immortal. There are many proofs of its immortality in Plato and the rest, but those are very difficult, hard to comprehend and scarcely well-understood (5) by those brought up in these sciences. For us let the teaching of the sacred books suffice as a proof of the soul's immortality, for it is reliable in itself, since it is divinely inspired. But for those who do not accept the Christian writings it suffices to prove that the soul is none of those things that perish. For if it is none of the things that perish, and is imperishable, (10) it is also immortal.[371] So this matter should be set aside as being in a satisfactory state.

370 Krause (1904) 23–24 compares Porphyry, *Sentences* 14 and Priscian, *Answers to Chosroes* 46.25. But the common source is Plato, *Phaedo* 78–79, and the presence of such a widespread idea shows little about Nemesius' sources.
371 Plato, *Phaedo* 106ce conversely argues from the immortality of the soul to its imperishability.

78   NEMESIUS

SECTION 3

ON THE UNION OF SOUL AND BODY

Souls are related to bodies while themselves preserving their own nature; analogy with the Incarnation.

We must inquire how the union of a soul and a soulless body comes about.[372] For this is a puzzling question. But if man is composed not only of these, but of an intellect also, as some contend,[373] it is yet more so. For all the ingredients (15) coming together to constitute a single substance are altogether unified, but all the unified are altered and do not remain what they formerly were, as will be shown in the case of the elements. For having been unified they have become something else. So how then does the body still remain a body when united with the soul, or, again, how is the soul, which is incorporeal and substantial in itself, united with a body and how does it become part of a living thing, while keeping its own substance unconfused and free

---

372 Dörrie (1959, 12–103), developing the discussions of von Arnim (1887), Domański (1900, 59–61) and Krause (1904, 5–11, 14–16), argues that Nemesius' discussion from here to 42.9 is based on Porphyry, with additions by Nemesius himself (e.g. 38.12–14 just below, referring back to section 1: Dörrie [1959] 41). This claim is based on the occurrence of much of the material, often in abbreviated form but in the same sequence, also in Priscian of Lydia, *Answers to Chosroes* 50.25–52.7, who cites Porphyry's *Miscellaneous Investigations* as a source at 42.16–17, together with Nemesius' citation of the same work of Porphyry at 43.2 below. Rist (1988), however, argued, citing in particular the absence of the slogan 'unified without being confounded' (39.19, 40.10; cf. Dörrie [1959] 55 and above, Introduction n.4) in the surviving works of Porphyry, that the source is not Porphyry but a fourth-century anti-Porphyrian Christian collection wrongly ascribed to Ammonius Saccas and excerpted by the Theodotus who is cited as a source by Priscian, *Answers to Chosroes* 42.15. See also Dodds (1960) 25; Theiler (1966) 105; Kallis (1978) 130–73; Schwyzer (1983) 72–73; Schroeder (1987) 512; Emilsson (1994) 5357–61; Sorabji (2004) vol. 1 204–05; Chiaradonna (2005) 132 n.7; Beatrice (2005) 260–66 and 272–73; Karamanolis (2006) 214, 289. See also below, n.390. In the course of his discussion Dörrie gives (39–99) a detailed commentary on this section, both the parts that have parallels in Priscian and those that do not. 38.12 (along with 38.20–23 below, *pace* Dörrie [1959] 45) ~ Priscian 50.25–28, 'At this point we must introduce the remaining question: in what way is the soul with the body, and through what kind of union or mixture or composition or even some other form of sharing a nature.' 38.20–43.16 here are printed in Sorabji (2004) vol.1 as 6(b)(1); cf. also Sorabji (2003), 158–61.

373 See above, nn.184–85. Telfer (1955, 293 n.1) suggests that the reference here is to followers of Apollinaris who made man not tripartite, as Apollinaris himself did, but quadripartite, distinguishing spirit from intellect on the basis of I Corinthians 14:15.

from destruction?[374] For body and soul must of necessity either be (20) unified, changed together and both perish together,[375] like the elements, or not be unified because of the absurdities previously stated, being beside each other like chorus-men in a dance or pebble by pebble, or else be mixed together like wine and water.[376] **[39]** But it has been proved in the section on the soul that the soul cannot lie alongside the body;[377] for only that portion of the body that was next to the soul would be animate, that not attached would be inanimate, in addition to the fact that one cannot call 'one' things placed together like pieces of wood, for example, or (5) iron or the like. Also the mixture of wine and water destroys both together; for the mixture is neither pure water nor wine.[378] However, such a mixture comes about by juxtaposition,[379] which escapes perception because of the smallness of

374 38.14–20 ~ Priscian, *Answers to Chosroes* 50.28–51.4, 'for we see that every being that is received into the substance of a single thing, animal it may be or body, is combined into the substance of some single thing [only] if it is first transformed and destroyed by something else. For it is not possible to understand it as being at one and the same time preserved without perishing and also combined into the substance of some single thing.' Dörrie (1959) 42–43.

375 I.e., lose their identity in the new mixture; see below, 39.6.

376 For these three types of mixture see Chrysippus the Stoic cited by Alexander of Aphrodisias, *On Mixture* 3 216.14–217.2 = *SVF* 2.473 = LS 48C; and for their application in discussion of the relation between body and soul Alexander, *Supplement to On the Soul (mantissa)* 3 115.33–116.1, 116.10–13; Calcidius, *On Plato's Timaeus* 221, p.234.6–235.6 Waszink and 227, p. 242.22–243.5 Waszink; Plotinus 4.7 [2] 8²; Priscian, *Answers to Chosroes* 44.15–28 (and cf 50.25–28; above, n.372); Krause (1904) 29; Emilsson (1994) 5343–44; Chiaradonna (2005). Waszink ad loc. argues that Calcidius is here dependent on Alexander via Porphyry, against Dörrie (1959, 33–35) who argued that the source of Calcidius, and of Priscian 44.15–28, was Middle Platonist. On the general context in Calcidius see also Mansfeld (1990) 3112–17, accepting the likelihood of Porphyry as source but noting that the source itself knew the doxographical tradition.

377 See above, 2 22.10–17.

378 39.5-11 ~ Priscian, *Answers to Chosroes* 51.4–9, 'For if they perish when they are united, they produce a single substance; but if they can be preserved, even if we cannot observe this, it does not seem that they are united into a single substance with a common nature, like the mixture of wine and water, if an oiled sponge drives the pure water out of the mixture, and papyrus similarly. From this one should judge that they are fitted together with each other, but not that they are unified in their nature'; Dörrie (1959) 47. The same objection to a mixture of soul with body at Alexander, *On the Soul* 15.5–8 and *Supplement to On the Soul (mantissa)* 3 116.5–13; Krause (1904) 29.

379 Alexander, *On Mixture* 15 231.22–232.6 expressly denies that the wine and water which (he agrees) can be separated by the sponge are mixed only by juxtaposition. Telfer (1955, 294 n.4) notes Bishop Fell as observing that some separation can be achieved – as is shown by the use of filter-paper in chemistry – but that it is only the first part of the water that can be separated in this way.

the parts of the things mixed, but is evident from the fact that they can be separated again from each other. For a sponge impregnated with olive oil raises up (10) the water pure, as does papyrus,[380] but it is altogether impossible to separate perceptibly things strictly unified.

But if they are neither united, nor adjacent, nor mixed, what is the explanation of the animal's being called one? Indeed because of this difficulty Plato does not consider a living being to consist of soul and body but to be a soul that uses a body[381] and, as it were, puts the body on like a garment.[382] But this explanation also (15) contains a difficulty. For how can a soul be one with its garment? For a tunic is not one with its wearer. Ammonius, the teacher of Plotinus,[383] gave the following solution to the question: he said that intelligible things had such a nature as to be both unified with things capable of receiving them, as are things which perish together with one another, and when unified, to remain unconfused and not perish, (20) like things which are juxtaposed. For in the case of bodies unification certainly brings about the alteration of the ingredients, since they are transformed into other bodies, as are the elements into their compounds, foods into blood, and blood [40] into flesh and the other parts of the body. But in the case of intelligible things unification occurs, but alteration does not follow with it; for intelligible things are not of a kind to be altered in their substance: either they depart or they perish into nothingness,[384] but they are impervious to change. But they do not perish into nothingness; if they did (5) they would not be immortal.[385] Also, if the soul, which is life, were to be changed when

---

380 Cf. Alexander, *On Mixture* 15 232.2; Stobaeus *Ecl.* 1.17, 155.5–11 = Arius Didymus *fragments on physics* 28 = *SVF* 2.471 = LS 48D; Philo, *On the Confusion of Tongues* 186. Dörrie (1959) 47–48; Todd (1976) 241.

381 Cf. Plato, *Phaedo* 79c; Dörrie (1959) 51, and above, n.189.

382 Cf., with Dörrie (1959) 52 and Sorabji (2004) vol. 1 204 and 206, Plato, *Gorgias* 523cd, *Cratylus* 403b, *Republic* 10 620c.

383 39.16–40.2 ~ Priscian, *Answers to Chosroes* 51.9–18, 'So this is remarkable in the case of the soul, in what way it itself is both mixed with something else, like those things [which are mixed by] perishing together, and also remains preserving its own nature, like those which are juxtaposed. For this is the nature of incorporeal things; the mixing of those things which are immaterial is not achieved by perishing, but without hindrance the things which are suitable to receive [each other] fill themselves throughout, and they pass through the whole of each other as not perishing, and they remain unmixed and without perishing together. For an incorporeal being unifies itself indivisibly and its presence to any body results in blending together, as a result of which the parts of the body too are unified one with another'; Dörrie (1959) 54.

384 Cf. Plato, *Phaedo* 102e–103a, 103d.

385 As Sorabji (2004, vol. 1 205 and 206) notes, this draws on Plato's *Phaedo* (105e–107a).

mixed, it would be altered and would not still be life. But what would it contribute to the body unless it provided it with life? Therefore the soul is not altered in unification.

However, now it has been shown that intelligible things are unalterable in their substance, it necessarily follows that even when they are unified they do not perish together with the things with which (10) they are unified.[386] The soul is, then, unified, and is unified to the body without being compounded with it. Their being affected together shows that they are unified; for a living thing is affected as a whole, since it is one. But it is clear that the soul also remains uncompounded from the fact that the soul is in a way separated from the body in sleep; it leaves the body lying like a corpse, and merely breathes life into it (15) lest it should perish utterly,[387] but in itself it is active in its dreams, foretelling the future and associating with things intelligible.[388] The same thing happens also when the soul reviews some reality on its own: for then also it separates itself as far as possible from the body and comes to be by itself in order that it may thus fix its gaze on realities. For being incorporeal it has permeated [the body] throughout as do things (20) that have perished together with one another,[389] while remaining incorruptible and uncompounded, preserving its own unity and making the things in which it comes to be conform to its life while not being transmuted by them.[390] For as the sun by its presence transforms the

---

386 40.8–10 ~ Priscian, *Answers to Chosroes* 51.18, '[incorporeal being] remains, therefore, unified without being compounded'; Dörrie (1959) 62.

387 40.11–15 ~ Priscian, *Answers to Chosroes* 52.13–16, 'that [soul] is unified [with body] is made clear by their being affected together; that it does not perish along with it is shown by the separation that occurs in sleep. For the soul returns to itself in a noble way and is only attached to [lit.: stretched out from] the body through a sort of vapour that gives life, like a flame hidden among ashes'; Dörrie (1959) 63–68.

388 The idea that the soul can foretell the future when it is freed from the body in sleep appears in Aristotle, *On Philosophy* fr.10 Rose (= Sextus Empiricus, *Against the Professors* 9.20–22) and is attributed to the Peripatetics Dicaearchus (4th century BCE) and Cratippus (1st century BCE) by Cicero, *On Divination* 1.70 (Cratippus only), 1.113 and 2.100 (both). See Sharples (2001b) 164–73. However, the association of this idea specifically with apprehension of the *intelligible* seems to be a specifically Platonist development; cf., perhaps, already Plato, *Republic* 9 572a.

389 40.19–20 ~ Priscian, *Answers to Chosroes* 51.25–26, 'it is unified without being compounded and spread throughout the whole, remaining most perfectly uncorrupted, since it is incorporeal'; Dörrie (1959) 69–73.

390 Dörrie (1959, 70) notes the similarity between this passage and 43.6–8 below, which is explicitly quoted from Porphyry's *Miscellaneous Investigations*. Schroeder (1987) uses the similarity to argue that Nemesius' source here is Porphyry, and suggests that Nemesius initially gave the name of Ammonius to avoid referring to the anti-Christian Porphyry.

air into light, making it have the form of light, and light is unified with the
[41] air, mixed with it without being compounded,[391] in the same way the
soul is unified with the body while remaining altogether uncompounded,
differing only in that the sun, being a body and circumscribed in place, is
not everywhere that its light is, as is also the case with fire. For fire remains
(5) in the wood or in the wick, tied down as being in a place.[392] But the soul,
being incorporeal and not circumscribed in place,[393] occupies as a whole
the whole of its own light and of its body,[394] and there is no part to which
it gives light in which it is not present *as a whole*. For it is not controlled
by the body,[395] but itself controls the body;[396] it is not in the body as in a
vessel or a wine skin,[397] but rather (10) the body is in it.[398] For things intelligible are not impeded by bodies, but spread throughout the whole body,[399] wander and move in and out, and so they cannot be constricted by bodily place. Being intelligible, they are also in intelligible places, either within themselves or in superior intelligibles, as the soul is sometimes in itself, in

---

391 Cf., with Dörrie (1959) 76 and 78 n.4 and Sorabji (2004) vol. 1 205, Seneca, *Letter* 41.5, and Plotinus 4.3 [27] 22.1–9, 1.1 [53] 4.14–16. Below, n.1040.

392 40.22–41.5 ~ Priscian, *Answers to Chosroes* 51.33–52.5, 'just as the sun turns air to light and adjacent fire warms; the light indeed is unified with the air, like those things which perish together, and remains present to it without being compounded. For this reason the activity of incorporeal things has its being and strength in itself, easily filling completely those things which are suited to receive it. For it is not the case that, as a flame burns on the wick, so the soul does in the body, but it is united like an attached flame'; Dörrie (1959) 74–79. The example of fire present in red-hot iron had been used by the Stoics to support the claim that two bodies can be present in the same place (Arius Didymus, *fr. phys.* 28 = *SVF* 2.471; Alexander, *On Mixture* 4 218.1–2 = *SVF* 2.473 = LS 48C, with the example of light and air at 218.8–9; see Todd [1976] 40–41); it was used to illustrate the Incarnation by Origen, *On Principles* 2.6.6 and *Against Celsus* 3.41, and by Apollinaris. See Raven (1923) 25 and Todd (1976) 193.

393 Porphyry, *Sentences* 27 (p.16.1–3 Lamberz), 31 (p.21.9), quoted at Sorabji (2004) vol. 1 6(b)(5)–(6).

394 Telfer understands the reference as to the sun's own body, and this is supported by the statement below that body is in soul rather than the reverse.The sun's light (it is argued) is present in the same way both in the sun's own body and beyond it.

395 Sorabji (2004, vol. 1 207) compares Plato, *Timaeus* 43a6–7, 44a7, and *Laws* 7 791a2.

396 See above, n.292.

397 Similarly Priscian, *Answers to Chosroes* 52.7, 'nor is it enclosed as in a bag': Dörrie (1959) 80–82. Sorabji (2004, vol. 1 205) compares Augustine, *On the Magnitude of the Soul* 5.7 p.139.9 Hörmann and *Literal Interpretation of Genesis* 8.21, p.261.8 Zyda.

398 Cf., with Sorabji (2004) vol. 1 207, Plotinus 4.3 [27] 22.7–10; Porphyry, *Sentences* 31, 'body is in soul and in mind and in god'.

399 Cf. Priscian, *Answers to Chosroes* 51.13, quoted in n.383 above: Dorrie (1959) 83–84.

discursive reasoning, sometimes in the intellect, in intellection.[400] So when (15) it is said to be in a body, it is not said to be in a body as in a place, but as in a relationship to it and by being present, as God is said to be in us. For we say that the soul is bound by the body in its relationship and inclination[401] towards something and disposition, as we say that the lover is 'bound' by the beloved woman, neither in a bodily sense nor in place but by their relationship. For since the soul has no size (20) nor bulk, nor parts, it is superior to spatial circumscription.[402] For by what sort of place can that which has no part be circumscribed? For place exists together with bulk: for place is the limit of the container,[403] by which **[42]** it contains the contained. But if someone were to say: 'Surely my soul is in Alexandria and Rome and wherever'[404] he fails to see that he counts himself a place. For what is in Alexandria and generally in a certain [place] is place. But it is absolutely not *in* place but *in relation* [*to* place]. For it has been proved that it cannot

---

400 Here Nemesius seems to have been led by his Platonist source into regarding the intellect as something other than an element in the soul.

401 Cf., with Sorabji (2004) vol.1 205 and 209, Porphyry, *Sentences* 3 (Sorabji 6(b)(4)) and Augustine, *Letter* 166, 551.7–12 (Sorabji 6(b)(10)). Porphyry too says that incorporeals are present in body by a relation or relationship (*skhesis*), the point being that a relation does not affect the thing itself; I can be taller than my growing child, and then shorter, without my own height changing. Alexander of Aphrodisias consistently defines illumination – and *light* (for which see above) is for him the illumination of the transparent medium – as a relation (Sharples [2004] 127, and references there). See also Theiler (1966) 107–08. The notion of relation was used in a Christological context (see below, n.406) by Nestorius, attacked for this by Cyril of Alexandria, *Letter to Acacius* 15 (*PG* 77.193D/*ACO* 1.1.4 p.27.8), 'he names two natures [in Christ] and distinguishes them from each other, putting God separately, and similarly man in turn, joined to God by a relation, according to equality of honour or authority only', and *Against Nestorius* 2, prologue (*PG* 76 60D/*ACO* 1.1.6 p.33.2–6), 'and how will it not be beyond doubt for everyone that, being God by nature, the Only-Begotten became man, not simply by conjunction, as [Nestorius] says, which is thought of as external, or by a relation'; Boulnois (2005) 456 nn.16–17.

402 See Porphyry, *Sentences* 27, 'what is completely without bulk and without size cannot be controlled by things that have bulk, and has no part in spatial movement', and 35; Domański (1900) 66 nn.1 and 2.

403 This is the definition of place given by Aristotle at *Physics* 4.4 212a6–6a Ross. Our Greek MSS of the *Physics* have nothing here to correspond to Nemesius' following 'by which it contains the contained', but Sextus Empiricus, *Outlines of Pyrrhonism* 3.131 gives Aristotle's definition and adds 'in that (*katho*) it contains' (only), and the commentaries of Themistius (*On Aristotle's Physics* 118.8), Simplicius (*On Aristotle's Physics* 580.3) and the medieval Arabic version add 'at which it is in contact with the contained' ('with the contained body', Themistius).

404 Literally 'everywhere'; but the point seems to be not that my soul is now everywhere (e.g. in the sense that I can think about a place other than that I am in) but that, wherever I may be, my soul is there at the time I am.

be surrounded by a place. So when an intelligible thing comes into relation with a place, or (5) with some thing that is in place, we rather incorrectly say that it is 'there' because of its activity there, taking the place instead of the relation and the activity. We ought to say 'it is active there', but in fact say 'it is there'.[405]

This account would fit more clearly and best with (10) the union of God, the Word, with man,[406] in which, while united, He remained uncompounded and uncontained, but not in the way the soul is. For the soul, being one of the things which are complex, seems both to be affected with the body in a way through its affinity with it, and sometimes to master it, sometimes to be mastered.[407] But God, the Word, is not in any way Himself altered by this affinity that concerns body and soul, (15) nor does He share in their weakness, but by giving them a share in His divinity He becomes one with them while remaining one as He was before the unification. This kind of mixture or unification is more novel.[408] He both is infused and remains altogether unmixed, uncompounded, uncontaminated and unchanged, not affected with them but only acting with them, neither perishing with them[409] and (20) altered with them, but increasing them without being Himself diminished by them, in addition to remaining immutable and uncompounded, since He is also pure and without share in any alteration. Porphyry, who raised his own voice against Christ, is a witness to this: the testimonies of

---

405 Cf. the similar move made concerning the divine Active Intellect by Alexander, *Supplement to On the Soul* (*mantissa*) 2 (*On Intellect*) 113.18–24.

406 In Christ. Telfer (1955, 300 n.1, and 304) argues that Nemesius, concerned with the nature of man and addressing himself to non-Christians (who by this date would have some knowledge of Christian controversies) as well as to Christians, uses the discussion of the Incarnation to support his general theory of the relation between soul and body in human beings generally, whereas the argument was more often in the opposite direction. Nonetheless, it would seem that what is said here about Christ can be seen as a deliberate culmination to the first three sections of the work. See Sorabji (2004) vol. 1 205; also Boulnois (2005) 454–59, who notes (457) that Nemesius does not actually take up in the Christological context the point about relation that he made in the anthropological one (above, n.401). See also Introduction, 3.a.

407 See above, section 2 21.19–22. Boulnois (2005) 458–59 (cf. 470) notes a difference between Nemesius' position concerning the human soul here and that attributed to 'the more highly reputed' philosophers in section 2, and attributes it to Nemesius' concern here to distance the Incarnation of Christ from the ordinary body–soul relation; but even in section 2 Nemesius seems to express doubts about the view that the human soul is not affected.

408 That is, 'exceptional'; but the point that the Incarnation was unprecedented is also apt.

409 From the context concerned with mixture, the point seems to be not just that Christ as divine did not perish with his human body and soul (which in any case did not perish) but that he was not blended with them in a way that destroyed the identity of both the divine and human, as the ingredients in a mixture lose their identity in the blending; above, n.375.

enemies **[43]** on our behalf are strong and permit no reply. Now this man Porphyry in the second book of his *Miscellaneous Investigations* writes in the exact words that follow: 'It is not to be denied that a certain substance can be received for the completion of another substance, and can be a part of [this] substance while retaining its (5) own nature together with completing another substance, and, while becoming one with another, can retain its own unity and moreover, while itself untransmuted, it can transmute those things into which it comes so that they gain its activity by its presence'. He says this about the unification of soul and body. But if this account is true of the soul because it is incorporeal, (10) still more is it so in the account of God Who is more uncompounded and truly incorporeal. This directly stops the mouths of those who try to attack the unification of God with man. For the majority of pagans make this an object of derision, saying that it is impossible, implausible and unseemly that the divine should come together with the mortal nature by (15) mixture and unification. But we make use of their own reputable witnesses and shrug off the accusation.

But it is said in some quarters, and particularly by the Eunomians, that God the Word is united to the body not substantially but through the powers of each. For it is not [they say] the substances that are united **[44]** or mixed, but the powers of the body are mixed with the divine powers. They say, with Aristotle, that it is the sensations that are the powers of the body,[410] no doubt simply 'the body with organs';[411] so, they say, the divine powers were mixed with these and brought about their unification. But I think that nobody (5) would agree with them when they declare that the senses are bodily powers. For it was previously made clear which are the properties of the body, which of the soul, which of their combination,[412] and we placed sensations by means of the organs among the properties of the combination,

---

410 For Aristotle sensation in fact involves both body and soul; sight is the soul of the eye, or rather that faculty of the soul of the whole creature that uses the eye as its instrument (above, section 2, 26.22–27.11). It is true that from the point of view of incarnational Christology the bodily senses are on the human rather than the divine side of the union even though they involve the soul. But this does not excuse what Nemesius says here, for he goes on to give, as a correction of the Eunomians, a view which is actually Aristotle's own. Telfer (1955, 301–02 n.3) well describes Nemesius' assimilation of Eunomius to Aristotle as 'more ingenious than ingenuous'.

411 The reference to organs may be dismissive, implying that the Eunomians are no better than Aristotelians. See above, 2 17.4–5.

412 It is unclear to what part of his discussion Nemesius is referring. Telfer suggests 1 9.22ff., which seems unlikely. For the general point concerning the relation between body and soul one might compare 1 5.19ff. or 2 28.4ff.; what, however, does not seem to have been said anywhere previously in the treatise is the point which follows, that sensation belongs to the soul–body compound.

but said that the organs themselves were bodily. So it is better to say, as we said before, that the union of the substances[413] comes about without composition through (10) the proper nature of the incorporeals, the more divine suffering no harm from the lower, while this is benefited by the more divine. For the purely incorporeal nature pervades the whole unchecked, while nothing pervades it. So they are unified because it pervades all, but because nothing pervades it, it remains unmixed (15) and uncompounded. But the means of the unification is not [God's] consent [to it], as is thought by some influential men,[414] but nature is the cause. For one may plausibly say that the reception of the body came about by consent, but that it is united without composition is through God's own nature and not by grace. For we should leave aside the ranks of souls, their risings and their descendings, which Origen introduces,[415] as not suited to the divine writings (20) nor in harmony with Christian dogma.

413 It is unclear how far Nemesius' discussion from here to the end of the section relates to the union of divine and human in Christ, and how far to the union of soul and body in each individual. The reference to the views of Theodore of Mopsuestia (see the next note) is certainly in the context of the former, and the reference to 'consent' in 44.17 is also more appropriate there; on the other hand the contrast with Origen's view on the descent of the soul (below, n.415) suggests the latter, and the passage is so interpreted by Verbeke and Moncho (1975) lx, seeing a contrast between 'nature' in the present sentence and Origen's view that the soul descends through a *fault*.

414 Theodore (bishop of Mopsuestia from 392 to 428), *On the Incarnation*, PG 66 973c, 'it is by consent that he also accomplishes the in-dwelling'; 992c, '[Mary] was the mother of God, because God was in the man that was born, not being circumscribed in him according to his nature, but being in him according to the condition of his will'; *Letter to Domnus*, PG 66 1013a, 'the account of unification by substance is true only of things that have the same substance, but false of those with a different substance; for [this sort of unification] cannot be free from confounding [of the two substances]. But the type of unification which is according to consent, preserving the natures unconfounded and undivided, produces one person of both, and one will, and one authority, and what follows from these, one dominion and one mastery ... for it is in the way that involves consent that the one born from the very womb of the Virgin, as we said, was united with the Divine Word'. Boulnois (2005) 457 n.18; cf. Streck (2005) 20. Telfer (1955, 303 n.6) notes that *On the Incarnation* was a notorious work from early in Theodore's career, and that he later modified his views. Beatrice (2005, 267–69) argues that Nemesius' use of the plural is not simply a literary device but indicates a reference to Nestorius (fr.201–02, pp. 66, 162, 219–20 Loofs [1905]), as well as to Theodore, and that Nemesius' treatise is therefore to be dated later than 429/430; Boulnois (2005, 457 n.18), however, questions Beatrice's argument, and Loofs himself questions whether these fragments of Nestorius are genuine.

415 Origen, *Against Celsus* 7.5, 156.22, *On Principles* 2.8, GCS 5.1 [22] 160.19–23 Koetschau, 'of rational beings those that had sinned, and as a result of this had fallen from the position in which they were, were cast into bodies for the sake of punishment corresponding to their individual sins; and being purified they are taken up again to the position in which they were before, altogether putting off wickedness and their bodies'. Cf. Kallis (1978) 170–73.

SECTION 4

ON THE BODY

The composition of the human body out of the four elements and the four humours, constituting the homogeneous and the heterogeneous parts.

Every body is a compound of the four elements[416] and has come into being from them.[417] The bodies of animals with blood are composed directly[418] of the four humours, (25) blood, phlegm, yellow bile and black bile.[419]

---

416 Earth, fire, air and water, the classical four elements first posited by Empedocles and subsequently adopted in the cosmological theories of Plato and Aristotle. Nemesius has already referred to them above, 1, 7.12–14, and will be discussing them in more detail in section 5 below. 'Compound' (*sunkrima*) does not necessarily refer to a chemical mixture but can also denote the relation or proportion between the components.

417 In this view, and in what follows, Nemesius broadly follows the theory of elementary physiology as expounded in Galen's *On the Elements according to Hippocrates*, *On the Doctrines of Hippocrates and Plato* (esp. 8.4), *On Mixtures* and *On Hippocrates' On the Nature of Man*, which itself, of course, is dependent in many respects on earlier thinkers, most notably the Hippocratic work *On the Nature of Man*, Plato's *Timaeus* and Aristotle's *On Coming to Be and Perishing*, *On the Parts of Animals* and *Meteorology*. Nemesius' dependence on Galen in this section has been analysed by Skard (1938), from whose study several parallels noted here are derived. However, we do not follow Skard's *Quellenforschung* in all details, nor in his tacit presupposition that Nemesius did not make any creative use of the material he found in his sources; and in some respects – e.g. his claims that Nemesius cannot have used Galen's *On the Elements according to Hippocrates* but drew on a Galenic work now lost (possibly his commentary on Plato's *Timaeus*) – Skard goes beyond what the evidence permits us to say (cf. Kallis [1978] 40–47; Telfer [1955] 305 n.2). It should further be noted that Galen's own physiological theory differs in important respects from Aristotle's – e.g. Aristotle did not adopt the four humour theory (something which Nemesius seems aware of in 45.12) – and indeed from Hippocratic views (e.g. nowhere in the Hippocratic writings is the four element theory expounded *as such*) or Plato's, but Galen has a habit of reading his own views on elementary physiology into earlier authorities; see van der Eijk (2001) 46–56.

418 The term 'directly' (or 'proximately', *prosekhôs*) is explained by Nemesius a few lines further down (45.2). The explanation there is remarkably close to that offered by Galen, *On the Elements according to Hippocrates* 10.7 (140.13–14 De Lacy, 1.493 K), also in relation to the elementary level of material organisation: '"Proximate" is the term customarily applied to the matter from which a thing first comes into being when it has no need of any other intermediate alteration' (tr. De Lacy [1996] 141).

419 The doctrine of these four humours had first been articulated in the Hippocratic work *On the Nature of Man* (c. 400 BCE), which correlates each humour to a particular season and specific combination of elementary qualities (hot, cold, dry, wet). Though the theory was just one among many humoural theories propounded in the 5th and 4th century BCE, it became canonical in later medical thought and was raised to authoritative status by Galen, e.g. in his *On*

The bodies of bloodless animals [45] are composed of the other humours and that which in them is analogous to blood.[420] We say 'directly' when something comes to be from those very things without an intermediate stage, in that the four humours are a compound of the four elements,[421] while the homogeneous things,[422] which are parts of the body, are a mixture of the humours. They[423] liken (5) black bile to earth, phlegm to water, blood to air and yellow bile to fire. Every compound of elements is either solid or liquid or airy.[424] Aristotle holds that the bodies of animals come to be directly from blood alone;[425] for [he thinks] it is directly from this that all the parts of the animal are nourished and grow, and [he thinks] sperm (10) has its origin in blood.[426] But since it did not seem correct that the hardest bones, the softest flesh and fat should come from one and the same thing, Hippocrates thought – and he was the first to do so – that the bodies of animals should be framed directly from the four humours, so that the

---

the Natural Faculties and his *On Hippocrates' On the Nature of Man*. The doctrine of the four 'temperaments', believed to correspond to each of the four humours, is a post-Galenic development (and there are no signs of this theory in Nemesius). For accounts of the history of Greek humoural theory see Schöner (1964); Flashar (1966); Klibansky, Panowsky and Saxl (1992).

420 The distinction between blooded and bloodless animals, and the reference to something 'analogous' to blood in the latter, is a standard Aristotelian formula; see, e.g., *History of Animals* 490b7; 505b27; *On the Parts of Animals* 678a33; for 'that which is analogous to blood' see, e.g., *On the Parts of Animals* 648a5.

421 Cf. Galen, *Elements* 10.3–6 (138.18–140.13 De Lacy, 1.492–493 K); *On the Doctrines of Hippocrates and Plato* 8.4.21–22 (502.21–25 De Lacy, 5.676 K). Skard's references – here and elsewhere in his study – to *On Hippocrates' On Nutriment* (in this case to ch. 1, 15.226 K) ignore the fact that this work is a Renaissance compilation.

422 Or 'homoeomerous' parts, a term first attested for Anaxagoras and adopted by Aristotle (see, e.g. *History of Animals* 486a14; 487a1–10) and subsequently also by Galen: see *Elements* 10.3 (140.2 De Lacy, 1.492 K); 6.29 (110.17–21 De Lacy, 1.465 K); 8.11 (126.1–5 De Lacy, 1.479 K).

423 The subject of this sentence is unspecified, but the view expounded is Galen's: cf. *Elements* 8.12 (126.5–9 De Lacy, 1.479–80 K): 'blood, phlegm, and the two kinds of bile, yellow and black; their genesis is from the things we eat and drink, which in turn were produced from air and fire, water and earth' (tr. De Lacy); *On the Doctrines of Hippocrates and Plato* 8.4.21 (502.22–25 De Lacy, 5.676 K); 8.6.41 (520.18–21 De Lacy, 5.698 K).

424 This distinction of these three states is standard; cf. Galen, *On Tremor, Palpitation, Convulsion and Rigor* 5 (7.597 K), where Galen attributes it to Hippocrates: 'For what constitutes man, as Hippocrates has taught us, are solids, liquids and gases'; *On the Method of Healing* 12.8 (10.865 K).

425 *On the Generation of Animals* 726b2–5; 726b9–10; 740a21; *On the Parts of Animals* 650a34–b13; 668a9–13.

426 *On the Generation of Animals* 726b3ff.; 726b31ff.; 727a26ff.; 728b33; 737a27–28; 739b25; 774a2–3; 776b11–12.

harder parts should come from the more earthy and compact, the soft parts from the softer.[427] (15) Often the four humours are found in the blood, as can be seen in phlebotomies,[428] when sometimes serous phlegm predominates in it, sometimes black or yellow bile.[429] Hence the authors somehow seem to agree on this with each other.[430] Now some parts of animals are homogeneous, others are heterogeneous.[431] Homogeneous are the brain, (20) [cerebral] membranes, nerve, marrow, bone, tooth, cartilage, glands, ligaments, membrane,[432] fibres, hair, nails, flesh, veins, arteries, passages,

---

427 For a close parallel to this perception of a disagreement between Aristotle and Hippocrates cf. Galen, *Elements* 14.1 (154.11–20 De Lacy, 1.506 K), where Aristotle is not mentioned but very likely included in Galen's reference to 'those physicians and natural scientists who asserted that the animal comes into being and takes nourishment from blood alone' (tr. De Lacy); for the attribution of this view to Hippocrates see also *Elements* 11.3 (140.20–22 De Lacy, 1.494 K, though, as de Lacy points out [p. 201], Galen's own view subsequently [as attested in *On the Seed*] changed to the effect that only some parts of the body derive from blood, others from semen). Although Aristotle was (held to be) chronologically posterior to Hippocrates, the latter is presented here as disagreeing with the former; but this kind of schematic presentation of positions disregarding chronological sequence is a standard procedure in ancient doxographical discourse; see van der Eijk (1999) 23–24.

428 Cf. Galen, *Elements* 11.16–19 (144.16–146.7 De Lacy, 1.498 K): 'And indeed if you cut the veins of persons still in good health, the blood from one person will flow yellow, from another red, and from one person blacker, from another whiter'. Venesection was a widespread therapeutic procedure in ancient medicine (with the exception of Erasistratus, who strongly rejected it). Its efficacy was, among other things, believed to lie in its withdrawing moistures from the body that were believed to be in excess, a view which presupposes the possibility that other moistures may be contained in the blood (see next note). For an account of the technique and a translation of Galen's works on the topic see Brain (1986).

429 See Galen, *Elements* 11.1 (140.16–17 De Lacy, 1.494 K); 13.9 (150.15–16 De Lacy, 1.503 K); *On the Doctrines of Hippocrates and Plato* 8.4.4 (498.26–28 De Lacy, 5.672 K). Skard refers to *On Black Bile* 4 (78.24–29 De Boer 5.119 K) and *On Plethos* 10.19–22 (66.9–23 Otte, 7.566–67 K).

430 I.e. Aristotle and Hippocrates. Telfer's translation, 'From this it appears how far men are uniform in constitution', seems not correct.

431 For this distinction, and some of the examples, see Aristotle, *On the Generation of Animals* 724b23ff.; *History of Animals* 486a13ff.; *On the Parts of Animals* 647b10ff.; Galen, *Elements* 6.29 (110.19–21 De Lacy, 1.466 K); 8.11–15 (126.1–18 De Lacy, 1.479–80 K); *On the Doctrines of Hippocrates and Plato* 8.4.2–3 (498.20–25 De Lacy, 5.671–72 K); *On the Affected Parts* 1.2 (8.26 K); *On Simple Medicines* 4.15 (11.670–71 K). Kallis (1978, 44 n.116) provides a tabular comparison between the lists given in the various passages, showing that brain, membranes, tooth, 'passages' (*poroi*), and yellow bile are not mentioned anywhere in Aristotle's or Galen's (extant) lists of homogeneous parts.

432 *Humenes*, membranes or fleeces within the body but distinct from the cerebral membranes (*mēninges*) referred to in line 20. Galen, *On Anatomical Procedures* 9.2 (561.17–25 Garofalo; 2.716 K) refers to a restricted usage of *mēninx* in the sense of cerebral membrane

fat, top-skin and what are, as it were, elements related to these: blood so far as it is pure blood, phlegm, black bile and yellow bile; for[433] a tendon is a composite of ligaments and sinewy fibres. Heterogeneous are the head, the chest, hands, [**46**] feet, and the other human parts. For the head does not divide up into head as nerve divides up into nerve, vein into vein and flesh into flesh. But everything heterogeneous is composed of homogeneous parts, as the hand is composed of nerves, flesh, bones and such things. These they also call (5) organic.[434] The definition of the homogeneous is this: things of which the parts are similar to the whole and to each other.[435] Here we have to understand 'similar' as equivalent to 'the same'.

Not every animal possesses all the parts of the body,[436] but some are deprived of some parts. For some have no feet, like fishes and snakes, some no heads like crabs,[437] crayfish and some swimmers (for they have their sense-organs in their breast, (10) since they have no head),[438] some have no lungs, like all those that do not breathe air; some have no bladder, like birds and all that do not urinate,[439] while shelled animals lack the majority of limbs; their animal nature resides in a few features.[440] Some animals that have parts appear to lack them, as deer appear not to have yellow bile,[441] since in fact (15) they possess it scattered through their entrails and not obvious. But man has them all and perfect, and in such a way that it could not have been well otherwise.[442]

---

which he perceives in medical writers of his time, and this may account for the terminology used by Nemesius here.

433 The use of 'for' (*gar*) seems motivated by the desire to account for the omission of 'tendons' (*tenontes*) from the list of homogeneous parts. As Kallis observes (1978, 44 n.116), tendons are not included in Aristotle's or Galen's lists of homogeneous parts, except in Galen's *On Unstable Imbalance* 2 (7.735 K), so their status in this regard may have been disputed.

434 Cf. Aristotle, *Parts of Animals* 647a3–5, 647b23; *Generation of Animals* 734b28; Galen, *Art of Medicine* 2.1 (279.5–6 Boudon, 1.310 K).

435 For this definition Morani refers to Galen, *On Hippocrates' On the Nature of Man* 1, prooemium (6,14 Mewaldt, 15.7 K); see also *Elements* 8.11 (126.4–5 De Lacy, 1.479 K).

436 Most of what follows here has parallels in Aristotle's zoological works; for the footlessness of fishes and snakes cf. *History of Animals* 505b12.

437 Cf. Aristotle, *Parts of Animals* 686a1.

438 Cf. Galen, *On the Usefulness of the Parts* 8.1 (1.442.9 Helmreich, 3.609–10 K) and 8.4 (1.454.6 Helmreich, 3.626 K).

439 Cf. Aristotle, *History of Animals* 506b26.

440 Telfer interprets slightly differently: 'for in few of them is there the reality of a living creature'.

441 Cf. Aristotle, *History of Animals* 506a20ff.

442 Skard refers to strikingly close parallels in thought and expression (man, or parts of the human body, being constituted as well as it possibly can be) in Galen's *On the Usefulness*

ON THE NATURE OF MAN 91

In the same way there is much difference between animals also in the disposition of their parts. For some have their breasts on the chest, others on the belly and others under the thighs;[443] some have two, others four and others even more than that.[444] For on the whole, (20) nature has distributed the number of breasts in proportion to the number of offspring.[445] If anybody should wish to sort out these matters in detail, let him read Aristotle's *History of Animals*.[446] For it is not appropriate for the present work to go into it in detail, but only to set out some sketches and outlines.

So let us move on to the account of the elements, which logically follows from this as a subject of inquiry.

SECTION 5

ON THE ELEMENTS[447]

The four elements, the four elementary qualities and their interrelations. The theories of Aristotle, Plato, the Stoics, the Hebrews, Hippocrates and some Pre-Socratic philosophers.

The element of which the universe is made[448] is the smallest part of the

---

of the Parts 14.6 (2.299.3 Helmreich, 4.161 K); 2.15 (1.106.15–16 Helmreich, 3.145 K); 3.10 (1.177.22–23 Helmreich, 3.242 K). Kallis (1978, 46 n.120) is more sceptical regarding the Galenic origin of this idea and points to parallels of the same idea in Aristotle's works, e.g. *On the Parts of Animals* 686a25–687b25.

443 Cf. Aristotle, *History of Animals* 500a25; Galen, *On the Usefulness of the Parts* 7.22 (1.437.13ff. Helmreich, 3.602 K).

444 Cf. Aristotle, *History of Animals* 486b25; 500a25.

445 Morani refers to Galen, *On the Usefulness of the Parts* 3.10 (1.171.7 Helmreich, 3.233 K), where a parallel expression ('Nature differentially distributing') is found (though not on the number of breasts but on the structure of the muscles). Kallis (1978, 46 n.121) refers to Aristotle, *History of Animals* 486b24–487a1; 500a13–32; *Parts of Animals* 688a18–b33.

446 As Kallis notes (1978, 45 n.122), this reference does not prove that Nemesius used Aristotle's work directly: information on its contents may also have been available to him through intermediaries (such as Galen or Athenaeus who quote from the work regularly) or summaries (such as Aristophanes of Byzantium's compendium).

447 For discussions of this section see Lammert (1953), who argues that Galen's work *On the Elements according to Hippocrates* is Nemesius' main source here; Siclari (1974) 137ff.; and Kallis (1978) 10–47.

448 The expression *stoikheion kosmikon* is found in Ps.-Galen, *Introduction or Physician* 9 (14.695 K, noted by Skard 1938, 39 n. 1) and in the pseudo-Galenic work *On Diagnosis and Treatment of Kidney Affections* 6 (19.688 K); but variants like *ta tou kosmou stoikheia* ('the elements of the universe') are found frequently in Galen's *On the Elements according to*

compound that constitutes (5) bodies. There are four elements, earth, water, air and fire, arranged in this ascending order.[449] They are themselves primary bodies, and simple in comparison with other bodies. For every element is homogeneous with the things of which it is an element: indeed, while a principle[450] is not homogeneous with the things that proceed from it, an element is altogether homogeneous [with the things of which it is an element].[451] It is clear that earth and water, (10) air and fire are the elements. For in them the qualities manifest themselves in their extreme form,[452] both potentially and actually.[453] Nor, again, is any of these perceptible elements[454] unmixed and uncompounded with another element. For in a way all these things are somewhat adulterated and partake of each other to a higher or lower degree,[455] but even in the mixture their nature is absolutely plain.

(15) Each of the elements has a combination of two qualities that determine its specific character.[456] For earth is dry and cold, water cold and wet, air wet and warm by its own nature, and fire is warm and dry. These qualities cannot be elements by themselves:[457] for bodies cannot be composed of

---

Hippocrates, e.g. 5.28 (100.6–7 De Lacy, 1.455 K) and 5.31 (100.15–16 De Lacy, 1.456 K), and in *On Hippocrates' On the Nature of Man* 1.18 (32.4 Mewaldt, 15.58 K).

449 I.e., earth is heaviest and therefore lowest, then water, then air and finally fire which is the highest element.

450 Such as the qualities hot, cold, dry or wet.

451 Cf. Galen, *Elements* 6.39 (114.21–23 De Lacy, 1.470 K): 'For element differs from first principle in this, that first principles are not necessarily homogeneous with the things whose first principles they are, but elements are entirely homogeneous' (tr. De Lacy); 8.13 (126.9–12 De Lacy, 1.480 K).

452 Or 'at their extreme, as extremities', i.e. the elementary qualities hot, cold, dry and wet are found here in their most basic, primordial and unmixed state. The use of *akros* ('extreme', 'ultimate') in relation to the elementary qualities finds numerous parallels in Galen's *Elements*, e.g. 6.35 (112.25 De Lacy, 1.468 K): 'If you are looking for an element that is simple in nature, it must be unmixed, unblended, and at the extreme in quality'; 6.40 (116.4 De Lacy, 1.470 K).

453 What is meant by 'actually' is illustrated further down in 47.24; for what is meant by 'potentially' see 49.1–5 below.

454 I.e. none of these elements in their perceptible state.

455 Skard (1938, 40) compares Galen, *Elements* 5.21 (98.9–11 De Lacy, 1.454 K): 'all have been adulterated by other kinds of things and mixed with them, and they have all received a larger or smaller share of each other' (tr. De Lacy).

456 The following account of the elementary qualities ultimately goes back to Plato's *Timaeus* (esp. 32Bff.) and Aristotle's *On Coming to Be and Perishing* 2.3–4, but contains parallels also to Galen's *Elements* and *Mixtures*. Nemesius' sources here have been studied by Skard (1938), Jaeger (1914) 73–96, and Lammert (1953).

457 As Lammert notes (1953, 489), the distinction between corporeal elements and incorporeal qualities is something on which Galen, Alexander of Aphrodisias and Plutarch insist and which they argue is ignored by the Stoics, who use the terms interchangeably.

incorporeal qualities,[458] but nor can other bodies that do not have the quality in extreme form and in actuality be elements. For the elements would be infinite, since all things possess a quality to a greater or lesser degree and could not be distinguished as to what sort were elements of what. So it is necessary that an element should be a body and a simple body, having its qualities in extreme form and in actuality. By qualities I mean warmth, cold, wetness and dryness, [48] for of qualities these alone change a substance throughout and completely,[459] whereas none of the others does that. White, for example, when associated with a body, does not whiten it throughout as warmth warms it and cold chills it, nor does anything else.[460]

The elements are contrary to each other if contrary (5) in their two qualities, as water is contrary to fire, being cold and wet and thus contrary to warm and dry, and as earth is contrary to air, being cold and dry and thus contrary to the warm and wet. But, since opposites could not be attached to each other without some intermediate bond assigned to bind them together, the Creator set water in between earth and air, which are contraries, and gave it (10) two qualities, coldness and wetness, by which it could be attached at each extreme and bind them together.[461] For it is made akin to earth by its coldness and attached to air by its wetness. Again, he assigned air as a mean between water and fire, which are also contraries, akin to water by its quality of wetness, by its heat to fire. Thus he attached contraries (15) to each other by certain intermediates that bound together both themselves and the things that they bonded. For that is the best sort of tie. So he attached each of them to the one before it by one of its qualities, to the one after it by the other. Thus water is cold and wet, but in so far as it is cold it is attached to earth, which is prior to it in the ascent,[462] and in so far as it is wet to air, (20) which is after it. Similarly air is attached to water, which is prior to it, in so far as it is wet, but to fire, which is after it, in so far as it is dry. Fire is attached to air, which is prior to it, in so far as it is warm, but to earth in so far

---

458 By 'bodies' Nemesius means the four elements.
459 Cf. Galen, *Elements* 7.3 (118.20–21 De Lacy, 1.473 K).
460 Cf. Galen, *Elements* 9.13 (130.13–16 De Lacy, 1.484 K): 'And if in fact it is affected, it will be affected when it is heated, cooled, dried and moistened; for not one of the other qualities is able to alter through and through [the body] that is close to it' (tr. De Lacy). Skard (1938, 40) compares Galen, *To Patrophilus on the Establishment of the Medical Art* 8 (1.252 K), where the wording is almost identical to what Nemesius says here.
461 Cf. Plato, *Timaeus* 31B5–32C8.
462 See 47.6 above (with note).

as it is dry by bending backwards[463] and turning back to the other extreme. Thus earth is attached to water in so far as it is cold, but to fire in so far as it is dry (25) by bending backwards. For in order that the elements should not be related only upward and downward,[464] but should have also a circular relationship, [49] he somehow bent back and returned the extremes to each other, I mean fire and earth. For fire, by merely losing its heat, becomes earth. This is illustrated by thunderbolts:[465] for when fire is carried down and cooled down from its extreme heat it turns into stone. Therefore every thunderbolt contains stone (5) and sulphur. Sulphur is like cooled-off fire which is no longer hot in actuality but only potentially, but is actually dry.

Only the elements have the qualities in actuality, everything else potentially unless associated with an element. But in order that neither the elements nor compounds of them should ever give out, the Creator wisely designed things in such a way that (10) the elements are both transformed into each other and into compounds, while conversely compounds are broken down into the elements, and thus, by continual mutual generation, are throughout preserved. For earth when condensed[466] becomes water, water when solidified and condensed becomes earth[467] but when heated and rarified becomes air, air thickened and condensed becomes water (15) but when dried is transformed into fire.[468] Similarly fire when it is quenched and loses its dryness becomes air. For air is the quenching of fire and the vapour of heated water. So from both cases it is clear that its generation comes from heat: for both water that is heated and fire that is quenched become air. So it is in its own nature hot, but it becomes cold (20) through its proximity to water and earth, so that its lower portions near the earth are cold, while the upper near fire are hot. This comes about from the softness and sensitivity of air: for it quickly

463 'Bending backwards' renders *kat' epiklasin*, bending round a straight line until it forms a circle; cf. Telfer (1955), 309 n. 7.
464 I.e. hierarchically.
465 Jaeger (1914, 75) compares Seneca, *Natural Questions* 2.21 and suspects Posidonian influence.
466 This renders the MSS reading *pilêtheisa* 'when condensed/compressed'; Matthaei prints *pêlôtheisa* 'having become mud', neither of which give satisfactory sense; Galen, *Elements* 4.2 (86.21–22 De Lacy, 1.443 K) talks of earth becoming water as a result of 'being moderately diffused' (*metriôs ... khutheisan*).
467 Skard refers to a close parallel in Galen, *Elements* 4.2 (86.16–17 De Lacy, 1.442 K): 'water when thickened and compressed, as it were, becomes earth, and if rarefied and diffused even more, fire' (tr. De Lacy).
468 On this whole sequence cf. Galen, *Elements* 4.2 (86.16–88.3 De Lacy, 1.442–43 K); *On Hippocrates' On the Nature of Man* 1.3 (17.5–15 Mewaldt, 15.28–29 K); Plato, *Timaeus* 49Bff.

departs from its own nature and is transformed.

Aristotle says that there are two kinds of air,[469] [50] one vapourish from the exhalation of water, the other smoky from the quenching of fire, and that the smoky is hot while the vapourish when it is generated is also itself hot, but as it moves on it is chilled part by part and progressively turns into water. (5) He proposed the dual nature of air in order to avoid certain other apparent absurdities, and in addition because of the fact that the higher parts which are distant from the earth appear to be colder.

All bodies come to be from the gathering of these four elements, including those of plants and those of animals, since nature (10) draws together the more pure elements into the generation of these [i.e plants and animals]. Aristotle calls these bodies natural,[470] since they are not constructed merely by aggregation but [their elements] are compounded throughout into a unity and make a body that is one and something additional to themselves. They are so united that it is not possible to separate out the elements nor to see earth on its own, or water, (15) air or fire on their own, since something has come to be that is one and beyond these through the gathering of the four elements, as in the case of the fourfold drug.[471] For in this case also the fourfold drug is other than the things composing it, but not in the same way. For it is not by the putting together of the smallest parts as in the fourfold drug that the elements make bodies, but through transformation and uniting. (20) As bodies perish they are resolved again into the elements, and in this way all things persist continually and are sufficient for the coming to be of things, without ever any increase or diminution. That is why they say that the coming to be of one thing is the ceasing to be of another, and the ceasing to be of one thing the coming to be of another, not only in the case of the soul, as was said previously,[472] but also in the case of the body.

(25) Plato[473] believes that three of the elements are transformed into

---

469 Aristotle, *Meteorology* 359b30–360b27 (not 340b4 as Morani says); see also *On Coming to Be and Perishing* 2.4.

470 Aristotle, *Meteorology* 378b1; *On the Soul* 412a12, 20, 28; *On the Heaven* 268b14, 270a30, etc.

471 Cf. Galen, *Elements* 5.14 (96.10 De Lacy, 1.452 K): 'the so-called *tetrapharmakos* is a compound of wax, resin, pitch and tallow'; 5.25 (98.19 De Lacy, 1.455 K); and *On Simple Medicines* 11.1.2 (12.328 K); for earlier attestations see Chrysippus, *SVF* 2.472,15; Philodemus, *Papyri from Herculaneum* 1005, col. V 8–13 (p. 173 Angeli); Philo, *On the Confusion of Tongues* 187; Erotian, *Lexicon of Hippocratic Words*, p. 72.18–19 Nachmanson; and Anonymus Londiniensis XIV 19–20.

472 31.23–32.13.

473 Cf. Plato, *Timaeus* 55Eff; for the exceptional state of earth see 55D8. For a discussion of

each other, but earth remains untransformed. For he likens to each element [51] the three-dimensionality of straight-sided figures. To earth is assigned the shape of a cube, since it is more immobile than the others; to water, the icosahedron because it is more difficult to move than the rest; the pyramidal shape to fire because it is most mobile, and the octahedron to air, because it is more easily moved than water, with more difficulty (5) than fire. From these figures he constructs the proof that the three are transformed into each other, but that this does not happen to earth. For the three, the pyramid, the octahedron and the icosahedron are composed of scalene triangles, but the cube out of equilateral triangles. Those that were composed of scalene triangles can be transformed into each other by coming to pieces (10) and being reconstructed. But neither can a resolved cube be transformed into one of the other three figures, since it consists of equilateral triangles, out of which none of the other three can be constructed, nor, again, one of the three figures into a cube. So it is also necessary that bodies given a form of these types be so related (15) to each other as the figures are. Of course, earth does not remain unaffected, but is divided by bodies with smaller parts into its elements, but is not transformed into those that divide it. For it comes together again and returns to itself, as can be seen in water. For if you throw a little earth into water and shake it the earth is dissolved in the water: but if you stop shaking it, (20) it falls to the bottom as the water becomes still: one must think in the same way about all earth. This is not change, but the separation of the mixed ingredients. Plato says that earth is loosened also by the sharpness of fire and the loose earth is carried with it, or in a mass of air, clearly when air breaks it up, or in water when it is dissolved by water.[474] Using another method of division, he says (25) that each of the elements has three qualities:[475] fire has sharpness, rarity and motion, [52] but the other extreme of the elements, i.e. earth, has the opposite qualities to these, bluntness, density and rest, so that earth and fire are opposites in regard to these qualities, which was not the case in regard to the other combinations of qualities. Qualities were taken from each of the extremes, and thus the intermediate elements were brought to be. For two qualities

---

the (in)accuracy of Nemesius' report see Kallis (1978) 26–27 n.50, who points out (following Bender 1898, 72 and Krause 1904, 38) that Nemesius fails to present the two basic triangles as rectangular and erroneously presents the isosceles triangle as equilateral.

474 *Tim.* 56Dff.

475 As Krause (1904, 38–39, following Bender 1898, 73) points out, this is not in the *Timaeus* but can be found in Calcidius' *Commentary on the Timaeus* 21; see also the discussion by Somfai (2004) 217 n.62.

are taken from fire, rarity and motion, (5) and one from earth, bluntness, and air is composed, having as its specific qualities bluntness, rarity and motion. Again, two qualities of earth are taken, bluntness and density, and of fire one only motion and water comes to be, it also being specified by bluntness, density and motion. So as sharpness to bluntness, so is fire to air; as (10) rarity is to density, so is air to water: as motion is to rest, so is water to earth; as fire is to air, so is air to water; and as air is to water, so is water to earth; for surfaces are naturally held together by one mean, i.e. ratio, but solids by two means.[476]

There is also another way in which they[477] say that the elements have qualities: (15) earth and water have heaviness, through which they naturally travel downwards, but air and fire lightness, through which they naturally travel upwards.

The Stoics say that some of the elements are active, some passive.[478] Air and fire are active, earth and water passive. (20) But Aristotle also introduces a fifth body,[479] which is ethereal and cyclic, since he does not hold that the heaven comes to be from the four elements. He calls the fifth body cyclic because it travels around itself in a circle. But Plato says outright that the heaven is composed of earth and fire. What he says is this:[480] 'What is becoming must be bodily, visible and tangible: (25) but without fire nothing would ever become visible, nor anything tangible without something solid, nor solid without earth. For this reason [53] the god at the beginning made the body of the universe to consist of fire and earth. But two alone cannot well hold together without a third: for there needs to be a bond between them both to join them. But the best of bonds is that which most creates a unit, of itself and the two it unites. And naturally a ratio brings this about best.' (5) By 'the bond' he means the two intermediate elements which are taken in the ratio stated above.

---

476 Cf. *Timaeus* 32B: the square root of 2 is given by 1:x::x:2, the cube root by 1:x::x:y::y:2.

477 The subject is unspecified; Kallis (1978, 19) refers to Aëtius/Pseudo-Plutarch, *Tenets* 1.12.4 which attributes this view to the Stoics.

478 *SVF* 2.418; Kallis (1978, 19 n.28) compares Aristotle, *On Coming to Be and Perishing* 323a6–10; 329b24–27; *Meteorology* 382b2–5; 389a29–31.

479 The terminology used here by Nemesius, though widespread in late antiquity (see Moraux 1963), is not entirely in accordance with Aristotle's own, which speaks of a 'first body', viz. aether (*On the Heavens* 269b4, 270b21, etc.) (we regard *On the Universe* 392b35 as post-Aristotelian).

480 *Timaeus* 31B4–C4.

Those who hold the doctrines of the Hebrews[481] in highest esteem differ about heaven and earth. For while almost all the others say that heaven and earth came to be from no previously existing matter – since Moses (10) says[482] 'In the beginning God created heaven and earth' – Apollinaris holds that God made heaven and earth out of the abyss.[483] For while Moses did not mention the abyss as having come to be at the coming to be of the world, in Job it says[484] 'He, who made the abyss'. So he claims that all other things came to be from this as their matter: the abyss was not uncreated but (15) came to be before all corporeal things laid down by the Creator with a view to the existence of everything else: the word 'abyss' indicates the infinity of matter. But how this is makes no difference: for in either case God is shown to be the Creator of everything and to have made everything out of nothing.

(20) What Hippocrates said will be sufficient in reply to those who say there is only one element,[485] either fire or air or water: 'If man were one [54] he never would feel pain: for being one, there would not be anything to be pained by; and even if he felt pain, one thing would cure him.'[486] For anything that is to feel pain must be in perceptible transformation. But if there were only one element there would be nothing into which it could be transformed: but if it did not become different but remained as it was nothing would feel pain, (5) even if it were perceptible. Also it is necessary that what is affected should be affected by something: but if there were only one element there would not be another quality other than that of the one element by which the living thing would be affected. But if it could be neither transformed nor affected how would it feel pain? Having shown that this is impossible he [i.e. Hippocrates] adds by way of concession: 'and even if he felt pain, one thing would cure him: as it is, (10) there is not one thing that cures but

481 On this expression see 6.6 and 11.15 above with note.
482 Genesis 1:1.
483 On Apollinaris see note 185 above; the present passage is fr. 171 Dräseke. See also the discussions by Dräseke (1886) 31–35 and Kallis (1978) 29. Dräseke notes the similar view in Julian the Emperor, *Against the Christians* 171.14–172.1 Neumann.
484 The expression is not literally to be found in Job, but certainly implied by passages such as 38:30 and 41:23–24.
485 Cf. the extensive discussion of this issue by Galen, *Elements* 2.9–3.64, who uses the Hippocratic passage a number of times (see next note) as support for his argument against those (such as the atomists) who argue that there is only one element.
486 *On the Nature of Man* 2 (168.4–6 Jouanna, 6.34–36 L.), alluded to and quoted by Galen, *Elements* 2.18 (62.13–14 De Lacy, 1.419 K); 2.52 (68.21–23 De Lacy, 1.426 K); 3.32 (76.21–78.2 De Lacy, 1.432 K). In the Hippocratic text, the opponents are Ionian and Eleatic monists (Melissus being mentioned by name).

many others.'[487] So man is not a single element.

But the best proof that there are four elements comes from what each says to establish his own particular doctrine.[488] For thus Thales, who says that water is the only element,[489] tries to show that the other three come from this: for he says that its sediment becomes earth, (15) that with lighter parts becomes air and the air with lighter parts becomes fire. Anaximenes, who says air is the only one,[490] likewise also himself tries to show that the other elements are brought to completion from air in the same way. Heraclitus[491] and Hipparchus[492] of Metapontus, who say it is fire, make use of the same proofs and say that fire gives birth to the other elements; and (20) of the others one says water, another air. In these ways it is proved that all the elements are transformed into each other, but since all turn into each other they must all be elements: for whichever of the four you may take, it will be found that this comes to be from another.

The faculties of the soul and their bodily instruments

The body is the instrument of the soul and it is divided up in correspondence with the faculties of the soul.[493] (25) For it is constructed to be serviceable and useful for these, so that none of the soul's [55] powers should be impeded by the body. At least, special parts of the body are assigned to each psychic power for its activity, as the argument will show as it continues. For the soul is in the position of a craftsman, the body of an instrument,[494] the

---

487 *On the Nature of Man* 2 (168.6–7 Jouanna, 6.36 L.), with slight textual variation.

488 On this doxographical account see Diels, *Doxographi Graeci* 212–13 (on Tertullian, *On the Soul* 5). Cf. also Galen, *Elements* 4.6 (88.13–14 De Lacy, 1.444 K), where Thales, Anaximenes, Anaximander and Heraclitus are mentioned. Krause (1904, 43) argues that Nemesius is dependent on Porphyry here.

489 Cf. DK 11 A 11.

490 Cf. DK 13 B 2.

491 Cf. DK 22 B 118.

492 Other versions of the doxographical tradition reflected here (e.g. Eusebius, Philoponus) have in this place the name of Hippasus of Croton (mentioned in one breath with Heraclitus in Aristotle, *Meta.* 984a7 = DK 18 A 7).

493 This paragraph marks a change of subject, and it clearly is a transition to the discussion of imagination and the senses in the next series of chapters. Skard (1938, 46) refers to Galen's designation of the body as the instrument of the soul in *On the Usefulness of the Parts* 1.2 (1.1.13–14 Helmreich, 3.1 K). Domański (1900, 13 n.1) refers to Aristotle, *On the Soul* 415b18–19.

494 For the view that the parts of the body are the instruments of the soul Skard (1938, 46) refers to Galen, *On Tremor, Spasm and Palpitation* 5 (7.606 K).

matter is what the action is concerned with, the completion is the action itself. For example, the woman is the underlying material, for the action[495] is concerned with her: the action is adultery or fornication or marriage. The faculties of the soul are divided into imagination,[496] thought and memory.

SECTION 6

ON IMAGINATION

Imagination and sensation, their objects and their location in the body.

Imagination[497] is a power of the non-rational part of the soul (10) that acts through the sense-organs. The imagined is that which is the object of imagination, as the sensed is the object of sensation. An image is an affection of the non-rational soul that comes about through something imagined. An apparition is an empty affection in the non-rational parts of the soul caused by nothing imagined. The Stoics[498] say that there are these four, the image, the object imagined, imagination and apparition; they say that an image (15) is the affection of the soul displayed within itself;[499] for when we see white an affection occurs in the soul through its reception; as an affection occurs

---

495 I.e. reproduction or at any rate sexual union; Nemesius here echoes the Aristotelian view that the woman constitutes or provides the matter in this process while the male provides the form; see *On the Generation of Animals* 716a7, 727b32, 729a11, etc.

496 Sense perception is included in imagination, as appears from 6, 56.5ff.

497 'Imagination' renders *to phantastikon* (the power or faculty), 'imagined' *to phantaston* (the object), 'image' *phantasia* (the experience, impression or effect caused by the imagined object), and 'apparition' *phantasma* (in the sense of an image not caused by an external object but merely a product of the mind). Nemesius notes a slight discrepancy between this definition of the terms and that of the Stoics below in 55.13.

498 Cf. Aëtius/Pseudo-Plutarch, *Tenets* 4.12 (= *SVF* 2.54), where this distinction is attributed to Chrysippus; Nemesius presents some verbal resemblances to this chapter, and clearly uses the same tradition (cf. also Pseudo-Galen, *Historia philosopha* p. 636 *DG*). The present section has been subjected to detailed *Quellenforschung* by Jaeger (1914, 4–27), who argues that Galen's lost work *On Demonstration* was Nemesius' chief source. See also Domański (1900) 92–99.

499 We follow Morani in square-bracketing *kai to pepoiêkos phantaston* (Aëtius/Pseudo-Plutarch 4.12, 900E1, has *to pepoiêkos* but omits *phantaston*). Telfer retains these words and translates the whole sentence as follows: 'they define imagining as that affection of the soul which both displays itself and points to the subject for imagination by which it is occasioned' (1955, 321).

ON THE NATURE OF MAN   101

in the sense-organs, when they sense, so in the soul when it thinks; for it receives in itself a replica[500] of the object of thought. The imagined, they say, is that which made the image sensible, (20) such as white and everything that can cause movement to the soul; imagination is the empty attraction[501] without an imagined object, and an apparition what we call up through the empty imagination, as in the case of people suffering from mania and melancholics.[502] **[56]** The disagreement here is merely about the interrelation of words.[503] The organs of imagination are the frontal cavities of the brain,[504] the psychic pneuma[505] within them, the nerves from them soaked[506] with the

---

500 The term used here in Greek is *eikôn*, often used in later Greek for mental images; cf. Plotinus 4.3 [27] 30; 5.3 [49] 13.

501 Gk. *ephelkusis*, lit. 'a carrying away' (cf. Sextus Empiricus, *Against the Mathematicians* 7.241 and 246; cf. Telfer (1955) 321 n.7: 'Mustering of images ... it clearly concerns mental imagery, but such as is undeliberate, though not necessarily involuntary.'

502 'Melancholics', people characterised by an excess of black bile in their bodies, which was thought to affect their cognitive capacities and functioning. The word is sometimes used in a broader sense of 'mentally disturbed', but here, since they are distinguished from the *memênotes* (people being in a condition of *mania*, a chronic mental illness believed to be often accompanied by hallucinations) a more specific clinical picture seems alluded to. Such a picture seems already presupposed in Aristotle, who refers to the melancholics' incapacity to keep their imagination under control (*On Memory* 453a19; *On Dreams* 461a22–23; *On Divination in Sleep* 463b15–17; *Nicomachean Ethics* 1150b25); and this had become a standard part of clinical accounts of melancholia in later Greek medical literature (e.g. in Rufus of Ephesus' work *On Melancholy* [fr. 127 Daremberg-Ruelle]) and in Galen, who discusses it in *On Affected Parts* 3.9–10 (8.182 K). For a discussion of the Aristotelian concept of melancholy see van der Eijk (2005a) ch. 5; for a discussion of the clinical picture of *mania* see Pigeaud (1987).

503 This seems to understate the difference: the Stoics used *phantastikon* in a different sense from Nemesius to refer to imagination unprovoked by external objects and *phantasma* to refer to pathological illusions, hallucinations etc. So they distinguished two kinds of non-externally triggered images, whereas Nemesius has only one category here.

504 On the location of imagination in the frontal cavities of the brain see also below, 13, 69.17–71.4 with note.

505 Aristotle introduced in *On the Generation of Animals* 736a–737a a notion of a *pneuma* or breath as a hot foamy substance centred on the heart and providing a link between the sense-organs and the sensitive soul (see Peck 1942, 592–93; for Theophrastus see Sharples 1995, 28; for Strato see fr. 128–29 Wehrli). A more specific use of the concept of *pneuma* is that of 'psychic pneuma', a notion first developed in Hellenistic medicine, especially by Erasistratus (but possibly already by Diocles of Carystus) and in Stoic psychological theory, and further systematised by Galen (and adopted by Nemesius). *Pneuma* is believed to flow through the nerves and to mediate sensory and motor signals between the sense-organs and the brain. On the role of *pneuma* in sense perception in Galenic medicine see Rocca (2003) ch. 6.

506 Domański (1900, 94) paraphrases this passage as 'die von demselben [i.e. the *pneuma*] ausgehenden Nerven', but this seems insufficiently specific a rendering of *diabrokhos*. The idea seems to be that *pneuma* 'relaxes' or 'loosens up' (*khalatai*) the nerves (or their ends)

psychic pneuma and the apparatus of the sense-organs.

(5) There are five sense-organs but one sense, that of the soul, which recognises through the sense-organs the affections that occur in them.[507] Through the most earthy and corporeal of the sense-organs, which is touch, [the soul] senses things of an earthy nature; through the most luminous, which is sight, it senses the most luminous; through the airy, <which is hearing,> it senses the affections of the air, (10) for air or the beat of the air is the substance of sound; through the spongy and watery, which is taste, it lays hold on flavours. For each object of sense is of a nature to be recognised by its own sense-organ. According to this account, however, there ought to be four senses since there are four elements. But vapour and the variety of odours have a nature between (15) air and water; for vapour has coarser parts than air, but lighter than those of water. This sort of thing becomes clear from the affection of a runny nose.[508] For those with a runny nose draw in air as they breathe in, but as they breathe it in they do not take in scents, since because of the obstruction that with coarser parts does not reach the sense. So for the sake of odours (20) a fifth sense organ, smell, was devised by nature, so that none of the things which is capable of being known should escape sense.

Sensation is not an alteration, but the recognition of an alteration:[509] for the sense-organs are altered and the sense recognises the alteration; often the sense-organs are called senses, but a sensation is the reception[510] [57] of objects of sense. But this definition seems to be not of the sensation itself

---

by 'moistening' them, thus enabling sensory awareness. Jaeger says that this is 'galensche Lehre' but does not give parallels; the only passages we have been able to find – Galen, *On the Composition of Drugs according to Places* 5.5 (12.871 K); *On Affected Parts* 3.9 (8.173 K) – refer to *pathological* conditions.

507 On the unity of sensation cf. Aristotle, *On Sleep and Waking* 455a20. The account that follows finds several close parallels in Galen's *On the Doctrines of Hippocrates and Plato* 7.5–6.

508 Gk. *koruza*. For the explanation (though with a slightly different example) cf. Galen, *On the Doctrines of Hippocrates and Plato* 7.6.27 (466.35–468.2 De Lacy, 5.635–36 K).

509 The view that sense perception is a kind of alteration or qualitative change (*alloiôsis*) is considered, albeit tentatively, by Aristotle (cf. *On the Soul* 415b24; 416b34; 417b5ff.; 418a1–3; 431a5; *On Dreams* 459b3–5; *On the Parts of Animals* 641b6; *On the Movement of Animals* 701b17–18), although Aristotle is anxious to stress that it is not an alteration in the full sense of the word (*On the Soul* 417b5ff.). The view that sensation is 'a recognition' or 'discernment' (*diagnôsis*) of alteration is found in Galen, *On the Doctrines of Hippocrates and Plato* 7.6.30–31 (468.15–16 De Lacy, 5.636 K)

510 *Antilêpsis*; for the terminology here (and in 57.4–5) cf. Aëtius/Pseudo-Plutarch, *Tenets* 4.8 (where it is attributed to the Stoics).

ON THE NATURE OF MAN 103

but of its functions, which is why they also define a sense as an intellective pneuma reaching from the authoritative element to the organs.[511] There is also this [definition of sensation]: a power of the soul to receive objects of sense, while a sense-organ is an instrument for the reception (5) of objects of sense. Plato says that sense is the community of soul and body in relation to the external;[512] for the power is of the soul, the organ is bodily, and together they receive the external through imagination.

Of the faculties of the soul, some are subordinate and act as spear-bearers,[513] others rule and command. The ruling are thought and understanding,[514] subordinate are those of sense, (10) movement according to impulse[515] and imagination. For movement and imagination[516] obey swiftly and almost instantaneously the wish of reason. For we wish and move at once and as one, needing no additional time between wish and movement, as can be seen in the movement of the fingers. Among natural things,[517] too, some are under (15) the authority of thought, such as the so-called affections.

---

511 This view ('intellective pneuma', *noeron pneuma*, proceeding from the ruling part of the soul) is attributed to the Stoics in Aëtius/Pseudo-Plutarch, *Tenets* 4.8; cf. Diogenes Laërtius 7.52.

512 This view is attributed, in virtually the same words, to Plato also in Aëtius/Pseudo-Plutarch, *Tenets* 4.8, 899E1–4. It is not literally found as such in Plato, but the idea is certainly Platonic; see esp. *Philebus* 34A5, *Timaeus* 43C, 46A, etc.

513 The terminology is Platonic (cf. *Timaeus* 70B), cited also by Galen in *On the Doctrines of Hippocrates and Plato* 3.1.31 (174.10–17 De Lacy, 5.292 K), 2.4.17 (120.1–7 De Lacy, 5.230 K) and 6.8.72 (422.14 De Lacy, 5.581 K). See also Galen, *On the Usefulness of the Parts* 8.2 (1.445.17 Helmreich, 3.614 K); *On the Formation of the Foetus* 3.26 (76.5 Nickel, 4.672 K); Philo, *On Special Laws* 3.111, 4.93, 4.123; Alcinous, *Didascalicus* 17.4; Gregory of Nyssa, *On the Creation of Man* 12 (*PG* 44 156D); above, Introduction 5.a.5 at n.133.

514 Morani prints *to dianoêtikon kai to epistêmonikon*; instead of *epistêmonikon*, one MS (D) reads to *mnêmoneutikon* ('memory'), but this is probably a later correction. As Domański notes (1900, 78 n.2), Nemesius does not refer to *to epistêmonikon* as a separate faculty anywhere else, whereas he does talk quite extensively about memory in section 13. However, he does not say there that memory is a commanding faculty.

515 This will be discussed in section 27.

516 The Greek text has *hê phantasia*; strictly speaking, according to the distinctions made earlier in this section, it would have to be *to phantastikon* (a reading possibly attested, and only indirectly, in the Arabic tradition).

517 'Natural' renders *phusikos*, as distinct from *psukhikos* ('psychic', 'belonging to the soul'); for this distinction see below 82.22.

SECTION 7

ON SIGHT[518]

Several theories of visual perception; Galen's account of optic pneuma mediating between the brain, the sense-organs and the external objects of vision. The transparent air as a medium. Colours and coloured objects; co-ordination between vision, memory and thought.

The word 'sight' is used in more than one sense; for it denotes both the sense-organ and the sensitive power [of sight].[519] Hipparchus says that rays extend from the eyes and with their own extremities lay hold on external bodies like the touch of hands, (20) and thus transmit their reception to the sense of sight.[520] Geometricians draw cones which are formed from the intersection of the rays sent out through the eyes.[521] For [they say that] [the

---

518 This section starts with a doxographical part (57.18–59.18 Morani), which shows strong similarities with the chapter on vision in Aëtius/Pseudo-Plutarch's *Tenets* 4.13 and with references to earlier authorities in Galen's discussion of vision in *On the Doctrines of Hippocrates and Plato* 7.5–7 (see relevant notes below); Nemesius' account of Galen's own views (58.14–59.13) may also be based on this Galenic work, although it is also possible, as Jaeger (1914, 27–53) has argued, that Nemesius used Galen's (lost) work *On Demonstration* (*Peri apodeixeôs*), to which Galen himself refers a number of times in *On the Doctrines of Hippocrates and Plato* 7 for fuller discussion of some of the points raised. The doxographical section ends with a report on Porphyry (59.13–18), but the theory of vision which Nemesius sets out after this continues to be heavily dependent on Galen. Nemesius' arrangement of the doxographical material may be motivated by the desire to present the Galenic (and Platonic) view as a synthesis of the two positions by explaining vision as a process involving both the faculty of vision emitting visual power from the eyes and the objects of vision responding to this; the reference to Porphyry may then be motivated by the role of thinking in the judgement of visual perception and the mechanism of error.

519 The various usages of the Greek word *opsis* which Nemesius refers to here can already be found in classical Greek (e.g. Hippocratic writings, Aristotle). In addition to the two senses given here, *opsis* is sometimes also used in Greek optics to refer to the visual 'ray' supposedly connecting the visible object with the eye – something which, in the next sentence on Hipparchus, Nemesius refers to by the word *aktis*.

520 Hipparchus of Nicaea, a 2nd-century BCE astronomer and geographer. The present passage is virtually identical to Aëtius/Pseudo-Plutarch, *Tenets* 4.13, where (as in Nemesius) also Epicurus and Plato are mentioned (as well as Democritus and Empedocles, not mentioned here by Nemesius).

521 The identity of these geometricians (or 'mathematicians') is unknown. Domański (1900, 99–100 n.2) refers to to Galen, *On the Usefulness of the Parts* 10.12, where a mathematical theory of vision is set out in which Galen frequently refers to geometry, mathematics, cones, etc.; see also *On the Doctrines of Hippocrates and Plato* 7.5.40 (460.24–28 De Lacy,

eyes] send out [58] rays, the right eye to the left, the left eye to the right, and as a result a cone is formed by their intersection, which is why sight can encompass many visible things all at once, but sees exactly [only] those parts where the rays intersect. This is at any rate how, when looking at (5) the floor, we often do not see the coin lying there, though looking hard, until the intersection of the rays falls upon that part where the coin lies, and then we gaze upon it as if we were then first paying attention. The Epicureans say that [vision occurs by] images of what appears falling upon our eyes.[522] But Aristotle says that it is not a corporeal image (10) but that a quality comes from the object of sight to [the organ of] sight through an alteration of the surrounding air.[523] Plato, however says that it is a meeting of the light from the eyes, so far as it flows into the air that is homogeneous with it, and of the light travelling in the opposite direction from bodies, while the light in the air between, which is easily diffused and changed, extends away to the fiery element of sight.[524] Galen, (15) in agreement with Plato, says in the seventh book of his work on the agreement [between Hippocrates and Plato], writing at various points of his discussion somehow as follows:[525] 'for if some part or power or image or quality of visible bodies arrived at the eye, we would not recognise the size of what we saw, perhaps even a huge mountain.[526] For it would be altogether unreasonable that such a great image should fall upon our eyes. (20) But moreover the optic *pneuma*,[527] when being emitted, also

---

5.626–27 K) and Alexander of Aphrodisias, *On Aristotle On Sense Perception* 28.2 (with the comments by Sharples 2004, 90–91).

522 The well-attested Democritean and Epicurean doctrine of *eidōla* or *simulacra*, images (consisting of particles, like films) emanating from the objects and striking the eyes of the percipient. Cf. Aëtius/Pseudo-Plutarch, *Tenets* 4.13. Morani refers to fr. 318 Usener and Epicurus' *Letter to Herodotus* 46.

523 Cf. Aristotle, *On the Soul* 2.7, esp. 419a13–21; Aristotle's theory of vision is not mentioned in Aëtius/Pseudo-Plutarch's *Tenets* 4.13, but Nemesius has possibly drawn this from Galen's discussion in *On the Doctrines of Hippocrates and Plato* 7.7.22 (474.16–17 De Lacy, 5.643 K): 'Aristotle is much superior to Epicurus; he does not bring a corporeal image but a quality from the visual object to the eyes through an alteration of the surrounding air' (tr. De Lacy).

524 Cf. Plato, *Timaeus* 45B–46C; but again (see note on 57.20), Nemesius is probably drawing on a summary of Plato's views like the one given in Aëtius/Pseudo-Plutarch, *Tenets* 4.13, with which the present passage is almost verbally identical.

525 What follows is a close paraphrase of Galen, *On the Doctrines of Hippocrates and Plato* 7.5.2-7 (452.35–454.16 De Lacy, 5.618–19 K), with further similarities to 7.5.32 (460.2–4 De Lacy, 5.625 K), 7.5.33–37 (460.4–16 De Lacy, 6.525–26 K) and 7.7.19 (474.4–5 De Lacy, 5.642 K). For a line by line comparison see Domański (1900) 101–02.

526 Morani's punctuation suggests that the quotation ends here, but this is misleading as the whole passage is a mixture of quotation and paraphrase.

527 In Galen's physiology of sense perception, optic *pneuma* is both located within the

would not be able to gain so great a strength to encompass all that was seen. So it remains that the surrounding air should become such an instrument for us at the time that we see, [59] as is the optic nerve in the body. For the air that surrounds us seems to be affected in some such way. For as the ray from the sun which touches the upper limit of the air hands on its power to the whole,[528] likewise also the ray as it travels through the optic nerve has the character of *pneuma* (5) and falls on its surroundings and brings about an alteration as soon as it touches them, and thus hands it on to the limit of what is continuous with it until it falls upon a resistant body. For air becomes an instrument for the eye for the recognition of visible objects such as is the nerve for the brain, so that the eye has the same relation (10) to the air that has been given soul power[529] by the sun's ray as the brain has to the nerve. That air naturally becomes like bodies near to it is clear from the fact that air, when something bright, red or blue or even shining silver travels through it, is altered by that which travels through it.'[530]

Porphyry in his [account][531] of sensation says that neither a cone nor an image, nor anything else is the cause of sight, (15) but that the soul itself, when it encounters visible things, realises that it itself is the visible things, since the soul contains everything there is, and that all the different bodies are the soul that contains them. For he holds that there is one soul of all things, the rational soul, and so he reasonably says that it recognises itself in all things.[532]

---

optic nerve – where it mediates between the eyes and the brain – and 'emitted' from the eye (*ekpiptein, ekkrinesthai*) in the act of vision and 'informing the air with soul power' (*empsukhoun*) thus enabling it to act as a medium between the eye and the visible object. See *On the Doctrines of Hippocrates and Plato* 5.3.7 (306.20 De Lacy, 5.446 K), 7.5.4 (454.5 De Lacy, 5.618 K), 7.5.6 (454.11 De Lacy, 5.619 K): 'It seems that the effect produced on the air around us by the emission of the pneuma is of the same sort as the effect produced on it by the light of the sun' (tr. De Lacy), and 7.5.40–41 (460.27 and 32 De Lacy, 5.627 K).

528 We follow De Lacy in reading *eis holon* both in Galen's text (454.12) and here in Nemesius. (Telfer has: 'it communicates the sun's power to the whole atmosphere').

529 The Greek is *empsukhoun*, 'ensoul', 'inform with consciousness'.

530 Cf. Galen, *On the Doctrines of Hippocrates and Plato* 7.7.1 (470.5–7 De Lacy, 5.637 K).

531 Fr. 264 Smith. A work by Porphyry on sensation does not survive (see Dörrie 1959, 155–58). Beatrice (2005, 273–76) in his discussion of this passage suggests that the reference 'on sensation' need not be to a treatise with that title but could also be an indication of the subject-matter; for parallels to the idea expressed here he points to Porphyry's *To Gaurus* 11.2 (p. 48 Kalbfleisch) and to *Sentences* 41 (see also *Sent.* 16).

532 We take it that at this point in the text, Nemesius' report of Porphyry's theory ends and that what follows is at least not presented as a theory held by other authorities (although in fact much of it goes back to Galen).

Sight sees in straight lines,[533] and perceives in the first instance (20) colours:[534] but it recognises together with them the coloured body, its size, its shape, the place where it is, its distance and its number, its motion and rest, whether it is rough or smooth, even or uneven, sharp or blunt, and its constitution, whether it is watery or **[60]** earthy, e.g whether it is liquid or solid.[535] Its own specific object of sense is colour, for we grasp colours through sight alone. But we simultaneously grasp, together with the colour, both the coloured body and the place in which the object of sight happens to be, as also the distance between that which sees and (5) the object of sight. For in however many perceptions a body becomes apparent, the place is at once recognised together with it, as with touch and taste, but these become aware of the place only when they are close to the body, except as will be described next, whereas sight does so also from afar. But since it grasps its specific objects of sense from afar it would necessarily follow that (10) it alone sees the interval as well, and that it alone recognises size, as long as it can encompass the object at a single observation. But in cases when the visible object is too big to be encompassed at one observation, sight needs also memory and thought.[536] For, since it sees a part at a time and not [the object of sight] as a whole, sight necessarily transfers [itself] from one to another (15) and what meets the eye on each occasion as it moves on is what is perceived, whereas memory preserves the parts seen before and thought brings together both what one has perceived and what one remembers. Therefore sight grasps size in two ways: sometimes on its own, sometimes together with memory and thought. But it never grasps on its own the number of things seen above three or four, which is not seen at one view, (20) [i.e.] motions and many-sided figures, but it always [requires the help of] memory and thought. For it cannot collect five, six, seven and

---

533 A standard point about vision since Aristotle: cf. *On the Soul* 418a29; *On Sense Perception* 437a5ff.; *On the Parts of Animals* 656b27ff.; *On Dreams*. 459b15; *Problems* 904b17. See also Galen, *On the Doctrines of Hippocrates and Plato* 7.5.40 (460.26 De Lacy, 5.627 K).
534 Cf. Aristotle, *On the Soul* 418a29; *On Sense Perception* 437a5–7; Galen, *On the Doctrines of Hippocrates and Plato* 7.5.33 (460.4–6 De Lacy, 5.625 K).
535 For this point, elaborated in the next sentence, cf. Galen, *On the Doctrines of Hippocrates and Plato* 7.5.33–39 (460.4–7 and 14–16 De Lacy, 5.625–26 K); *On the Usefulness of the Parts* 16.3 (2.383.7–8 Helmreich, 4.273 K). At the background is Aristotle's theory of 'common sensibles' (*koina aistheta*), i.e. properties perceived with more than one sense: *On the Soul* 418a10ff.; 425a14ff.; 428b22; *On Sense Perception* 437a8–9; 442b4ff.; *On Memory* 450a9; *On Sleep and Waking* 455a14ff., though Nemesius seems to extend this list by adding liquid and solid.
536 Cf. Galen, *On the Doctrines of Hippocrates and Plato* 7.6.24 (466.27 De Lacy, 5.634 K).

more without memory, and thus not hexagons and octagons and many-sided figures either. Also motion occurs through transference, and has an earlier and a later portion. But where there is a first, (25) a second and a third, memory alone can preserve it. Above and below and uneven and even, as well as the rough and smooth and the [**61**] sharp and the blunt, are common to touch and sight, since the latter are also the only [senses] that recognise place. But they also need thought: for only that which is the object of sense at one view is the task of the sense alone. What is acquired through multiple views is not the task of it alone but also of memory with thought, as was shown before.

(5) Sight is of a nature to pass through transparent things to the end, primarily and mainly air, which it passes through completely, secondly through water that is still and clear (at any rate we see fishes swimming), less through glass and other things of that sort, clearly because they admit light. This, too, is specific to sight. Nobody should be under the delusion that (10) the grasping of hot things is through sight because when we see fire, we immediately know that it is also hot. For if you reduce the account to the first sight of it you will find that then, when sight first observed fire, it received only its colour and shape; but when touch also approached it we recognised that it is hot, and this was preserved by memory, (15) which took it from touch. So now, when we observe fire, we see nothing other than the colour and form of the fire, but thought adds on heat as well through the memory, in addition to what is seen. The same reasoning applies to apples. For if an apple is not identified by colour and shape alone, but also by its smell and its characteristic taste, (20) sight knows that it is an apple not by grasping these as well, but [because] the soul calls up the memory gained from smelling and tasting and, at the time of observation, attends to these along with shape and colour. So when we believe that an apple made of wax is a real apple, it is not sight that is deceived but thought. For sight (25) was not mistaken about its specific objects of sense; for it recognised both the colour and shape.

[**62**] So three of the senses, sight, hearing and smell grasp external objects which are not adjacent, through the medium of the air. But taste does not perceive in any other way than through being in close contact with the object of sense. The case of touch is ambiguous; for it occurs both when it is in contact with bodies and also sometimes through the medium (5) of a stick.[537] So sometimes sight needs additional evidence from the other senses, when what is viewed is crafted in order to deceive, as is the case with pictures:

---

537 Nemesius is presumably alluding to the fact that if we feel the contours of a body at the end of a stick we do not appear to observe pressures on the fingers but the shape of the body.

for what painting does is to deceive sight with non-existent projections and hollows, if that is the nature of the thing. Hence for discernment there is need of grasping, especially by touch, but sometimes also by taste and (10) smell, as in the case of a waxen apple. But sometimes sight by itself vividly presents things seen, when it sees them from not far off. Thus it sees the square tower as round from a distance, and it is deceived when we look through mist or smoke or something similar of a kind that obscures sight.[538] It is the same when one looks through moving water,[539] for in the sea (15) an oar is seen as broken, and when one looks through a transparent material, as in the case of mirrors[540] and glass and other things of that nature, or when the object seen moves swiftly; for fast motion disturbs sight, so that we see as round things that are not round, and as stationary things that are moving.[541] One is also deceived when thought is preoccupied with other things, as in the case of one who has arranged to (20) meet a friend and, on meeting him, walks past, because his mind is on other things. But this also is not the fault of sight but of the mind. For sight saw and reported, but the mind did not attend to what was reported. Sight needs especially four things for clear recognition, an unimpaired sense-organ, suitable movement (25) and [suitable] distance, clear and bright air. **[63]**

SECTION 8

ON TOUCH

Touch and tangible qualities; touch the most fundamental sense to all animals and present in the whole body; its co-ordination with the brain through the nerves and the pneuma.

---

538 These are stock examples of observational illusion; cf. Lucretius, *On the Nature of Things* 4.353–55; Sextus Empiricus, *Against the Mathematicians* 7.208.

539 Strictly speaking, the water does not need to be moving in order to create the illusory effect mentioned: cf. Lucretius, *On the Nature of Things* 4.436–42; Aëtius/Pseudo-Plutarch, *Tenets* 3.5.

540 Mirrors are of course not transparent but reflecting; but the point probably is that they present a distorted view of the object reflected (cf. Telfer 1955, 330 n.12: 'in a mirror, left and right are reversed').

541 Nemesius may be referring here to the illusion created by a moving boat: cf. Lucretius, *On the Nature of Things* 4.387; Aristotle, *On Dreams* 460b26–27; *Problems* 872a18–26. For an example of the opposite (seeing stationary things as being in motion) see Aristotle, *On Dreams* 459b18–22.

NEMESIUS

The Creator constructed each of the other sense-organs double and confined it in a certain place and portion of the body.[542] For He made two eyes, two ears and two channels for sensation in the nose. (5) Also He implanted two tongues in all animals, but in some they are divided, as in snakes, in some they are joined together into one, as in men.[543] For this reason He also made two frontal cavities in the brain, so that the sensitive nerves should descend from each of the cavities to make the sense-organs double.[544] He made them double (10) from superabundant care, so that if one of them suffered, the remaining one would preserve the sense.[545] Yet when most of the sense-organs are destroyed an animal is in no way vitally impaired, whereas if touch perishes the animal perishes with it. For touch alone of the senses is common to all animals.[546] For while every animal has touch, (15) not all have

---

542 For the twofold nature of the sense-organs and the special status of touch see Aristotle, *On the Parts of Animals* 656b32ff.; see also Galen, *On the Usefulness of the Parts* 8.10 (1.481.16–17 Helmreich, 3.663 K); 9.8 (2.23.18–20 Helmreich, 3.714 K); 10.1 (2.55.1–3 Helmreich, 3.759 K); 11.10 (2.140.22–25 Helmreich, 3.881 K).

543 For the 'double' or 'split' (*eskhismenos*) nature of the tongue in general see Aristotle, *On the Parts of Animals* 657a2, and Galen, *On the Usefulness of the Parts* 11.10 (2.140.22ff. Helmreich, 3.881 K); the double, or rather 'forked' (*dikroos*) nature of the tongue in snakes (and also in seals) is observed by Aristotle in *On the Parts of Animals* 660b6 (see also 691a6–8 and *History of Animals* 508a25) and given a teleological explanation (to enhance their sense of taste so as to put a check on their 'inordinate appetite'); see also Galen, *loc. cit.*: 'In certain animals, indeed, such as the snake, the tongue too is divided, but in man, since it was not better that it should be, for either eating or speaking, the parts of it are properly united and come together to form one part.' (tr. May). Telfer (1955, 331–32 n.1) argues that Nemesius goes beyond Galen in arriving at the view that the tongue is 'genetically' double on embryological grounds derived from a source other than Galen, possibly 'the advanced anatomical knowledge of the Alexandrine school of surgery'. We see little support for this view, as Nemesius' view is fundamentally that of Galen in the passage from *On the Usefulness of the Parts* just quoted, and Telfer's comment that Galen was weak on embryology, if true at all, seems irrelevant for this issue; see also Nutton (1984) 4 n.27.

544 See also below, 64.2. Although Galen often says that the frontal cavities of the brain are the place where psychic pneuma is produced, which is obviously essential for sensation (see e.g. *On the Usefulness of the Parts* 8.10 [1.481.6–8 Helmreich, 3.663 K, with reference to *On the Usefulness of Respiration* 5, 4.501–11 K]; *On the Doctrines of Hippocrates and Plato* 1.6.5–6 [78.31–80.4 De Lacy; 5.185–86 K]), the localisation *as such* of sense perception (and/or imagination) in the frontal cavities of the brain is not found in Galen and seems a post-Galenic development; see below, n.607, and Rocca (2003) 245–47.

545 Cf. Galen, *On the Usefulness of the Parts* 8.10 (1.481.14–19 Helmreich, 3.663–64 K).

546 On the fundamental nature of touch for the definition of animalhood see Aristotle, *On the Soul* 413b4–10; 434b23; 435b4; *On Sleep and Waking* 455a6–7, 23–32; *History of Animals* 489a17–18. Nemesius in a sense reverses the Aristotelian position in that he argues that because

ON THE NATURE OF MAN 111

all the other senses, but some have some and the higher animals have them all. Since, therefore, an animal's being an animal or not was at risk on this matter, the Creator did not assign one part to touch, but almost the whole body of the animal: for except for bones, nails, horns, ligaments, hair and other similar parts,[547] every part of the body has a grasp of touch.[548] (20) So it happens that each of the sense organs has two kinds of sensation, the one being of its specific sense-objects, the other being touch, as in the case of sight; for it both distinguishes colours and participates in the sensations of hot and cold, but of these latter in so far as it is body, of colours in so far as it is sight.[549] The same holds of taste, **[64]** smell and hearing.

So how can touch belong to the whole body, when we say that sensations are from the frontal cavities of the brain?[550] Surely it is obvious that

---

touch is essential therefore it was given to every part of the body, for maximal protection as it were, whereas Aristotle's position is that because touch is present throughout the body (*On the Soul* 435b13), and involved in every sense, *therefore* it is essential for life (*toinun*, 435b4).

547 Cf. Aristotle, *On the Soul* 435a24–25; Galen, *On the Usefulness of the Parts* 16.2 (2.379.2–18 Helmreich, 4.268 K).

548 Aristotle (*On the Soul* 423a26ff.) had pointed out that the distribution of the sense of touch throughout the body is due to flesh being the medium of touch (the organ of touch being an inner sense, located in the region of the heart: see *On the Soul* 422b22–23; *On Sleep and Waking* 455a23–b2).

549 Cf. Aristotle, *On the Soul* 435a18–19: 'The other senses perceive also by means of touch, through a medium, whereas touch perceives by means of itself only'; Galen, *On the Usefulness of the Parts* 16.2 (2.381.7–11 Helmreich, 4.271 K): 'Accordingly, parts such as the eyes, ears, and tongue, that are not only moved simply in obedience to the will but also have sensation over and above that sense of touch common to all the parts, have both the hard and the soft kinds of nerves' (tr. May).

550 On the location of sensory power in the brain see above, 63.7 (with note), and below, 69.25–70.10 and 89.5–7 (where, however, sensory nerves are said to originate either from the frontal or from the middle ventricles). The question Nemesius addresses here is how the presence of the sensation of touch throughout the body is related to the presence of sensory powers *in general* in specific ventricles of the brain. Strictly speaking, this question could be raised with regard to the other senses as well (e.g. does smelling take place in the nose or in the brain?); but in the case of touch, its distribution over the whole body and the local nature of the sensations it experiences (i.e. of its being aware of the affections) presents itself most clearly. Nemesius answers the question by saying that the sensory nerves are part of the brain and that this would explain the simultaneous awareness of an affection both at the place where it touches the body and in the brain. (This is the Galenic position; see notes below). Further down in 64.13–15, however, he considers a further possible answer to this question to the effect that a distinction can be made between the 'affection' (*pathos*, i.e. the presentation of the stimulus to the sense organ), which is localised, and the awareness or reporting (*sunaisthêsis, apangelia*) of this affection, which is sent on to the brain (cf. below, 66.9), a distinction that goes back to Aristotle (cf. *On Memory and Recollection* 450b11–18; *On Dreams* 459a26; 461a26–b7).

the sensation of touch supervenes[551] when nerves descend from the brain and divide themselves over the whole of the body. Yet since often, (5) when our foot hits a thorn, the hairs on our head immediately shiver, some have thought that the affection, or the sensation of the affection, is sent upwards to the brain. Yet if this account were true, it would not be the part that is cut that suffers pain, but the brain. It is therefore better to say that the nerve *is* the brain; for it is a part (10) of the brain, which has psychic *pneuma* all throughout itself, just as iron that has been heated in the fire contains the fire; well, for this reason, then, wherever a sensitive nerve grows, this part has a share in sensation because of this, and it becomes sensitive.[552] But perhaps there is nothing absurd about saying that what is sent upwards to the brain, the origin of the nerves, is not the affection but some kind of awareness[553] (15) and a report about the affection.

The proper[554] sense object of touch is the hot and the cold, the soft and the hard, the sticky and the crumbly, and the heavy and the light; for these are known through touch only.[555] Common to touch and sight are the sharp and the blunt, the rough and the smooth, the solid and the liquid, the fat and lean, upwards and downwards, and position and size, whenever it is of such nature (20) that it is grasped by one apprehension of touch, as well as the

---

551 The verb used here is *prosginetai*, which indicates that the sensory power comes in addition to the physical structure of the nerves descending from the brain: the latter is a material condition on which the formal faculty supervenes, and changes to the material condition also affect the functioning of the faculty; cf. Galen, *On the Doctrines of Hippocrates and Plato* 7.5.13–14 (456.7–14 De Lacy, 5.621 K).

552 Cf. Galen, *On the Doctrines of Hippocrates and Plato* 7.5.13 (456.5–11 De Lacy; 5.621 K): 'Now all the sensory powers (*aisthêtikai dunameis*), having as they do their beginning in the brain, have this in common, that they are carried through the nerves all the way to their proper organs. And the nerve is also homogeneous in substance (*homoeidês kata tên ousian*) with the brain' (tr. De Lacy).

553 The terms rendered here as 'affection', 'awareness' and 'report' are *pathos, sunaisthêsis* and *apangelia* (cf. below, 66.9).

554 The distinction between sense objects that are 'proper' (*idia*) to one particular sense and those that are 'common' (*koina*) to more than one sense was first made by Aristotle, *On the Soul* 418a10ff.; 425a14ff.; 428b22; *On Sensation* 437a8–9; 442b4ff.; *On Memory* 450a9; *On Sleep* 455a14ff. Typical examples of the latter as mentioned by Aristotle are shape, size, movement, rest, number, unity, roughness and smoothness.

555 Lists of the proper objects of touch can be found in Aristotle, *On the Soul* 423b28–29 (hot, cold, dry, wet), 435a23 (hot, cold, 'and others') and Galen, *On the Natural Faculties* 1.6 (109.7–12 Helmreich, 2.12 K) (hot, cold, dry, wet, hardness, softness, stickiness, brittleness, lightness, heaviness, density, rarity, smoothness, roughness, thickness and thinness). Yet contrarily to Galen, Nemesius lists rough and smooth, and dry and wet, fat and lean and dense and rare under the common sensibles. Cf. Aristotle, *On Sensation* 442b5.

dense and the rare and the curved, whenever it is small, and other shapes as well. Likewise, touch also senses the movement of the neighbouring body, together with the memory and thought of it,[556] and likewise also number, but only up to two or three, and these [only] when [the things] are small and easily graspable; (25) it is sight rather than touch that grasps these, as is the case with what is even or uneven; for this belongs to the class of the smooth [65] and the rough; for harshness combined with unevenness produces roughness, evenness combined with density produces smoothness.[557]

It is clear from what has been said that the senses have much in common with each other; for indeed, the errors of the one are pointed out by the other. At any rate in the case of painting, sight (5) sees certain projections, [e.g.] of the nose and of other things, but when touch gets closer to it, it exposes its illusion. Just as sight always sees everything through the medium of air, likewise touch through the medium of the stick perceives objects that are hard or soft or liquid, but inferentially and with the aid of thinking; for man has the most accurate sense of touch.[558] In this [i.e.touch] and also in taste he (10) is superior to other living beings, even though he is inferior in the three others.[559] Other living beings are superior to man in one of these three senses, while dogs are so in all three simultaneously; for they have a keener sense of hearing, vision and smell, as is evident from tracker dogs.

The whole body is the organ of touch, as has been said before,[560] especially (15) the interior parts of the hands, and even more than these the extremities of the fingers; for we have these as accurate indicators of touch.[561] For the Creator not only crafted hands as an instrument for grasping

556 Cf. Galen, *On the Doctrines of Hippocrates and Plato* 7.6.23–24 (466.21–30 De Lacy, 5.633–34 K): 'As for those qualities found in resistant bodies that are (as we saw) peculiar to their own special character, one cannot perceive them with every member that shares the nerves, because not every (part) is suited to be affected by contact with an earthy body ... The rest are incidental: size, shape, motion, number [cf. Plato, *Theaetetus* 186C–D.]; they require reasoning and memory, not merely sensation – at least, in the case of touch and sight...' (tr. De Lacy). Galen refers here to his (lost) work *On Demonstration*, and it is possible that Nemesius (who mentions the work in 82.7) has drawn on this work for the present passage.

557 Cf. Plato, *Timaeus* 63E10–64A1.

558 See Aristotle, *On the Soul* 421a18–22; *On Sense Perception* 440b21–441a3; *History of Animals* 494b16.

559 Cf. Aristotle, *On the Soul* 421a18–22; *On Sense Perception* 440b30–441a2.

560 Above, 63.17.

561 For this passage and what follows, there is a close parallel in Galen, *On Mixtures* 1.8 (34.20–35.16 Helmreich, 1.563–65 K): 'Human skin is an object of this sort [i.e. well-balanced], being exactly midway between all extremes – hot, cold, hard, and soft. And this is especially true of the skin of the hands. For this part was designed to be the instrument of

things, but also to touch things; therefore they have a more delicate skin, and muscle is spread out within beneath the whole of them, and they do not have hair, so that they better grasp the objects of touch. (20) The reason that no hair grows on them is the muscle that is stretched underneath it. Rough hands are stronger for grasping, softer ones are more accurate for touch,[562] just as in the case of the nerves the rough are more suitable for movement, the soft ones for sensation.[563] These, then, are the instruments of touch; for through these (25) the sensation of touch comes about.[66]

[Sections 9–11] Discussions of taste, hearing and smell, their location in the body; the connection between their respective sense organs and the brain; and the great variety of their objects.

SECTION 9

ON TASTE

We have said above that vision sees along a straight line.[564] Smell and hearing perceive not only along a straight line, but from all directions,[565] while touch and taste perceive neither along a straight line nor from all directions, (5) but only then when they come into contact with their proper objects of sense themselves, except in those cases already defined.[566] Taste is concerned with

---

assessment [*gnômôn*, a term also used by Nemesius here – PJvdE] of all perceptible objects; it was created as the organ of touch suited to the most intelligent of animals. It therefore had to be equidistant from all extremes, whether of hot, cold, dry, or wet ... man is the most balanced, not only of all animals, but in fact of all bodies generally, and, furthermore, the skin on the inside of the hand is immune to the extremes suffered by the other parts' (tr. Singer).

562 Cf. Galen, *On Mixtures* 1.8 (37.5–7 Helmreich, 1.567 K): 'For there are two functions for which hands were created, that of touching and that of holding; soft hands are better equipped for accuracy in the sense of touch, hard hands for strength in grasping objects' (tr. Singer).

563 Cf. Galen, *On the Usefulness of the Parts* 16.2 (2.381.1–3 Helmreich, 4.270 K), and *On the Doctrines of Hippocrates and Plato* 7.5.16 (456.17–21 De Lacy, 5.622 K).

564 Above, 59.18–19.

565 Cf. Aristotle, *On the Parts of Animals* 656b26–31: 'Nature has located the sense-organs in a very satisfactory manner. The ears are half-way round the circumference of the head, because they are to hear sounds from all directions alike and not only from straight before them. The eyes face front: this is because sight is along a straight line' (tr. Peck).

566 As Telfer notes, the only type of case that has been mentioned is the sense of touch via the intermediary of a stick in the previous section (65.7–8).

the grasping of flavours, and its instruments are the tongue,[567] especially the tip of it, and along with that also the palate,[568] in which the nerves that descend from the brain are widened[569] and report[570] to the ruling part[571] the apprehension that has taken place.

The so-called taste-qualities of flavours are as follows:[572] sweetness, sharpness, bitterness, astringency, harshness, pungency, saltiness and oiliness: for it is these that taste distinguishes. It is, furthermore, with regard to these qualities that water is said to be without qualities, because it reveals none of these qualities to taste: for in regard to the other qualities, such as coldness and wetness, the quality is natural to it.[573] (15) Astringency and harshness differ from each other by the degree that they dry up the mouth.[574]

These are about the only simple qualities of taste, but there are thousands of compound ones: for each sort of animal and plant has distinguishing qualities: for we get one taste from perhaps pork and another from goat. This is why (20) we recognise from the taste what kind of meat is being served without being told. This would not be the case if each thing tasted had not a different quality. Hence one could not include them in a list of kinds, since they are countless and altogether different from each other. For even in those cases in which one of the simple tastes is dominant **[67]** the difference in each kind of thing tasted is recognisable. At least in the cases of dried figs, raisins and dates one quality, sweetness, is dominant, but taste distinguishes the difference between the kinds.

---

567 Cf. Aristotle, *On the Parts of Animals* 660a1–2; 690b29–31.

568 Cf. Aristotle, *History of Animals* 492b26.

569 Cf. Galen, *On the Usefulness of the Parts* 9.16 (2.47.1–15 Helmreich, 3.747 K); 16.3 (2.384.5–7 Helmreich, 4.275 K).

570 For the terminology cf. above, 64.15.

571 For the terminology cf. above, 57.3.

572 For similar lists of flavours see Plato, *Timaeus* 65D3–66C7; Aristotle, *On the Soul* 422b10–14; *On Sense Perception* 4; Theophrastus, *On the Causes of Plants* 6.1 and 6.4 (with the discussion by Sharples 1985); Galen, *On the Doctrines of Hippocrates and Plato* 7.6.25–26 (466.30–35 De Lacy, 5.634 K); *On Hippocrates' On the Nature of Man* 1.7 (22.30–23.2 Mewaldt, 15.40 K); *On Simple Medicines* 1.37 (11.445 K) and 1.38–39 (11.450–54 K).

573 For the exceptional case of water cf. Galen, *On Simple Medicines* 1.5 (11.390 K) and 1.8 (11.394 K).

574 Cf. Galen, *On Simple Medicines* 4.7 (11.639–40 K); *On the Affected Parts* 2.9 (8.113 K).

SECTION 10

ON HEARING[575]

(5) Hearing perceives voices and sounds. It discriminates their height, their depth, their smoothness and roughness and their volume.[576] Its organs also are the soft nerves coming from the brain[577] and the apparatus of the ears, particularly the cartilaginous type. For the cartilage is suitable for noises and echoes. Only man and (10) the ape do not move their ears,[578] while all other animals that have ears move them.[579]

SECTION 11

ON SMELL

Smell comes about through the nostrils and penetrates as far as the limits of the frontal cavities of the brain. For these are very vaporous (15) in their nature and readily receive vapours.[580] For it has been said already[581] how each of the sense-organs grasps its specific objects of sense through a certain likeness and kinship. But the brain has not sent down a nerve of sensation to

---

575 The order in which Nemesius discusses the five senses (vision, touch, taste, hearing, smell) is unusual, especially the position of hearing in between taste and smell (but see Aristotle, *History of Animals* 533a14). But it is probably partly motivated by his discussion at 6, 56.5–21, where he lists them in the order touch, vision, taste, hearing, smell; and his actual order of discussion may further be motivated by the fact that the primacy of vision was standard. Galen, *On the Causes of Symptoms* 1.6 (7.115 K) ranks vision, touch, taste, smell and hearing in order of intensity of pleasantness or unpleasantness.

576 Cf. Plato, *Timaeus* 67B; Aristotle, *On the Soul* 422b28; Galen, *On the Doctrines of Hippocrates and Plato* 5.3 (306.12–13 De Lacy, 5.446 K).

577 As in the case of touch; see above, 63.7–8. Cf. Galen, *On the Usefulness of the Parts* e.g. 8.3 (1.451.18–28 Helmreich, 3.623 K); 16.2 (2.381.7–13 Helmreich, 4.271 K).

578 Cf. Aristotle, *History of Animals* 492a22, 28 (man only); Galen, *On the Usefulness of the Parts* 16.6 (2.399.12 Helmreich; 4.295 K): man and apes.

579 We do not follow Morani in omitting this phrase, which is attested in all Greek MSS, although admittedly it is somewhat redundant.

580 Cf. Galen, *On the Doctrines of Hippocrates and Plato* 7.5.45 (462.13–17 De Lacy 5.628 K): 'the organ of smell, which is not in the nasal passages, as the majority believe, but in the tips of the anterior ventricles of the brain, to which the nasal passages ascend; for at this point its ventricles are most vaporous' (tr. De Lacy). Galen refers for more extensive discussion to his treatise on the organ of smell.

581 Above, 56.12.

ON THE NATURE OF MAN 117

smell as it has done to the other senses, but it satisfies its need and receives the (20) exhalation of vapours with the ends of its own nerves. The most general difference of vapours is their smelling well or badly and the mean between these, which is smelling neither well nor badly.[582] **[68]** Good smell comes from the moisture of properly concocted materials,[583] a moderate state when they are cooked moderately, a bad one when they are insufficiently cooked or incompletely.

SECTION 12

ON THOUGHT[584]

The various kinds of discursive thinking, including divination by dreams; its location in the central cavity of the brain and in the pneuma.

The power of the imagination, its organs, its parts (5) and the kinship and difference of the parts has been sufficiently described so far as is possible in a short account.[585] The different kinds of thought are judgement, assent, avoidance and impulse:[586] specifically there are the concepts of things,

582 Cf. Aristotle, *On the Soul* 421b22; Sextus Empiricus, *Against the Mathematicians* 7.300; Galen, *On Simple Medicines* 4.22 (11.699 K).
583 Domański refers to [Aristotle], *Problemata* 907b9.
584 This discussion of (discursive) thought (*to dianoêtikon*) is very brief; but more details follow in section 13 on memory and in section 14 on different kinds of reason (*logos endiathetos* and *logos prophorikos*). Earlier on (57.11), Nemesius had distinguished between *to dianoêtikon* and *to epistêmonikon*: and this perhaps corresponds to the distinction made below in 68.22 (and attributed to Plato) between *dianoêsis* and *noêsis*: the latter has as its objects 'the proper objects of thought' (*ta kuriôs noêta*) which have no basis in sense-perception as opposed to the *dianoêta* which do go back to sensory experience. In making this distinction, Nemesius once again harmonises Plato and Aristotle.
585 This had been done in section 6 above; but the reason for this concluding phrase here is probably that in Nemesius' view sensation is somehow subordinated to imagination; and thought follows after imagination in the listing of faculties mentioned above (n.496).
586 I.e. the drive to pursue something. The division here between generic and specific kinds of thought is Stoic in origin; cf. Sextus Empiricus, *Outline of Pyrrhonism* 1.65: 'Immanent reason according to the Stoics ... is concerned with the choice of things proper to it (*hairesis tôn oikeiôn*) and the avoidance of what is alien to it (*phugê tôn allotriôn*), with the knowledge of the skills that lead to this (*gnôsis tôn eis touto sunteinousôn tekhnôn*) and with the apprehension of the naturally appropriate virtues concerning the emotions (*antilêpsis tôn kat' oikeian phusin aretôn tôn peri ta pathê*).' Cf. also Aëtius/Pseudo-Plutarch, *Tenets* 4.21: 'The Stoics say that the ruling part is the highest part of the soul, which creates imaginations and assents and sensations and impulses; they call it reasoning (*logismos*).'

the virtues, the sciences, the rationale of the [relevant] skills, deliberation and choice. It is this [i.e thought] also which foretells (10) the future to us through dreams,[587] which the Pythagoreans say is the only true method of divination,[588] following the Hebrews.[589] Its organ is also the central cavity of the brain and the psychic pneuma within the cavity.[590]

SECTION 13

ON MEMORY

Memory and its relation to imagination. Sense-objects the proper objects of memory. Recollection of innate ideas. The location of memory in the posterior cavity of the brain. Empirical evidence for the localisation of sensation/imagination, thought and memory in the anterior, the middle and the posterior cavity of the brain respectively. A Galenic case-history of phrenitis.

---

587 Divination in sleep had been discussed by Aristotle in his treatise with the same title, but regarded as an activity of imagination, not of thinking, and of little cognitive or practical significance. But in Hellenistic and early Imperial philosophy (esp. the Peripatetic philosophers Dicaearchus and Cratippus, as well as Cicero), divination in sleep was upgraded (as was imagination) and the soul's divinatory capacity was related to its intellectual faculties (see Sharples 2001b). Nemesius reflects this later development also in 71.11, where he mentions the possibility that in our dreams we can have rational conversations (*kai en tois oneirois dialegometha*) that may be superior to those of the waking state since in sleep we are not distracted by sensory impressions.

588 Nemesius' reference to the Pythagoreans is puzzling. Cicero, *On Divination* 1.3.5 and 1.50.113, mentions Dicaearchus (and Cratippus) as those who recognised only natural divination (through dreams and ecstatic inspiration); and Aëtius/Pseudo-Plutarch, *Tenets* 5.1 likewise says that of all types of divination Aristotle and Dicaearchus acknowledged only divination through dreams and ecstatic inspiration. Aëtius/Pseudo-Plutarch also mentions the Pythagoreans in the same chapter but says that they acknowledged all forms of divination except the one through sacrifice (*to thutikon*), which seems to be confirmed by Cicero, *On Divination* 1.50.102. Telfer (1955, 338–39 n.3) suspects that Nemesius may be relying on Origen's characterisation (in his *Commentary on Genesis* and his *Against Celsus*) of Numenius as a Pythagorean philosopher who claimed that Pythagoras borrowed ideas from the Jews and who followed Jewish methods of allegorical interpretation (probably those of Philo).

589 This is probably a reference to Philo ('the Hebrews' is Origen's characteristic way of referring to Philo), who in his (partly extant) work *On Dreams* acknowledges the divine origin and prophetic value of at least some dreams. The Old Testament rejects most other forms of divination: see Deuteronomy 18:10–11; Leviticus 19:26, 31; Isaiah 8:19.

590 For this concept, and its physical location, see above, 56.3 and 64.10.

ON THE NATURE OF MAN 119

(15) The faculty of memory is the cause and storehouse of memory and recollection.[591] According to Origen[592] memory is the imagination left

---

591 In Greek *mnêmê* and *anamnêsis*. The difference is not always clear (and not always defined in the same way by all authors). Aristotle in his work *On Memory and Recollection* treats the former as a faculty by which humans (and animals) hold on to things they have experienced, store them somehow in their souls and are passively reminded of them by other stimuli (sensations or images or thoughts), whereas recollection is an active (and rational, hence confined to humans) process of searching for information one knows to have learned before but which is temporarily inactivated.

592 All manuscripts (as well as the Latin, Armenian and Arabic translations) read *Ôrigenês* here except the late ms. D, which reads *Aristotelês*; the latter reading is accepted by most editors and interpreters (Matthaei, Morani, Domański), though not by Einarson (TLG) nor by Jaeger (even though Jaeger goes on to point out that this section is a concatenation of quotes and half-quotes from Aristotle's treatise *On Memory and Recollection*). On palaeographical grounds it is hard to reject *Ôrigenês* and it is very likely that *Aristotelês* is a scribal correction (there are more such examples in D; see note on 57.9); whether the reference is to the Christian Origen or to the Neoplatonist philosopher of the same name is still debatable (apart from the present passage, the Christian Origen is mentioned only twice by Nemesius, and on both occasions rather negatively: in 44.20, he is criticised for his heretical views on the reincarnation of the soul; and in 95.18, he is said to have sacrificed to other gods; however, Skard [1936] has claimed that Origen's *Commentary on Genesis* was one of Nemesius' major sources). Domański's counter-argument that in the Christian Origen's extant writings this reference finds no correspondence proves little as many of Origen's works have not survived (besides, see *Selected Comments on the Psalms* vol. 12, p. 1272.16–17, and *Commentary on John's Gospel* 20.24.208 for some similar points); and this applies even more to the Neoplatonist Origen of whom virtually nothing survives (and who is mentioned nowhere else by Nemesius). Besides, the reference does not *exactly* correspond to anything specific in Aristotle's treatise (at any rate not to 450a23 quoted by Morani, for that just links memory to imagination), even though it may be said to summarise its chapter 1 reasonably faithfully (see esp. 450a31, *hoion tupon tina tou aisthêmatos*, and the account of memory images in 450b21–451a2; incidentally the phrase *apo tinos aithêseôs tês kat' energeian phainomenês* comes remarkably close to Aristotle's expression in *On Dreams* 461b21–22: *hupoleimma tou en têi energeiai aisthêmatos*, 'a remnant of the sense image when it was active', but this is said of dream images, not of memories; cf. also 460b2–3: *apelthontos tou thurathen aisthêtou emmenei ta aisthêmata aisthêta onta*, 'when the sense-object from outside has gone away, the sense images remain present and are perceptible'). On the other hand, Nemesius' attribution of specific views to Plato here also goes considerably beyond what can be found in Plato's writings, so one should not expect word-by-word similarity (and it is possible that Nemesius is drawing on an intermediary source here). Furthermore, there are several striking similarities with Aristotle further down (see notes below), and while we have no reason to suppose that either Origen was regarded as an authority on the subject of memory, Aristotle's treatment of memory and recollection was certainly well-known in late antiquity, as witnessed by, e.g., Plotinus, Porphyry, Philoponus, etc. So from the point of view of contents the reading 'Aristotle' is more satisfactory, though palaeographically it is unlikely that this is what Nemesius wrote and we may have to content ourselves with an unverifiable reference (cf. the similar case of Dinarchus in section 2 above, 17.10).

behind by an actually appearing sensation, according to Plato the preservation of sensation and thought.[593] For the soul grasps objects of sense through the sense-organs and an opinion is formed,[594] while it grasps things intelligible through the (20) intellect and intellection[595] comes about: when the soul preserves the imprints[596] of what it has experienced and of what it has conceived it is said to remember.[597] In this context Plato seems to use the word intellection not for intellection proper, but for thought.[598] For objects of sense are remembered as such, but intelligibles incidentally, since **[69]** memory of objects of thought as well seems to come about by previously attained imagining.[599] But as for intelligibles in the strict sense, we remember that we learned or heard of them but we do not have memory of their being. For the acquisition of intelligibles is not by preceding imagination but from learning or natural intuition.[600]

If we are said to remember (5) what we previously saw or heard or got to know in some other way, while 'previously' has a reference to time past, it is clear that what is remembered is things which come to be and pass away and are formed in time, and memory is of absent things but is not brought about by absent things. There is said to be recollection when forgetting interrupts memory:[601] for (10) recollection is the regaining of lost memory: but it becomes lost through forgetting. Forgetting is loss of memory, but the loss is sometimes continuous, sometimes for a period, in which case there

---

593 Plato, *Philebus* 34A10, defines memory (*mnême*) as 'preservation of sensation' (*sôteria aisthêseôs*); but *Theaetetus* 191D5–6 speaks of memory being concerned with 'what we have seen or heard or thought' and with 'sensations and thoughts' (*aisthêsesi kai ennoiais*).

594 Opinion being concerned with perceptions is standard Platonic theory: cf. *Philebus* 39B10; *Theaetetus* 161D3, 179C2–3.

595 'Intellection' renders *noêsis*, the activity of the intellect, the *nous*.

596 'Imprints' renders *tupoi*, a term used in the context of memory by Plato in *Theaetetus* 191D6 and 192A4, and metaphorically by Aristotle (*On Memory* 450a31).

597 Plato, *Theaetetus* 191D5–6.

598 The distinction is between *noêsis* and *dianoêsis*, which is similar to the distinction made by Plato in *Republic* 511D6–E2 (*noêsis* vs. *dianoia*), 534A5. Here, the relevance of the distinction is not made very clear, but it seems that Nemesius wishes to reserve *noêsis* for the thinking of the eternal forms which is by recollection of things the soul experienced prior to its descent into the body and into the world of coming to be and passing away.

599 This point is made by Aristotle in *On Memory and Recollection* 450a12–14 and 24–25: the proper object of memory is sense-objects which are being imagined (*phantasia*); thought-objects can be remembered but only in the form of appearances (*phantasmata*). However, the context is quite un-Aristotelian in that it refers to the recollection of innate ideas.

600 This is because imagination (*phantasia*) is not involved in their cognition.

601 Cf. Plato, *Philebus* 33E3.

ON THE NATURE OF MAN 121

is recollection. There is another sort of recollection which is forgetting[602] not of the matter of sensation and intellection but of natural concepts.[603] We call natural those present in all without teaching, such as the existence of God. (15) This sort Plato says is recollection of forms (what a form is we shall say later on).[604]

Thus the faculty of imagination hands on things imagined to the faculty of thought, while thought or reasoning, when it has received and judged them, passes them on to the faculty of memory.[605] The organ of memory, too, is the posterior cavity of the brain, which they call the cerebellum and the enkranis, and the (20) psychic pneuma within it.[606]

Since we say that the frontal cavities of the brain are the origin and roots of sensation, that of thought the central cavity and the posterior of memory, it is necessary to demonstrate whether this is the state of affairs, lest we should seem to believe what is being said without having a good reason for it.[607] The

---

602 This must mean 'concerned with forgetting'; it is understandable that Jaeger wished to delete *lêthê* here, but the text can probably stand.

603 This is the well-known Platonic concept, familiar from the *Meno* (81Cff.), of learning as recollection of what the soul experienced prior to its incarnation. 'Natural' renders *phusikos*, a term which Plato does not use in this connection. *Phusikê ennoia* is a Stoic term (see Diogenes Laertius 7.54), also used frequently in Albinus' *Epitome of Platonic Doctrine*, e.g. 4.6, 4.8, 5.7, etc; sometimes *koinai ennoiai* is used to express the same idea: see Philoponus, *On Aristotle on the Soul* 3.24ff.; 5.17–19.

604 This promise will remain unfulfilled (the Forms reappear in 125.1 below, but this is hardly an explanation). On the unfinished state of the work see Introduction, section 2.

605 This sentence concludes the epistemological account of memory and returns to the original claim of memory as a 'manager' (or 'storehouse', *tamieion*) of memories and recollections (68.15–16).

606 Cf. above, 68.12 with note.

607 In this paragraph, Nemesius provides empirical evidence for his claims about the location of imagination/sensation, thought and memory in particular parts of the brain – claims that have already been made (but not empirically substantiated) earlier on in 56.2 (imagination), 64.2 (sensation), 68.12 (thought) and 69.18 (memory). The passage that follows finds a very close parallel in the fragments of the late 4th-century medical writer Posidonius of Byzantium as preserved in the early Byzantine author Aëtius of Amida's *Medical Books* 6.2 (vol. 2, p. 125 Olivieri): 'Phrenitis is an inflammation of the membranes surrounding the brain during acute fever, causing insanity and loss of reason ... There are several different kinds of phrenitis, but the following three are most important. Either only imagination is affected and reasoning and memory are spared; or only reasoning is affected and imagination and memory are spared; or imagination and reasoning are affected and memory is spared. Furthermore, loss of memory due to febrile diseases usually destroys the faculties of reason and imagination as well. A disorder of the anterior part of the brain affects only the imagination; a disorder of the middle ventricle leads to aberration of reason; a disorder of the posterior part of the brain near the occiput destroys the faculty of memory, usually together with the other two.' The same idea is

most adequate demonstration is gained from the activity of the parts. (25) If the frontal cavities are damaged in any way **[70]** the senses are impaired but thought remains unharmed. If the central cavity alone suffers thought is overthrown but the sense-organs continue to preserve their natural [power of] sensation. If both the frontal and the central cavities suffer, reason (5) is damaged together with the senses. But if the cerebellum suffers, memory alone is lost together with it without sensation and thought being harmed in any way.[608] But if the posterior suffers together with the frontal and central ones, sense, reason and memory also are destroyed, in addition (10) to the whole creature being in danger of perishing.

This becomes clear from many affections and symptoms, particularly from phrenitis.[609] For the senses of some of those with phrenitis are preserved and thought alone is harmed. Galen[610] records such a sufferer from phrenitis who, when a certain wool-worker was working in his house, sprang up and took (15) some glass utensils, rushed to the windows and, calling each of

---

reflected in Philoponus, *On Aristotle On the Soul* 155.20–30: 'It is also evident that from the affections of the body something proceeds to the soul, too. For when the one suffers, the other suffers, too, and when the one is in good mood, the other cheers with it. Also the fact that the body, when it is in this or that condition, hinders the soul or does not hinder it, is known to everybody, whereas this hindering of the soul through the body would not happen if not some sort of sympathetic reaction proceeded from the soul's relationship with the body to the soul in this way, just as memory is affected when a particular cavity at the back of the brain is affected, as is the rational part of the soul when some other cavity is affected, and when it is in a certain state the soul is easily affected by imagination, but when it is in a different state, it is very difficult for it to imagine' (tr. van der Eijk 2006). In spite of Nemesius' reference to Galen below, the specific localisation of different cognitive functions in different parts (or ventricles) of the brain is not found in Galen, or at least not in his extant works, and may well be regarded as evidence for an awareness, on Nemesius' part, of post-Galenic medical ideas; cf. Rocca (2003) 245–47; Flashar (1966) 123–24; Sudhoff (1913); Grunert (2002).

608 We follow Morani and a number of textual witnesses in omitting the sentence 'It is clear that we are not talking now of movement according to impulse'.

609 In ancient classifications of disease from the Hippocratic writings onwards, 'phrenitis' was regarded as one of the most dangerous forms of acute mental disturbance. It was believed to manifest itself in high fever, delirium and the plucking of threads from the patient's clothes. Opinions on its causes, physical location and the reason for its nomenclature differed: some doctors believed the name of the disease was related to the part that was believed to be affected, viz. the *phrenes* or diaphragm, while others related it to the cognitive function (*phronêsis*, intelligence) that was believed to be disturbed. See, e.g., the discussion in ch. 1 of the so-called Anonymous of Paris (a medical text on diseases presumably dating from the 1st or 2nd century CE; ed. Garofalo 1997) and the elaborate account by the 5th-century CE medical author Caelius Aurelianus, *Acute Affections* 1.8.53–56, with the discussion by van der Eijk (2005b) ch. 4. The identification of 'phrenitis' with a modern concept is problematic: see van der Eijk (2001) 144–45.

610 What follows corresponds very closely to Galen, *On Affected Parts* 4.1–2 (8.226–28 K).

ON THE NATURE OF MAN 123

the instruments by name, asked the passers by if they wanted it to be thrown down below. When bystanders said they did want it, he first hurled each of the utensils and then asked those present if they also wanted the wool-worker to be thrown down. They thought the affair was a joke and so (20) said that they did want it. So he took the wool-worker and pushed him down from above. This man was sound in his sensations, for he knew that the things were instruments and the man was a wool-worker, but his thinking was diseased. Others are prone to imagining and think that they see what they do not see, but are rational in other matters. These were impaired only in the frontal cavities while the central one remained unaffected. Through the affections **[71]** that result in each part, their activities are impeded: for the creature is damaged with respect to that activity which the part that suffers naturally carries out, just as when the foot suffers we are hindered from walking: for that is the activity of the foot. (5)

SECTION 14

ON IMMANENT AND EXPRESSED REASON

An alternative division of the rational faculties of the soul. Immanent and expressed reason as two different forms of 'speech'. The organs of speech.

This, then, is one way of dividing the power of the soul, viz. according to the division of certain bodily parts.[611] With regard to the rational element of the soul, there is another division, which is made in a different way, viz. into the so-called immanent and expressed reason.[612] Immanent reason is a motion of

---

611 It is striking to see that Nemesius here presents the differentiation according to bodily parts as the *criterion* of the division of soul faculties he has been using in the preceding sections. Something similar had been suggested in 55.24 above; but while it is true that in most sections specific attention was given to the 'organs' of the relevant faculties (e.g. in 54.24; 56.2; 65.17, 24; 66.7; 67.7; 68.4, 11; 69.18), they could hardly be regarded as a criterion of division.

612 *Logos* here is difficult to translate: it primarily refers to linguistic ability or articulateness, the capacity to express thoughts and feelings in language, either through speech or internally. Neither 'speech' nor 'reason' cover this entirely, while 'discourse' (Urmson) in English seems to refer too much to a process or external entity rather than an internal faculty. Our 'immanent' renders *endiathetos* (lit. 'belonging to someone's internal disposition'), 'expressed' *prophorikos* ('uttered', 'bringing forth', 'productive'). The distinction is Stoic: cf. *SVF* 2.135 and 2.223 (= Sextus Empiricus, *Against the Mathematicians* 8.275); see also Sextus, *Outline of Pyrrhonism* 1.65ff.; Plutarch, *That a Philosopher ought to converse especially with Men in Power* 777C; *The Cleverness of Animals* 973A; Porphyry, *On Abstinence* 3.3.

the soul which occurs in the speech function (10) without any speaking aloud, which is why we often go through a whole reasoning process by ourselves in silence and converse in dreams.[613] In that way in particular we are all gifted with reason: for we are less so in expressed reason than in this. For both those who are dumb from birth and those who have lost their voice through accident or disease are none the less gifted with reason. (15) Expressed reason has its activity in speech and in conversation. There are many organs of speech:[614] for the intercostal muscles[615] within the thorax, the lung, the windpipe, the larynx, and of these especially the cartilaginous element,[616] the returning nerves,[617]

613 On the role of reason in sleep see also above, 12, 68.9–10.
614 As in previous sections (see n.611 above), after discussing the faculty as such Nemesius relates it to its physical organs. The account that follows owes much to Galen, although not all details can be paralleled: in *On the Usefulness of the Parts* 7.5 and 7.11, Galen deals at great length with the organs of speech, but he also refers there for even more extensive treatment to his work *On the Voice*, which survives only in fragments (collected by Baumgarten 1963) but an excerpt of which may be preserved in Oribasius, *Medical Collections*, Books of Uncertain Order, ch. 62 (CMG VI 2.2, pp. 165–71 Raeder), which contains a number of elements also found in Nemesius here (e.g. section 5, p. 165.27 ff. Raeder, on the organs of speech; sections 21–23, p. 167.20–37, on the distinction between sound production and speech production; and section 50, p.171.23–25 Raeder, on the role of the nostrils); yet the fact that Nemesius has also preserved Galenic elements not mentioned in Oribasius' abstract indicates that it cannot have been through Oribasius alone that Nemesius had access to Galenic ideas. See Baumgarten (1963) 89–90, who argues that it is unclear whether Nemesius has used this Galenic treatise. See also Galen, *On the Affected Parts* 1.6 (8.50–53 K) and 4.9 (8.266–68 K): 'the formation of voice (*phônê*) is the function of the sound organs, but the production of speech (*dialektos*) of the speech organs, the most important of which is the tongue, while nose, lips and teeth support speech considerably. I also want to mention that the larynx and the muscles which move it are phonetic organs, and so are the nerves which conduct the power of the brain to these (parts)' (tr. Siegel 1976, modified).
615 These are discussed by Galen in *On the Usefulness of the Parts* 7.20 (1.433 Helmreich, 3.595–96 K), where he also refers for more details to his work *On the Causes of Respiration* (they are discussed in ch. 2, 4.467 K of the surviving [short] work with that title; however, several other references by Galen to a work of this title do not find correspondence in the extant treatise that bears this name, and there may have been a longer version).
616 This is discussed by Galen at some length in *On the Usefulness of the Parts* 7.17.
617 For these nerves (the so-called *nervi recurrentes*) cf. Galen, *On the Usefulness of the Parts* 16.4 (2.389.6–390.4 Helmreich, 4.282–83 K): 'She [i.e. Nature] decided to bring nerves down from the brain, like the others I have spoken of earlier, by way of the sixth pair, from which nerves must also be given to the heart, stomach, and liver, but to make them run a sort of double course, carrying them first to parts below the thorax and then bringing them back up again to its most important muscles. They could not run back (*palindromêsai*) without making a turn, so that Nature was forced to seek a turning-post, so to speak, for the nerves, around which she might bend them ... and it became necessary for Nature to bring the pair of nerves down into the thorax and look for the turning-post there' (tr. May); see also Galen, *On*

ON THE NATURE OF MAN 125

the glottis[618] and all the muscles that move these parts are organs of sound production, (20) and of speech the mouth: for in this speech is moulded, given shape and as it were, a form: the tongue and the uvula have the function of a plectrum, the palate of the mouth that of a sound-board,[619] the teeth and the formation of the mouth's opening that of the complement of strings in a lyre, [72] while even the nose contributes something to the euphony or cacophony, as is clear from the case of singers.

SECTION 15

ANOTHER DIVISION OF THE SOUL

Further divisions of soul faculties; the vegetative, sensitive and rational. The divisions of Zeno the Stoic, Panaetius, and Aristotle.

They[620] also divide up the soul in another way into powers, or kinds or parts, into the vegetative, (5) which is also called nutritive and affective,[621] into

---

the Affected Parts 1.6 (8.53–55 K), where he presents the term *palindromountes* as his own coinage, and 4.9 (8.267 K).

618 On this see May (1968), vol. 1, 357 n.41 (on *On the Usefulness of the Parts* 7.13): 'The whole inner structure of the larynx comprising ventricular folds, ventricles, and vocal folds is called *glôttis* by Galen.'

619 Cf. Galen, *On the Usefulness of the Parts* 7.5 (1.382.1–6 Helmreich, 3.526 K): 'I pointed out in the same book [= *On the Voice*] that the (rough) artery [i.e. the windpipe] provides a preliminary regulation and preparation of the voice for the larynx, and that when the voice has once been produced in the larynx, it is amplified by the roof of the mouth lying in front (of the larynx) and acting as a sounding board and by the uvula acting as a plectrum' (tr. May). Cf. also *On the Doctrines of Hippocrates and Plato* 2.4.27 (122.4–6 De Lacy, 5.233 K): 'The expelled breath becomes voice on being struck by the cartilages of the larynx as by a kind of plectrum' (tr. De Lacy, slightly modified). See also *On Hippocrates' Epidemics I* 1.2.80 (94 Wenkebach; 17A.187 K), where the same metaphor is used.

620 The Greek just uses the impersonal third-person plural here (*diairousi*) and the holders of this division remain unspecified; it is likely, however, that the Stoics are meant. See nn. 621 and 622 below.

621 This use of *pathêtikon* as identical with the vegetative and distinct from the sensitive part of the soul may cause surprise, since in most ancient psychological divisions passions, emotions and affections are connected with the sensitive rather than the vegetative domain (except sexual desire, which is linked to the reproductive/nutritive part of the soul); see Nemesius below 73.8 and 74.2–3, and Aspasius, *On Aristotle's Nicomachean Ethics*, p. 35.17–20, who explicitly distinguishes the *pathêtikon* from the *threptikon* part of the soul, the difference being that the latter is completely devoid of reason, whereas the former can partake in reason when it is obedient

the sensitive and the rational.[622] Some of the organs for these have already been stated,[623] others will be stated in what follows. Zeno the Stoic says that the soul has eight parts, dividing it into the controlling element, the five senses, speech and the generative faculty.[624] But the philosopher Panaetius (10) claims that speech belongs to movement according to impulse,[625] and quite rightly so, but that the generative function is not a part of the soul, but

---

to it. It may be, however, that this distinction is too subtle for the present context. In the next section, Nemesius uses the term *pathêtikon* in relation to the non-rational (*alogon*) part of the soul as a whole, though still specifically in relation to appetite, *orektikon* (see Domański [1900] 76 n. 2; Domański quotes a passage in Plutarch, *On Moral Virtue* 3, 441B–C, where Aristotle is credited with a distinction between *to pathêtikon* and *to aisthêtikon*, but where the *pathêtikon* is also distinguished from the *threptikon kai phutikon*, whereas the affective and the nutritive are identified by Nemesius here). Further down in section 22, this 'non-rational [part] that is not capable of obeying reason' is identified with the functions of nutrition, generation and pulsation. This perhaps explains the association of *pathêtikon* with the lowest soul functions and its being distinguished from the sensitive part here (although the division mentioned here is not necessarily one that Nemesius would endorse: Nemesius himself, in accordance with Panaetius, does not regard vegetative/generative functions as belonging to the soul but to 'nature'). For parallels for the use of *pathêtikon* as synonymous with *alogon* see Galen, *On the Doctrines of Hippocrates and Plato* 2.7.18 (156.2–3 De Lacy, 5.271 K): 'the part which is called non-rational and affective'; 3.7.23 (216.18–19 De Lacy, 5.340 K); 4.7.40–41 (290.5–9 De Lacy, 5.425–26 K); 5.5.32 (324.8–10 De Lacy, 5.466 K) and 5.6.22 (330.18–19 De Lacy, 5.473 K); most of these passages deal with Stoic views, either those of Chrysippus (whom Galen criticises) or Posidonius (with whom Galen is in broad agreement; see Tieleman [2003] 72–76); see Posidonius F33 Edelstein-Kidd *ad loc.*; see also Theodoret, *Cure of Greek Diseases* 3.48.3: 'They [the Greeks] deify the part [of the soul] which they call the affective and the non-rational (*pathêtikon kai alogon*), which they recommend to the service of reasoning. Desire (*epithumia*) they call Aphrodite and Eros, spirit (*thumos*) Ares, drunkenness Dionysus, theft Hermes, reasoning (*logismos*) Athena.' There is also the discussion of *pathos* in the sense of 'accident' i.e. something that happens to one, regardless of one's experience of it, in Nemesius 73.20ff.

622 Having discussed divisions of the soul 'according to their bodily parts' (71.6–7), and having referred to an alternative division of the rational part of the soul (previous section), Nemesius now considers alternative divisions of the whole soul. The criterion here seems to be function or 'faculty' (*dunamis*). The first division mentioned here seems, broadly speaking, the Aristotelian division (see note 628 below) except for the inclusion of emotions among the vegetative functions, which rather suggests a Stoic background (see n.621 above).

623 The organs involved in imagination and sense perception have been discussed in sections 6–11 (56.2–4; 59.7–10; 65.24; 66.7; 67.7), those involved in memory in section 13 (69.18–20) and those involved in rational thinking in section 12 (68.11–13). The organs involved in nutrition and reproduction will be discussed in sections 23 and 25.

624 Zeno of Citium (333/2–262 BCE), the founder of the Stoics; see *SVF* 1.143 (this passage) and 2.827a (= Aëtius/Pseudo-Plutarch, *Tenets* 4.4.4); Stobaeus, *Anthology* 1.49.34 (p. 369.6 Wachsmuth, derived from Iamblichus' work on the soul).

625 On this concept see section 27 and the discussion by Inwood (1985) 253–54 and Verbeke (1945) 94–95.

of nature.[626] Aristotle in his works on natural philosophy[627] says that there are five parts of the soul, the vegetative, the sensitive, the locomotive, the appetitive and that concerned with thought:[628] he calls vegetative that of nutrition and growth and (15) what causes generation and the formation of bodies. He also calls the vegetative the nutritive, naming the whole from its most important element, nutrition, to which the other elements in the vegetative owe their existence. That is what he says in the works on nature, but in his ethical works[629] he divides the soul into the two primary and basic kinds, the rational and the non-rational, and he subdivides the non-rational into (20) that which is capable of obeying reason and that which does not listen to reason.

Reason has been discussed in earlier sections,[630] but we shall now make distinctions about the non-rational. [73]

SECTION 16

ON THE NON-RATIONAL PART OR KIND OF THE SOUL, WHICH IS ALSO CALLED THE AFFECTIVE AND APPETITIVE

Appetite, affection and movement according to impulse. Distinction between what is capable of obeying reason and what is not. Spirit and desire and their location in the heart and the liver. Various definitions of 'affection' and 'activity'.

626 Panaetius of Rhodes (185–109 BCE), main representative of the so-called 'middle Stoa'; the present passage is fr. 86 van Straaten. For this correction in Stoic doctrine cf. Tertullian, *On the Soul* 14.2, who says that Panaetius divided the soul into six parts (see the discussion by Waszink [1947] 210–11 and Verbeke [1945] 95). 'Movement according to impulse' (*kinêsis kath' hormên*) is discussed by Nemesius in the next section (73.9ff.), generation in section 25 (85.23ff.), where it is said to belong to the part of the soul that is not capable of obeying reason, even though the activity of sexual intercourse belongs to the soul and is within our control.

627 I.e. *On the Soul*, the *Parva Naturalia* and the zoological works (esp. *On the Parts of Animals* and *On the Generation of Animals*).

628 Aristotle sometimes divides the soul into three 'parts', the nutritive (which includes reproduction and growth), the sensitive (which involves locomotion and appetite) and the intellectual parts (*On the Soul* 415a17), but he also sometimes presents locomotion and appetite as separate faculties (*On the Soul* 413b12–13, 414a31–32). The term *phutikon* ('vegetative') is not found in *On the Soul* nor indeed in any of the works on nature (but see 411b28–29; 414a33; 415a3), but it is used in *Nicomachean Ethics* 1102a33, 1102b29; *Eudemian Ethics* 1219b37.

629 *Nicomachean Ethics* 1.13, esp. 1102a27ff. and b28ff.

630 Sections 12 and 14.

128   NEMESIUS

Some say that what lacks reason is self-contained,[631] as being a non-rational soul and not a part of the rational one, first because it is found self-contained in non-rational animals, (5) from which it is clear that it is something complete and not part of another soul, next because it is the height of absurdity for the non-rational to be a part of the rational. But Aristotle both calls it a part and a power and divides it into two, as we said.[632] He calls these in common also the appetitive:[633] for to this belongs movement according to impulse.[634] For appetite is the origin of change. For it is through appetite (10) that animals hasten to movement according to impulse.

Of the non-rational, one part does not obey reason, the other is capable of obeying reason.[635] Further what is capable of obeying reason is divided into two, the desirous and the spirited.[636] The organ of the faculty of desire, which

631 *Kath' heautên*, i.e. 'on its own', not part of something else. As Domański notes (1900, 114 n.1). this may be a reference to Numenius of Apamea, the 2nd-century CE Neopythagorean philosopher (cf. Stobaeus, *Anthology* 1.19, p. 350.26–351.4 Wachsmuth: 'some thinkers, among whom Numenius, think that there are not three parts of one soul, or two, the rational and the non-rational, but that we have two souls, as the others do, the one being rational, the other non-rational').

632 In the previous section (72.18–19); in *On the Soul*, Aristotle uses both *morion* and *dunamis*, although he is anxious to specify that 'part' should not be understood in a spatial sense (432a23ff.).

633 In *On the Soul* 3.9–11, Aristotle discusses appetite (*orexis*). He begins by considering this under the rubric of locomotion, and he asks whether this is a separate power of the soul, or even a separate soul altogether (432a18–22). He identifies *orexis* (or, to be more precise, the object of appetite, *to orekton*) as the motive force both for rational and non-rational movement, hence common to animals and humans, and he indicates that *orexis* can also be contrary to reason (433a22–30). As such, Nemesius' account of the Aristotelian position is not wholly inaccurate (contra Domański [1900] 75–76 n.1 and Telfer [1955] 348 n.2).

634 *Kinêsis kath' hormên*, a term of Stoic origin (sometimes also rendered as 'conative movement'), a movement arising from within the organism (as opposed to external force); further down in 87.20ff., Nemesius defines it as a movement which it is in our power to exercise or not exercise (e.g. locomotion, speaking, breathing, as opposed to growing and pulsation which, although arising from within us, are beyond our control); see also section 27 for fuller treatment of this type of movement.

635 Cf. Aristotle, *Nicomachean Ethics* 1102b29: 'the part that is non-rational appears twofold, too: for the vegetative (*phutikon*) has no part in reason at all, but the desiring and, in general, appetitive part (*to epithumêtikon kai holôs orektikon*), in some way do partake of reason in so far as they are capable of obeying reason and open to persuasion by it'; cf. also 1098a4.

636 Cf. Aëtius/Pseudo-Plutarch, *Tenets* 4.4 and the discussion by Vander Waerdt (1985) 375. These faculties (*epithumia* and *thumos*) and their corresponding physical organs (liver and heart) correspond to the two non-rational faculties of the soul identified by Plato in the *Republic* and the *Timaeus*. We take *epipeithês* in the sense of 'capable of obeying to reason', 'open to persuasion' (cf. Aristotle, *Nicomachean Ethics* 1094a4), for it is quite possible for desire to go against reason.

works through the senses[637] is the liver, that of spirit the heart, a harsh part which permits vigorous motion assigned to a harsh service (15) and intense impulse, just as the liver, which is a tender internal organ, is the organ of tender desire.[638] These are called capable of obeying reason, because they are of a nature to obey reason, to be subordinate to it, and to cause movement as reason dictates in the case of men who are in a natural condition.[639] These affections, too, constitute the existence of a living being:[640] for without them (20) life cannot be sustained.

But since 'affection' has more than one meaning, the ambiguity must first be resolved.[641] For [the word] 'affection' is applied both to what is bodily, such as diseases and wounds, and also what belongs to the soul, which is the subject of the present discussion, which is desire and spirit. An affection of animals is in general that on which pleasure or pain follows.[642] For while pain follows upon an affection, (25) the affection is not itself pain.[643] If it were so, then everything affected would also suffer pain, but

637 As opposed to the spirited element, whose desires presumably arise from thoughts.
638 See previous notes for the Platonic background of this location of spirit in the heart (cf. esp. *Timaeus* 70B1, C1 and D3) and of desire in the liver (ibid.; for the purpose of the liver's softness see *Timaeus* 71D2). This view on the location was adopted by Galen, and the contrast between the 'harsh' (*sklēros*) heart and the 'tender' (*hapalos*) liver is a commonplace in Galen (e.g. *Art of Medicine* 12.6 (311.3–13 Boudon, 1.338 K); *On Mixtures* 1.9 (38.20–21 Helmreich, 1.570 K), but we have been unable to find the psychological application that Nemesius here gives to this in Galen.
639 Cf. Aristotle, *Nicomachean Ethics* 7.5 and Alexander, *Supplement to On the Soul* 23 (175.14–15 and 21–22 Bruns), with the comments by Sharples (2004) 214–15; (2001a) 588–92.
640 Through the desire for food and drink (individual) and sexual desire (species).
641 The word *pathos* in Greek can be used for anything that happens to something (e.g. an accident) or is an attribute of something (e.g. a property). When the affected entity is an organism, it can be translated as 'experience' or 'feeling', and in ethical contexts it is usually rendered as 'emotion' or 'passion'; but the word can also be applied to lifeless objects; and it can refer both to the process of being affected and to the result. Distinctions between these various usages can already be found in Aristotle (e.g. *Metaphysics* 1022b15–21). For the distinction between psychic and somatic affections see Anonymus Londiniensis I.29–II.6, and Galen, *On the Causes of Pulses* 4 (9.157 K); *On Hippocrates' Epidemics VI* 4.26 (242.25–26 Wenkebach, 17B.210 K); and in medical contexts *pathos* very often refers to physical illness or injury. See Tieleman (2003) 15–16.
642 Cf. Aristotle, *Nicomachean Ethics* 1104b15; 1105b23; Anonymus Londiniensis II.34–36: 'Of the affections of the soul the two most general ones according to the ancients are pleasure and discomfort'; and Aspasius, *On Aristotle's Nicomachean Ethics*, p. 42.27ff. (which presents a debate with various positions being taken on the classification and hierarchy of emotions); see Sorabji (2004), vol. 1, 275–80. See also Plotinus 3.6 [26] 4.
643 Cf. Galen, *On the Elements according to Hippocrates* 2.18 (62.15–16 De Lacy, 1.419 K): 'Surely something that is to feel pain must necessarily meet these two requirements: it

as it is [74] things without sensation are affected without suffering pain: so the pain is not the affection but is the perception of the affection; and this must also be significant if it is to fall under sensation.[644] A definition of an affection of the soul is this: an affection is a perceptible movement in the faculty of appetite on the occasion of an imagination of good or evil.[645] (5) Another is: an affection is a non-rational movement in the soul on account of a supposition of good or evil.[646] Generally they[647] define an affection as follows: an affection is a movement in one thing received from another.[648]

---

must be capable of undergoing change and capable of sensation' (tr. De Lacy, modified); 2.43 (66.24–68.2 De Lacy, 1.424 K): 'if you grant that they are subject to affections but are not sentient, they will not feel pain because they will have no feeling. For, as I said, a thing that is going to feel pain must be affected and must feel the affection (*kai paskhein kai tou pathous aisthanesthai*)' (tr. De Lacy); see also *On the Causes of Symptoms* 1.7 (7.137 K).

644 Telfer (1955, 348) translates: 'and must be marked enough to call attention to itself'; see also 75.2 below.

645 Exactly this definition is also found in the anonymous commentary *On Aristotle's Nicomachean Ethics* (CAG 20 p. 130.19, on 1105b19ff.), but it is cited without attribution to a specific authority.

646 Exactly this definition is also found in Aspasius in his commentary *On Aristotle's Nicomachean Ethics* p. 44.21–24, where it is attributed to the Peripatetic thinker Andronicus (1st century BCE; and Aspasius himself rejects Andronicus' definition as too Stoic because of the presence of 'supposition', and goes on to give another of his own (45.13–14: 'a movement of the irrational [part] of the soul by the pleasant or the painful'), which is not noted by Nemesius (see Sorabji [2000] 133–34, and Gottschalk [1987] 1114), which may suggest that Aspasius himself is not Nemesius' (direct or indirect) source, or else that he or his source did not read Aspasius very carefully. For similarities with the Stoic thinker Chrysippus cf. Diogenes Laërtius, 7.111 (= SVF 2.456) and Galen, *On the Doctrines of Hippocrates and Plato* 4.2.8 (240.11–17 De Lacy, 5.367–68 K), 4.2.19 (242.12–14 De Lacy, 5.370 K), 4.4.32 (256.32–258.1 De Lacy, 5.389 K), and 5.2.2 (294.29–30 De Lacy, 5.432 K), who, however, criticises Chrysippus for the apparent inconsistency between calling affections 'non-rational' and regarding them as forms of judgement involving a 'supposition' (*hupolêpsis*, the term used here by Nemesius) of something good or evil. See De Lacy (1984), vol. 3, 642 (note on p. 240.5–6) and Domański (1900) 118 n.2.

647 No subject is specified in the Greek.

648 From here onwards to p. 75.1, Nemesius follows almost literally the distinctions made by Galen in a number of his writings, esp. in *On the Doctrines of Hippocrates and Plato* 6.1.5–17 (360.22–364.10 De Lacy, 5.506–09 K), of which we quote the relevant sections: 'Now *energeia* (activity) is an active motion, that is, motion that comes from the moving object itself; but *pathos* (affection) is a motion in one thing that comes from another thing ... In the same way anger is an *energeia* (activity) of the spirited part of the soul but a *pathêma* (affection) of the other two parts, and of our whole body besides, when our body is forcibly driven to its actions by anger ... They have another meaning when we think of *energeia* (activity) as a motion according to nature, and *pathos* (affection) as a motion contrary to nature ... The movement of the heart in pulsation is an *energeia* (activity), but in palpitation it is a *pathos*

An activity is a movement involving action. 'Involving action' means 'self-initiated'. Thus anger is also an activity of the spirited element, but also an affection of the [other] two parts of the soul, and further of the whole of our body, (10) when one is led forcibly to actions by anger. For the movement is received by one thing from another, which we said was what an affection was. An activity is also said to be an affection in another way, when it is unnatural. For activity is natural movement, affection the unnatural. And also, according to this account, activity when the movement is not natural is called an affection, (15) whether the movement be self-initiated or by something else. For the motion of the heart, when it moves by pulsation is an activity, but that through palpitations is an affection, for even the motion through palpitation is self-initiated, but is not natural, while that of pulsation is also self-initiated, but natural.[649] So it is nothing to wonder at that one and the same thing is called both an affection and an activity: (20) in so far as they are movements arising from the affective element in the soul itself they are a sort of activities: in so far as they are immoderate and unnatural they are not activities but affections. Thus a movement in the non-rational part is an affection [75] in both meanings of the word. But not every movement in the affective part is called an affection, but those that are more violent and reach the senses: for those that are small and unnoticed are not yet affections.[650] For an affection must have a significant size, which is why the definition of an affection includes being a (5) perceptible movement.[651] For slight changes escape being noticed and do not produce affections, as said above.

(affection). Palpitation too begins within the heart itself yet is not according to nature; while pulsation, which also arises in the heart, is according to nature ... Therefore it is not surprising that a single thing may happen to be called both *pathos* (affection) and *energeia* (activity) ... In this way, then, the terms *energeia* (activity) and *pathos* (affection) will both be used of anger, distress, fear, desire, inflamed anger and the like, but each in a different sense; and besides, inasmuch as the whole body along with the soul is carried away by them, the movement of the animal will be a *pathos* (affection) in both senses of the word' (tr. De Lacy). Other parallels for the distinction between activity and affection in Galen are listed in De Lacy's apparatus (p. 360); see also Plotinus 3.6 [26] 4.

649 For the unnaturalness of palpitation (*palmos*) see Galen, *On the Causes of Symptoms* 2.2 (7.159 K); *On Tremor, Palpitation, Convulsion and Rigour* 5 (7.594 K and 598 K).

650 This picks up what was said in 74.2-3, although there is some margin for ambiguity here as in 74.1-2 affection was distinguished from the perception of the affection, while here Nemesius suggests that in order to count as an affection, the movement has to be significant; see the definition cited in n.645, and Gottschalk (1987) 1115.

651 See n.645.

SECTION 17

ON THE DESIROUS PART

Desire, pleasure and distress; good and bad desires.

As we said, the non-rational part of the soul that is capable of obeying reason is divided into two, the desirous and the spirited elements.[652] In its turn the desirous part is divided (10) into two, into the pleasant and the distressing: for a fulfilled desire brings pleasure, an unfulfilled one distress.

Again, in another way desire can be divided up to contain four types, including itself;[653] for since some things are good and some bad, and some are already present, some expected, in these ways, multiplying two by two, (15) the different kinds of desire become four. For there is good and evil and further the present and the expected. Desire is [concerned with] the expected good, pleasure [with] the good that is already present: again, fear is [concerned with] the expected evil, distress is [concerned with] its presence. For pleasure and desire revolve around what is good, fear and distress around what is bad. This is why some[654] divide affection[655] (20) into four, desire, pleasure, fear and distress.

We call good and bad either what is really so or what is thought to be so.[656] Bad affections come to be in the soul for the following three reasons: bad training, ignorance and a bad state of the body.[657] For if we are not

---

652 Above, 73.11–12.

653 I.e., 'desire' (*epithumia*) would be the designation of one of the four species as well as the designation of the genus; see below, 75.19–20.

654 Presumably the Stoics are meant here: cf. Aspasius, *On Aristotle's Nicomachean Ethics* 45.16–22; Stobaeus, *Anthology* 2.6.166.

655 There are two possible ways of taking *to pathos* here, either specifically 'this affection', i.e. desire, in which case this sentence picks up what was said above in 75.12 ('including itself'), or in the generic sense, i.e. 'affections'.

656 This distinction is often made in Aristotle (e.g. *Nicomachean Ethics* 1155b26; *Rhetoric* 1369b18ff.; *On the Soul* 433a27) and also by the Stoics (see Stobaeus, *Anthology* 2.6.166).

657 This division of sources of evil is reminiscent of Plato's account (*Timaeus* 86B–87B) of 'diseases of the soul' arising either from a bad condition of the body (*dia ponêran hexin tina tou sômatos*) or from bad upbringing (*apaideuton trophên*, 86E1–2, 87B2–9), even though it does not quite match Plato's categories since Plato treats *amathia* as one type of mental illness next to *mania* (86B4 and 88B5); furthermore, in his treatment of mental illness, Plato gives ample space to medical intervention by diet and drugs (89A5ff.) alongside intellectual pursuits (87B2ff.; see n.662 below). Nemesius' division further corresponds broadly to the division of the counterparts of these three factors as sources of good moral achievement, viz. training,

brought up well from childhood so as to be able to master our affections, we fall into immoderation about them. From ignorance bad (25) decisions are implanted into the rational element of the soul, so that we think that bad things are good and good things bad.[658] Sometimes bad affections are the result of a bad state of the body:[659] for those with bitter bile are irascible,[660] and those heated and moist in their bodily mixture are prone to sexual activity.[661] **[76]** A bad habit is to be cured by a good habit, ignorance by learning

---

education and natural endowment, as found from Plato (*Meno* 70A) and Aristotle onwards (*Nicomachean Ethics* 1099b18–20 and 1179b20ff.; *Eudemian Ethics* 1214a15–21). Domański (1900, 120 n.2) refers to Timaeus of Locri, 103: 'the beginnings of the virtues arise from nature, but their middle and end from exercise of the body through gymnastics and medicine, and from exercise of the soul through education and philosophy'. *Kakhexia* denotes general bad physical health; in later medical Greek literature it acquired a more specific sense referring to a particular kind of chronic disease. It is mentioned several times in the fragments of Chrysippus as an example of an overall poor state of the body analogous to a similar state of the soul (fr. 471.25; Diogenes Laertius 7.106); and according to Tieleman (2003, 159 and 165), the medical language in Stoic sources goes further than just analogy, since within the Stoic conception of the soul and emotions as corporeal (cf. *SVF* 2.886) it makes perfect sense to speak of the state of the body as a source of moral corruption, and of regimen as a contributing factor to moral health (cf. also *SVF* 1.285–87 on the Stoic Zeno's melancholic temperament, and see Tieleman 2003, 165–66). Finally, a parallel may be noted in Clement of Alexandria, *Miscellanies* 7.16.102, about God wishing people to turn away from evil caused by *amathia*, *abelteria* and *kakhexia* ('ignorance, stupidity and bad bodily health').

658 In the background here is the Platonic view that no one does evil knowingly, which is referred to also in Plato's discussion of mental illness in *Timaeus* 86D7–E2.

659 Bodily mixture (*krasis*, i.e. a proportion between elementary qualities) as a predisposing factor towards immoderate behaviour is already found in Aristotle's discussion of 'the melancholics' as examples of people prone to lack of self-control (*akrasia*) and to pursuing bodily pleasure as a result of their physical state; see *Nicomachean Ethics* 1150b25, 1152a17ff. and 1154b3ff; see van der Eijk (2005b) 149–52 and (2005a) 133–35 (and above, n.502). The idea, as well as its corollary that one can improve one's ethical and intellectual performance by physical measures such as regimen and drugs, is central to Galen's work *That the Faculties of the Soul Follow the Mixtures of the Body* and was well-known in late antiquity; see van der Eijk (2005a) 133–35.

660 The association of anger with (bitter) bile was common in Greek thought from Homer onwards (cf. *Iliad* XVIII.108–10) and is noted by Nemesius below in 81.3; the specific association between those with a bodily mixture determined by bitter (yellow) bile and irascibility is found in the 1st-century CE medical writer Aretaeus of Cappadocia, *Causes and Signs of Acute Diseases* 1.5.1.

661 Telfer translates *katôphereis* 'lewd' (cf. LSJ s.v.), while Burgundio has *tristes*; the latter, however, is unlikely considering that in ancient temperament theory sadness and despondency were usually associated with the elementary qualities cold (and dry). Sexual immoderateness is related to a moist constitution also by Plato, *Timaeus* 86C–D (esp. D3–5: *tên henos genous hexin ... rhuôdê kai hugrainousan*).

and knowledge, while a bad state of the body is to be cured bodily, changing it as far as possible into a mean bodily mixture by a suitable mode of life, by exercise, and by drugs if we need them as well.⁶⁶² (5)

SECTION 18

ON PLEASURES⁶⁶³

Pleasures of the body and pleasures of the soul. Natural and necessary pleasures. Intellectual pleasures. Plato's distinction between false and true pleasures. The Epicurean definition of pleasure criticised. Differentiation of pleasures according to the different senses and the different activities of the mind.

Some pleasures are of the soul, some of the body.⁶⁶⁴ Those are of the soul which belong to it by itself, such as those involving study and contemplation, for these and similar pleasures belong to the soul alone.⁶⁶⁵ Those are bodily which come about through the joint involvement of the body and the soul and are therefore called (10) bodily, such as those involving eating and sexual intercourse. There are no specific pleasures to be found that belong to the body alone, only affections⁶⁶⁶ such as cuts, discharges and those involving

---

662 Cf. Plato, *Timaeus* 87B7–8: 'one should try to avoid evil both by upbringing and by intellectual pursuits'; 87D1–3: 'In order to bring about health and disease, virtue and vice, no balanced proportion (*summetria*) or lack of proportion (*ametria*) is of greater importance than that of the soul itself in relation to the body itself'; and 89A6: 'In order to restore and sustain the body, the movement of the body by means of exercises is best ... Second is the movement through sea travel ... The third type of movement is useful if it is really necessary but should not by any means be tolerated by anyone who is sensible, viz. medical purgation by means of drugs.' Curability of ethical faults by physical means seems also implied by Aristotle (*Nicomachean Ethics* 1154b12 with the discussion by Demont 2005) and in Stoic moral theory (*SVF* 3.229) with the discussion by Tieleman (2003) 162–66.

663 This section presents a good example of Nemesius' way of reworking traditional material: he draws from a range of sources (though possibly through intermediaries), especially Aristotle's discussion of pleasure in *Nicomachean Ethics* 7 and 10, Plato's *Philebus* and Epicurus, but he uses this material to suit his own Christian argument. For an analysis of Nemesius' sources for this section see Evangelides (1882) 1–20; see also Domański (1900) 120–21.

664 Cf. Aristotle, *Nicomachean Ethics* 1117b28, where 'ambition' (*philotimia*) and 'love of learning' (*philomatheia*) are given as examples of pleasures in which the body is not affected.

665 On the pleasures derived from 'contemplation', i.e. theoretical study, see Aristotle, *Nicomachean Ethics* 1153a1, 1153a22, 1174b21.

666 *Pathê*: see n.641 above. Presumably, Nemesius thinks of bodily affections and processes which we are not aware of, such as involuntary emission of semen during sleep (cf. 85.23–24),

the mixture of qualities. For every pleasure includes sensation and we have shown that sensation belongs to the soul.[667] It is clear that 'pleasure' is one of those [words] that have many senses: for they fall under different genera, such as (15) good and bad pleasures, or the false and the true,[668] or some that are of thought alone, involving knowledge, and some that are together with the body involving sensation, or among those involving sensation some that are natural, some that are not. Again, the pleasure of drinking is opposed to the distress of thirst, but nothing is opposed to the pleasure of contemplation. All these points show that 'pleasure' has many senses.

(20) Of what are called bodily pleasures some are both necessary and natural,[669] without which life is impossible, such as nourishment which satisfies a need and necessary clothing: some are natural but not necessary, such as natural and lawful sexual intercourse. For this contributes to the survival of the whole race, but it is possible to live without it in abstinence. (25) But some pleasures are neither necessary nor natural, such as drunkenness and lewdness and **[77]** gorging beyond need. For these neither contribute to the continuance of our race, as does lawful sexual intercourse, nor to the maintenance of life, but even harm them. But one who lives a godly life should pursue only those pleasures that are both necessary and natural, while he who comes after him (5) in the second rank of virtue[670] may pursue those that are natural but not necessary in a way, to a degree, at a time and at a place which is fitting: others are altogether to be avoided.

---

digestion etc. For being cut cf. Aristotle, *Nicomachean Ethics* 1173b12–13 (but note that this phrase is obelicised by Bywater); see also Nemesius' rendering of Cleanthes' argument in 2, 21.5–6 above and his response in 21.19–22.

667 Above, 56.5.

668 See below, 77.20ff.

669 The terms 'necessary' and 'natural' are applied to desires for specific types of pleasure by Epicurus in his *Letter to Menoeceus* 127ff. (see Long and Sedley [1987] vol. 1, Texts 21B and 21I, pp. 113ff.), as indeed is the whole threefold distinction. Nemesius' understanding of the types – (1) necessary and natural: food and clothing; (2) natural but non-necessary: sex; (3) neither necessary nor natural: excess in (1) and (2) – is the same as that attributed to Epicurus by the Anonymous commentator *On Aristotle's Nicomachean Ethics* (*CAG* 20, p. 171.23–28 Heylbut = Usener 456), except that there (3) is concerned rather with *specific types* of (1) and (2). By contrast, in the scholion on Epicurus, *Principal Doctrines* 29 (= Long and Sedley [1987] 21I), (1) is exemplified by drinking when thirsty, (2) by expensive food, and (3) by political honours. Against Nemesius' and the Anonymous' interpretation is Epicurus' subdivision of the necessary desires; cf. Sharples (1996) 86–87 and 143 n.6. See also Evangelides (1882) 13 n.25.

670 Telfer notes (1955, 353 n.1) that this hierarchy probably reflects Nemesius' belief in degrees of moral perfection according to a Christian scale of asceticism. It may be added also that in Platonic and Aristotelian philosophy there is a tendency to regard the contemplative life as superior and the active life secondary (cf. *EN* 1178a9ff.).

Generally speaking, one should estimate those pleasures to be good that are not associated with distress, do not lead to regret, do not bring about some other harm, are not (10) excessive, and which do not draw us away far from good works or enslave us. Pleasures in the most proper sense are those somehow arising with or bound up with the knowledge of the divine, the sciences and the virtues, which should be included in those which are to be especially sought after in the first instance, not as simply pleasant nor as contributing to the survival of the race, but because they contribute to our well-being and our being (15) worthy and beloved by God and to the very fulfilment of man in soul and intellect. These are neither cures for sufferings, as are those that fill a need,[671] nor do they have any distress that precedes, follows or is opposed to them, but they are pure and unmixed with any material ingredient and are purely of the soul.

Furthermore, according to (20) Plato,[672] some pleasures are false, some true. Those are false which come about with sensation and false belief and are involved with distress;[673] those are true which are of the soul itself and by itself, involving knowledge, intellect and wisdom, pure and unmixed with distress and on which no repentance ever follows.[674] They call those pleasures that follow on (25) contemplation and good deeds not affections but experiences.[675] Some **[78]** say that such a pleasure is properly called joy.[676] They

671 The so-called 'restorative pleasures': see 78.3–5 below and Aristotle, *Nicomachean Ethics* 1153a1; 1154a26ff.; 1173b8–10.
672 *Philebus* 36C–42C.
673 Nemesius seems to be interpreting the false pleasures of the *Philebus* in terms of the contrast that follows them in the text, that between mixed pleasures and pure pleasures – a view which has found some support among modern interpreters of the *Philebus*, though it may be questioned whether it is an accurate interpretation of Plato to assimilate the two notions of false pleasure and mixed pleasure in this way.
674 This seems to amount to the views of Antisthenes: cf. Athenaeus 12, 513A, and Plato, *Philebus* 51B–52B.
675 According to Telfer, this is a Stoic distinction, but we have been unable to find occurrences except in Sextus Empiricus, *Against the Mathematicians* 7.384, where, however, the distinction between *pathos* and *peisis* is quite different from what it is here in Nemesius. Chrysippus (*SVF* 2.934) makes a distinction between *poiêsis* and *peisis* but again this is different from what we find here. (Psellus, *Short Works on the Soul* 28.4, refers to Plato for the distinction, but this seems to be dependent on Nemesius). See, however, next note.
676 According to Diogenes Laertius (7.116), the Stoics distinguished between *khara* (philosophically founded rational elation) and *hêdonê* (a false emotion relating to what is only apparently good); cf. Chrysippus, *SVF* 3.434; see also Galen, *On Hippocrates' Epidemics VI* 4.26 (242.26 Wenkebach, 17B.210 K) and Plutarch, *On the Impossibility of Living Pleasantly according to Epicurus* 1092D. See also Epicurus fr. 7.1.3 Arrighetti (= Diogenes Laertius 10.136), where *khara* is defined as kinetic, *hêdonê* as static.

define pleasure as a perceptible process of becoming a natural state.[677] But this definition seems to be of bodily pleasure only: for this is a certain replenishment and cure of bodily deficiency and of the distress brought about by the deficiency. (5) For, when we are cold or thirsty, as we treat the distress arising from the cold and thirst, we take pleasure in being warmed and in drinking. So these pleasures are contingently good, not such in themselves nor naturally.[678] For as being brought to health is contingently a good, while being healthy is naturally good and good in itself, so these pleasures are contingently good since they are a kind of cures, but (10) the pleasures of contemplation are good in themselves and naturally so; for they do not arise from a deficiency. It is clear from this that not every pleasure is a replenishment of a deficiency.[679] If that is the case the definition saying that pleasure is a perceptible process of becoming a natural state is not sound: for it does not include all pleasures, but leaves out that arising from contemplation.

(15) Epicurus also, by defining pleasure as the gradual removal of everything that causes distress,[680] says the same as those who say that it is a perceptible process of becoming a natural state. For he says that pleasure is freedom from what causes distress. But since no process of becoming is the same or similar in kind to its own products,[681] the process of a pleasure's coming to be cannot be thought to be pleasure, but something else beside pleasure. For a (20) process of becoming consists in coming to be, but nothing that is coming to be simultaneously comes to be and has come to be: it clearly does so gradually, whereas what is found pleasant is found pleasant all at once. So pleasure is not a [matter of] coming to be.[682] Further, all coming to be is of something that is not [yet] present, whereas pleasure is something that is already present. Further, all coming to be is said to be

---

677 This view, presumably held by Aristippus (cf. Plato, *Philebus* 53Cff.), is referred to by Aristotle in *Nicomachean Ethics* 1152b17, but subsequently criticised in 1153a13–15.

678 For 'contingent' (*kata sumbebêkos*) pleasures see Aristotle, *Nicomachean Ethics* 1154b17–20: 'By "contingent" I mean pleasures that are curing (*iatreuonta*); for in such cases cure takes place through the agency of something underlying which is healthy, and that is why it appears to be pleasant; but naturally pleasant are those that bring about the action of a given nature.'

679 Cf. Aristotle, *Nicomachean Ethics* 1173b15–18.

680 *Principal Doctrines* 3 (Arrighetti, p. 121): 'The definition of the extent of pleasures is the removal of all that causes distress. For where what is pleasant is present, as long as it is present, there is no pain nor distress nor the combination of the two.'

681 Cf. Aristotle, *Nicomachean Ethics* 1152b13.

682 Cf. Aristotle, *Nicomachean Ethics* 1174a13–b14.

quick or slow, but pleasure is not.[683] Further,[684] of things that are good some are dispositions, some (25) activities, some instruments: a disposition is as an excellence, an activity as action in accordance with the disposition; and again, vision is a disposition, but seeing is an activity. Instruments are the means to our activity, as are the eye, the foot and the like. All powers of the soul that are concerned with things good and bad are powers of certain dispositions: **[79]** so whether a pleasure is something good or something bad will depend on these alone, but it is not a disposition: for it is neither so as an excellence (if it were it would not so easily fall into its opposite, distress), nor as that which is opposed to a deficiency:[685] for there cannot be a disposition towards and a deficiency with regard to the same matter, whereas some people simultaneously experience pleasure and (5) distress, like those who scratch themselves.[686] So pleasure is not a disposition. But nor is it an instrument: for instruments are for the sake of something else and not for their own sake, whereas pleasure is not for the sake of something else but for its own sake. Therefore it is also not an instrument.[687] It remains that it is an activity, which is why Aristotle defines it[688] as the activity of a natural disposition that is unimpeded: for things which impede a natural disposition are distressing. But (10) happiness is also the unimpeded activity of a natural disposition.[689] So it comes about that according to this definition happiness is pleasure, and the definition is faulty. Therefore he corrected it by defining pleasure as the goal of a living being's unimpeded natural activities, so that pleasure is bound up with and exists with happiness, but happiness is not [the same thing as] pleasure.[690] Yet not every (15) activity is a movement, but

683 Cf. Aristotle, *Nicomachean Ethics* 1173a31–b7.

684 The argument that follows uses ideas from Aristotle's *Nicomachean Ethics* to reject the Epicurean view of pleasure as a process of coming to be. It strongly breathes a Peripatetic atmosphere, though exact parallels in the commentary tradition on the *Nicomachean Ethics* are difficult to find.

685 We adopt Morani's text here and see no reason to follow Evangelides in deleting the section *oute gar hôs arête sterêsis* (1882, 16–17 n.37).

686 For the example see Plato, *Philebus* 46A–B.

687 Aspasius (*On Aristotle's Nicomachean Ethics* 42.13–20) argues that pleasure and pain are not the instruments of virtue.

688 Cf. Aristotle, *Nicomachean Ethics* 1153a14–15; cf. 1173a30.

689 Cf. Aristotle, *Nicomachean Ethics* 1153b14–19.

690 *Nicomachean Ethics* 1153b9. It is interesting to note that, while Aristotle certainly provides an argument for *eudaimonia* being *a* pleasure, (i) he uses the expression 'what is best' (1153b7, 13), not *telos* (though he does use *teleios* at 1153b16–17); (ii) he does not present the formulation including *telos* or 'what is best' as a general definition of pleasure as such, and certainly not as a 'correction' of the more general definition; (iii) the argument is dialectical and

there is also an activity which is without movement, through which the first God acts:[691] for the first author of movement is unmoved.[692] The activity of men in contemplation is also of that sort: for it is without change. For what is contemplated and the thinking of him who contemplates remain always one and the same. For contemplation is about what is one and the same. But if the pleasure of contemplation, which is the greatest, (20) most proper and true, is without change, it is clear that those pleasures which involve lesser changes are superior and greater proportionally as the changes are lesser.

Pleasures are divided into different species in conjunction with their activities, for there are as many species of pleasure as there are of activity, and the pleasures of good activities are good, those of bad activities are bad.[693] It is also clear that the pleasures arising from each of the different senses are also different in kind.[694] (25) For the pleasures of touch and taste are different, and those of sight, [80] hearing and smell are different. The purer pleasures are those of the senses that give pleasure without being in close proximity to the object of sense, such as sight and hearing and smell. There are also two species of intellectual activities: one intellectual activity is practical, one theoretical: so it is clear that there are also two species of pleasures which follow upon these activities, (5) and of these the theoretical is purer than the practical.[695] The intellectual pleasures are peculiar to man as such. For those that are of the senses he has in common with the other animals, as an animal. But since some delight in some, some in other pleasures of the senses, it is not those that appear good to bad men but those that appear good to good men that are good in themselves.[696] For in all matters the good judge is not just anybody but the (10) man of understanding and in a natural state.

(arguably) expressed in hypothetical form (*eiê an*, 1153b12), even if Aristotle would not reject the conclusion. Aspasius, interestingly (*On Aristotle's Nicomachean Ethics*, 150.31), presents this argument in Aristotle as directed against those who say that pleasure is not a *telos* or 'what is best', but he does not go so far as building *telos* into the definition.

691 The Greek text reads *kath' hên ho prôtos energei theos*, a remarkable expression for a Christian writer to use; but rather than following Evangelides (1882, 18 n.39) in emending the text to *kath' hên prôtos energei ho theos*, we prefer to think that Nemesius is following the terminology used by his (presumably Peripatetic) source or arguing dialectically.

692 Cf. Aristotle, *Nicomachean Ethics* 1154b24–26.
693 Cf. Aristotle, *Nicomachean Ethics* 1175b25ff.
694 Cf. Aristotle, *Nicomachean Ethics* 1176a1ff.
695 Cf. Aristotle, *Nicomachean Ethics* 1139a27–36; 1175a15.
696 Cf. Aristotle, *Nicomachean Ethics* 1176a15ff.

SECTION 19

ON DISTRESS[697]

Different kinds of distress. Contemplation and moderation as means of overcoming distress.

There are four kinds of distress:[698] shock, grief, envy and pity.[699] Shock is distress that renders one speechless, grief is distress that weighs one down, envy is distress (15) over the goods of others, pity distress over the evils of others. All distress is bad of its own nature. For even if a good man[700] will sometimes be distressed when worthy men or children perish or a city is sacked, still it is not in a primary way or purposely but because of the circumstances. Even in these matters the man given to contemplation[701] will be altogether unmoved, having made (20) himself a stranger to the things of this world and bound himself to God, while the good man will have moderation in his emotions in such circumstances, without excess and without making himself a captive of them, but rather overcoming them.

Distress is opposed to moderate pleasure as evil to good, but to excessive pleasure as evil to evil.[702] But there are excesses only in bodily pleasures: for the pleasures of contemplation,[703] which are a kind of extreme and attain perfection, do not admit of excess, nor is distress their opposite, nor do they occur as a cure of preceding distress.[704] **[81]**

697 The word here, and elsewhere in this version, translated as 'distress' is *lupê*. It is commonly translated as 'pain': but 'pain' is the name of a certain type of unpleasant sensation which, like many others, is distressing. Nemesius is discussing some kinds of emotional states that are distressing, not just pain. Contrary to the Peripatetic Andronicus, who in his book *On Affections* lists 25 varieties of distress, Nemesius lists only four (see next note).

698 What follows is essentially a Stoic account of distress (see Stobaeus, *Anthology* 2.7.10 [p. 92.7ff. Wachsmuth] and Diogenes Laertius 7.111–12), although Nemesius mentions only four of the nine different kinds of distress recognised by Zeno; see also Domański (1900) 121–22.

699 Greek *akhos, akhthos, phthonos, eleos.*

700 *Spoudaios*, distinguished in the next sentence from the man devoted to contemplation, who is superior. This reflects the same hierarchy as above, 77.3–4 and 11–19.

701 Cf. above, 77.3–4 and 11–14. This characterisation strongly reflects that of the Stoic sage. Gillian Clark points out to us that the influence of the philosophical tradition on Nemesius is here so strong that it may raise problems from the Christian point of view.

702 This reflects the Aristotelian idea of virtue as a mean between two extremes. The same point is made at Alexander, *Ethical Problems* 7 (127.35–128.2); see also 5 (125.5–6, 126.3–5) and 16 (137.5–9) with the discussion in Sharples (2001a) 599 n.594.

703 See above, 76.8 with note.

704 Aristotle, *Nicomachean Ethics* 1154b15–17 combined with 1154a28–29 comes close to

SECTION 20

ON ANGER[705]

Different kinds of anger; the relationship between anger and reason; righteous anger.

Anger is the boiling of the blood in the region of the heart[706] arising from an evaporation of bile or from turbidity. That is why it is called bile[707] and also anger.[708] Sometimes anger is also the appetite for retaliation.[709] For when we are wronged, or think we are, (5) we are angry and then our feeling becomes a mixture of desire and anger.[710] There are three sorts of anger, wrath[711] (which is also called bile and anger),[712] grievance[713] and vindictiveness.[714] For anger

---

implying this. Aspasius (*On Aristotle's Nicomachean Ethics* 156.26 and 157.1) makes the reference to contemplation in the Aristotle passage explicit; and the point is also made explicitly at Alexander, *Ethical Problems* 6 (126.20–32) and 7 (127.23–28, 127.34–128.2); see Sharples (2001a) 598 n.586.

705 We follow Morani and all MSS in printing the present section on anger before that on fear – contrary to Matthaei and Telfer, who put the section on fear first. (On the reasons for the latter see Burkhard [1910]: Matthaei claimed that two Munich MSS [A and a in Morani's discussion (1981)] had the reverse order, but according to Burkhard this is in fact false. Burkhard suggests that Matthaei got his ordering from Ellebodius, and that he in turn got it from John of Damascus; Burkhard ends his paper by arguing that John changes the order of items in the lists within sections and may well have changed the order as well.)

706 This definition is given, e.g., by Aristotle in *On the Soul* 403a31 and is often cited in philosophical discussions of anger (*thumos* or *orgê*) as illustration of what Aristotle calls the 'material cause' of anger; the addition 'arising from an evaporation of bile or from turbidity' presumably derives from a medical source (for the association of bile and anger see next note), although we have been unable to identify an exact parallel (it is also mentioned by Eusthatius in his commentary on the *Iliad*, vol. 4.113); see Domański (1900) 127 n.1.

707 Gk. *kholê*, which usually refers to the bodily fluid 'bile' associated with anger.

708 Gk. *kholos*, a term used for anger since Homer.

709 This definition also stems from Aristotle's *On the Soul* 403a30, where it is given as an example of the formal definition of anger (as opposed to the material; see note 706 above).

710 The word translated here as 'anger' is *thumos*, which Nemesius uses throughout this section; but here, the specific combination with *epithumia* ('desire') suggests that we may have to think of the 'spirited' (*thumoeides*) and the 'desiderative' (*epithumêtikon*) parts of Plato's non-rational soul.

711 Gk. *orgê*.

712 Again *kholê* and *kholos* are used here.

713 Gk. *mênis*, the term used by Homer for Achilles' wrath in the *Iliad*. The definition given here is also found in Arius Didymus (?), '*Doxography B*', in Stobaeus, *Anthology* 2.7.10c,3 (p.75.8), in an account of Stoic ethics, and in the Scholia on Aristophanes' *Frogs* verse 844.

714 Gk. *kotos*. The definitions given here in the following sentence are also found in Arius

that has a beginning and changes[715] is called wrath or bile or anger; grievance is bile that broods, for it is called that because it lasts and is stored in the memory; vindictiveness is anger that watches for a chance for vengeance, and is called that because it lies in wait.[716] But anger is the guard of reason:[717] for when reason judges an event worthy of resentment, then anger comes forth against it, if they maintain their natural and proper relationship.[718]

SECTION 21

ON FEAR

Different kinds of fear. Its physical reactions. Galen's view on the abdomen as the seat of distress.

(15) Fear is divided into six kinds, into hesitation, modesty, shame, terror, consternation and anguish.[719] Hesitation is fear of approaching action, terror is fear from an overwhelming impression, consternation is fear from an unusual impression, anguish is fear of failure and misfortune (for we feel anguish when we fear that we will be unsuccessful in our activities), modesty (20) is fear in expectation of blame (which is a very good feeling), shame is fear because of evil done (and this also is not without hope of redemption). Modesty differs from shame in this way, that he who is ashamed is depressed by what he has done, [82] but the modest person is afraid to suffer some loss of reputation.[720] The men of old often call both modesty shame and shame

---

Didymus (?), 'Doxography B', in Stobaeus, *Anthology* 2.7.10c,3 (p.75.9).

715 I.e. a process which develops, as opposed to a stationary state.

716 *Keisthai*, a pun on *kotos* also mentioned by Eusthatius in his commentary on the *Iliad* (2.615; 3.618; 1.401) and in the Scholia on Sophocles' *Ajax* (41a.2)

717 Cf. Plato, *Timaeus* 70B2–C1.

718 This, again, reflects the Platonic view of the 'spirited' (*thumoeides*) part of the soul being the executor of the instructions of the rational part. It is interesting to see that Nemesius sees a proper place for anger and does not regard it as something to be avoided at all cost. Cf. Romans 12:19.

719 The terms used here are *oknos, aidôs, aiskhunê, kataplêxis, ekplêxis* and *agônia* respectively. As in section 19, these distinctions and their definitions are probably Stoic in origin, even though they do not entirely correspond with the relevant lists given in Diogenes Laërtius 7.112–13 (*deima, oknos, aiskhunê, ekplêxis, thorubos, agônia*) and Stobaeus 2.7.10 (*oknos, agônia, ekplêxis, aiskhunê, thorubos, deisidaimonia* and *deos*).

720 Exactly the same contrast between *aidôs* and *aiskhunê* is found in the anonymous commentator *On Aristotle's Nicomachean Ethics* (CAG 204.7–9). A similar point, though not the contrast between *aidôs* and *aiskhunê*, is found in Alexander, *Ethical Problems* 21 (142.1).

modesty, abusing the terms.[721] Fear arises through a chill, as all warmth runs together into the heart, seeking that which rules over it,[722] just as (5) the people, when they are afraid, take refuge with their rulers. The organ of distress is the mouth of the abdomen:[723] for it is this that feels the bite when one is in distress, as Galen says in the third book of his work on proof[724] in this sort of way: 'When people are distressed, not a little of the yellow bile runs down into the stomach, which produces the bite they feel, and they do not cease to be (10) distressed and to feel the bite until they vomit the bile out.[725] For the bite occurs for them below the cartilage at the middle of the

721 This seems to be a correct observation: cf. Aristotle, *Nicomachean Ethics* 1128b29–30. But distinctions between the two (though different from the one here) were made by Aristoxenus, fr. 42a.4 (*aidôs* being more restricted in application to age group, virtue, experience and reputation) and also in Ptolemy the Grammarian, *Differences between Words* p. 395.10 (*aidôs* being used more generally, *aiskhunê* in relation to errors one has made oneself).

722 The association between fear and cold was very common in Greek thought (Aristotle, Galen, etc.; see references in Domański [1900] 124). 'That which rules over it' renders *to arkhikon*, the control centre of bodily heat, i.e. the heart. Thus there is no need to take this as a reference to the Stoic view of 'the ruling part of the soul' (*to hêgemonikon*) and its location in the heart (as implied by the inclusion of this passage as a fragment of Chrysippus in *SVF* 3.416.23), which would force one to suppose that Nemesius inadvertently, by adopting the terminology from his Stoic source, implies the cardiocentric view here as opposed to the Galenic-Platonic encephalocentric view to which he seems committed elsewhere (and which Galen forcefully defends in the passage in *On the Doctrines of Hippocrates and Plato* that Nemesius seems to have been using; see next note).

723 Cf. Galen, *On the Doctrines of Hippocrates and Plato* 2.8.4–5 (158.7–13 De Lacy, 5.273 K): 'Thus I pointed out that the argument based on speech [as used by the Stoics] starts from position, and this is true also of the argument based on inhalation and exhalation. And you will find that it is the same with the argument from the pain that accompanies distress of the mind; for the pain is clearly at the mouth of the stomach, but they [the Stoics] refer it to the heart. Now if they hold that because the heart is placed close to the mouth of the stomach, therefore the affection begins from the heart, they are arguing from position; but if they think that the pain is actually in the heart itself, they are quite mistaken.' See also *On the Causes of Symptoms* 2.3 (7.168 K).

724 Galen's lengthy work *On Proof* or *On Demonstration* (*Peri apodeixeôs*, in 15 books) has not been preserved, but is referred to by himself on numerous occasions, especially in *On the Doctrines of Hippocrates and Plato*; the fragments and testimonies have been studied by Müller (1895); his discussion of the present passage is on pp. 457–58. Nemesius refers to it also in 23.25 (above), and it has been argued by Jaeger and Skard that this work served as a source for Nemesius (see our Introduction, 5.b, and n.226 above).

725 Cf. Galen, *On the Doctrines of Hippocrates and Plato* 2.8.17 (160.12–14 De Lacy, 5.276 K): 'For yellow bile collects in the stomachs of persons who are distressed or have exercised too strenuously; and being irritated by it, they suffer heartburn (*daknomenoi kardialgousin*)' (tr. De Lacy). For similar points see *On the Properties of Foods* 1.1.9 (204.26 Helmreich, 6.459 K), which speaks of a sense of 'irritation', *dêxis*, in the stomach caused by yellow bile; *On the*

sternum which is called ensiform.[726] The heart is situated much above it. For the abdomen is below the diaphragm and the heart above it. The ancients were accustomed to call heart the mouth of the abdomen as well,[727] as did Hippocrates,[728] and (15) Thucydides in his account of the plague, saying: "Sometimes it established itself in the heart and upset it, and all the purgings of bile that have been given a name by physicians followed on".[729] For what was upset is the mouth of the abdomen which was forced to vomit, not the internal part that is the heart.'[730]

Usefulness of the Parts 5.4 (1.260.19–21 and 264.20–22 Helmreich, 3.355 K and 3.361 K); *On Hippocrates' Aphorisms* 1.2 (17B.359 K). Morani prints the closing quotation mark here, but it may well be that the quotation continues until the end of the section, for all the following points coincide almost verbally with points made by Galen (see next notes).

726 See Galen, *On the Doctrines of Hippocrates and Plato* 2.8.6 (158.13–15 De Lacy, 5.274 K): 'For the pain is below the thorax under the cartilage of the sternum' (tr. De Lacy); on the term 'ensiform' (*xiphoeidês*) see Galen, *On Anatomical Procedures* 5.7 (313.23 Garofalo, 2.513 K; 314.3 Garofalo, 514 K; 317.9 Garofalo and 516 K).

727 *Kardia*, the word translated as 'heart', was also used to refer to what in modern anatomy would be called the orifice of the stomach. Galen himself comments on this usage in *On the Doctrines of Hippocrates and Plato* 2.8.7–12 (158.17–30 De Lacy, 5.274–75 K): 'Nor does the term heartburn signify that the heart enclosed in the thorax suffers pain; there is an identity of names that deceives no one who is familiar with the writings of the ancients. For the ancients called not only the organ in the chest but also the mouth of the stomach "heart", and they often use the word in this meaning.' Galen goes on to refer to passages in Nicander, Hippocrates' *Epidemics* 2 and the Thucydides passage mentioned by Nemesius (see below), which he also quotes in *On Hippocrates' Prognostic* 3.35 (360.21 Heeg, 18B.286 K). See also Hippocrates, *Prorrheticon* 1.72 (186 Potter, 5.528 L.); Galen, *On the Preservation of Health* 6.14 (194.30 Koch, 6.444 K); *On the Affected Parts* 5.6 (8.339 K); (Ps.?)Galen, *Introduction or Physician* 13 (14.735 K); Caelius Aurelianus, *Acute Affections* 2.30.161; Alexander of Aphrodisias, *On the Soul* (98.22–24). See Harris (1973) 114 n.2.

728 See previous note; Galen refers to *Epidemics* 2.2.1 (5.84 L.), where the verb *kardialgein* ('suffer heartburn') is used. We see no compelling reason to follow Morani's bracketing of this reference and the one to Thucydides (on the strength of its absence in the Armenian version).

729 Thucydides 2.49.3 (with slight textual variations), also quoted by Galen in the passages from *On the Doctrines of Hippocrates and Plato* 2.8.11 and *On Hippocrates' Prognostic* cited in n.727 above.

730 Cf. Galen, *On the Doctrines of Hippocrates and Plato* 2.8.6 (quoted in n.726 above) and 2.8.18 (160.15–21 De Lacy, 5.276 K): 'my only purpose at present is to show that neither heartburn nor the irritation in distress is an affection of the heart – the internal organ – but that the symptom is in the mouth of the stomach' (tr. De Lacy). On the question as to where the quotation from Galen ends see note 725 above.

ON THE NATURE OF MAN 145

SECTION 22

ON THE NON-RATIONAL ELEMENT THAT IS NOT CAPABLE OF OBEYING REASON

Nutrition, generation and pulsation; the former called natural, the latter vital.

(20) This, then, is the condition of the part that is capable of obeying reason. To that which is not capable of obeying reason belong the nutritive, the generative and pulsation. The nutritive and generative are called natural;[731] pulsation is called vital. [83]

SECTION 23

ON THE NUTRITIVE FACULTY

The four faculties of nutrition, and the bodily parts involved in the processing of nutriment and the disposal of waste products.

There are four faculties of the nutritive element, those of attraction, retention, alteration and separation.[732] For each part of an animal's body naturally

---

731 The distinction between *phusikon* ('natural') and *zôtikon* ('vital') is first attested in Galen (but may be of older, Hellenistic origin) and became widespread in late antique physiological theory: while the latter is the most basic function (as constituted by heartbeat and pulsation), the former is more complex and involves sustenance and long-term preservation; cf. *On Prediction from Pulses* 4.12 (9.424 K), with the same distinction between nutrition being natural and pulse vital; *Synopsis on Pulses* 21 (9.492 K), where heartbeat is called 'vital' and nutrition 'natural' and associated with the liver; *On Hippocrates' Prorrheticon* 2.4 (56.4–8 Diels, 16.598 K); and *On Hippocrates' Epidemics VI* 1.3 (18.4–13 Wenkebach, 17A.821 K). It is also found in Ps.Alexander's *Medical Problems* 1.16–17 Ideler and *On Fevers* 6.1–2. (The distinction between 'vital' pneuma on the one hand and 'psychic [*psukhikon*] pneuma' or 'rational [*logikon*] pneuma' on the other is already found in the fragments of Erasistratus, Zeno and in the works of Philo.) Nemesius differs from Galen in that the latter relates nutrition and pulsation to the spirited part of the soul and reproduction to the desiderative part of the soul (cf. *On the Doctrines of Hippocrates and Plato* 6.1.15, 364.2–6 De Lacy, 5.509 K) whereas Nemesius classifies both as belonging to nature rather than soul and as incapable of obeying reason.

732 The account that follows is the standard Galenic doctrine of nutrition and digestion as set out in *On the Natural Faculties*, esp. 1.5, 1.6, 1.8, 1.10–12 and summed up in 3.8 (229.14–22 Helmreich, 2.177 K): 'Thus ... we have demonstrated each of these four faculties

draws to itself its appropriate nourishment, and, having attracted it, retains it, and, having retained it, (5) transforms it into itself and thus extrudes the waste.[733] These are the faculties which provide the nourishment of the parts of the body, and from them come growth both in height and in girth. Waste is separated out through the stomach, through urine, through vomiting, through sweat, through the mouth, through the nostrils, through the ears, through the eyes, through breath and through the invisible channels.[734] The (10) other forms of excretion are very obvious: that through the ears is what is called wax, which is the dirt of the ear, from the eyes come tears and rheum, from breathing out the smoky breath from the heat of the heart.[735] Invisible channels is the name they give to the respiration of the whole body, through which most of the vapours from the depths of the body and the contraction of the arteries come out through the porosity of the skin.[736] (15) The organs

---

existing in the stomach – the attractive faculty in connection with swallowing, the retentive with digestion, the expulsive with vomiting and with the descent of digested food into the small intestine – and digestion itself we have shown to be a process of alteration' (tr. Brock); see also 3.13 for a summary of the whole process of digestion. See further *On the Usefulness of the Parts* 4.1–6 (which focuses more on the anatomical structures facilitating nutrition and digestion), *On the Doctrines of Hippocrates and Plato* 6.8 and the summary of the latter in Oribasius, *Medical Collections*, Books of uncertain order, ch. 8, which may have been an additional source for Nemesius in the present section. The present distinction between the various faculties (*helktikê, kathektikê, alloiôtikê, apokritikê*) is also referred to in *On Hippocrates' Epidemics VI* 5.1 (256.17–19 and 259.2–3 Wenkebach, 17B.228 and 233 K); *On Hippocrates' Epidemics III* 1.17 (46.13–14 Wenkebach, 17A.558 K); *On Hippocrates' On the Nature of Man* 2.5 (64.22 Mewaldt, 15.124 K); *On Affected Parts* 5.8 (8.358 K); *On Mixtures* 3.1 (91.3–5 Helmreich, 1.654 K); *On Differences between Symptoms* 4 (7.63 K), and *On Differences between Fevers* 2.14 (7.381 K).

733 Cf. Galen, *On the Natural Faculties* 3.9 (230.1–3 Helmreich, 2.178 K): 'These four faculties have been shown to be necessary for every part that is to be nourished'.

734 This is the doctrine of skin-breathing, explained below in 83.12–14, which Galen adopted from predecessors; its history goes back to Empedocles; see Furley and Wilkie (1984) 3–39.

735 The use of the term *lignuôdes* ('smoky'), and of *aithalôdes* ('sooty') further down (85.19), suggest a Peripatetic-style oven analogy, according to which the heart is the location of a quasi-combustion process central to the entire functioning of the organism. Although Galen's physiology differs in some ways from the Aristotelian picture, Galen did adopt the theory of the role of innate heat in the processing of nutriment and the heart's role in the generation of natural *pneuma*.

736 Cf. Galen, *On the Natural Faculties* 1.17 (152.21–22 Helmreich, 2.70 K): 'that which passes off as sweat or imperceptible perspiration' and 2.6 (172.13–14 Helmreich, 2.98 K): 'what is evacuated through what doctors call imperceptible perspiration'; *On Hippocrates' Aphorisms* 6.2 (18A.10 K): 'The perspiration called invisible by doctors empties [the body] of its finest residues in the form of vapours (*atmoeidôs*)', and *On Black Bile* 4 (77.25–26 De Boer, 5.117 K).

ON THE NATURE OF MAN 147

of the nutritive faculty are the mouth, the stomach, the abdomen, the liver, all the veins, the intestines, both kinds of bladder[737] and the kidneys. For the mouth first prepares the food for the abdomen by cutting it up into small portions with the teeth and the tongue. For the tongue provides the greatest assistance for chewing by aggregating (20) the food and placing it under the teeth, in the way that corn-girls provide corn to the mill-stones with their hands:[738] for in a way the tongue is a hand in the chewing process.[739] When the food has been worked on in this way it is sent to the abdomen through the stomach: for the stomach is not only the organ that is sensitive of lack of food,[740] but also a channel for foods.[741] For it reaches up to the gullet, (25)

---

737 There are two possible ways of interpreting *hai kholai amphoterai*: (i) to take it to refer to the gall bladder and the urinary bladder, or (ii) to the two fluids yellow bile and black bile. The former is probably preferable here in the light of what is said further down in 84.11–12 about the role of the gall-bladder (there is no reference to the urinary bladder there, but its function is probably subsumed under that of the kidneys: cf. Galen, *On the Formation of the Embryo* 5.18 [90.9–10 Nickel, 4.686 K]). However, it is strange, on this interpretation, that Nemesius would use the expression *kholai amphoterai* instead of *kusteis amphoterai*, the latter of which would have been the Galenic way of referring to the two bladders (cf. *On the Natural Faculties* 3.4 [214.12–13 Helmreich, 2.156 K]: *kusteis amphoterai ... kholêdokhos ... hetera*; cf. also Galen, *On the Formation of the Foetus* 5.18 [90.8 Nickel, 4.685 K], which speaks of *kusteis duo*, and Ps.Alexander, *Problems* 2.60 [I.71.2–3 Ideler], which distinguishes between the *kholêdokhos kustis* and the *ourêdokhos kustis*), whereas *amphoterai kholai* in Galen normally refers to the two fluids yellow bile and black bile (cf. *On Differences between Fevers* 2.11 [7.374 K]). So linguistic usage would support the other interpretation, which gains further plausibility from what Nemesius says below in section 28 (92.2–7), where the fluid yellow bile is given an important role in the digestive process (see note *ad loc.*). There is, however, no discussion of any digestive role of black bile in Nemesius neither here in section 23 nor in section 28. It is likely, therefore, that Nemesius mistakenly wrote *kholai amphoterai* when he meant *kusteis amphoterai*.

738 For a related food distribution metaphor cf. Galen, *On the Usefulness of the Parts* 4.2 (1.196.1–7 Helmreich, 3.267 K): 'Just as city porters carry the wheat cleaned in the storehouse to some public bakery of the city where it will be baked and made fit for nourishment, so these veins carry the nutriment already elaborated in the stomach up to a place for concoction common to the whole animal, a place which we call the liver' (tr. May).

739 Cf. Galen, *On the Usefulness of the Parts* 11.4 (2.122.7–13 Helmreich, 3.855 K): 'Now the tongue plays no small part in this action, moving the nutriment about like a hand und turning it in the mouth so that every part of it may be equally broken up, and on the outside this massetic muscle, one on each side, has been prepared as a second hand to help the tongue' (tr. May).

740 Cf. Galen, *On the Usefulness of the Parts* 4.7 (1.201.23–202.2 Helmreich, 3.275 K): '[Nature] has granted to the stomach alone and particularly to the parts of it near its mouth the ability to feel a lack which arouses the animal and stimulates it to seek food' (tr. May); *On the Method of Healing* 10.4 (10.681 K).

741 Cf. Galen, *On the Usefulness of the Parts* 4.1 (1.195.13–18 Helmreich, 3.267 K): 'This storehouse, a work of divine, not human, art, receives all the nutriment and subjects the food to

seizes on the food and transmits it to the abdomen.⁷⁴² When the abdomen has received the food it separates what is good and nourishing from the stony and woody and what does not nourish,⁷⁴³ transforms the good part into juices,⁷⁴⁴ and sends them on to the **[84]** liver through the veins which draw [the juices] from [the nutriment] and channel them to the liver.⁷⁴⁵ These veins are like roots of the liver that draw the food from the stomach, as the roots of plants draw it from the earth.⁷⁴⁶ For the abdomen is like the earth which provides food to plants,⁷⁴⁷ (5) the veins which carry up the juice to the gates and hollows of the liver from the abdomen and the intestines through the intestinal membrane are like roots, the liver itself is like a stem,⁷⁴⁸ while the veins that are divided off from the hollow vein which grows off the bulging parts of the liver are like twigs and branches.⁷⁴⁹ For the liver, when it has

---

its first elaboration, without which it would be useless and of no benefit whatever to the animal; *On the Method of Healing* 4.7 (10.297 K).

742 Cf. Galen, *On the Usefulness of the Parts* 7.7 (1.387.3–11 Helmreich, 3.532 K).

743 Cf. Galen, *On the Natural Faculties* 3.4 (213.24-214.1 Helmreich, 2.156 K): 'Then, when [the food] has been completely digested, the lower outlet opens and the food is quickly ejected through it, even if there should be amongst it abundance of stones, bones, grape-pips, or other things which cannot be turned into juice' (tr. Brock, modified); *On the Usefulness of the Parts* 4.1–4 (1.195–98 Helmreich, 3.266–72 K).

744 This is the process of *khulôsis*, conversion of nutriment into bodily juices, referred to by Galen in *On the Natural Faculties* 3.4 (213.18 Helmreich, 2.155 K).

745 Cf. Galen, *On the Usefulness of the Parts* 4.1.

746 For this metaphor see Galen, *On the Anatomy of Veins and Arteries* 1 (2.780 K): 'The veins arriving into the stomach and the intestines are similar to roots', and 9 (2.817 K): 'the vein at the gate of the liver, which ... like roots takes up the nutrition with its extremities'; *On the Doctrines of Hippocrates and Plato* 8.1.27 (486.17–20 De Lacy, 5.656 K); *On Hippocrates' Prorrheticon* 3.8 (117.11 Diels, 16.728 K).

747 Cf. Aristotle, *On the Parts of Animals* 650a25; Galen, *On the Affected Parts* 6.3 (8.395 K): 'The liver attracts the food from the stomach through the veins in the mesenterion just like trees attract [water] from the earth through their roots.'

748 Cf. Galen, *On the Doctrines of Hippocrates and Plato* 6.3.41 (382.24–28 De Lacy, 5.532 K): 'The veins that descend to the stomach, then, are like roots, as Hippocrates himself pointed out when he said "For as the earth is to the trees, so the stomach is to the animals" (Hp. *On Humours* 11 [5.490 L.]), and the vena cava is as it were the trunk that grows from the convex surface of the liver and moves directly from the liver to both parts of the animal, the upper and the lower' (tr. De Lacy); *On the Usefulness of the Parts* 16.2 (2.377 Helmreich, 4.266 K); *On the Anatomy of Veins and Arteries* 1 (2.780 K).

749 Cf. Galen, *On the Doctrines of Hippocrates and Plato* 8.1.27 (486.17–20 De Lacy, 5.656 K): 'For it was shown that in plants the parts are thickest where they grow out from their source, and that in the case of the two previously demonstrated sources, that of the nerves and that of the arteries, some parts were trunks, as it were, close to their sources, and others, like branches, were generated as the trunk advances' (tr. De Lacy); *On Hippocrates' On the Nature of Man* 2.6 (73.25 Mewaldt, 15.143 K).

received the juice from the abdomen, cooks it and makes it like itself,[750] (10) and since its flesh is very similar to blood it transforms the juice into blood, as one would expect.[751] The blood is purified through the spleen and the gall-bladder and the kidneys.[752] The spleen draws off the dregs and makes them its own food,[753] the gall-bladder takes off the bitter element that remains in the juices from the food,[754] the kidneys remove the serous matter along with (15) what remains of the bitter,[755] so that what remains and becomes blood

750 Cf. Galen, *On Black Bile* 7 (89.10–23 De Boer, 5.139–40 K).
751 Cf. Galen, *On the Usefulness of the Parts* 4.3 (1.197.5–9 Helmreich, 3.269 K) and 4.12 (1.218.24–219.2 Helmreich, 3.298 K): 'There remains, then, as the principal instrument of sanguification and source of the veins, only the so-called flesh of the liver, ... Indeed, if one observes carefully the nature of this flesh, it obviously seems very closely akin to blood' (tr. May), and further passages in 4.13 (1.222.15–16 Helmreich, 3.303 K and 1.224.21–24 Helmreich, 3.306 K); see also *On the Doctrines of Hippocrates and Plato* 6.8.27 (412.26–30 De Lacy, 5.570 K).
752 Cf. Galen, *On the Natural Faculties* 2.9 (201.15–16 Helmreich, 2.138 K): 'the blood is purified both by the spleen and by the bladder beside the liver' (tr. Brock); for the role of the kidneys see *On the Usefulness of the Parts* 4.6 (1.200.11–22 Helmreich, 3.273–74 K).
753 For the role of the spleen see *On the Usefulness of the Parts* 4.15 (1.232.14ff. Helmreich, 3.316ff. K); *On the Natural Faculties* 2.9 (197.11 Helmreich, 2.132 K). 'Dregs' is a frequent metaphor in Galen in contexts of nutrition: see *On the Usefulness of the Parts* 4.2 (1.197.23 Helmreich, 3.270 K); *On the Natural Faculties* 2.9 (139.10 Helmreich, 2.135 K); *On Hippocrates' Aphorisms* 4.21 (17B.682 K); *To Glauco on the Method of Healing* 2.12 (11.139 K); *On the Composition of Drugs according to Places* 10.2 (13.237 K). See also [Aristotle]/ [Alexander] *Supplementary Problems* 1.9 Kapetanaki and Sharples (2005) = [Aristotle], *Probl. ined.* 1.9 Bussemaker = [Alexander], *Problems* 3.9 Usener: 'The spleen, attracting the dregs of the blood from the liver, attracts a larger quantity of blood along with it because there is an abundance, and this happens more, when it has its attractive [faculty] strengthened; for it is from "attracting" (*epispan*) that it has been called "spleen"', with their note ad loc. comparing Meletius, *On the Nature of Man* 20 (*Anecdota Oxoniensia* 3 103.13–14 Cramer) and Leo, *Synopsis on the Nature of Man* 68 (CMG 10.4 52.7–8 Renehan), using the same term as here for 'dregs'; also Orion, *Etymologicum* s.v. *splên* (143.27–28 Sturz); *Etymologicum Magnum* s.v (724.17–18 Gaisford); and ps.-Zonaras, *Lexicon* s.v. (1663.16–17 Tittmann). 'Spleen' and 'attract' are used in close proximity, without any explicit allusion to the etymology, by Galen, *On the Method of Healing* 11.16 (10.796 K); also [Ar.]/[Alex.] 1.17 (= 1.17 = 3.17) ad fin.: 'Blood is analogous to wine in blending and substance. For as we have explained that wine has four parts, in the same way also does blood. For it has the watery part which the kidneys attract, and similarly what is analogous to a bloom, which the gall-bladder attracts, and *the thick [part] like dregs which the spleen attracts*, and the wine-like and pure part [itself] of the blood which is given off in the body like wine and nourishes the parts.'
754 Cf. Galen, *On the Natural Faculties* 2.12 (235.18–236.11 Helmreich, 2.185–86 K); *On the Doctrines of Hippocrates and Plato* 6.4.13–14 (386.10–21 De Lacy, 5.536 K).
755 I.e. once the spleen has done its work. Cf. Galen, *On the Usefulness of the Parts* 14.13 (2.330.3–10 Helmreich, 4.201 K).

is pure and good to be shared out as nutriment to the other parts of the body through the veins that are divided off to go to them. Thus each part draws in the blood, retains it and transforms it into its own specific nature, and sends on what is superfluous to the neighbouring parts when it has become nourishment suitable to them.[756] (20) In this way all parts are fed and grow and continue on blood, while the liver is directing this.[757]

This part of the non-rational part is said not to be capable of obeying reason since it carries out its specific work not according to our judgement or choice, but naturally.[758]

SECTION 24

ON PULSATION

The origin of pulsation in the heart, and its expansion and contraction through the arteries. The threefold structure of veins, arteries and nerves.

(25) The pulsating motion is also called a vital power, since it originates from the heart[759] and especially from its left cavity which is **[85]** called the pneumatic,[760] and it distributes the natural and vital warmth to every part of the body through the arteries,[761] as the liver distributes nourishment through the veins.[762] Therefore, when the heart becomes abnormally[763] hot the whole

---

756 Cf. Galen, *On the Natural Faculties* 3.6 (216.24–217.9 Helmreich, 2.160 K)

757 The image is of the liver as a *khorêgos*, a conductor of a chorus. Again, this image derives from Galen: *On Hippocrates' Epidemics VI* 5.9 (277.16–17 Wenkebach, 17B.258 K); *On the Method of Healing* 7.13 (10.527 K); *On the Doctrines of Hippocrates and Plato* 6.4.1 (384.2 De Lacy, 5.532 K).

758 This looks like a structuring comment by Nemesius linking different material found in his sources. The distinction between 'natural' and 'psychic' is developed further below, 25, 85.23–24, the whole of section 27, and 28, 89.19.

759 For the connection between 'vital' (*zôtikê*) and 'heart' in Galenic physiology see n.731 above.

760 Cf. Galen, *On the Usefulness of the Parts* 7.8 (1.391.8–9 Helmreich, 3.538 K): 'the left cavity of the heart is the only one to contain pneuma'; *On the Doctrines of Hippocrates and Plato* 6.8.37 and 41 (5.473–4 K); *On Differences between Pulses* 4.2 (8.702 K).

761 On the role of the heart and the arteries in regulating innate heat throughout the body cf. Galen, *On the Usefulness of the Parts* 4.12 (1.220.11–12 Helmreich, 3.300 K), 4.13 (1.222.12–13 Helmreich, 3.303 K) and 6.21 (1.372.1–2 Helmreich, 3.511 K).

762 This has just been shown in the previous section, 84.1–5.

763 'Abnormally': the words *para phusin* are left out here by the Ms. H and deleted by Matthaei, and by Matthaei also (but apparently not by H) in the next line. But they give good

body also immediately becomes abnormally hot, and it grows cold when the heart grows cold. For (5) the vital breath[764] is scattered from the heart through the arteries into the whole of the body. In most cases,[765] these three, vein, artery and nerve, are divided off in conjunction with each other from the three principles that manage the body, the nerve from the brain which is the principle of motion and sensation, the vein which is the vessel for blood from the liver which is the principle of blood and nutrition, the artery (10) which is the vessel for breath from the heart which is the principle of life.[766] Being together with each other they gain each other's help. For the vein provides blood for the nerve and the artery, the artery shares with the vein the natural warmth and vital breath.[767] Hence it is not possible to find

---

sense, for both excessive heat and cold are unnatural states compared to the mean of natural heat (cf. Galen, *On the Causes of Pulses* 1.5 (9.7 K); and the next sentence ('For the vital breath...') is appropriate as an explanation if *para phusin* is kept, whereas it would be redundant if these words were deleted.

764 The word translated 'breath' is *pneuma*. This process of 'scattering' is achieved by pulsation.

765 I.e. in most animals.

766 This tripartition of organs (brain, heart and liver) with their corresponding connecting vessels (nerves, arteries and veins) and functions (motion and sensation; sustenance of basic life functions; blood supply and nutrition) is, again, standard Galenic doctrine and can be found throughout Galen's work, especially in *On the Doctrines of Hippocrates and Plato* (particularly books 6, 8 and 9, e.g. 6.1.2 [360.7–13 De Lacy, 5.506 K] and 9.9.7 [598.28–600.4 De Lacy, 5.793 K]), *On the Natural Faculties* 1.6–7 and *On the Usefulness of the Parts* (e.g. 1.16; 15.6). Galen builds on the Hellenistic medical distinctions between veins and arteries (Praxagoras, late 4th century BCE) and the discovery of the nervous system (Herophilus and Erasistratus, early 3rd century BCE); Erasistratus' notion of a threefold texture, the *triplokia*, constituted by veins, arteries and nerves, is especially of interest here (frs. 86–90 Garofalo). But Galen makes important modifications, e.g., concerning the natural presence of blood in the arteries, which was denied by Erasistratus (except in some non-natural circumstances) but affirmed by Galen – and, following him, by Nemesius here. By contrast, Lammert (1941, 129–31, followed by Telfer 1955, 366 n.1) has argued that Nemesius draws not on Galen but on Hellenistic medical sources here and represents an 'important departure' ('bedeutende Abweichung', p. 131) from Galenic teaching on this very point – the natural presence of blood in the arteries: 'Galenos selbst hat zwar auch die Dreiteilung der Gefässe, jedoch keineswegs in dieser Zuspitzung des Erasistratos, die ja gerade Galenos, wie wir sahen, in einer besonderen Abhandlung [i.e. *On Whether Blood is Naturally Present in the Arteries*] so leidenschäftlich bekämpt hat, mit ihrem Betonen des Pneuma in den Arterien. An Galenos als Quelle für Nemesios c. 24 Peri sphugmôn ist also nicht zu denken', p. 129). However, we feel that this is inconsistent with 85.18–20, where Nemesius subscribes to the possibility of there naturally being blood in the arteries in full accordance with Galen (see n.768).

767 In the Ms. D the sentence continues 'and the nerve provides sensation to these and to the whole of the body', and this is included in the text by Matthaei. We follow Morani (and all the other textual witnesses.) in leaving it out. See also note after next.

an artery without (15) light[768] blood nor a vein without vaporous breath.[769] The artery expands and contracts strongly according to a certain rhythm and ratio, the origin of its motion being from the heart. As it expands it draws light blood forcibly from the adjacent veins, which is vaporised and becomes food for the vital breath.[770] As it contracts it empties the sooty element[771] (20) in it through the whole body and through the invisible channels,[772] just as the heart thrusts out its smoky impurities through the mouth and the nose in exhalation.[773]

768 *Lepton haima*; cf. Galen, *On the Doctrines of Hippocrates and Plato* 6.8.36 (414.30–33 De Lacy, 5.572–73 K): 'But the blood that is yellow, warm, fine-parted (*leptomeres*), resembling *pneuma*, is first generated in the left ventricle of the heart, and the arteries distribute and carry this kind of blood to the whole animal' (tr. De Lacy). The natural presence of blood in the arteries is argued for by Galen in a separate treatise, *Whether Blood is Naturally Present in the Arteries*.

769 In the Ms. D the sentence continues 'nor a nerve without sensation', which is included in the text by Matthaei. We follow Morani (and all the other textual witnesses) in leaving it out.

770 Cf. Galen, *On the Usefulness of the Parts* 6.10 (1.328–30 Helmreich, 3.450–52 K), 6.17 (1.361–63 Helmreich, 3.496–98 K); *On the Usefulness of Pulses* (5.156 K); *On the Doctrines of Hippocrates and Plato* 6.8.38–39 (416.6–9 De Lacy, 5.573 K).

771 On this evacuating effect of systolic movement see Galen, *On the Usefulness of the Parts* 7.9 (1.396.17–23 Helmreich, 3.545 K): 'It is likewise proper to sing [Nature's] praises because in the contraction of the heart she pours off all that is sooty and smoky in it [*aithalôdes en autêi kai lignuôdes*, the same terms as those used by Nemesius here; PJvdE] through these same arteries and even more through the great artery into the others, thus providing safely that the heat in the heart should never be smothered by noxious residues and quenched' (tr. May, slightly modified); *On the Doctrines of Hippocrates and Plato* 8.8.7 (528.32–33 De Lacy, 5.709 K): 'by their contraction the arteries squeeze out as much of the humours in them as has become sooty and smoky (*aithalôdes kai kapnôdes*)' (tr. De Lacy); *On the Causes of Pulses* 1.5 (9.7 K); *On Prediction from Pulses* 2.1 and 3.7 (9.272 and 9.384 K); *Synopsis on Pulses* 9 (9.459 K); *On the Causes of Diseases* 3 (7.15–16 K); *On Hippocrates' Epidemics VI* 5.5 (274.10–11 Wenkebach, 17B.253 K).

772 See above, 83.9 and 12 with note.

773 See above, 83.7–9, and the passage from Galen's *On the Usefulness of the Parts* 7.9 (1.396.17–23 Helmreich, 3.545 K) quoted in n.771, which provides an almost verbal resemblance to what Nemesius is saying here.

SECTION 25

ON THE GENERATIVE OR SEMINAL FACULTY

Generation and its organs, the veins and arteries. The formation of semen out of blood, its transmission through the body. The female contribution, and Galen's correction of Aristotle's theory on this.

The generative faculty also belongs to that part which is not capable of obeying reason; for we eject semen in dreams without wishing to, and the desire for (25) sexual intercourse belongs to nature,[774] for we are moved towards it when unwilling. But the activity is incontestibly up to us and involves the soul: for it is accomplished through the organs that are subject to impulse,[775] and it is in our power to abstain and conquer the impulse. **[86]**

The organs of the seminal power are, to start with, the veins and the arteries.[776] For in these the seminal fluid is first generated by the transformation of blood, as milk is in the breasts. Indeed, this fluid is the nourishment of these vessels,[777] for originally they come to be from semen. (5)

---

774 I.e. not to the soul, as distinct from the act of sexual intercourse mentioned in the next line.

775 For 'movement according to impulse' see section 27 below.

776 The account that follows is, again, Galenic and shows strong, sometimes verbal similarities to Galen's *On Semen* and sections from *On the Usefulness of the Parts* 14.9–14 (see also the summary of this in Oribasius, *Medical Collections*, Books of uncertain order, ch. 9, which may have been an additional source for Nemesius). For the role of veins and arteries in the production of seed see *On Semen* 1.12.3–12 (106.20–108.14 De Lacy, 4.555–57 K): 'An artery and a vein are observed to go to each of the testicles, not in a straight path, as they do to all other parts, but twisting first in many shapes, like grape tendrils or ivy ... And in these many twists that they make before reaching the testicles you can see the blood gradually growing white', and 1.14.6–10 (114.5–21 De Lacy, 4.562–63 K); *On the Doctrines of Hippocrates and Plato* 7.3.29 (446.3–8 De Lacy, 5.608 K): 'Nature, needing to fashion semen and milk with precision, ... contrived for them a lengthy stay in the organs of coction and for that reason provided for semen the spiral (*helix*) before the testes and for milk the length of the vessels that go to the breasts...' (tr. De Lacy); and *On the Usefulness of the Parts* 14.10 (2.316.5–318.15 Helmreich, 4.183–86 K) and 16.10 (2.419.9–420.25 Helmreich, 4.321–23 K): 'both milk and semen are generated from perfectly concocted blood. It is the length of time which the blood spends in the vessel conducting it that permits the perfect concoction of these ... In the brain, these arteries nourish the psychic pneuma.' As in section 24, we are unable to follow Lammert (1941, 132ff.) in arguing that Nemesius is departing from Galenic doctrine and drawing on Hellenistic medical theory.

777 *Tôn angeiôn toutôn* can be taken as a reference either to the veins and the arteries in general (Telfer) or to the breasts (as seems to be Urmson's view: 'for the nourishment of these

The arteries and veins, then, cook the blood into seminal fluid for their own nourishment, but the superfluity of their food becomes seed.[778] For first it is carried up over a long period to the head, and again it is carried down from the head through two veins and two arteries. For this reason, if someone cuts out the veins beside the ears and beside the (10) carotid arteries he makes the animal sterile.[779] These veins and arteries become the spiral and varicose bundle[780] beside the scrotum, whence the seminal fluid drops out into each of the testicles:[781] in these it is finally turned into semen,[782] and through

---

receptacles is this fluid'). The use of *toutôn* ('these') might seem to favour the second option; moreover, on the first interpretation it is difficult to see how veins and arteries can both be said to originate from semen ('for originally they come to be from semen') and to be the generators of semen – which is also the problem for which Galen criticises Aristotle in *On Semen* 1.12.15 (108.19–23 De Lacy, 4.557 K). But perhaps this difficulty can be resolved by assuming that veins and arteries, like all parts of the body, come to be from semen (at the formation of the body) and then subsequently, once in existence, start producing semen in turn (from blood) which serves them as nutriment: the point about the veins' and arteries' origin in the seed is then that its suitability as nutriment to the veins and arteries is made clearer by the consideration that they stem from this themselves.

778 Cf. Galen, *On Semen* 1.17.5 (140.26–142.2 De Lacy, 4.590 K).

779 These veins and arteries are mentioned by Galen in *On Hippocrates' Epidemics VI* 5.22 (301.3–7 Wenkebach, 17B.283 K, on the Hippocratic passage *Epidemics* 6.5.15 [5.320 L.], where the cutting of these vessels is recommended in the treatment of *kedmata*, an affection of the hips), and in *On the Dissection of Veins and Arteries* 9 (2.823 K); and their cutting is discussed in *On Affected Parts* 3.12 (8.202 K), *On the Composition of Drugs according to Places* 4.1 (12.706 K), and in *On Venesection* 23 (11.313 K). However, that the cutting of these vessels might damage fertility – an idea found in the Hippocratic treatises *Airs, Waters, Places* 22.3 (2.78 L.) and *On Generation* 2 (7.472 L.) – is rejected by Galen in his commentary on the passage in *Airs* (cited by Jouanna 1996, 340). Thus in this respect, Nemesius draws on a different tradition and seems to be at odds with Galen.

780 On this structure see Galen, *On Semen* 1.15.8–10 (116.14–23 De Lacy, 4.565 K): 'The artery and the vein, starting out from the vessels along the spine, are carried down through the flanks until they reach the so-called epididymis. That is a part of the animal placed at the head of the testicle, as the name itself indicates, and many tubes full of seminal fluid extend from it to the testicle. The artery and the vein grow alongside this epididymis at the convolution (*helix*) mentioned a little earlier [1.14.8–10, 114.10–21 De Lacy, 4.563 K], and they send a short branch from themselves to it before they grow into the testicle. Indeed the spermatic duct, which some call the varicose helper, draws the semen from there and carries it up to the outgrowth of the pudendum' (tr. De Lacy); 1.15.65–74 (130.1–132.7 De Lacy, 4.578–80 K); and *On the Usefulness of the Parts* 9.4 (2.12.23 Helmreich, 3.700 K).

781 We follow Morani (and Matthaei) in omitting the next sentence 'one artery and one vein full of semen', which is clearly a gloss.

782 The role of the testicles in the formation of semen is a point on which Galen insists throughout *On Semen* (against Aristotle), especially in 1.14–16.

ON THE NATURE OF MAN 155

the varicose helper[783] behind the testicles it is separated out (15) with air, because an artery, too, is involved in emitting it.[784] That it is transmitted also from a vein is clear from lewdness. For when men have intercourse over a long period and use up the seminal and generative fluid, they then emit pure blood through the violent suction.[785]

Women have all the same parts as men, but inside and not outside.[786] Aristotle (20) and Democritus maintain that female sperm contributes nothing to the generation of offspring.[787] For they maintain that what is given off by women is sweat of the relevant part rather than seed.[788] But Galen

783 *Kirsoeidês parastatês* is a technical term first attested for Herophilus (see von Staden 1989, frs. T 101–03, T 105, T 189–90, and his discussion on pp. 166–67, 296 and 392) probably referring to what in today's anatomy is called the *ductus deferens*; the 'assistance' provided by this structure was presumably believed to consist in the transportation of the semen to the testicles and to the penis. The term is mentioned several times by Galen in *On Semen*, e.g. in 1.15.11 (116.22 De Lacy, 4.565 K), 1.16.5 (134.5–6 De Lacy, 4.582 K): 'Herophilus gave the name "varicose helper" to the part of the spermatic vessel that lies close to the penis'; 1.16.25 (138.8 De Lacy, 4.587 K); and *On the Usefulness of the Parts* 14.11 (2.321.10–11 Helmreich, 4.190 K).

784 As mentioned above (85.5), the arteries were believed to be the natural channels for the transmission of breath (*pneuma*). The view that, during ejaculation, *pneuma* is emitted from the body together with the semen, is found also in Aristotle (*Generation of Animals* 728a10; *History of Animals* 586a15; *Problems* 953b38–39).

785 Cf. Aristotle, *On the Generation of Animals* 726b7; Theophrastus, *Enquiry into Plants* 9.18.9; Galen, *On Semen* 1.16.23 and 25 (136.25–27 and 138.10–11 De Lacy, 4.586–87 K); Herophilus, T 191.16–19 von Staden 1989 (with discussion on pp. 292–95); and [Ar.]/[Alex.], *Supplementary Problems* 2.28 (= 2.28 = 4.28: cf. above, n.753), 'Why do those who engage in intercourse more often sometimes emit blood? Because when the substance of seed has been exhausted there is no moisture more ready than blood.' Cf. *Bamberg Problems* 37 (cited by Kapetanaki and Sharples [2005] 133 n.249), which simply says 'the substance of semen (i.e., blood) is discharged'.

786 The view that the woman also contributes 'seed' to the reproductive process is attested in the Hippocratic Corpus (*On Generation* 6; see Lonie [1984] and Lesky [1951]) but became a contested issue (see Pseudo-Plutarch, *Tenets* 5.5), with Aristotle rejecting it. Galen, however, reinstates it and defends it at great length in book 2 of *On Semen* (and in sections of *On the Usefulness of the Parts* 14.10), where he discusses the female 'testicles', 'spermatic vessels' and the female 'seed' itself.

787 It is certainly true that Aristotle vigorously denied that women contribute seed to generation: see especially *Generation of Animals* 1.20. But for Democritus, precisely the opposite view is attested in Pseudo-Plutarch, *Doctrines* 5.5.1 (the inconsistency is listed by Diels in his note to DK 68 A 143; see also Lesky [1951] 1297).

788 Aristotle frequently refers to a secretion of fluid by women during intercourse, but he does not call it 'sweat' but 'moisture' (*hugrasia* or *hikmas* or *hugrê apokrisis*), e.g. in *Generation of Animals* 727b36ff., 739b1. Only in *History of Animals* 635b19 (whose Aristotelian authorship is not certain) is the moisture a woman experiences in the orifice of the uterus during intercourse compared to a 'local sweating' (*hidrôma tou topou*).

156   NEMESIUS

condemns [87] Aristotle and says that women have seed and the mixture of both seeds makes the embryo.[789] That, he says, is why copulation is also called mixture in Greek.[790] But, [according to Galen], women do not have perfect seed like a man's, but it is still uncooked and rather watery.[791] As such the woman's seed becomes nourishment for that of the man.[792] From (5) it a portion of the fetal membrane[793] round the horns[794] of the womb is solidified, and also the so-called sausage-like membrane which is a receptacle for the residues from the embryo.[795]

789 Cf. Galen, *On Semen* 2.1 and 2.4.
790 Galen frequently uses words such as *mixis* and *meignunai* in *On Semen*, e.g. in 1.7.4 (86.20 De Lacy, 4.536 K), 2.6.3 (198.3 De Lacy, 4.643 K) to denote sexual intercourse; and in 2.3.4–5 (168.2–6 De Lacy, 4.616 K) he speaks (though in a polemical context) of 'an inborn desire for uniting and combining' (*henôseôs kai mixeôs*). See also *On Hippocrates' Epidemics VI* 5.26–27 (304.14ff., 308.25ff. and 309 Wenkebach, 17B.284 K) and *On the Preservation of Health* 6.14.2 (194.32ff. Mewaldt, 6.444 K).
791 Cf. Galen, *On Semen* 2.4.24 (176.13–14 De Lacy, 4.624 K): 'Indeed the female is wetter and colder, the male hotter and dryer. It is reasonable then that the one lacks something for the precise perfection of the semen, and the other cannot have a residue of blood because by its heat and dryness it expels all the moisture' (tr. De Lacy); see also 2.2.2 (162.4 De Lacy, 4.610 K) and 2.2.22 (166.5–11 De Lacy, 4.615 K).
792 Cf. Galen, *On Semen* 2.4.33 (178.6–10 De Lacy, 4.625 K): 'It has been shown, therefore, that the wetness and coldness of the female are necessary in those animals in which nature fashions the animal in the uterus to resemble the conceiver. For what earth is to plants, this the mother is to such animals, irrigating them with nutriment until the whole animal has been completely formed' (tr. De Lacy).
793 This is the so-called *khorion*, discussed by Galen in his work *On the Anatomy of the Uterus*, ch. 10 (50–58 Nickel, 2.902–08 K); it has been suggested by Nickel (1971, 91ff.) that Galen postulated the existence of this membrane in humans on the basis of animal uterine anatomy, esp. in pigs (*placenta diffusa*); and certainly the function Galen attributes to it is similar to that of the placenta, although his description of it is not entirely in accordance with human uterine anatomy. See also n.795.
794 These are the so-called 'horns' (*keraiai, kerata*) of the uterus, which in Galen presumably are to be identified with the Fallopian tubes (although again, as with the *khorion*, his description may have been inspired by animal rather than human anatomy): see *On the Anatomy of the Uterus* 3.1–3 (38.2 Nickel, 2.890 K, with the discussion by Nickel on pp. 69–71), *On Semen* 2.1.5 (144.14–15 De Lacy, 4.594 K), and *On the Usefulness of the Parts* 14.11 (2.323.18–22 Helmreich, 4.193 K): 'the horns, which are for the semen from the female's own testes. The horns accordingly tend upward toward the flanks, become gradually narrower and have extremely narrow ends where they are attached each to the didymus of its side' (tr. May). They are referred to also by Soranus (*Matters Related to Women* 1.14) and already attributed to Diocles (frs. 23a–e van der Eijk, although there is considerable confusion in the sources as to what exactly Diocles meant by this: see the discussion in van der Eijk [2001] 38–42). For the history of the concept 'horns of the uterus' see Holl (1921).
795 Cf. Galen, *On Semen* 1.7.15–19 (88.20–90.5 De Lacy, 4.538–39 K): 'Then in time …

ON THE NATURE OF MAN 157

The female in each kind of animal accepts the male when she is able to conceive. Therefore those that are always able to conceive always accept intercourse, as do hens and doves and humans.[796] (10). But the others avoid intercourse when they are pregnant, while a woman always admits it. For while hens accept intercourse almost every day because they give birth almost every day, women have free will about intercourse after conception as in other matters. For non-rational animals are ruled not by themselves but by nature, and receive limits and a determined season. (15)[797]

SECTION 26

ANOTHER DIVISION OF THE POWERS CONTROLLING LIVING BEINGS

Psychic, natural and vital powers – the former being within our control, the latter two beyond control.

They[798] divide the powers of living beings in yet another way,[799] calling some psychic, some natural, some vital, with psychic those involving choice, natural and vital those not involving choice. The psychic are of (20) two sorts,

---

a vessel is formed, which is attached to the vessel of the uterus and similar to it. ... This outer membrane is called the *khorion*; through it pass the arteries and the veins that bring matter from the uterus to the fetus. The other membrane, which reaches up to the horns, was given its name from its shape, being similar to a sausage. It also got a name taken from that source. Its usefulness to the embryos in the first days is that which I just now mentioned, but as they grow it serves as a receptacle for one of the liquid wastes' (tr. De Lacy). On the functions of these membranes see also *On Semen* 1.10; *On the Usefulness of the Parts* 14.7.

796 Cf. Aristotle, *On the Generation of Animals* 749b15; *History of Animals* 544a31; 558b12–13; 558b21.

797 We do not follow Morani's bracketing of lines 10–15, which are absent from the Armenian tradition.

798 As in previous cases (e.g. section 15) no names are mentioned. The distinction between 'psychic', 'natural' and 'vital' in relation to three different kinds of *pneuma* goes back to Hellenistic physiological theory (Erasistratus' distinction between *pneuma zôtikon* and *pneuma psukhikon* and Chrysippus' distinction between *pneuma phusikon* and *pneuma psukhikon*; see Galen, *On the Doctrines of Hippocrates and Plato* 1.6), and is systematised by Galen (see n.505 above and *On the Movement of Muscles* 2.5 [4.440 K]). The distinction between 'vital' and 'natural' has already been referred to above in 82.22 and throughout section 24. 'Psychic' pneuma has been mentioned above in 56.3, 64.10, 68.12 and 69.20.

799 Previous divisions had been in accordance with 'the parts of the body' (cf. 71.7), and according to 'functions' or 'faculties' (72.4)

158   NEMESIUS

movement according to impulse and sensation.[800] The kinds of movements according to impulse are those of change of place and movement of the whole body, speech and breathing. For it is in our power to do these things and not to do them. The natural and the vital are those not in our power but occur both when we want it and when we do not want it, like nourishment and growth and production of seed, which are natural, (25) and pulsation, which is vital.[801] The organs of the rest have already been described,[802] and we shall now describe those of movement according to choice.

SECTION 27

ON MOVEMENT ACCORDING TO IMPULSE OR CHOICE, WHICH BELONGS TO THE APPETITIVE PART

The physiology of voluntary movement: brain, nerves, muscles, tendons, hands and feet. Combination of the 'psychic' and the 'natural'; sensory and motor nerves.

The brain and the spinal cord, which is itself part of the brain, are the origin of movement according to choice or to impulse:[803] the organs which (5) grow from these are the nerves, the ligaments and the muscles.[804] Muscles

---

800 Sensation was called 'psychic' in 56.5 and 76.13 above.
801 See above, 82.20–22.
802 See above, 83.15ff.; 86.1ff.
803 Cf. Galen, *On the Movement of the Muscles* 1.1 (4.369–73 K); *On the Affected Parts* 2.5 (8.129 K) and 3.14 (8.209 K); *On the Doctrines of Hippocrates and Plato* 1.6.5–6 (78.31–80.4 De Lacy, 5.185–86 K), 2.4.42 (126.14–17 De Lacy, 5.238 K), and 8.8.11 (530.8–11 De Lacy, 5.709–10 K): 'The spinal cord itself comes from the brain, so that the nerves carry voluntary motion from the brain by way of the spinal cord to the muscles of the thorax' (tr. De Lacy); *On Hippocrates' Epidemics VI* 5.5 (271.7–8 Wenkebach, 17B.247 K). On the expression 'movement according to impulse' (*kinêsis kath' hormên*) see Inwood (1985) 250–55, who points out that the term, though Stoic in origin, in later antiquity lost its specific Stoic significance and came to stand for voluntary movement in general; that is certainly also the case in Nemesius here.
804 The relationship between these structures is set out by Galen in *On the Movement of Muscles* 1.1–2 (4.367–76 K) and summarised in *On the Doctrines of Hippocrates and Plato* 1.9 (94.11–96.11 De Lacy, 5.302–05 K); see also *On the Usefulness of the Parts* 1.17 (1.33.16ff. Helmreich, 3.47ff. K); 12.2 (2.187.21ff. Helmreich, 4.9–11 K); *On Anatomical Procedures* 1.3 (21.19–20 Garofalo, 2.233 K) and 14.2 (pp. 169–70 Simon); *On the Method of Healing* 6.4 (10.408–09 K).

consist of flesh, sinewy fibres and tendons interwoven with the fibres of the nerves: this is why some have thought them to be sensitive,[805] because of the sensation from the nerves bound up with them. A tendon is a compound of ligaments and thin nerves. A tendon (10) differs from a nerve in that every nerve is sensitive, round, rather soft and originates from the brain, while the tendon is harder, [originates] from bone, and is insensitive in itself and sometimes flat.[806]

The hands are an instrument for taking hold and very suited to the crafts. For if one takes away the hands, or only the fingers of the hands, (15) it makes a man totally useless for almost all crafts: that is why man alone, since he is rational and can acquire skills,[807] received hands from the Creator.[808] The feet are an instrument for moving about, for it is by means of them that we change our place.[809] Man alone sits down without needing any support: for he alone (20) bends his legs at the hip and the knee at two right angles, one inwards and one outwards.[810] So all movements by means of nerves and muscles belong to the domain of the soul[811] and are brought about by choice:

---

805 This is said of the nerves of the larynx by Galen in *On the Usefulness of the Parts* 7.14 (1.420.8–11 Helmreich, 3.578 K); but the general point of the muscles' lack of sensation is stated in *On the Movement of the Muscles* 1.1 (4.373 K).

806 We do not follow Morani in bracketing these lines (9–13: 'A tendon is ... band-like') on the strength of their absence from the Armenian tradition. For flat tendons see Galen, *On Anatomical Procedures* 1.5 (35.16 Garofalo, 2.246 K) and 5.2 (283.21 Garofalo, 2.489 K).

807 The connection between having intelligence and the possession of hands is given a teleological explanation in Aristotle, *On the Parts of Animals* 4.10 (687a2–23), a point taken up by Galen in *On the Usefulness of the Parts* (1.3.25ff. Helmreich, 3.5–7 K), the whole first book of which is a eulogy on the hand as the prime example of purpose in natural creation.

808 We do not follow Morani in bracketing these lines (14–17: 'For if ... Creator') on the strength of their absence from the Armenian tradition.

809 Cf. Galen, *On the Usefulness of the Parts* 3.4 (1.134.19ff. Helmreich, 3.184 K).

810 We do not follow Morani in bracketing these lines (18–21: 'Man alone ... outwards') on the strength of their absence from the Armenian tradition. The connection between man's being able to sit and man's being biped (and consequently his being able to stand right) is developed by Galen, *On the Usefulness of the Parts* 3.1 (1.126.22–127.4 Helmreich, 3.173 K): 'For in addition to all the other advantages man enjoys, he is the only one of all the animals who can conveniently sit down on his hip bones. This fact has indeed escaped most people; they believe that man alone stands erect but do not perceive that he is also the only animal that can sit' (tr. May) and 3.3 (1.131.15–134.18 Helmreich, 3.179–85 K). Aristotle makes the point about bending of joints in opposite directions at *On the Progression of Animals* 13 712a13ff. and *History of Animals* 2.1 498a3–31, and the point that only man sits down by implication at *On the Parts of Animals* 4.10 689b19ff., but he does not actually connect the two anywhere.

811 Lit. 'psychic' (*psukhikos*), the same term as that used in section 26 (87,18).

we have shown that sensations and speech are among these.[812]

That, then, is the rational distinction of the soul functions and the natural functions. The Creator, (25) in accordance with his supreme foresight, wove the functions of the soul together with the natural and vice versa.[813] For since the evacuation of superfluities is the task of the excretive **[89]** faculty, which is one of the natural faculties, in order that we should not unwillingly behave in an unseemly way by such ejection where, when and in circumstances in which we should not, he established muscles as warders over evacuations, thus bringing natural functions into the domain of the soul: so we can hold back evacuations on that account, (5) both often and for a long time.[814]

The sensitive and soft nerves are sent down from the central and frontal cavities of the brain, the harder ones governing movement from the posterior cavity and the spinal cord.[815] Those from the spinal cord are harder, and of

---

812 Sensation is called 'psychic' in 56.5, 76.13 and 87.20; speech was called 'part of movement according to impulse' in 72.10 and 87.21–22 and was discussed as a rational and deliberative faculty in 71.6ff. (If in 57.8 *phônêtikon* is read instead of *phantastikon*, the reference might be also to this passage.) As for sensation being up to us, the meaning must be that we can choose whether to look at something, to touch something, to taste something etc. But clearly it is not up to us what we see when we do look at something, nor can we switch off our senses of touch or hearing or smell in the same way that we can close our eyes. So, just like the case of respiration discussed in the next section, sensation is 'up to us' only in some respects.

813 For a discussion of this passage see Debru (2005) 95–97, who argues that for Galen the excretion of residues is an activity of the epigastric muscles and those of the diaphragm rather than, as Nemesius thinks, a 'mixed' activity involving both soul and nature. However, Nemesius just says the functions of nature and soul are 'woven together' and that the natural functions are 'brought into the domain' of the soul; neither – perhaps – goes quite as far as saying that the faculty of excretion is not just a natural one, and this might be deliberate. See also next note on the Galenic position.

814 The role of the muscles in keeping the evacuation of residues under control is set out by Galen in *On the Movement of Muscles* 2.8 (4.454–58 K); Galen calls the relevant muscles 'guards' (*phulakes*, 455 K) and 'overseers' (*ephistôtes*, 458 K, cf. the expression *pulôrous epestêse* here in Nemesius 89.3) and makes the same distinction between instruments/faculties of the soul (*psukhês*) and instruments/faculties of nature (*phuseôs*) (455 K) as Nemesius; see also *On the Usefulness of the Parts* 4.19 (1.245.25–246.18 Helmreich, 3.324–25 K): 'Nature has arranged all these matters admirably, and in addition to them there are the muscles which close the two outlets for the residues and are like bars to prevent continual and untimely elimination ... For all the muscles, being instruments of voluntary motion, do not allow the residues to be evacuated except at the command of reason, and here at the two outlets for the residues is the only instance in this whole long course of the natural instruments where there is an instrument of the soul' (tr. May, modified).

815 Galen, in *On the Usefulness of the Parts*, frequently says that the soft nerves have their origin in the brain whereas the harder ones originate from the spine; see e.g. 9.11 (2.30.24–26 Helmreich, 3.724 K); 9.14 (2.42.23ff. Helmreich, 3.741–43 K): 'the spinal medulla is the

these still more so the nerves from the lower portions of the spine. For the further (10) the spine extends from the brain, it itself and the nerves growing out from it are so much harder.

As we received our senses double, so also we have double growths of nerves:[816] for each vertebra of the spine sends out a pair of nerves, one of which goes to the right hand parts of the body, the other to the (15) left.[817] For almost the whole of our body is divided into two, to right and to left. For so are our feet and hands and each other part, as well as each sense-organ.

SECTION 28

ON RESPIRATION[818]

Respiration another combined activity of the psychic and the natural. The usefulness of respiration: preservation of innate heat and nourishment of psychic pneuma. The bodily parts involved in breathing: muscles, bronchial tubes, lungs, vessels, the nose and the mouth.

Respiration, too, is one of the functions belonging to the soul: for it is muscles that (20) expand the thorax,[819] which is the most important organ of respiration, and the panting sighing breath occurring in great distress shows it to be an activity of the soul.[820] It is also within our power at need to control changes

source of all the hard nerves and the lower end of it gives rise to the hardest; the brain is the source of all the soft nerves and the median part of its anterior portion is set aside for the softest; the region where that brain and the spinal medulla meet is the source of the substance of the intermediate nerves' (tr. May, slightly modified); and 16.3 (2.385.12–15 Helmreich, 4.276 K); but, once again, the differentiation between different cavities/ventricles of the brain as sources of different kinds of nerves (and corresponding activities) is not found in Galen and seems to represent a later development (see above, n.607).

816 Cf. Galen, *On the Usefulness of the Parts* 6.4 (1.308.15–18 Helmreich, 3.422 K); *On the Doctrines of Hippocrates and Plato* 9.8.19–21 (594.30–596.4 De Lacy, 5.789 K).

817 Cf. Galen, *On the Usefulness of the Parts* 13.5 (2.253.1–255.12 Helmreich, 4.98–101 K).

818 This title applies only to the first part of this section (up to 91.22); what follows is a general account of the way in which parts of the body serve a specific purpose within the overall system they are part of.

819 Muscular movement having been demonstrated to be an act of the soul in the previous section, Nemesius now uses their role in respiration as an argument for the 'psychic' nature of respiration as well. In this, he once again follows Galen's view that respiration belongs to the soul rather than to nature: cf. *On the Movement of Muscles* 2.5 (4.443 K) and 2.6 (4.448 K).

820 I.e. it is affected by states of the mind such as anxiety or excitement. But in the next sentence, 'belonging to the soul' is specified in the sense of 'being within our power.'

in respiration. For if part of the breathing apparatus is painful or parts that move together with them, such as the diaphragm or the liver or the (25) spleen or the abdomen and the lesser intestines or the colon, we then breathe little and often: little in order not to press too hard on the **[90]** painful part, often in order that frequency should compensate for the deficit in size.[821] Indeed, also when we have a pain in the leg, we stretch it out [only] a little way as we walk, for the same reason as in the case of respiration. So as walking is an activity of the soul, so also is the function of respiration,[822] yet if we remain at rest (5) and do not walk we can live for a very long time, while we cannot hold our breath for even a few minutes.[823] For the heat in us is choked and extinguished by its smoke[824] and this immediately leads to death.[825] Indeed, also if someone were to enclose fire in a container with no vent he would extinguish it as it was choked by the smoke.[826] So on account of this (10) necessity the soul is active in this part no less when we are asleep, since it knows that if it should slacken even for a very short time the living being would perish.[827] So here again the natural is implicated with the domain of the soul:[828] for it is

---

821 The same point is made by Galen in *On Difficulty of Breathing* 1.9 (7.787 K).

822 Cf. Galen, *On Difficulty of Breathing* 1.9 (7.775 K).

823 Literally: 'the tenth part of an hour'. Cf. Galen, *On Difficulty of Breathing* 1.12 (7.790–91 K); 3.6 (7.914 K).

824 See above, 83.12, 85.15, 85.19 and 85.21.

825 In chapter 3 of his treatise *On the Usefulness of Respiration* Galen states that respiration is for the purpose of cooling and fanning innate heat and that breathing out discharges the smoke generated by internal heat; see esp. 3.8 (108.20–24 Furley-Wilkie, 4.491–92 K); and he concludes in 5.8: 'It remains, then, that we breathe for regulation of heat. This, then, is the principal use of breathing, and the second is to nourish the psychic pneuma. And the first is brought about by both parts of breathing, both in-breathing and out; to the one belong cooling and fanning, and to the other, evacuation of the smoky vapour; the second is brought about by in-breathing only' (132.14–19 Furley-Wilkie, 4.510 K). See the discussion by Debru (1996) 144.

826 Galen has a similar analogy in *On the Use of Respiration* 3.8 with an oven quenched through lack of draught (4.491 K); for the choking of fire cf. also Theophrastus, *On Fire* 11 and 23.

827 As Telfer notes (1955, 375 nn.2–3), the knowledge attributed here by Nemesius to the soul (rather than to nature) is what we would call instinctive or subconscious knowledge (or perhaps even knowledge possessed by the *body*) rather than the result of reasoning. Debru (2005, 98) refers to Galen, *On the Movement of Muscles* 2.6 (4.446 K), where Galen points out that in sleep the soul continues to be vigilant in order to ensure that the muscles maintain their tonic activity (see also *On the Affected Parts* 5.1, 8.300–01 K).

828 As above in 88.25–26. It has been argued by Larrain (1994) and (1996) that Nemesius has borrowed this concept of 'mixed' (*sumpeplegmenon*) faculties from Galen's treatise *On Unclear Movements* (lost in Greek but preserved in Arabic and in two Latin translations): see p. 197.95–97 Larrain. But the concept can also be found in *On the Usefulness of the Parts* and *On the Movement of the Muscles*: see the passages mentioned in n.814 above.

ON THE NATURE OF MAN 163

through an artery,[829] a natural organ that is in continual motion,[830] that [the soul] creates the activity of breathing, so that its task should never fail, nor that of the other arteries. For this reason (15) some who did not understand have thought breathing to be a purely natural function.[831]

There are three causes[832] of respiration, the usefulness,[833] the power and the organs.[834] The usefulness is twofold, the preservation of the natural heat and the nourishment of the psychic pneuma; the preservation of the natural heat consists in breathing in and out, with breathing in cooling and moderately rekindling (20) the heat, while breathing out expels the smoky element in the heart.[835] The nourishment of the psychic pneuma is by breathing in alone: for some portion of air is drawn into the heart through its expansions.[836] The faculty [of respiration] belongs to the soul: for it is this that sets in motion the respiratory organs by means of the muscles:[837] first the thorax, and with

---

829 I.e. the windpipe, which the Greeks referred to as the 'rough artery' (*artêria tracheia*, hence the use of *trachea* in modern anatomy).

830 I.e. also in sleep. On this passage see Debru (2005) 98–99, who argues that, although Nemesius heavily leans on Galen here, he goes beyond Galen in assuming a permanent natural movement of the trachea, whereas in Galen the movement of the trachea in respiration is a consequence of the activity of the thoracic muscles and hence belongs to the domain of the soul rather than nature. But the reference to the 'naturalness' of the arteries (in this case the 'rough artery', i.e. the trachea) is standard Galenic theory: see *On the Movement of Muscles* 1.1 (4.372 K).

831 Galen, *On Anatomical Procedures* 8.2 (2.657 K) refers to a group of thinkers who hold that respiration is entirely natural without any 'psychic' involvement; Garofalo ad loc. (1991, vol. 2, 719 n.15) suggests that this may refer to Herophilus (see von Staden 1989, 261–62) and to Asclepiades. Skard (1939, 51) refers to Galen's argument against a similar position at *On Difficulty of Breathing* 2.2 (7.827 K).

832 'Causes' in the Aristotelian/Galenic sense of final cause, efficient cause and material cause.

833 *Khreia* is the standard term in Galen's works for 'that for which something is needed', i.e. the purpose or usefulness. As such, it figures frequently in the titles of Galen's works, e.g. *On the Usefulness of the Parts, On the Usefulness of Respiration, On the Usefulenss of the Pulses*.

834 Cf. Galen, *On the Causes of Respiration* 1 (4.465 K).

835 As mentioned in n.825 above, this is exactly the Galenic conclusion of *On the Usefulness of Respiration*.

836 Evangelides (1882, 46 n.21) points out that Nemesius is in accordance with Galenic physiology here in that the production and nourishment of psychic breath is brought about by the influx of air into the thoracic region and by the subsequent processing of this in the cerebral plexus (*On the Doctrines of Hippocrates and Plato* 7.3.26–29 [444.26–446.10 De Lacy, 5.608 K]). For a different view see Lammert (1941) 131, followed by Telfer (1955) 376 nn.5 and 7, who deny usage of Galenic ideas by Nemesius here and suggest that the account goes back to the Hellenistic medical writer Chrysippus.

837 Cf. Galen, *On Difficulty of Breathing* 1.4 (7.761 K).

164   NEMESIUS

this the lung and the rough arteries,[838] which are a portion of the lung, are also set in motion.[839] For the cartilaginous part of the rough artery **[91]** is the organ of speech,[840] and its membraneous ligatures the organ of respiration:[841] but the artery[842] which consists of both is at once the organ of speech and of respiration.[843] So the lung is a complex consisting of four things, the rough artery, the smooth one,[844] a vein[845] and the (5) frothy flesh of the lung itself: this flesh fills up like a pad the spaces between the complex of the two arteries and the vein, so that it becomes a base and a ligature for them. The flesh in the lung naturally cooks the breath[846] in the same way as the liver does the juice from the abdomen, and by this means, as the liver surrounds the abdomen (10) that needs heat with its extreme lobes, so the lung also embraces the heart that needs the surrounding cold from respiration.[847]

The bronchial tube is joined on to the rough artery continuously:[848] it consists of three large cartilages,[849] and to this is attached the throat, and then

---

838 I.e. the pulmonary artery and the trachea. What follows is probably based on Galen's detailed account of the anatomy of the lung, the bronchial tubes and the pharynx, and the physiology of speech and breathing as set out in *On the Usefulness of the Parts* 7.1–12; for an analysis of the sometimes verbal similarities see Skard (1939) 52–53. See also *On Difficulty of Breathing* 1.11 (7.782 K) and 1.18 (7.802 K).

839 Evangelides (1882, 48 n.23) compares Aristotle, *On the Parts of Animals* 669a13; Ps.Aristotle, *On Breath* 482b21; Galen, *On Affected Parts* 3.8 (8.172 K).

840 Presumably this refers to what in today's anatomy is called the upper laryngeal cartilage. Cf. Galen, *On the Usefulness of the Parts* 7.3–5 (1.376–84 Helmreich, 3.523–28 K).

841 Cf. Galen, *On the Usefulness of the Parts* 7.3 (1.378.17 Helmreich, 3.521 K).

842 I.e. the windpipe.

843 This is said of the lung by Galen in *On the Usefulness of the Parts* 6.2 (1.300.15–16 Helmreich, 3.411 K), 6.9 (1.322.24–25 Helmreich, 3.442 K) and 7.1 (1.375.5–6 Helmreich, 3.516 K), and of the cartilaginous larynx connecting the rough artery and the pharynx in *On the Usefulness of the Parts* 7.5 (1.381.20–25 Helmreich, 3.525 K).

844 Presumably, the pulmonary artery is meant here.

845 Presumably, the pulmonary vein is meant here.

846 Cf. Galen, *On the Usefulness of the Parts* 7.8 (1.392.11–17 Helmreich, 3.539–40 K): 'When conditions are normal, very little actual air is taken over from the rough into the smooth arteries and the flesh of the lung appears light and full of air, showing plainly that it was made to concoct the air, just as the flesh of the liver was made to concoct the nutriment' (tr. May).

847 Cf. Aristotle, *On the Parts of Animals* 665a15.

848 Cf. Galen, *On the Usefulness of the Parts* 7.11 (1.400.22–26 Helmreich, 3.551 K): 'I should next speak about the parts of the larynx, for it too is an instrument of the pneuma. As I have said before [7.3, 1.376.26–377.1 Helmreich, 3.518 K], it is called not only larynx but head of the windpipe (*bronkhos*) as well; for the rough artery itself is also called the *bronkhos*' (tr. May).

849 Cf. Galen, *On the Usefulness of the Parts* 7.7 (1.389.13–16 Helmreich, 3.535 K): 'the lung's artery, which is composed of *bronkhia*, for that is what physicians usually call the carti-

the mouth and the nose. For we draw air from outside with both of these: from thence it flows (15) through the perforated or spongiform bone,[850] which was perforated in order that the brain should be in no way harmed by excesses in the quality of the air as the breath fell upon it all at once. The Creator also used the nose here for both breathing and for smelling, just as he used the tongue both for voice and taste and chewing. Thus the (20) most important parts for existence itself and for the necessities of life are divided up among the powers of the soul. If anything has been omitted it will easily be gathered from what has already been said.[851]

The purposiveness of the organs of the body; yellow bile, the spleen, the kidneys, the glands, the flesh, the skin, the bones, the nails, the hair.

As in the case with all things that have come into being, some have done so for their own sake, some for themselves and for something else, some for something else alone, some as incidental consequences, (25) so in the case of the parts of a living being one will find the same progression. For all the organs mentioned of the three principles that control a living being[852] came about for themselves. For these, **[92]** which are called 'in accordance with nature' in the most proper sense, were constructed as primary and highest in rank, and take their birth in the womb from the seed itself,[853] as also the bones. But yellow bile exists both for itself and for another purpose, for it contributes to digestion, stimulates excretion, and thus in a way becomes

---

lages of the artery, just as they call the whole artery the *bronkhos*, and its upper end the head, another name for which is the larynx' (tr. May).

850 Cf. Galen, *On the Usefulness of the Parts* 8.7 (1.472.22–26 Helmreich, 3.652–53 K): 'These bones lying in front of the cerebral membranes, the intricately perforated, porous bones that anatomists call *êthmoid* ['like a colander'], were made to guard against such injury [i.e. as a result of breating in excessively cold air]. It would be better, however, to call them not *êthmoid* but *spongoid* ['spongelike'], which was Hippocrates' comparison [*On Places in Man* 2, 6.278 L.; *On Fleshes* 16, 8.604 L.]; for their perforations are intricate like those in a sponge, and are not bored through in straight lines like those in a colander' (tr. May).

851 Skard (1939, 53) points out that even this phrase is almost literally identical to the conclusion of Galen's discussion of respiration in *On the Usefulness of the Parts* 7.21 (1.437.9–11 Helmreich, 3.601 K).

852 The brain, the heart and the liver, their respective functions and connecting structures: see above, 24, 85.6–11.

853 Cf. Galen, *On the Usefulness of the Parts* 15.6 (2.359.9ff. Helmreich, 4.241–42 K) discussing the emergence and prominence of the liver, the brain and the heart during embryonic development.

one part of the nutritive powers:[854] but (5) indeed it also provides a certain heat to the body,[855] as does the vital power. For these reasons it seems to have come to be for its own sake, but in so far as it purifies the blood it seems to be for something else in one way. The spleen, too, contributes not a little to digestion: for being porous and rigid in its nature[856] it pours out the separated excess of black bile (10) into the stomach, contracts it, strengthens it, and excites it to help in digestion.[857] In addition to this it purifies the liver: for this reason it too seems to exist in one way for the sake of the blood.[858] The kidneys also are a purifying agent for the blood[859] and are responsible for the appetite for sexual intercourse.[860] For the veins, which we said descended into the testicles come out through the kidneys and draw out thence (15)

854 In attributing this role to yellow bile, and especially in designating yellow bile as 'one part of the nutritive powers', Nemesius seems to be stretching standard Galenic doctrine to the limit (as the wording 'in a way becomes', *ginetai ... tropon tina*, may indicate), for in Galen, it is usually the *secretion* of yellow bile from nutriment that contributes to digestion: cf. Galen, *On the Natural Faculties* 2.2 (157.17ff. Helmreich, 2.78 K), and *On the Usefulness of the Parts* 4.13 (1.223.17 and 225.12–13 Helmreich, 3.303 and 307 K). However, Galen does grant yellow bile a certain expulsive power in *On the Usefulness of the Parts* 5.3 (1.256.9–13 Helmreich, 3.349 K): 'the energy of the expulsive action is increased when the bile is not yet mixed with residues but circulates, still pure, along the tunics of the intestines, irritating and stimulating them to evacuation' (tr. May); 5.4 (1.259.3–11 Helmreich, 3.353–54 K; 1.261.4–11 Helmreich, 3.356 K; 1.263.23–264.8 Helmreich, 3.360 K); and 5.12 (1.284.1-2 Helmreich, 3.387–88 K). Galen further speaks of yellow bile stimulating excretion in reaction to certain foodstuffs: cf. Galen, *On the Properties of Foods* 1.1 (209.7–8 Helmreich, 6.467 K): 'honey mixed with water (melicrat) stimulates excretion, just as yellow bile does on account of the bitterness and sharpness it has within itself'.

855 Yellow bile is by nature hot: cf. Galen, *On the Natural Faculties* 2.8 (187.1 Helmreich, 2.118 K).

856 Cf. Galen, *On Black Bile* 7 (87.6–8 De Boer, 5.135 K).

857 Cf. Galen, *On the Natural Faculties* 2.9 (197.10ff. Helmreich, 2.132–34 K); *On the Usefulness of the Parts* 4.15 (1.232.16–18 Helmreich, 3.316 K).

858 Cf. Galen, *On the Natural Faculties* 2.9 (197.10ff. Helmreich, 2.132–34 K); *On the Usefulness of the Parts* 4.4 (1.199.1–15 Helmreich, 3.271–72 K); 5.6 (1.271.18 Helmreich, 3.370 K).

859 See section 23 above, 84.12–14 and cf. Galen, *On the Natural Faculties* 1.16 (148.21–149.5 Helmreich, 2.65 K); *On the Usefulness of the Parts* 5.5 (1.268.17–21 Helmreich, 3.366 K); 5.6 (1.271.8–12 Helmreich, 3.370 K).

860 With this statement, Nemesius is, again, stretching Galenic doctrine: for while Galen had recognised the existence of connections between the kidneys and the testicles (e.g. *On the Usefulness of the Parts* 14.7, 2.306.3–18 Helmreich, 4.170–71 K; 14.13, 2.330.25–331.1 Helmreich, 4.202 K; 16.12, 2.419.1–7 Helmreich, 4.321 K) and the possibility of 'irritation' in the kidneys stimulating the desire for excretion of residues in pathological cases (e.g. *On the Affected Parts* 6.3 [8.396–98 and 401 K], he does not talk about a *normal* contributive role of the kidneys in the generative process.

ON THE NATURE OF MAN 167

some sharp element that stimulates the appetite, just as the sharpness that comes to be under the skin causes an itch. In as much as the flesh of the testicles is softer than the skin, so much more are they bitten by the sharpness and make the desire for the emission of the seed frantic. These organs, then, and similar ones, exist in a way for their own sake and for something else, (20) but the glands and the flesh for the sake of other things alone. For the glands are a conduit and support for the vessels in order that they may not be ripped apart when carried aloft in violent motions,[861] while flesh is a protection for the other parts, so that in summer it may cool the animal by extruding sweat and in the winter may supply the need of a coat of wool.[862] The skin also is a protection (25) both of the soft flesh and of all the other internal parts; [93] it has the nature of flesh, which has been made callous by what surrounds it and by bodies it has come into contact with.[863] The bones are a support of the whole body, especially the spine, which they also call the keel of the animal.[864] The nails both satisfy the need to scratch for all that have them, and (5) other special needs that vary from one case to another: they were given to many animals as a weapon of defence, as to those with curved claws, and are like an instrument of the spirited part, to many as at once a weapon of defence and a support for walking, as for horses and all single-hoofed animals. To men they were given not only for scratching and tearing the hardness of the skin but also for picking up of small objects: (10) for we lift up very small things with them and by supporting the tips of the fingers by pressing from behind they support their grasp.[865] But hair came into being in addition and incidentally: for the more smoky sweats

---

861 Cf. Galen, *On Semen* 2.6.15 (200.24–26 De Lacy, 4.648 K, a report by Galen of the views of his teacher Marinus); *On the Usefulness of the Parts* 3.9 (1.155.6 Helmreich, 3.211 K).

862 The terminology here closely resembles Plato, *Timaeus* 74B–C, a passage also cited by Galen, *On the Usefulness of the Parts* 1.13 (1.26.25ff. Helmreich, 3.37 K), which may well be Nemesius' source.

863 We do not follow Morani in bracketing this line (93.1-2: 'it has ... with') on account of its absence from the Armenian tradition.

864 A frequent metaphor in Galen: cf. *On the Usefulness of the Parts* 3.3 (1.131.6–7 Helmreich, 3.179 K); 12.10 (2.211.17ff. Helmreich, 4.41 K): 'Nature has made the spine for animals to be like the keel of the body that is necessary for their life; for it is thanks to the spine that we can walk erect and each of the other animals can walk in the posture that is the better one for it' (tr. May); *Art of Medicine* 10.5 (303.5 Boudon, 1.333 K). The metaphor of the brace of a ship (*hupozôma*) is applied to the diaphragm by the physician Aristo (presumably 5th century BCE) in Anonymus Parisinus 10.

865 Cf. Galen, *On the Usefulness of the Parts* 1.7 (1.10.19ff Helmreich, 3.14–15 K).

that are emitted from the body cohere and incidentally stick together.[866] But the Creator did not make them altogether useless, but, (15) although they came to be incidentally, he provided them to contribute to the protection and beauty of animals, a protection to goats and sheep, an adornment to men, and to some animals at once an adornment and a protection, as to the lion.[867]

SECTION 29

ON THE INTENTIONAL AND UNINTENTIONAL[868]

The distinction between intentional and unintentional actions.

(20) Since we have often made reference to the intentional and the unintentional[869] it is necessary to treat of these also, in order that we may not fail to gain an accurate understanding of them. He who is going to discuss the intentional and unintentional must first set out certain standards and criteria by which it will become recognisable whether what comes about is intentional or unintentional. Everything intentional (25) involves some action, and what is thought to be unintentional also involves some **[94]** action – this will be demonstrated shortly: but some posit that what is really

---

866 Cf. Galen's extensive account of the formation of hair in *On Mixtures* 2.5 (66.10–70.27 Helmreich, 2.614–21 K), which uses very similar language.

867 Cf. Galen, *On the Usefulness of the Parts* 11.14 (2.153.27–155.16 Helmreich, 3.899–901 K), building on Aristotle, *On the Parts of Animals* 658b3–10, which presents the same combination of mechanical necessity and purpose.

868 The Greek words here translated as 'intentional' and 'unintentional' are *hekousion* and *akousion*. They are in some contexts very reasonably translated as 'willing' and 'unwilling'. They are sometimes, most unsuitably, translated as 'voluntary' and 'involuntary'. Thus in some contexts what one does in ignorance of the facts might be said to be unintentional, but not involuntary, and there is no reason to suppose that at the time of action it was done unwillingly. But this is a prime example of the *akousion*. Nemesius at times gets confused about whether he is talking about the unintentional or the unwilling. Thus he defines one kind of unintentional action as that which is done in ignorance of the facts, but later says that the discovery of treasure is *hekousion,* no doubt because one is not unwilling to stumble upon it.

869 For the specific contrast see section 26 above. This suggests that intentional movements have been discussed in sections 27–28 and unintentional ones in sections 23–25; though digestion (for example) is hardly '*un*-intentional' in the same way as (say) poisoning someone through giving them a drink unaware that it was poisoned, a point that Nemesius makes at 32, 98.10–14 below.

unintentional, too, involves not only being affected but action as well.[870] So before everything else we must define what action is. Action is rational activity: actions attract praise and blame, and some of them are done with pleasure, some (5) with distress; some are worthy of choice by the agent, some to be avoided, and of those worthy of choice some are always so, some at a given time, and similarly in the case of those to be avoided. And again some actions are pitied and are thought deserving of pardon, some are hated and punished. So let the criteria of the intentional be that it always attracts praise or blame; that they are done (10) with pleasure; and that the actions are worthy of choice by the agents either always or at the time when they are done. The criteria of the unintentional are that it is thought deserving of pardon or pity: that it is done with distress: and that the actions are not worthy of choice. Now these distinctions have been made, let us talk first about the unintentional.

SECTION 30

ON THE UNINTENTIONAL

An account of actions which are intentional in themselves but are undertaken because of compulsion. [871]

(15) Of what is unintentional some is done under force, some on account of ignorance. The productive origin[872] of the unintentional under force is external: for something else is the cause of the force and not we ourselves. So the definition of the unintentional under force is that it is that of which the origin is external, while he who is under force contributes nothing by

---

870 Aristotle, *Nicomachean Ethics* 3.1 1110a2 (though the extent to which truly unintentional 'actions', as opposed to the 'mixed' actions discussed in section 30 below, can really be regarded as *actions* at all is questionable).

871 The account of the unintentional, choice and deliberation in sections 30–34 derives ultimately from Aristotle, *Nicomachean Ethics* 3.1–3, but apparently filtered through later Peripatetic sources; see the Introduction, 5.c. Section 29 clearly forms part of the same discussion even though it has no such close parallels in Aristotle himself; it is likely that it has been prefixed to what follows it in the course of scholastic elaboration and systematisation of Aristotle's account. Some of the examples Nemesius gives (Origen, Susanna, Joseph) may be his own contributions.

872 I.e. the initiating cause. Streck (2005, 50) notes the use of the same expression in the same context by Alexander of Aphrodisias, *Ethical Problems* 12 133.1; see the next note.

his own impulse.⁸⁷³ Here it is the productive cause that is spoken of as the origin. There is a question whether such (20) actions as throwing goods overboard which are done by sailors beset by a storm, or accepting to suffer something disgraceful, or to do it, in order to save one's friends or one's country are unintentional. They appear rather to be intentional; for that is why 'while he who is under force contributes nothing by his own impulse' is added to the definition. For in such circumstances they by themselves **[95]** intentionally move their bodily parts and in that way throw the goods into the sea. The case of those who endure something disgraceful or horrific for a greater good is similar, as that of Zeno who bit off his own tongue and spat it out at the tyrant Dionysius in order not to reveal in any way to him what was forbidden.⁸⁷⁴ (5) Similarly Anaxarchus the philosopher endured being pounded in a mortar by Nicocreon the tyrant⁸⁷⁵ in order not to betray his friends. So generally, when one either chooses the lesser evil through fear of greater evils or accepts a lesser evil through hope of a greater good which is not otherwise attainable, it is not unintentionally that one is accepting the doing or suffering of something; for one acts by (10) choice and selection, and [such actions] are worth choosing at the time of action, though not worthy of choice in themselves. So they are a mixture of the intentional and unintentional,⁸⁷⁶ unintentional in themselves but intentional at the time

---

873 So (but without the reference to impulse, the term for which is later and of Stoic origin) Aristotle, *Nicomachean Ethics* 3.1 1110b15–17. Streck (2005, 50) notes that Aristotle's definition is cited at the start of Alexander of Aphrodisias, *Ethical Problems* 12 132.19–20 and that this too refers to 'own impulse' (133.9).

874 This example, and the following one of Anaxarchus, occur in the same context in Anonymous, *On the Nicomachean Ethics* (*CAG* 20) 143.1ff., 'similarly for Anaxarchus who was being pounded in a mortar and enduring the most dishonourable things, it would be shameful if he had not endured, and for Zeno who bit off his tongue and spat it out and did not reveal what was forbidden'; Koch (1921) 26. The anonymous commentator does not name the tyrant in either case in the present context, though Nicocreon is named as the persecutor of Anaxarchus later in the commentary, at 177.30. The story of Anaxarchus is in Diogenes Laertius 9.26–27, where this version is attributed to Antisthenes' *Successions of Philosophers*, but the tyrant is named (earlier, in the context of a variant version where it is the tyrant's ear that Zeno bites off) Nearchus or Diomedes. The name of the tyrant resisted by Zeno is given as Dionysius, as here, by Tertullian, *Apology* 50 = DK 29A19; Tertullian also there gives the Anaxarchus story without naming the tyrant. Other identifications in Clement of Alexandria and in Valerius Maximus: DK 29A8; see Streck (2005) 50–52. Should we suppose that Nemesius used the anonymous commentary and added material from elsewhere in it and from other texts that he had read? Or should we rather suppose the existence of a common source on which both the anonymous commentary and Nemesius drew selectively?

875 Cf. Diogenes Laertius, 9.59 (Anaxarchus 72A1 DK).

876 Streck (2005, 49) notes that this wording appears in Aspasius' commentary (61.5–6)

because of the special circumstances: for nobody would make these choices except in special circumstances.[877] The praise or blame bestowed on such actions also shows that they are intentional. For (15) there will be no praise or blame for what is done unintentionally.

It is not easy to determine what is worth choosing rather than what: but for the most part one should prefer the distressing over the shameful, as did Susanna and Joseph.[878] But this is not always so: Origen at least, through not accepting the shame of the Ethiopians, sacrificed and lost everything;[879] so decision on such matters (20) is not easy. It is even harder than that to

---

while Aristotle himself refers to the actions as 'mixed' but leaves it to the reader to infer from what they are mixed.

877 Similarly Aristotle, *Nicomachean Ethics* 3.1 1110a4–19, 1110b3–7. On these so-called 'mixed actions' see e.g. Urmson (1988) 43–45. Streck (2005, 49–50) discusses this passage and shows that Nemesius' formulation, using the terminology *peristasis* (special circumstance) is closest to pseudo-Heliodorus (42.18) among the extant commentaries on the *Nicomachean Ethics*; Streck speaks of Nemesius 'modifying' the wording of pseudo-Heliodorus, but it is not clear whether he intends to imply that pseudo-Heliodorus was actually Nemesius' source, or only to make a comparison between the wording they use; the uncertainty of pseudo-Heliodorus' date is noted by Streck (2005) 82. Nemesius and pseudo-Heliodorus may in any case be making independent use of a common source.

878 Susanna chose to be accused of adultery with a young man rather than avoid the accusation by committing adultery with her accusers (Susanna [= Daniel 13] 19–23): Joseph refused to lie with his master's wife and so was falsely accused by her of attempting what he had in fact refused to do (Genesis 39:7–18).

879 The story is given by Epiphanius – who denounced Origen's doctrines – in *Panarion*, haeresis 64.2.2–5 (*GCS* vol.2 404.4–12 Holl and Dummer). Telfer (1955, 385 n.5) suggests, as do also Holl and Dummer ad loc., that Epiphanius is Nemesius' source. The *Panarion* was written between 374 and 376, which fits the probable date of Nemesius well enough. The persecutors of the Christians forced Origen to sacrifice to the pagan gods by threatening him with sexual abuse by an Ethiopian; Epiphanius specifically makes the point that even after Origen had chosen to sacrifice, he did not do so willingly (*ou ... hekousiâi gnômêi*; Telfer suggests that Epiphanius indicates that the story was malicious hearsay, but in fact the qualification in Epiphanius seems to apply only to the specific point of Origen's unwillingness). As a result, according to the story, Origen was expelled from the church in Alexandria; hence 'lost everything' here. That Origen left Alexandria because of quarrels with the ecclesiastical authorities there may be the only true part of the story, which subsequently appears in Georgius Monachus (Georgius Hamartolus), *Chronicle* 2 457.20–458.7 de Boor; Constantine Pophyrogenitus, *Excerpts on virtues and vices*, vol.1 140.1–9 Buettner-Wobst and Roos; Cedrenus, *Compendium of Histories*, vol.1 446.22–447.8 Bekker; and the Suda, s.v. 'Origenes' (Ω 183, vol.3 622.8–18 Adler; cf. also Suda s.v. *parakhratai* (Π 493, vol.4 46.3–6 Adler; references from Arnold [2000]). All the reports apart from Nemesius' refer to 'an Ethiopian' in the singular. Telfer suggests Nemesius thought that the persecution actually took place in Ethiopia, but the plural may rather be deliberately allusive, reducing the emphasis on the single individual and the threatened act.

stand by one's decisions: for evils that are anticipated and are being brought upon oneself are not frightening in [just] the same way,[880] and sometimes we desert the decision we have made when we are in trouble, as happened in the case of some at the time of martyrdom: for they were strong in their aim at the beginning, **[96]** but gave in at the end, weakened by the experience of hardship.

Let nobody think that the desire for licentiousness, or anger, are among unintentional faults, on the ground that they have an external initiating origin,[881] since the beauty of the prostitute goaded to licentiousness (5) the one who saw her,[882] and the man who provoked stirred to anger. For even if these men have an external origin of their action, still they act themselves, through themselves and their bodily organs, and do not fall under the definition of the unintentional: for they provide for themselves the cause of the origin because, through their poor training, they are easily made captives by emotions. So those who behave in this way are blamed as (10) accepting an intended evil. That it is intended is clear, for they enjoy what they do, while the unintentional was shown to be distressing. So much for the unintentional under force: it remains to speak of that which is on account of ignorance.

SECTION 31

ON THE UNINTENTIONAL THROUGH IGNORANCE

When ignorance does, and when it does not, render an action unintentional.

We do many things on account of ignorance about which we are glad when they are done, as when one (15) unintentionally kills an enemy, but is glad about his slaughter. These and similar actions are called 'not intentional', but

880 I.e., they are more frightening.
881 Literally, 'productive origin'. See n.872 above. Streck (2005, 53) compares this paragraph with Aristotle, *Nicomachean Ethics* 3.1 1110b9–15, noting that Nemesius uses a specific example while Aristotle refers to 'fine and pleasant things' in general, and that in introducing 'desire ... or anger (*thumos*)' – which in Nemesius' Greek word-order are adjacent to one another – Nemesius is introducing (Platonic) psychology into the discussion. One may ask whether this was already present in Nemesius' source, and whether that source was Platonising, Christian (compare the next note) or both.
882 A similar example is used by Origen, *On Principles* 3.1.4 (*SVF* 2.988): 'for example, the woman who showed herself to the man who had determined to control himself and abstain from sexual relations, and invited him to do something contrary to his intention, is not the sufficient cause of his rejecting his intention'.

not also 'unintentional'. Again, we do some things on account of ignorance and are distressed about what happened: these they[883] called unintentional, those which when done are followed by distress. So there are two types of actions done on account of ignorance, one being the not intentional, the other the unintentional. (20) Our task is now to discuss the unintentional alone, for what is not intentional is closer to the intentional, being mixed; for its origin is unintentional, but its result is intentional. As a result of the outcome what was unintentional has become intentional. Therefore they also give the following definition of the unintentional: the unintentional is what is distressing and regretted as well as not intentional.

Again, it is one thing (25) to do something on account of ignorance and another to do it in ignorance.[884] For if the cause of our ignorance is something that is up to us we act in ignorance, not through ignorance. For he who does something base when drunk or angry has drink or anger as the cause of what he brought about, and these were intentional. For it was in **[97]** his power not to get drunk; therefore he became the cause of his own ignorance. So one is said to do such things not through ignorance but in ignorance, and these are not unintentional but intentional, which is why those who do these things are blamed by good men. For if he had not got drunk he would not have done it: but he got drunk (5) intending to, so he did what he did, too, intending to. We do things through ignorance when we do not ourselves bring about the cause of the ignorance, but when it happens as follows, for example if somebody shooting arrows in the accustomed place killed his father by hitting him when he happened to be passing by. So they demonstrate by the foregoing that it is not he who is ignorant of what is suitable or thinks that what is bad is good who has (10) the unintended experience; for the ignorance is [part] of[885] his wickedness: so he also is blamed, and blame is for what is intended. So the ignorance of universal and general truths or of what is by choice is not unintentional, but that of particular facts is. For we are ignorant of single matters unintentionally, but of the universal intentionally.

Now these distinctions have been made, we must next make clear of what sort particular facts are. (15) They are what the rhetoricians call circumstan-

---

883 I e. Aristotle, *Nicomachean Ethics* 3.1 1110b18–24.
884 The distinction is Aristotle's: *Nicomachean Ethics* 3.1 1110b24–27.
885 Or '[a result] of'. Streck (2005, 59–60) notes that Aristotle (*Nicomachean Ethics* 3.1 1110b31–32) in the corresponding context says the opposite: 'ignorance in choosing is the cause not of what is unintentional but of wickedness'.

tial parts:[886] who did what to whom with what, where, when, how, why, such as a person, a deed, an instrument, a place, a time, a manner, a reason. The person is the subject or object of the action, as when a son has struck his father in ignorance; the deed is that which was done, as when someone has caused blindness when wishing to slap; the tool as when one threw a stone thinking it was (20) pumice; place, as when someone has bumped into someone he did not know was there when turning round a narrow path; time, as when in the night someone has thought a friend was an enemy and killed him; manner, as when someone has killed someone by hitting him gently and not violently (for he did not know that he would die if hit gently); cause, as when someone has given someone a drug to cure him, but he who took it died because the drug was found to be harmful. (25) Not even a madman would be ignorant about all these at the same time: but he who **[98]** has been ignorant of most or the most important of these matters has acted on account of ignorance. Amongst them the most important are the purpose and nature of the action, i.e. the reason and the deed.

SECTION 32

ON THE INTENTIONAL

Which actions are intentional.

(5) Since the unintentional is twofold, that through ignorance and that under force, the intentional is opposed to both.[887] It is what occurs neither under force nor through ignorance, and it is not under force if the origin is in the agents, and it is not through ignorance if no particular facts about the act and its circumstances are unknown. So we define the intentional by

---

886 E.g. Anon. in Hermogenes, *On Invention, Rhetores Graeci* vol. 7.2 756.12–13, 760.9 Walz; Anon. in Hermogenes, *On Styles (De ideis), Rhetores Graeci* vol.7.2 920.14 Walz. Streck (2005, 58) notes that the terms used by Nemesius here ('person', 'deed', 'instrument' etc.) appear in pseudo-Heliodorus' commentary on the *Nicomachean Ethics* (44.4–8) but not in Aristotle; nor, we may add, does the list appear in this form in the other ancient commentaries on the *Ethics* at this point. See above, n.877, and Introduction, n.152.

887 Aristotle, *Nicomachean Ethics* 3.1 1111a22–24, but without the explicit point about opposition. Alexander of Aphrodisias, *Ethical Problems* 11 discusses how the latter is to be reconciled with the general thesis that each thing has only one opposite; so too do Aspasius, *On Aristotle's Nicomachean Ethics* 65.33ff., and Anonymous, *On Aristotle's Nicomachean Ethics* 141.10–20. Cf. Sharples (1978) 265–66 n.229; (1985a); Streck (2005) 60 and n.190.

combining the two: it is that which has its origin in the agent who knows (10) the particular facts concerning the action.[888] People enquire whether natural events such as digestion and growth are intentional. But it is shown that they are neither intentional nor unintentional: for the intentional and the unintentional are both up to us, but digestion and growth are not up to us; so even if we are not ignorant of the particular facts, they are neither intentional nor unintentional since they are not up to us. But actions (15) done through anger or desire were shown to be intentional, since if right they are praised and if wrong they are blamed or hated, and pleasure and distress accompanies them, and their origin is in the agents. For it was in their power not to be easily trapped by their emotions: such things are corrected by habit. In any case, if such actions are unintentional, no non-rational animal (20) does anything intentionally, and nor do little children; but, as it is, this is not the case, for we see them going to their food intentionally and neither under force (for these are those that are set in motion through themselves)[889] nor in ignorance[890] (for they are not ignorant of their food). At any rate, when they have seen their food they are pleased and go to it as something familiar, and they are distressed if they do not get it: and it is a mark of the intentional that success (25) pleases and failure distresses. From this it is clear that the intentional includes both **[99]** desire and anger; for even anger is accompanied by pleasure. And in any case, if one says that acts done on account of anger and on account of desire are not intentional, one abolishes the moral virtues: for they are in a mean with regard to the emotions.[891] But if emotions are unintentional then actions in accord with the virtues are also unintentional; for these also are done (5) in accordance with an emotion. But nobody calls unintentional that which is done in accordance with reason and with choice, and under one's own impulse and aim with knowledge of the particular facts, and it was shown that the origin too is in the agents.

---

888 So Aristotle, *Nicomachean Ethics* 3.1 1111a22–24, followed by Alexander, *Ethical Problems* 29 159.20–21; but Nemesius is closer to Aristotle's wording than Alexander is. Sharples (1978) loc. cit.

889 For the Stoics living creatures move not just 'through themselves' (a description that applies to all self-motion) but 'from themselves' (*SVF* 2.499). Nemesius is not using technical Stoic terminology. See below, n.923, and on the whole topic the classic discussion of Hahm (1994).

890 Strictly, the argument requires 'nor *on account of* ignorance' (see section 31 above). But not being *in* ignorance implies not acting on account of ignorance *a fortiori*.

891 Cf. Aristotle, *Nicomachean Ethics* 2.6 1106b24–28. This particular argument does not explicitly appear among those advanced by Aristotle himself against the claim that actions due to anger or desire are not intentional (*Nicomachean Ethics* 3.1 1111a24–b3).

Therefore they are intentional.

But since we have referred to choice in many places,[892] and to what is up to us,[893] we must also explain choice (10).

SECTION 33

ON CHOICE

Choice is a combination of deliberation, selection and appetition.

What then is choice? Is it the intentional, since everything chosen is also intentional? But they are not convertible, as would be the case if choice and the intentional were the same. But as it is we find that the extension of the intentional is greater. For every choice is intentional, but not everything intentional involves (15) choice. For both little children and non-rational animals act intentionally, but they do not also choose [what they do]; also what we do through anger without previous planning we do intentionally, but by no means also through choice. Or a friend suddenly met us; this was intended,[894] since we were pleased, but we did not choose it. And a man who found a treasure unexpectedly (20) came upon a windfall intentionally, but not choosing to do so. From all these cases the conclusion follows that intention is not the same as choice.

So is choice appetition? But it is not that either. For appetition is divided

---

892 12, 68.9; 23, 84.23; 26, 87.18–19; 27, 88.1, 3, 22; 30, 95.10; 31, 97.12; 32, 99.5.

893 25, 85.27; 26, 87.23; 28, 89.22; 31, 96.25; 32, 98.12–14. Streck (2005, 41) notes that, while Nemesius deals with choice in the next section, he does not discuss what is up to us until sections 39–41; Streck therefore raises the possibility that this sentence has been taken over by Nemesius from his source. Perhaps, however, the discussion of fate in the intervening sections was regarded by Nemesius as a part of the treatment of what is up to us.

894 Plainly 'intended' here and below is unsuitable as a translation. Perhaps 'willingly' would do. The deliberately unacceptable translation indicates that Nemesius has changed the subject. What he produces here are in fact prime examples of what is *non*-intended because of ignorance of the facts. The examples of the chance meeting – but with a debtor rather than a friend – and of the treasure come from Aristotle (*Physics* 2.5 196b33–197a5 and *Metaphysics* Δ 30 1025a15–19 respectively), but Aristotle does not mention chance events in his own argument in *Nicomachean Ethics* 3.2 for the distinction between choice and what is intentional. The example of meeting a friend *does*, however, occur in a context similar to the present at Anonymous, *On Aristotle's Nicomachean Ethics* 148.1, 'We also say that sudden things [happen to us] "willingly". For in this way when a friend suddenly came up to us we were willing, but did not choose or plan it'; Koch (1921) 32.

into three kinds, desire, anger and wish.⁸⁹⁵ But that choice is neither anger nor desire is evident from the fact that there is no kinship between man and **[100]** non-rational animals regarding choice, but there is with regard to desire and anger. For if we are akin to them in those ways, but differ with regard to choice, it is clear that choice is one thing, anger and desire another. The person who lacks self-control also shows this to be the case, since he is overpowered by desire and acts in accordance with it, but not (5) in accordance with his choice; for in his case choice opposes desire: but if they were the same they would not conflict. And the person who is self-controlled acts in accordance with his choice, but not in accordance with his desire.⁸⁹⁶

That wish also is not the same as choice is clear from the following: it is not fitting to say 'wish' in all cases where it is to say 'choose'.⁸⁹⁷ For we say that we wish to be healthy, but nobody (10) would say that he chooses to be healthy, and one says that one wishes to be rich but not also that one chooses to be rich. Also 'wish' can be used with reference to the impossible, but 'choose' only with reference to what is up to us. For we say 'I wish to become immortal', but do not say 'I choose to become immortal'. For wish is for the end but choice (15) of what leads to the end, in the same relationship as what is wished for has to what is subject to deliberation. For what is wished for is the end, what is subject to deliberation is the things which lead to the end. Also we choose only those things that we think that we can ourselves accomplish; but we wish also for what we cannot ourselves accomplish, as a general may wish for victory.

It has been sufficiently demonstrated that choice (20) is neither desire, nor anger, nor wish. That it is also not belief becomes clear both from the same proofs and from others. For belief is not only about things that are up

---

895 So Aristotle, *On the Soul* 2.3 414b2 and elsewhere (Bonitz [1870] 522a6); the classification is found in the *Eudemian Ethics* (2.7 1223a26) and the *Magna Moralia* (1.12 1187b37). The *Nicomachean Ethics* argues that choice is not desire, anger or wish (3.2 1111b10–12), but does not present these as species of appetition; they are, however, so treated in Aspasius' commentary on the latter, at the point corresponding to the present text (67.21: Koch [1921] 32, Streck [2005] 64). The arguments that follow are based on *Nicomachean Ethics* 3.2.

896 Cf. Aristotle, *Nicomachean Ethics* 3.2 1111b13–16, with Streck (2005) 65; and for the person who lacks self-control see in general Aristotle, *Nicomachean Ethics* 7.1–10.

897 One might rather expect 'it is not fitting to say "choose" in all cases where it is so to say "wish".' The point at issue here is not yet that we can wish for things that are not in our power – that point comes later. Rather, it is being taken for granted (oddly, for a bishop? – but Nemesius reflects his pagan sources) that wealth is obviously preferable to poverty, so to say that one *chooses* wealth is simply redundant.

to us but also about things that are eternal.[898] Also we say that belief is true and false, but we do not say that choice is true and false. Also belief is about the universal,[899] but choice is of the particular;[900] for choice is concerned with (25) what one may do, and such matters are particular.

Choice is also not deliberation;[901] for deliberation is enquiry about what one might do; **[101]** what is chosen is what has been selected as a result of deliberation.[902] So it is clear that deliberation is concerned with things that are still under investigation, choice with such things as have already been selected.

So it has been stated what choice is not: let us state what it actually is. It is a mixture of deliberation, selection and appetition, and (5) it is neither appetition as such nor mere deliberation, but something composed of them.[903] For as we say that an animal is composed of soul and body, but is neither body as such nor soul on its own, but both together, so is the case with choice. That it is a sort of plan and deliberation with selection, even if it is not a plan itself, is clear from its etymology; (10) for what is chosen is one thing that is taken before another.[904] Nobody prefers something without having deliberated, nor selects without having decided. But since we do not propose to put into practice everything that seems good to us, choice [occurs], and that which is preferred after deliberation becomes chosen, only when appetite is added. So choice is necessarily concerned with the same matters as is (15) deliberation. The conclusion from the above is that

898 And we do not deliberate about what is eternal; *Nicomachean Ethics* 3.3 1112a21. Cf. below, section 34.

899 Contradicted by Aristotle, *Nicomachean Ethics* 7.3 1147a25; Streck (2005, 67) takes *Nicomachean Ethics* 3.2 1112a3–5 also, in the context corresponding to Nemesius here, to indicate that belief can be concerned with particulars.

900 This contrast is not made by Aristotle in *Nicomachean Ethics* 3.2 (1111b34–1112a1 is different).

901 Omitting *hoion boulê* ('like taking counsel') with the Armenian version, as a gloss.

902 Aristotle, *Nicomachean Ethics* 3.3 1113a4–5.

903 That choice is a composite is asserted (but using the term *suntheton* rather than *sunkeimenon* as here), and with the same analogy of an animal, by Aspasius, *On Aristotle's Nicomachean Ethics* 75.9ff. (Koch [1921] 33; Streck [2005] 70). However, Aspasius mentions only two of the three factors mentioned by Nemesius, namely deliberation and appetition; cf. Verbeke and Moncho (1975) lxxx and n.80. They compare Nemesius' own formulation rather with that of Alexander of Aphrodisias; but he analyses choice in terms of deliberation, appetition and *impulse* (*On Fate* 12 180.9); closer is Alexander, *Ethical Problems* 29 160.19–25, compared here by Streck (2005) 73 and n.235. Choice is described as 'mixed' (from intelligence and appetition) by the anonymous commentary on the *Nicomachean Ethics* (153.15–17); cf. 101.4 here (Streck [2005] 70).

904 The Greek word for 'chosen' literally means 'taken before'.

choice is deliberative appetition of things that are up to us,[905] or appetitive deliberation about what is up to us. For in choosing we aim at what has been preferred through deliberation. But since we say that choice is about the same things as is deliberation, let us make it quite clear what deliberation is concerned with and about what we deliberate. (20)

SECTION 34

ABOUT WHAT THINGS DO WE DELIBERATE?

We deliberate about things which are up to us, come about through us and have an equal possibility of coming about or not.

Before saying about which things we deliberate it is better to determine how deliberation differs from inquiry.[906] For deliberation and inquiry are not the same thing, even if he who deliberates is inquiring when he deliberates: but there is a great difference. For we inquire whether the sun is bigger than the earth, but nobody says 'I am deliberating whether the sun is bigger [102] than the earth'.[907] For inquiry is the genus of deliberation, for it also has a greater extension. Thus on the one hand all deliberation is inquiry, but not all inquiry is deliberation.[908] That has been demonstrated. We speak of investigating sometimes with regard to deliberation, for example 'I am investigating whether we ought to sail', and sometimes with regard to understanding, for example (5) 'I am investigating the mathematical sciences', but not 'I am deliberating the mathematical sciences'. We are often confused by the uncritical understanding of words, thinking what is not the same to be the same.

Now that the difference between them has become clear, we must next

---

905 Aristotle's definition: *Nicomachean Ethics* 3.3 1113a10–11. Streck (2005, 71–72) argues that for the Aristotelian commentators, unlike Nemesius, deliberation precedes appetition; but Aspasius, *On the Nicomachean Ethics* 3.24–27, which Streck cites, seems to go against this.

906 Aristotle in *Nicomachean Ethics* 3.3 proceeds directly to the question about which things we deliberate. As often in these sections, Nemesius' account bears the marks of a scholastic tradition which has elaborated and systematised Aristotle's remarks. See below, n.909.

907 The Greek word, unlike the English, is restricted to cases of deciding what to do, and does not have the wider sense of 'consider'.

908 A point made by Aristotle later in his discussion (*Nicomachean Ethics* 3.3 1112b21–23); cf. Streck (2005) 76.

say about what things we deliberate. We deliberate, then, about things that are up to us and can come about through us, and of which the outcome is unclear, that is, it can come about in (10) one way or in another. 'Up to us' was said because we deliberate only about practical matters, for it is these that are up to us. For we do not deliberate about what is called theoretical philosophy, since we neither do so about God, nor about things that happen from necessity ('from necessity' I apply to those things which always happen in the same way, such as the cycle of the year), nor about those things that are not always (15) present but always happen in a similar

Aristotle, *Nicomachean Ethics* 3.3	Anon. *On Aristotle's Nicomachean Ethics* 149.14ff.	Aspasius, *On Aristotle's Nicomachean Ethics* 71.16ff.	Alexander, *Ethical Problems* 29.160.5ff.	Nemesius
Eternal things: world, incommensurability of diagonal	Eternal things: existence of world or God, incommensurability of diagonal	Eternal things: world, incommensurability of diagonal	Eternal things	God
				Things from necessity, always in the same way: cycle of year
Always in the same way: solstices and risings	Always in the same way	Always in the same way: risings, settings, solstices	Always in the same way: risings, settings, solstices	Always in a similar way, sunset and sunrise
	natural, for the most part: grey hair, growing teeth			natural, for the most part: grey hair, beard
differently at different times: drought, rain		natural but less orderly: drought, rain	differently at different times: drought, rain	natural and unpredictable, rain, drought, hail
chance: finding treasure	chance: finding treasure	chance: finding treasure	chance	chance
not through us or up to us: constitution of Scythians	not through us or up to us	not up to us: constitution of Scythians	constitution of Scythians	not through us: constitution of enemies or those far away
exact sciences	definite, determined sciences	exact and self-sufficient skills		definite, determined sciences and skills

way, such as the sunset and sunrise, nor about things that are natural but do not always occur in the same way, but do so for the most part (e.g. whether a sixty-year-old becomes grey-haired or a twenty-year-old grows a beard), nor about things that are natural but occur unpredictably at different places in different ways, such as rain and drought and hail; but nor do we deliberate about those things that are said (20) to come about by chance, which are among things that may happen less frequently.[909]

For those reasons, then, we said 'up to us'; we said 'through us', since we do not deliberate about all people or about all matters, but only about what is up to us *and* comes about through us.[910] For we do not deliberate how our enemies or those living a long way away from us might have a good constitution, although (25) that is a matter for deliberation among them. But neither do we deliberate about all things that come about through us and are up to us, but 'of which the outcome **[103]** is unclear' must be added: for if that is clear and undisputed we no longer deliberate. For we also do not deliberate about the products and activities of science and skill: for their rules are determined, except for a few skills that are called stochastic, such as medicine, physical training and navigation.[911] (5) For it is not about these

---

909 This list of things about which we do not deliberate derives from Aristotle, *Nicomachean Ethics* 3.3. Nemesius' version is closer to Anonymous, *On Aristotle's Nicomachean Ethics* 149.14ff. than to Aspasius, *On Aristotle's Nicomachean Ethics* 71.16ff., or Alexander of Aphrodisias, *Ethical Problems* 29 160.5ff. (*see preceding table*); in particular, Nemesius shares with the anonymous commentary, but not with Aristotle himself or Aspasius, God as an example of something about which we do not deliberate (Koch [1921] 34; Streck [2005] 76–77 and n.252). Cf. Sharples (1978) 265 n.229. Aristotle does not in *Nicomachean Ethics* 3.3 refer explicitly to natural occurrences which are usual (neither does Aspasius; 71.31), but the anonymous commentary does so with one example, grey hair, being the same as Nemesius' (Anon. 149.22: Koch [1921] 35). On the contrast between what happens for the most part and what happens for the least part see also below, n.916; it is significant, as noted by Streck (2005) 77 and n.253, that Nemesius is here already using the terminology ('may happen less frequently', where 'may' renders *endekhomenon*) that appears in the final part of the present section.

910 The first part of the present sentence suggests that 'and' here is to be understood in a strong sense; for Nemesius what is up to us includes, but is wider than, what comes about through us. This distinction does not appear in any of the parallel texts, and seems implausible; a change in the constitution of the Scythians certainly cannot come about *through* us (armed intervention apart), but it does not seem appropriate to describe it as up to us either.

911 On stochastic arts – those in which the outcome is not entirely determined by the art – see Ierodiakonou (1995). The anonymous commentary on the *Nicomachean Ethics* refers explicitly to stochastic arts but only mentions medicine and navigation (149.31; Koch [1921] 35); Aristotle himself (*Nicomachean Ethics* 3.3 1112b2–8) does not draw a distinction between arts where we deliberate and those that we do not, but says that we deliberate about what comes about through us but in a variable way, about medicine, money-making and navigation more

things only that we deliberate, but we do so about those things that are up to us, come about through us and of which the outcome is unclear, and which can be carried out in one way or in another.

But it was shown that deliberation was also not about the end but about what contributes to the end: for we deliberate not about being rich but how and by what means we may become rich. To sum up, we deliberate only about (10) those things that have an even chance of coming about.[912]

On this matter one must be careful that nothing is lacking in our discussion from the point of view of clarity.[913] Those things are called powers through which we are able to do something:[914] for we have the power to do everything that we do; on matters where we do not have power we perform no actions. So action depends on power and power on substance: for action comes from power and power (15) comes from substance and is in substance. So those three things, as we said, depend on each other – being able, power and possibility: what is able is the substance, power is that from which we are able, the possible that which is of a nature to come about through power. Of things possible some are necessary, some contingent. Those things are necessary which cannot be prevented, or those of which also the opposite is impossible; (20) the contingent is what is able to be prevented or of which also the opposite is possible.[915] Thus it is necessary for a living person to

---

than gymnastics because they are more uncertain, and (with the usual MSS reading) more about (practical) arts than about sciences; similarly Aspasius, 72.19–73.5, except that he is aware of a variant 'more about opinions than about sciences' (favoured by Barnes [1999] 42–43).

912 Nemesius is following the common, but artificial, identification of what is up to us with what has an equal chance of coming about or not; see below, n.916.

913 What follows is no longer from *Nicomachean Ethics* 3. The distinction between what is able, power and possibility also occurs at pseudo-Plutarch, *On Fate* (probably 2nd century CE) 571a; Nemesius, or his source, has switched to the middle-Platonist source which also underlies section 38 below. See above, Introduction 5.c.; Domański (1900) 148 n.1; Streck (2005) 77–81; and Dillon (1996) 298 and 323, who describes this particular piece of doctrine as 'superfluous scholastic trumpery'. Streck (2005, 78 n.258) notes the similarity between Nemesius' 'that nothing is lacking in our *discussion* (*logos*) from the point of view of *clarity*' here and pseudo-Plutarch's 'you will understand *clearly* what I am *saying* (*to legomenon*)' (6 570f, near the start of the discussion of possibility). He also (2005, 78) relates pseudo-Plutarch's discussion of possibility and contingency to the section of the *Nicomachean Ethics* (3.5 in his numbering, 3.3 in the English numbering) that Nemesius has been discussing; the connections may be more complex (see Introduction n.83 and below n.916), but at any rate the connection between the two parts of the present section is a natural one and could have been present already in a single source (see Introduction nn.161–62).

914 Plato, *Republic* 5 477c.

915 [Plutarch], *On Fate* 6 571bc (with different examples), 'of things that are possible some could never be prevented, like celestial phenomena, risings and settings and things like

breathe; of this the opposite also, for a living person not to breathe, is impossible. There being rain today is contingent, but its opposite also, there being [104] no rain today, is possible. Further, of the contingent some things are said to be for the most part, some rarely, some with an equal possibility: for the most part is e.g. a sixty-year-old having grey hair; a sixty-year-old not having grey hair is rare; and going for a walk and not going for a walk, and simply (5) doing something or not doing something, have an equal possibility.[916] So it is only about those contingent things that have an equal possibility that we deliberate. That is contingent with an equal possibility which we are able to do and its opposite: for if we could not do both, both it and its opposite, we would not have deliberated. For nobody deliberates about what is agreed upon or the impossible. If we had been able to do only (10) one of the opposites, that would have been agreed upon and in no way in doubt and its opposite impossible.

[Sections 35–36] Rejection of the claim that everything is determined by the stars, and of the Stoic view that fate and human freedom are compatible.

these; others can be prevented, like many human affairs and many meteorological phenomena. The former are called "necessary" because they come about of necessity, those that in addition admit their opposite are called "contingent". They might also be defined in this way; the necessary is the possible that is opposed to the impossible, the contingent the possible of which the opposite is also possible. For that the sun sets is both necessary and possible ... but that when the sun sets it should rain or not rain are, both of them, possible and contingent.' Cf. also, but with a reference to prevention not forming part of the formal definition, Calcidius, *On Plato's Timaeus* 155 189.16–190.5, '"necessary" is also applied to what is constrained by necessity, and, because very many possible things cannot be prevented from happening, but some are prevented and avoided by judgement, they are indicated by definitions of the following sort: the necessary is the possible of which the opposite is impossible, for example that everything that comes to be perishes and [everything] that grows grows old ... the contingent (*dubium*) is the possible whose contrary is also possible, for example that today it will rain after sunset.' The Stoics defined what is possible as what *is not* prevented (*SVF* 2.201 = LS 38D). For Aristotle's 'two-sided' notion of the contingent – that which excludes both the impossible *and* the necessary – see *On Interpretation* 13 23a15–16, *Prior Analytics* 1.13 32a18–29. See Mansfeld (1999) 144–49, on the Platonist use of Peripatetic sources to 'neutralise' Stoic modal notions.

916 This 'tripartition of the contingent' is standard in Peripatetic and Middle- and Neoplatonist texts (including [Plutarch], *On Fate* 571cd; Calcidius, *On Plato's Timaeus* 156 190.8ff.). Cf. Sharples (2001a) 549–51, and further references there. It derives ultimately from a combination of Aristotle, *Prior Analytics* 1.13 32b5–18 with the standard contrast between what is for the most part and what is for the least part, e.g. at *Physics* 2.8 198b36. The identification of what is up to us with that which we can do or not is prominent in Alexander of Aphrodisias (Sharples [2001a] 546–49) and derives from Aristotle: *Nicomachean Ethics* 3.5 1113b7–8, *Eudemian Ethics* 2.6 1223a2–9. However, the idea that what is up to us is intermediate in frequency between what is usual and what is infrequent is hardly plausible.

184   NEMESIUS

SECTION 35

ON FATE

Those who ascribe the cause of everything that happens to the rotation of the stars[917] are not only in conflict with accepted ideas but also exhibit (15) the whole of social activity as useless. For laws are absurd, law courts are out of place since they punish those who are in no way responsible, blame and praise are irrational, and prayers are senseless, since everything happens according to fate.[918] Providence is also banished[919] together with piety, while man is found to be a mere instrument of the rotation above. For by this (20) not only the bodily parts but also all the thoughts of the soul are said to be stimulated to action. In general, those who maintain these views annihilate both what is up to us and the nature of the contingent, and thus simply degrade the universe. The stars themselves are also unrighteous, making some men adulterers, some murderers, and, prior even to these, their creator, God, (25) bears the responsibility if he framed such a state of affairs which inevitably [105] places on us a burden of evils, so that not only does this absurdity bear on social activity but also God is displayed as the cause of the greatest evils, in addition to their hypothesis being proved to be impossible. But one must not even listen to these ideas, which are clearly blasphemous and (5) absurd.

Some say that both our freedom and fate are preserved.[920] For fate [they say] contributes something to each thing that happens, such as to water its chilling, to each plant its bearing a certain fruit, to stone its downward

917 A general reference to believers in astrology. Some ancient astrologers, like their modern successors, countered these objections by saying that astrology only indicates tendencies; cf. e.g. Ptolemy, *Tetrabiblos* 1.3.4, but contrast Manilius, *Astronomicon* 4.12–22, 106–18.

918 These are standard objections to determinism, and in particular to astrological determinism, in both pagan and Christian authors, traced back to Carneades in the second century BCE by Amand (1973); on this passage specifically see Amand (1973) 568–69. Cf. Verbeke and Moncho (1975) lxiv n.5.

919 This is the first appearance in the treatise of Nemesius' view that providence is incompatible with necessitation, the latter rendering the former redundant. But there are difficulties here; see the Introduction.

920 For the contrast between astrological determinism, in what has preceded, and Stoic compatibilism, in what follows, cf. e.g. Tacitus, *Annals* 6.22, 'others think that there is indeed a fate in accordance with events, but that it does not come from wandering stars but is to be found in the principles and interweavings of natural causes; and they leave to us the choice of life, (though), when you have chosen this, there is a fixed sequence of things that follows'; Plotinus 3.1 [3] ch.2.25–36, and also ibid. chs. 5 and 7 respectively.

motion and to fire its upward motion, and in the same way to a living thing its assenting (10) and having impulse; so when nothing external and fated obstructs this impulse, then it is entirely up to us to walk and we shall by all means walk. Those who say this, of the Stoics Chrysippus and Philopator and many other famous men,[921] prove nothing other than that everything happens by fate: for if they say that our (15) impulses are given to us by fate and these are sometimes hindered by fate, sometimes not, it is clear that everything happens by fate, including what seems to be up to us. We shall again use the same arguments against them to show the absurdity of their opinion. For if, in the presence of identical causes, as they themselves say, there is every necessity that the same things (20) should happen,[922] and it is not possible for them to happen at one time this way, at another differently, because things have been thus ordained from eternity, then it is necessary that also the appetition of a living thing should utterly and wholly occur in this way in the presence of the same causes. But if impulse also follows from necessity where is what is up to us left? For what is up to us must be free. But it would be free if in the same **[106]** circumstances it were up to us sometimes to have impulse, sometimes not to. But if impulse also follows by necessity, it is clear that the result of impulse will also come to be by fate, even if it is brought about by us and in accordance with our nature, our impulse and our decision. For if it were possible for our impulse also not to

---

921 Chrysippus (c.280–207 BCE) is the third head of the Stoic school; Philopator is referred to by Galen (*On the Diagnosis of the Affections of the Soul*, 5.41 K) as the teacher of one of his teachers, which places him early in the 2nd century CE. The same argument is attributed to unnamed determinists by Alexander of Aphrodisias (*fl.* c.200 CE), *On Fate* ch.13 (LS 62G); cf. also Plotinus, 3.1 [3] 7.14ff., and Boethius, *On Aristotle's On Interpretation, second version*, 195.10ff.; Sharples (1978) 253–59. Nemesius must derive from the common source independently of Alexander, for he names Philopator, while Alexander does not. It seems likely that Philopator claimed to be giving the views of Chrysippus (cf. Bobzien [1998a] 368–69), and that he is the source both for Nemesius (via Pophyry?) and for Alexander. Partly on the basis of this passage, Bobzien (1998a, 359–412) argues that the terms of the debate on determinism and free will were substantially altered in the 2nd century AD; see above, Introduction 4.c.

922 This formulation of the determinist position – apparently anticipating Laplace – is again parallelled in Alexander (*On Fate* ch.22 = LS 55N) and there is a lack of exact parallels in our evidence for earlier Stoic doctrine. See Bobzien (1998a) 372–75, who also argues that this formulation is similar to Chrysippus', and differs from modern ones, in not appealing to general empirical laws. How far there is any substantial difference from Chrysippus in the conception of determinism here may indeed be questioned; on the use of the term 'necessity' see Bobzien (1998a) 140–42. Bobzien argues against the view that Alexander has imposed the term 'necessity' on the Stoic position (1998a, 366 n.14); the strongest argument for her view is the occurrence of the term in a similar context here in Nemesius, who must be independent at least of Alexander's treatise *On Fate* (above, n.921).

occur, (5) the proposition saying that in the presence of the same causes the same results must necessarily follow would be false. It will be found that the same also holds in the case of non-rational and inanimate things. For if they assign impulse to us because we have it by nature, what stops us saying that burning is up to fire, since fire burns by its nature, as perhaps Philopator seems to hint in his book on (10) fate? So what is brought about through us[923] by fate is not up to us, for by the same argument something will be up to a lyre, a pipe and other instruments, and all non-rational and inanimate things, when people act through them. But that is absurd.

SECTION 36

ON WHAT IS FATED THROUGH THE STARS

(15) The wise men of the Egyptians say that fate is truly [predicted] through the stars, but that it can be averted by prayers and expiatory sacrifices:[924] for there are certain services to the stars themselves which soften them, and other superior powers that are able to divert them, and that is why prayers, and services (20) of the gods and expiations have been devised. In reply to them we shall say that they make fate something contingent and not something necessary. But the contingent is undetermined, the undetermined unknown. So by this all prophecy is destroyed,[925] especially that of the so-called 'nativity-casters', which these men value above other methods as a powerful and true activity. (25) If they should say that the effects on our fortunes of the astral configurations are clear and recognized by those who understand, but when the aspect does not result in accordance with its own power a god has prevented it, we shall say that this also is absurd. First

---

923 'through' is similarly used in the statement of the Stoic argument at Alexander, *On Fate* 13 182.12. See above, n.889 to section 32.

924 Telfer (1955, 402), followed by Wyller (1969, 140–41), sees a reference here to the Egyptian priest Abammon in Iamblichus, *On the Mysteries*. (Telfer regards the work as actually by Abammon rather than by Iamblichus, but that view is now generally rejected.) As Polites (1979, 70) points out, the idea that prayer can release us from fate is attributed to 'the Egyptians' by Porphyry, *Letter to Anebo* 25.3–7 Sodano = Eusebius, *Preparation for the Gospel* 3.4.2 (*GCS* 8.1 [43.1] 117.2-6 Mras; the reference to the Egyptians at 24.1 Sodano/116.13 Mras). On the notion here that fate can be altered see Bobzien (1998a) 187 n.24, who compares Seneca, *Questions concerning Nature* 2.36f.

925 For the expression 'all prophecy is destroyed', Polites (1979, 71) compares Diogenianus at Eusebius, *Preparation for the Gospel* 4.3.11 (*GCS* 8.1 [43.1] 172.5–7 Mras) = *SVF* 2.939 270.34-36, and Alexander, *On Fate* 17 188.11–12, 31 201.28.

because they make prayer alone and the service of the gods up to us, but nothing else. Then we shall raise with them the question how it is that, while all other **[107]** human activities and pursuits stand in some sort of relation to the stars, prayer alone is up to us. For it is puzzling from what cause this is so and why it is necessary. Next, if there is some skill and method of expiation which wards off the effects of fate, (5) is the method attainable by all men, or by some and not by others? For if by all, nothing in the argument prevents fate being altogether averted when all have learned the skill which prevents its fulfilment; if it can be attained by some and not by others, what sort of being is he who determines this? For if fate itself makes some servants (10) of the divine, but not others, everything will be found once again to be fated; for the matter of prayer and service is revealed as not only no more up to us than is fate, but as less so.[926] But if it is not fate, and there is some other cause of this state of affairs, that will rather appear as fate:[927] for the whole power of fate is bounded by one's being able or (15) not being able to succeed by prayer. For fate is nothing to those who are able [so to succeed], but for those who are not able everything is according to fate. So it will be found that for some men everything is according to fate, for others nothing according to fate. And it is clear that he who determines this is himself the supreme fate, and so once again everything will be found to be according to fate, in addition to the fact that he who so distributes (20) will be unjust, whether he be some divinity or some other fate. For he does not distribute the method of serving the gods among men according to merit. For why is this person more meritorious than that when all are instruments of fate and none does anything from his own initiative, or rather does not choose? For in things that happen in this way no one (25) is righteous or unrighteous, so that no one is worthy or unworthy of favour. But he who makes an unequal distribution to equals is unjust. **[108]**

[Sections 37–38] Rejection of the view that choices are up to us but their consequences are fated and inevitable, and of the Stoic belief that all events are endlessly repeated. God is superior to necessity.

926 Literally, 'as not only no less not up to us than is fate, but more so'.
927 Polites (1979, 73) compares Gregory of Nyssa, *Against Fate*, 48.5–9 McDonough (1987), though there the regress involves not humans' ability to pray but the power of the stars themselves: 'if it is not from choice that each of these things [*sc*. the power of the astrological signs] is as it is thought to be, but as a result of some necessity, then some other fate again above these determined the peculiarities of their natures and powers; so it will be necessary to look for other stars above these'.

SECTION 37

ON THOSE WHO SAY THAT CHOICE OF ACTIONS IS UP TO US

Those who say that the choice of actions is up to us, but the outcome of our choices depends on fate – and they are the wisest of the pagans[928] – are right on the one count and mistaken on the other.[929] For in positing that choices (5) of practical matters are up to us, but their outcome not completely so, they are completely right, but they are wrong to attribute the outcomes to fate. They will be shown to be wrong first as making fate incomplete, if it has the

---

928 Literally 'Greeks'
929 It is not clear who these are. Telfer (1955, 404) and Verbeke and Moncho (1975, lxvi–lxvii) take the reference to be to the Stoics; Amand (1973, 565), Polites (1979, 74) and Bergjan (2002, 197) regard the theory criticised here as Platonist. The position described is similar to the Middle-Platonist doctrine of conditional fate discussed in the next section (38), but is presumably to be distinguished from it, unless this part of Nemesius' work is to be regarded as more than usually in need of editorial revision. The Stoic doctrine of co-fated events is sometimes illustrated by similar examples to those used by the Platonists; the latter make the point that Laius, the father of Oedipus, was told that *if* he had a son that son would kill him (Alcinous, formerly identified as Albinus, *Instruction Manual [Didascalicus]* 26, 'So the soul has no master, and it depends on her to act or not, and this has not been necessitated, but the consequence of the action will be brought about in accordance with fate. Thus "Paris will carry off Helen", which depends on him, has as consequence "the Greeks will go to war over Helen." For this was how Apollo, too, prophesied to Laius, "If you beget a son, the one who has been born will kill you." The oracle includes Laius and his begetting a child, but what was fated was the consequence'; Calcidius, *On Plato's Timaeus* 153: 'This is how Apollo gave the prediction to Laius: "Beware of sowing the forbidden furrow of children; the son who is born will slaughter you impiously and all your house will be stained with blood." By this oracle he showed that it was in Laius' power not to sow, which is what preceded; what then followed was no longer in Laius' power but rather a matter of fated necessity according to what was deserved by what had preceded. If it had been necessary for that destiny to befall Laius, or if that disaster had already been threatening for a long time as the result of unavoidable necessity, the prediction would have been pointless. But [Apollo], since he knew in advance what would follow, forbade him to become a sower according to fate, knowing that it was in his power to abstain if he wanted to; but Laius, as a human being not knowing the future, enquired what he should do from the one who did know, but nevertheless he sowed, not enticed by fate but overcome by his own lack of temperance'), and the former that Laius would not have had a child if he had not slept with a woman (Cicero, *On Fate* 30 = *SVF* 2.956 = LS 55S; cf. Origen, *Against Celsus* 2.20 = *SVF* 2.957 = Sorabji [2004] vol.2 5(k)(3), Diogenianus in *SVF* 2.939, and Alexander, *On Fate* 31). Bozbien (1998a, 219) (cf. 181 n.6, 216 n.103) argues that the connection between conditional oracles and co-fated events is post-Chrysippean and the result of a confusion; see, however, Sharples (2007b). The appeal in what follows to the Stoic doctrine of fate (below, n.931) has particular *ad homines* relevance against the Stoics.

ON THE NATURE OF MAN 189

one but not the other, and then making it a consequence of our judgment. For they say that the works of fate follow upon our judgment, (10) and thus it will be found to be manipulated by us rather than manipulating us, and man, who moulds it through his choice, is more powerful than fate.[930] But one must say that providence is the cause of the outcome of actions; for this is the work of providence rather than of fate. For it is peculiar to providence to assign to each according to what is suitable for each, and for that reason the outcome (15) of choices will sometimes be advantageous and sometimes will not. But fate is a concatenation of causes, for this is how the Stoics define it, i.e. as an order and binding together that admits of no exception.[931] It does not produce its ends according to utility, but rather through its own necessary process.[932]

But what would they say about those who are altogether dim-witted and foolish and therefore (20) incapable of choice? Is it fated for them to be such or is it not? If it is not they will fall outside the limits of fate: if it is fated, it necessarily follows that not even choice is up to us. For if what is not chosen is subject to fate, necessarily what is chosen is so as well, and thus they fall back among the first group (25) who say that everything is fated. Also the battle between **[109]** reason and desire in the case of the one who has self-control and the one who lacks it is superfluous; for if it is determined of necessity that one will act and the other abstain, what is the use of his inner conflict and quarrelling? However, this also is included in what is fated, not

---

930 This remark, cited by Verbeke and Moncho (1975) lxvii n.18, is sufficient on its own to show the falsity of the claim in their main text (lxvi–lxvii, and again at lxxviii) that for the Stoics our autonomy extends only to our internal attitude to events and does not involve any ability to influence them. There are *some* cases where we have no power to influence the course of events (and the Stoic Epictetus, for rhetorical purposes, tends to emphasise these); but this is not the normal human condition, in the Stoics' view any more than in anyone else's. See Sharples (1986) and (2005).

931 *SVF* 2.917, cf. 918–21; LS 55JKL.

932 Again Nemesius characteristically requires that providence, by contrast with fate, excludes necessity and admits of discretion. See the Introduction. There is, however, no reason why a predetermined fate should not give to each what is suitable for each, if it is designed by a providence which knows in advance what this will be; and this was in fact the Stoic position, identifying providence and fate (*SVF* 1.176, 2.528, 2.937) or seeing the latter as the working out of the former (*SVF* 2.913 = LS 55M). The objection that the Stoic theory, if such it is, in effect reduces providence to fate is the characteristic complaint made by the Platonists against the Stoics, according to Boys-Stones (2007); on the other hand, the Platonists who put forward the conditional-fate doctrine of section 38 would hardly want to deny that the outcomes of choices are fated. If then there is a Middle-Platonist basis to Nemesius' argument here, it would seem that it has been overlaid by other considerations.

merely that he should act, but also that he should act in this manner. What does he who holds this say (5) other than that choice also is something decreed? For choice is that which fights with desire and wins in the case of those who have self-control, but loses in the case of those who do not. So their basic hypothesis is destroyed: for choice is no longer up to us.[933]

SECTION 38

ON PLATO'S ACCOUNT OF FATE

(10) Plato has a double account of fate, one concerning its substance, the other concerning its activity. In substance it is the soul of the universe: in activity it is the divine law that admits of no infringements on account of an ineluctable cause. This he calls the decree of Nemesis.[934] He holds that

---

933 The objection in this paragraph could again come from a Platonist source insisting that the Stoics cannot escape the implication of their theory that everything alike is due to fate. Cf. Boys-Stones (2007).

934 Literally 'Adrasteia', a title of the goddess Nemesis; Plato, *Phaedrus* 248c, one of the Platonic 'proof-texts' for the doctrine of conditional fate also cited by [Plutarch], *On Fate* 4 570a (cf. Calcidius, *On Plato's Timaeus* 143, 182.8 Waszink). Both aspects of the doctrine of fate here, fate as substance and fate in activity as a conditional law, are found in pseudo-Plutarch, *On Fate* 568c–70e: '[Fate] as substance seems to be the whole soul of the world divided in three ways, into the part that does not wander and the [part] that is thought to wander and thirdly into that which exists beneath the heaven in the region of the earth. The highest is called Clotho, the one after her Atropos, and the lowest Lachesis, receiving the heavenly activities of her sisters and weaving these together and transmitting them to what is assigned to her, the region of the earth. ... Next let us define what is conditional, and [show] that fate too is like this. By "conditional" we mean what is not laid down by itself, but in a way really subjoined to some other thing, in all cases that indicate a consequence. "This is the ordinance of Necessity (Adrasteia): whatever soul accompanies a god and sees something of the truth is to be free from suffering until the next revolution, and, if it can always do this, it will always be free from harm." [Plato, *Phaedrus* 248c] ... In addition to this let it be distinguished in what way "Everything is in accordance with fate" is true, in what way false. If it indicates that everything is included in fate, it is true ... but if, as it rather implies, it indicates not all things, but just what is a consequence of fate, we should not say that everything is in accordance with fate, even if everything is in accordance with fate [in a sense]. For not all the things which are included in law are lawful or in accordance with law, for it includes treachery and desertion and adultery and many other things like that, none of which anyone would call lawful.' Both aspects are also found in Calcidius, *On Plato's Timaeus* 143–54, especially 152: 'Fate regarded as a substance, then, is the soul of the universe, but there is also assigned to this as its structure the law of doing all things rightly, which incorporates fate regarded in terms of function and action, and which has the following content and consequence: "if this is the case, this will follow". So in these

this law was given by the first and highest god to the soul of the universe for the ordering of everything, and according to it (15) everything that happens proceeds. He says that this active fate is also in accordance with providence, for fate is delimited by providence. For everything that occurs by fate does so also in accordance with providence, but everything providential is not also fated.[935] The divine law itself, which he says is providence together with fate, contains everything within it, (20) some things as a condition,[936] some things as a result of a condition. For it includes the antecedent[937] causes, as it were as certain causes which are conditions, and these are up to us – assents and judgments and impulses.[938] Those matters that follow on from these of

---

things what precedes depends on us, but what follows is according to fate, and is called by a different term, "fated", very different from fate; so that there are three things – what depends on us, and fate, and what awaits us by the law of fate according to our deserts. Then he sets out the words of the law itself: "the soul that has made itself the companion of a god and has seen something of those things which really exist will be safe up to the time of another revolution, and if it always does this, it will always remain safe" [Plato, *Phaedrus* 248c]. So this whole law and announcement is what is properly called fate.' Fate as a conditional law also in Alcinous, *Instruction Manual (Didascalicus)* 26: 'Concerning fate [Plato's] opinion is something like this. He says that all things are in fate, but not all things are fated. For fate, which has the status of a law, does not say "because this person will do this, this person will suffer this". For this is infinite [in extent], since the people who are born are infinite [in number], and so are the things that happen to them. For what depends on us will be no more, and praise and blame and everything like these. Rather, [it says that] whichever soul chooses such a life and does certain things, will incur certain consequences. So the soul has no master, and it depends on her to act or not, and this has not been necessitated, but the consequence of the action will be brought about in accordance with fate.' See below, nn.935, 939, 940; also *Timaeus* 41de; Theiler (1946); Dillon (1996) 294–98, 320–23; Mansfeld (1999); Bergjan (2002) 198–99; and Boys-Stones (2007), who persuasively argues, against the dominant view, that the Middle Platonists shared the Stoic belief in the compatibility of determinism and human responsibility, and that their disagreement with the Stoics turned rather on what they saw as the impossibility, within the Stoic system, of distinguishing between divine and human agency.

935 Cf. Calcidius, *On Plato's Timaeus* 144–45, 183.10–184.3 Waszink; Dragona-Monachou (1973).

936 The Greek word used here, *hupothesis*, can mean both 'purpose' and 'supposition'. The doctrine of conditional fate adopted by the Middle Platonists and followed here interprets fate as the law that certain actions which we choose to perform have certain inevitable consequences; the antecedents in the conditionals that express these connections are indeed both suppositions, in the context of the general conditional statements, and purposes, in the context of actual human action, but we have chosen to translate in a way that brings out the theory of conditional fate.

937 Or possibly 'primary'. On the term *prohêgoumenos* in such contexts cf. Sharples (2001a) 538 n.188, and the discussions referred to there.

938 Verbeke and Moncho (1975, lxviii n.25) connect this formulation with that of Alexander of Aphrodisias, influenced by Stoic terminology, in his *On Fate*. See above, n.903 to section 33.

necessity are because of the condition. And the choice of things that are done is up to us, as a condition; when the things that are up to us are established, what is fated follows on from these themselves (25) as from a condition. For example, it is up to us whether to sail; that is the condition: but on the basis that we sail, there follows what results from this condition, that we shall or shall not be shipwrecked. That is why he calls what accompanies **[110]** and follows from conditions up to us, i.e. beginnings and actions, 'as a result of the condition'. So what precedes and is up to us is as a condition, the consequences are as a result of the condition and not up to us, but of necessity. For what is in accordance with fate is not, he holds, determined from eternity, but follows upon what (5) precedes and is up to us. His 'Responsibility lies on him who has chosen. God is not responsible'[939] is also in accord with this, as is also that 'virtue has no master'[940] and the existence of prophecy. All his argument tends towards choices and some actions in accordance with choice being up to us, but what results from them and the outcome being necessarily in the hand of fate.

But this was shown in the foregoing (10) to be unsatisfactory. In so far as he calls fate the ordinance and will of God, and in so far as he subordinates fate to providence he varies little from the sacred oracles which say that providence alone controls all; but he differs greatly in saying that the outcome follows what is up to us of necessity. For we say that the acts of providence do not come about of necessity, (15) but contingently;[941] for if they do come about of necessity, in the first place the greater part of prayer is cut away, for according to Plato prayer will extend only to beginnings of actions, so that the better things are chosen,[942] but after they are chosen prayer will for the rest be pointless, since consequences follow entirely from necessity. But we determine that prayer has power (20) over these also. For it is in the hands of providence whether the sailor is shipwrecked or not; neither, however, is of necessity, but contingent. For God is not subordinate to necessity, nor is it lawful to say that his will is the slave of necessity: for he is even the creator of necessity. For he placed a necessity upon the stars,

---

939 Plato, *Republic* 10 617E, also alluded to by Calcidius, *On Plato's Timaeus* 143, 182.9–10 Waszink and quoted by Theodoret, *Remedy for Greek Attitudes* 6.57.

940 Plato, *Republic* 10 617E; also quoted by Theodoret *Remedy for Greek Attitudes* 6.57 and (in the form '*soul* has no master') by Alcinous, *Instruction Manual (Didascalicus)* 26.

941 See the Introduction, 4.d.

942 The Greek could also mean 'the more important'. But that is out of place – the point is that prayer will have a *restricted* place – and the idea that we pray for guidance to make the better choice is appropriate to the context.

so that they always move in the same courses, and he laid bounds upon the sea, (25) and he placed a necessary limit on the universal and generic. If they want to call him fate, since things come about wholly and completely in accordance with necessity in such a way that everything that comes to be ceases to be in its turn, it is of no account. **[111]** For we do not quarrel with them about words. God himself is not only set outside all necessity, but is also its lord and maker. He is authority and his nature is authoritative, and he does nothing either by natural necessity nor by the dictate of law: everything is possible to him including what is necessary. (5) In order that this should be shown to be, he once stopped the course of the sun and the moon which travel of necessity and are always the same, to show that nothing comes about for him of necessity, but everything contingently according to his authority. He made such a day once, as the scriptures also signified, so that he should only exhibit and not break the decree that he made in the beginning of (10) the necessary course of the stars.[943] Also he preserves some men alive, such as Elijah and Enoch, who are mortal and subject to passing-away, in order that we should recognize through all these acts his authority and unfettered will.[944]

The Stoics say[945] that the planets are established again into the same (15) sign according to magnitude and longitude in which each was in the beginning when the universe first was formed, and at set revolutions of time they bring about the conflagration and destruction of what exists and again establish the universe anew in the same state, and, as the stars travel once again in the same way, each of the things that came to be in the previous cycle is brought to be (20) unchanged. For Socrates and Plato will exist again, and each person with the same friends and fellow-citizens, and they will have the same experiences, meet with the same events and undertake the same activities, and every city and village and field will be reconstituted as before. The reconstitution of the universe occurs not once but many times, or, rather, to infinity, and (25) the same things will be re-established without end.[946] But, they hold, the gods who are not subject to this destruction, having observed one cycle, know from **[112]** it everything that will come about in the following cycles. For there will be nothing foreign beyond

---

943 Joshua 10:12–14, 'Sun, stand thou still upon Gibeon'.
944 II Kings 2:11, 'And Elijah went up by a whirlwind to heaven'; Genesis 5:24, 'And Enoch walked with God, and he was not, for God took him', quoted at Epistle to the Hebrews 11:5.
945 111.14–112.3 = *SVF* 2.625; LS 52C.
946 For this Stoic doctrine (also attributed to Pythagoreans) cf. LS § 52.

what happened before, but everything will be the same without change even in the least detail. Some say that the Christians imagine the resurrection because of this reestablishment, far (5) wide of the truth. For the sayings of Christ foretell that the resurrection will occur once and not cyclically.[947]

[Sections 39–40] Which things are up to us; the extent of our autonomy.

SECTION 39

ON WHAT IS UP TO US, OR ON AUTONOMY

The account of autonomy, i.e. of what is up to us,[948] includes first an investigation whether anything is up to us; for there are many who oppose this. (10) The second investigation is about what things are up to us, and over what we have control. The third is to discover the reason why the God who made us made us autonomous.

So let us resume and speak first about the first problem, and prove that there is something up to us from what even the opponents accept. They say that of everything that happens the cause is either God, or necessity, or fate, or nature, (15) or luck, or spontaneity;[949] but of God the work is existence and

---

947 Luke 20:36. For the contrast between Christian belief and the pagan doctrine of eternal recurrence cf. Origen, *Against Celsus* 5.20–23; Siclari (1974) 265; Polites (1979) 89.

948 'up to us' renders *eph' hêmin*, as previously; 'autonomy' renders *autexousion*. See Bobzien (1998a) 355 and n.73, and above, Introduction 4.c.

949 Streck (2005, 91–92) compares the lists at Aristotle, *Nicomachean Ethics* 3.3 1112a31–33 and Anonymous, *On Aristotle's Nicomachean Ethics* 149.33 and 155.19. Only Nemesius includes God among the causes. The anonymous commentary and Nemesius distinguish 'spontaneity' (*automaton*) from luck; Aristotle does not do so here, but the later writers have clearly incorporated the distinction from Aristotle, *Physics* 2.5–6 in a typical piece of systematisation. Neither Aristotle nor the anonymous commentary includes fate, but for the apparent addition of fate to lists of causes attributed to Aristotle (and to Theophrastus) and deriving ultimately from *Nicomachean Ethics* 3.3 1112a31–33 one may compare Aëtius 1.29.2 and 1.29.4. (We are grateful to Bill Fortenbaugh and David Runia for discussion of these passages; see Fortenbaugh's forthcoming commentary on Theophrastus fr. 503 FHS&G). Verbeke and Moncho (1975, 143) and Streck (2005, 91–92) note a similar list (necessity, fate, choice, chance, spontaneity) attributed to Anaxagoras and the Stoics at Aëtius 1.29.7, in the context of the Stoic theory of chance as 'a cause obscure to human reason'. The list in Aëtius includes choice and excludes nature, since for the Stoics everything is in a sense due to nature, identified with fate. Neither pseudo-Plutarch nor Calcidius introduces their account of chance with an argument by elimination of this type. What is up to us and what is due to chance are contrasted by Basil the Great, *On the Six Days [of Creation]* 2.5 (*PG* 29 40A).

providence: of necessity the process[950] of things that are always the same; of fate to bring to pass of necessity what is fated (for it too is a kind of necessity); of nature birth, growth, decay, plants and animals; of luck the rare and unexpected. For they define luck as the conjunction and (20) meeting of two causes originating from choice that bring about something other than what is usual,[951] such as finding a treasure when digging a grave.[952] For he who put the treasure there did not do so in order that he who found it would do so, nor did he who found it dig in order to find the treasure: rather, the former acted so that he could get it out when he wanted it, the latter in order to dig a grave. But something came to pass other than what both had proposed. To the (25) spontaneous belong incidental occurrences to the inanimate or non-rational involving neither nature nor **[113]** skill.[953]

Under which then of these are we to include what occurs through men, if man is not the cause and origin of his actions? But it is not permissible to ascribe deeds that are sometimes evil and unjust to God; nor to necessity, since they are not among things that are always the same; nor to fate, since what is fated (5) is among things necessary rather than contingent; nor to nature, for it is living creatures and plants that nature produces; nor to luck, for the deeds of men are not rare and unexpected; nor to spontaneity, for it is occurrences to the inanimate or non-rational that just happen. It remains that the man who acts and makes is himself the origin of his own works and is autonomous.

---

950 Or 'movement'. If the reference is to the heavenly bodies, as it appears to be (and cf. Aristotle, *Nicomachean Ethics* 3.3 1112a23–26) locomotion is in fact the only process they can undergo.

951 Literally, 'what is natural'.

952 The example is Aristotle's (above, n.894, except that Aristotle has digging in order to plant rather than digging a grave; the change to the latter is presumably for heightened rhetorical contrast with the good fortune, though we may note that two MSS here have *taphron* 'ditch' rather than *taphon* 'grave': cf. Morani [1982] 39. Basil, cited in n.949, has digging to make a well.). Cf. Alexander, *On Fate* 8. But the doctrine of chance as the conjunction of *two* causes is distinctively Platonist: [Plutarch], *On Fate* 572c, 'it resulted from a certain concurrence of causes, each having come about with a different end in view', Calcidius, *On Plato's Timaeus* 159 192.17–19, 'when two causes which have their origin in our intention come together in such a way that there happens not what was intended but something very different and unexpected, this is the sport of fortune', followed by the example of buried treasure, and Boethius, *Consolation of Philosophy* 5.1, again of the treasure example, 'it has its own proper causes, the unforeseen and unexpected concurrence of which seems to have produced the chance event'. Cf. Sharples (1991) 214–16; Streck (2005) 93–94.

953 So Aristotle, *Physics* 2.6.

Moreover, if man (10) originates no actions, deliberation is superfluous.[954] For what will be the use of his deliberation if he is not master of any action? But to exhibit what is fittest and most valuable in man as superfluous would be an extreme absurdity. Accordingly, if he deliberates he deliberates for the sake of action. For all deliberation is for the sake of action and because of action. Further, where activities are up to us, there our actions (15) through the activity are up to us. But activities exhibiting virtue are up to us, so the virtues are also up to us. That activities exhibiting virtue are up to us is made clear by what Aristotle well says about the excellences of character;[955] for what we learn to do through action, that we do through having learned. For by having learned mastery over pleasure we become self-controlled, and when we have become self-controlled (20) we master pleasures. One may also put it this way: all agree that it is up to us to practice and train; but practice is master of our dispositions, for custom is second nature.[956] But if practice is master of disposition and practice is up to us, then so is our disposition: but where our dispositions are up to us there our actions in accordance with our dispositions are also; for our actions **[114]** contribute to our dispositions. For he who has a right disposition will act rightly, he who

954 For this argument compare Alexander, *On Fate* 11 178.8–15, 'if everything that comes about will do so through certain causes which are laid down beforehand and defined and pre-existing, it follows that men deliberate pointlessly about what they should do. But if deliberating is pointless, it will be pointless for man to be capable of deliberation. And yet, if nature does nothing that is primary pointlessly, and man's being an animal capable of deliberation is brought about by nature in a primary way, and not as some consequence and concomitant of the things that come about in a primary way, the conclusion will be that men's capacity for deliberation is not pointless'; Ammonius, *On Aristotle's On Interpretation* 148.11–15, '[if contingency is excluded, Aristotle] will accuse nature of pointless labour in having made us capable of deliberation; for it is clear that if nothing depends on us, it is pointlessly that we will attempt to deliberate about the things that are not in our power, and we will do something like those who deliberate how the sun might rise or not rise' (cf. above, n.909); Boethius, *On Aristotle's On Interpretation, second version*, 220.10–15, 'everything which is by nature is not pointless; but it is by nature that men possess [the power] to deliberate; but if necessity alone is going to rule affairs, there is no reason for deliberation; but deliberation is not pointless, for it is by nature; therefore necessity does not have complete power in affairs.' Domański (1900) 153 n.1.

955 *Nicomachean Ethics* 2.1 1103a32–33: 'things we must do by having learned, these we learn by doing'. Cf. Streck (2005) 94–95, who notes that Nemesius omits Aristotle's non-ethical examples (building and lyre-playing) retaining only the ethical ones, and that Nemesius' clause 'when we have become self-controlled, we master pleasures' is an addition to what Aristotle says here; however, it explicates 'we do by having learned', and may reflect a desire for rhetorical symmetry. For the argument that follows compare *Nicomachean Ethics* 3.5 1114a4–b25; Streck (2005) 95 n.311 (his 3.7).

956 Literally: 'an acquired nature'.

has a wrong one wrongly: so it is up to us to be righteous or unrighteous. Encouragement and advice make clear that some things are in our power. For nobody encourages a man not to be hungry or thirsty or to fly:[957] for these things are not up to us. (5) So it is clear that things to which there is incitement are up to us. Further, if nothing is up to us laws are superfluous; but every society naturally uses some laws, knowing that they have the power to do as the law says, and the majority of societies record gods as their lawmakers, as the Cretans do Zeus and the Lacedaemonians Apollo. So a knowledge of what is up to us is naturally inbred (10) in all men. The same as the above is to be said about blame and praise and everything else that disproves that everything happens by fate.

SECTION 40

CONCERNING WHAT THINGS ARE UP TO US

It has been sufficiently proved that certain things are up to us and that we are in control of some actions. It remains to say what things are up to us. (15) Accordingly we say that in general everything that is done by us intentionally is up to us (for it would not be said to be an intentional action if the action were not up to us), and without qualification whatever is followed by praise or blame and in regard to which there is encouragement and law; for this also was earlier shown to be so.[958] All things involving soul and about which we deliberate are up to us in the proper sense: for we deliberate on (20) the basis that it is up to us to perform or not to perform the envisaged action. Deliberation was shown in what preceded to be about matters having an equal possibility. What has an equal possibility is that where we are able to do both the thing itself and its opposite.[959] Our intellect makes a choice of this and it is the origin of actions, and these things that have an even possibility are the ones that are up to us, things such as moving and (25) not

---

957 Similar examples (but with 'persuasion', rather than 'encouragement') at Aristotle, *Nicomachean Ethics* 3.5 1113b26–29 and Anon., *On Aristotle's Nicomachean Ethics* 156.6–7 (growing hot, being in pain, being hungry); Aspasius, *On Aristotle's Nicomachean Ethics* 77.4–5 (growing hot near a fire, being hungry). Koch (1921) 40.

958 Above, section 29 and the first part of section 35.

959 Above, latter part of section 34. For the formulation in terms of its being up to us to do a thing or not to do it cf. Aristotle, *Nicomachean Ethics* 3.5 1113b6–11; Donini (1987) 1250–52 (who argues that the formulation in terms of doing the *opposite*, as here, is that of Alexander of Aphrodisias rather than of Aristotle himself); Sharples (2001a) 547–49.

moving, being moved to act or not,[960] trying or not trying to obtain what is not [115] necessary, lying and not lying, giving and not giving, rejoicing and not rejoicing in what one should, and all matters in which virtue and wickedness are displayed. In these matters we are autonomous. The crafts are also concerned with what has an even possibility;[961] for every craft is concerned with the production of what (5) may or may not exist and of which the origin is in the power of the maker, not of the product. For nothing either of the things that are eternal and exist of necessity, nor of those things that come to be of necessity, is said to come to be by skill, and also nothing that comes to be among those things that may be otherwise but has its productive cause in itself, as in the case of animals and plants, is said to come to be (10) by skill. For they come to be naturally and not by skill.[962] But if the productive cause of the products of crafts is external to the products, who is the cause of the products of craft except the craftsman who produces them? For to produce them is up to the craftsman; so he is the origin and cause of what was done. So therefore skilled activity, the virtues and all actions involving the soul and reason are up to us.

It was shown (15) earlier[963] which sort of activities involve the soul. But most people, who think that autonomy is ascribed to every action, possession and chance, naturally discount the importance of reason; the most severe even introduce scripture into the argument such as 'it is not in man that walketh to direct his steps',[964] and they say 'My good people,

---

960 More literally, 'having an impulse or not', in the sense not just of having an initial inclination but of acting upon it. See above, n.873, and section 35.

961 Streck (2005, 97) notes that the conflict with 34, 103.2–5 above is only apparent; here the point is that the crafts are concerned with what may or may not come about, there that, to the extent that they have fixed rules for bringing about the desired outcome, deliberation is not required.

962 With 115.4–10 Streck (2005, 95–97) well compares Aristotle, *Nicomachean Ethics* 6.4 1140a10–16, and notes that Nemesius says of plants and animals that they have their productive cause in themselves, where Aristotle speaks rather of their having their *principle (arkhê)*; Streck suggests that Nemesius modifies Aristotle's wording from a Christian perspective. He further notes that in their wider contexts the aims of Aristotle and Nemesius in the two passages are different; Aristotle discusses craft (*tekhnê*) in order to contrast it with action (*praxis*), while Nemesius wants to emphasise that both are up to us.

963 Above, section 26.

964 Jeremiah 10:23. It is not clear who 'the most severe' are, but that the verse had been used in this way may also be suggested by the fact that Theodoret, writing some years later than Nemesius, argues that the following verses show that Jeremiah is not here 'submitting our freedom of judgement to a physical (or 'natural') slavery, or what subordinating what is according to us to the necessity of fate' (Theodoret, *On Jeremiah* 10:24–25, *PG* 81

how is man autonomous, when it is not in his power to direct his steps?' (20) They also quote 'the thoughts of men, that they are vanity',[965] as if we could not accomplish what we have in mind. They say many such things, in ignorance of what is meant by 'autonomy'. For we do not have the power to be rich or poor, or always be healthy, or be naturally strong, or to rule, or in general to have any of the goods that are called instrumental or fortuitous, or things (25) whose end is determined by providence: but we can perform acts of goodness and badness, choose them, and move and do those things whose opposites we are equally able to do; for choice precedes every action, and not only action but choice also is liable to judgment. A passage in the gospel **[116]** makes this clear: 'Whosoever looketh on a woman to lust after her hath committed adultery with her already in his heart',[966] and Job made sacrifices to God on account of the wrongdoings of his children in their thoughts.[967] For choice is the beginning of sin and of righteousness; for the *deed* is sometimes permitted by providence and is sometimes (5) prevented.[968] For since some things are up to us and there is providence, of necessity both of these outcomes occur. For if they happened in only one way the other would not exist; but since what happens is of both kinds, sometimes the result will be as we choose, sometimes according to the word of providence and sometimes both.

But since providence is in a way general, in a way individual, (10) it is inevitable that the particular should be affected in the same way as the universal; for, if the surroundings are dry, bodies become dry, if not all in the same way, and if a mother lives an unhealthy life and is luxurious her children will in consequence be born with a poor bodily temperament and wayward in their impulses.[969] So it is clear from what has been said that people may find themselves with an unfavourable bodily temperament either

---

col.572.10–14 Migne). Telfer (1955, 415 n.5) similarly notes that the use of this passage of Jeremiah to argue against human autonomy is tendentious, but does not suggest who might be referred to; he also translates *drimuteroi* not by 'the most severe' but by 'men of sharper wit', which seems too positive a characterisation for the context.

965 Psalm 94[93]:11.
966 Matthew 5:28.
967 Job 1:5.
968 For Nemesius' view that necessity and providence are incompatible see the Introduction, 4.d. For Nemesius, unlike the Platonists, the consequences of our actions are not inexorably determined once we have acted, but providence can intervene.
969 The effects of bodily temperament on behaviour are emphasised by Galen, *That the Faculties of the Soul follow the Mixtures of the Body* (*Quod animi mores*) (see above, nn.298, 300); but they are already indicated by Plato, *Timaeus* 86–87, cited by Galen at *That the Faculties of the Soul follow the Mixtures of the Body* 6, 49.12–51.11 Müller (4.789–91 K).

(15) through the general environment or through the preferred life-style of their parents or through themselves being damaged by luxuriousness, so that poor constitutions may sometimes be brought about from an intended beginning, and providence is not altogether responsible for such things. So when the soul gives in to the bodily temperament and abandons itself to desires and anger, or is oppressed or puffed up (20) by chance circumstances, such as poverty or wealth, intended evil has existence. For the soul that does not give in corrects and conquers the poor temperament, so that it alters rather than is altered, and sets its psychic dispositions into a good state by good behaviour and a favourable regime. So it is clear from those who do get things right that those who do not **[117]** do so err intentionally. For it is up to us either to go along with a poor constitution or to oppose it and conquer it. But the majority who use their poor constitution as an excuse, [saying that it is] the cause of their condition, ascribe their wickedness to necessity and not to choice, and therefore say that the virtues also are not up to us, a ridiculous (5) statement.

SECTION 41

FOR WHAT REASON WERE WE BORN AUTONOMOUS?[970]

That we have autonomy is the result of our rational nature. Man and the immaterial beings.

It remains to say for what reason we were born autonomous. So we say immediately that autonomy enters in together with the rational [element of the soul],[971] and that change and transformation[972] are naturally implanted in all things that come to be, especially those which (10) come to be from underlying matter. For transformation is the origin of coming to be: for coming to be is through the alteration of the underlying matter. One might recognise what is being described by turning one's eye to all plants and animals, land, winged and aquatic, for their change is continuous. That

---

970 The combination of Neoplatonist and Aristotelian ideas in this section is discussed by Streck (2001).
971 Cf. above, 2, 36.26–37.1 with Streck (2005) 73 n.237, and Introduction 4.c; Alexander, *On Fate* 14, 184.15–20. The ultimate source of the connection between reason and the ability to choose between opposites may be traced back to Aristotle's contrast between rational and non-rational potencies in *Metaphysics* Θ 5.
972 *tropê*, literally 'turning', and so in the next sentence.

autonomy enters in together with reason is easy for those who have paid attention (15) to see from what was said about something being up to us: but it is perhaps not at all out of place if we recall the same things, since the chain of thought requires it.

Of the rational element one aspect is theoretical, another practical; that which comprehends the nature of what there is is theoretical, the deliberative element that determines the right rule for practical matters is practical. They also call the theoretical element (20) intellect, the practical one reason, and the former wisdom, the latter sagacity.[973] But everyone who deliberates does so on the basis that choice in practical matters is up to him, so that he may choose what is preferred as a result of the deliberation and, having chosen, may do it. So there is every necessity that he who is able to deliberate should also be in control of his actions; for if action were not in his power his capacity to deliberate would be superfluous.[974] If that is the case (25) autonomy necessarily exists alongside the rational element: for either the rational element will not exist, or if the rational element exists it will be in control of actions. But if it is in control of actions **[118]** it must certainly be autonomous.

It was also demonstrated that things that come to be from underlying matter are changeable.[975] From both considerations it follows that man is necessarily autonomous and is changeable.[976] He is changeable because he comes to be, and autonomous because he is also rational. So those who accuse God because he did (5) not make man incapable of evil, but autonomous, fail to notice that they accuse God because he made man rational and not a non-rational [animal]. For one of the two is inevitable, that he should be made non-rational, or, as rational and concerned with practical matters, autonomous. So of necessity all of a rational nature is autonomous and changeable in its own nature, (10) but those that come to be from underlying matter have a changeable nature in two ways, in regard to matter and in regard to birth itself; but those that did not come to be from underlying matter are changeable in only one way, that of birth.[977] Again,

---

973 'Sagacity'=*phronesis*, sometimes translated 'practical wisdom'. Aristotle, *Nicomachean Ethics* 6.7 and 6.5 respectively.
974 Cf. above, n.954.
975 Above, 117.9–10.
976 Literally, 'subject to turning' (*trepton*). Above, n.972.
977 That is, the only change that is possible for immaterial beings is the one involved in their being created in the first place. For Aristotle and the Neoplatonists immaterial beings are not created at a particular moment in time, having previously not existed; but Nemesius adopts a Christian perspective, and has in mind angels and other spiritual beings. However, he qualifies

of these immaterial beings those in regions surrounding the earth and by their association with men busying themselves with practical matters are more (15) changeable than others. But those [immaterial beings] who from the exaltation of their nature are more closely related to God and attain to blessedness by their knowledge of him, being turned only to themselves and to God, have altogether made themselves strangers to practical affairs and to matter and have made themselves akin to contemplation and to God,[978] and they remain unchanged, autonomous (20) through their being rational, but unchanging for the reasons given. And no wonder; for of men also those who have become contemplative and have separated themselves from practical matters have remained unchangeable.[979]

I think that it has been demonstrated also by what has been said that in the beginning all rational natures were created in the best possible way; and if they had remained as they were first made they would have been free from (25) all evil. Their evil comes to them by their choice; and thus at least those who have remained as they originally came to be have blessedness. Of the incorporeal **[119]** only angels were changed, and not all of them, but some of them who inclined towards things below and acquired a taste for earthly things, distancing themselves from their relationship with things above and with God.[980]

It is surely clear from what has been proved that we have (5) changeable powers of choice[981] so that we may be changeable in our nature, and

---

what he says here by immediately indicating in the next sentence that some immaterial beings *can* change once they already exist.

978 Verbeke and Moncho (1975, lxxxiv n.99) note that the terms translated here by 'made themselves strangers' and 'made themselves akin' are in origin technical terms of Stoic ethics.

979 elfer (1955, 419 n.3) compares Athanasius, *Life of St. Antony*, 14, where the saint after twenty years in solitude is described as 'governed by reason and stable [established, fixed: *hestôs*] in what concerns nature'; *hestôs* corresponds to 'unchangeable' (*atreptoi*; above n.976) here. Streck (2005, 112 n.360) argues that Nemesius may be referring alike to pagan and to Christian ascetics here. See also section 19 above, with Streck (2005) 39 and n.114.

980 On the fall of the angels compare Augustine, *City of God* 11.11 and 13, 12.1–9; also above, section 1 6.14–16, 10.14–19 and nn.215, 230 there. The point of '*only* angels' here is not clear; Telfer (1955, 420 n.4) takes it to exclude archangels, but as he himself indicates this is inconsistent with the view that Satan was a fallen archangel. Is the point rather that inferior spirits (118.13–15 above, i.e. *daimones*) always had a more lowly status?

981 Streck (2001, 561 n.7 and 2005, 103–04) notes that the anonymous commentator on the *Nicomachean Ethics* connects choice with disposition and contrasts this with power: 199.15–23 (on 4.7 1127b14–15, see the next note), 'that is, [being boastful is not located in] having the power to pretend to have greater things that one does not possess (for everyone can do *that*), but in having a disposition of such a sort and being of such a sort as to do this. For it is not powers

one surely cannot blame God for our being bad through having powers that admit of change. For vices do not reside in powers but in dispositions, and our dispositions follow our choice.[982] So we become bad through our choice, and we are not bad by nature.[983] One may understand better what is being said as follows: in what preceded (10) we said that a power was that as a result of which we are able to do each thing that we do.[984] But every power of choice is the same for both opposites;[985] for the power to lie and to tell the truth is one and the same, and there is one and the same power to be temperate and to be licentious. But there is not also the same disposition towards opposites,[986] such as to be licentious and to be temperate, to lie and (15) to tell the truth, but it is opposite dispositions that are [directed] towards opposites. For being temperate is from a virtuous disposition, being licentious from a bad one. So vices do not relate to powers, but to dispositions and to choice.[987] For it is not the power that prepares us to be licentious or to lie, but choice; for it is up to us to tell the truth and not to lie. So, (20) since vice is not a power but a disposition, He who gave us the power is not the cause of our evils, but the disposition which is acquired in us, through us and because of us; for it was possible for us to acquire the opposite disposition by practice, and not the bad one.

A power differs from a disposition in that all powers are natural but dispositions are acquired, and in that powers cannot (25) be taught, but

---

that are responsible for [people] being like this or like that, but rather choices, since powers themselves are for opposites, and opposites cannot co-exist ... the liar is not the one who has the power to lie, but the one who chooses [to do so] and who lies and [does so because] he delights in the act of lying itself.' As Streck observes, the commentator here implies that choice follows disposition, while Nemesius says the reverse; for Aristotle each implies the other. See above, Introduction 4.c.

982 With this and 119.16–17 below Streck (2005, 100–01) compares Aristotle, *Nicomachean Ethics* 4.7 1127b14–15: '[being] boastful is not [a matter] of power but of choice; for it is according to his disposition and by being of a certain sort that [someone] is boastful'.

983 With the second half of this sentence Streck (2005, 101) compares Aristotle, *Nicomachean Ethics* 2.5 1106a9–10; Aristotle has mentioned choice earlier in the context (1106a2–4).

984 Above, section 34 103.11.

985 Cf. Aristotle, *Metaphysics* Θ 2; *Nicomachean Ethics* 5.1 1129a13–14, and the anonymous commentary on the *Nicomachean Ethics* 199.17–23 (cited in n.981 above) and 206.1–2 (on 5.1). Streck (2005) 102–05, suggesting from the parallels with the anonymous commentary that Nemesius may be reliant on the commentary tradition rather than on Aristotle directly.

986 Cf. Aristotle, *Nicomachean Ethics* 5.1 1129a14–15, and the previous note: Streck (2005) 102.

987 Aristotle, *Nicomachean Ethics* 2.5 1105b19–1106a12.

dispositions are acquired by learning and habit. So if a power is natural and untaught, but a disposition is acquired and taught, nature is not responsible for evils but our bad training, and thereby **[120]** the possession of a bad disposition. For it has been shown that every disposition is acquired. It is clear that all powers are natural from the fact that we all have the same powers save the disabled. It is clear that dispositions are not natural from the fact that we do not all have the same dispositions, but different people different ones; for the things that are natural are the same for (5) everyone.[988]

SECTION 42

ON PROVIDENCE

Arguments for the existence of divine providential care.

It has been sufficiently stated in the foregoing that man is autonomous, in what matters he is autonomous and for what reason he was born autonomous. But since not everyone who proposes to kill always actually kills, but (10) sometimes he does, sometimes he does not, since his action is thwarted and does not proceed as envisaged, and we said that providence was the cause of these events and not fate,[989] the appropriate discussion after those on what is up to us is the discussion about providence. This discussion divides into three: first whether there is providence, second what it is, third what it is about. (15) But a Jew, even if he were mad, would not be unaware of providence, knowing the wonders in Egypt, having heard of those in the wilderness in which providence appeared to man more far-shining than things visible, and having become aware in the prophets and in Babylon of many works of providence that admit of no ambiguity. Christians are taught by all these things too that (20) there is a providence, but most of all by the most divine and incredible work of providence through its love for man, the incarnation of God for our sake. But since this discussion is not directed

---

988 'Nature' must here be understood as referring to human nature in general. For the argument compare Alexander of Aphrodisias, *On Fate* 27 198.12–20, though Alexander does say 'all or at any rate most'.

989 See above, 40, 116.4. Verbeke and Moncho (1975, lxxi at n.33) see a different connection; because human action itself (though not its consequences) is excluded from the scope of providence (see above, Introduction, 4.c–d.) it is appropriate to go on to discuss providence after dealing with human agency. This connection is not explicit in the text, but is reasonable enough.

to these alone,[990] but also to the pagans, then let us demonstrate that there is providence by other things as well in which they too believe. One might then prove that there is providence by the same arguments as those by which we also showed (25) that there is a God. For the permanence of all things and especially of those that come to be **[121]** and pass away, the position and order of things which is always preserved in the same way, the motion of the stars that never alters in any way, the yearly cycle, the return of the seasons and the yearly equality of days and nights, each in turn – increasing and decreasing with a (5) measure which is never less nor more – how would this have continued in the same pattern if no one exercised providence?[991] Furthermore, retribution for sins, and still more the revelation of sins themselves, when they become manifest through some circumstances when nobody has been able to discover them, show that there is providence. The Hebrew scriptures (10) are full of such stories, as well as pagan writings. Like this is the experience of Susanna narrated in the scripture,[992] and among the Greeks that of the poet Ibycus; for while he was being murdered by some men and had no ally nor witness of the plot he saw some cranes and said 'Do you, O cranes, avenge my murder.' When his (15) city was searching for the murderers and could not find them, some cranes flew across as the theatre was closing and the people were seated; the murderers saw them, laughed and said 'Behold! the avengers of Ibycus'. One of those who were seated near them heard them and reported it to the authorities, and the murderers were arrested and admitted the murder.[993] There is a mass (20) of similar stories written down by the ancients, and if one wished to collect them the account would be endless in length. If the same kind of conviction does not follow for all the guilty, and some even seem to escape altogether, let none deny providence on that account: for it does not watch over mankind in only one manner, but in (25) many different ways.

The existence of providence is proved not least by the **[122]** structure and harmonious relationship of bodies that come to be and pass away,

990 See the Introduction, 3.a. As Telfer (1955, 424 n.3) points out, 'these' could refer either to Jews and Christians, or just to Christians, but the former is more likely.

991 Cf. Plato, *Laws* 10 886a. The connection of providence with the maintenance of order in the universe is difficult to reconcile with the contrast between providence and necessary fate on which Nemesius elsewhere insists (see the Introduction). The two can be reconciled by arguing that providence is above fate and hence not itself subject to necessity even when it creates it; see below, n.1007.

992 Above, 30, 95.17.

993 For the story see Plutarch, *On Garrulousness* 509e–510a. Ibycus' city was Reggio di Calabria in southern Italy.

which is preserved throughout in a consistent way. For the foresight of providence is revealed in every part of the body, which the industrious can catalogue from various works.[994] Also the variety of colours in (5) animals which always retains the same pattern shouts out that there is providence. Again, the need for prayer and service to the divine by votive offerings and precincts acknowledged in common by all men is indicative of providence. For if the universe were without providence who would pray, and to whom would anyone pray? Also the care for good works which is naturally exhibited by all who are not perverted[995] (10) displays providence: for while eagerly expecting the reward from this we also choose to benefit those who are unable to reciprocate.

But if providence be abolished injustice is permitted to those who are able to act unjustly: charity and the fear of God are abolished and with them virtue and reverence. For if God is not provident he neither punishes (15) nor bestows rewards on those who act well, nor does he ward off harm from those unjustly treated. So who would then worship a god who helped us in no way about anything?[996] Prophecy and all foreknowledge are also abolished. But nothing of this is consonant with what happens almost every day. For there have been many divine epiphanies in times of need, many remedies are given (20) to the sick in dreams, many predictions have been fulfilled in every generation, and many murderers or evildoers are terrified by night and by day. Moreover, God is good, and, being good, He is beneficent: but if He is beneficent He also exercises providence. What need is there to speak of the works of creation, its harmonious (25) relationships, its position and order and the help that each part provides for the whole, and how it could not be in a good state other than that in which it now is, and how it permits no addition to or subtraction from what there is, but all is complete and good and **[123]** providentially constructed?

But let us postpone to the account of the creation[997] our exposition of these matters in order that we may not suffer what many who have written about providence have suffered. For they sing the praises of the creation

---

994 Telfer (1955, 425 n.7) suggests that Nemesius may have in mind, among others, Galen, *On the Usefulness of the Parts*; see above, n.367.

995 For parallels see Sharples (2001a) 588–89 n.524.

996 Cf. the complaint against Aristotle of Atticus (the Middle Platonist) fr.3: 'we are looking for a providence that makes a difference to *us*'.

997 No account of creation follows. The abrupt end of the treatise may suggest that it was left unfinished or that the end is lost, though there is no evidence, beyond the abrupt ending, to indicate that this is so. See the Introduction, section 2.

instead of providence, though creation, while leading us to the account of providence, is very different (5) from it. For creation and providence are not the same thing. For to creation belongs the making well of things that come to be, to providence the good care of things that come to be.[998] But these do not altogether co-exist, as can be seen from the men engaged in each craft and procedure. For some go only so far as to make things well and have no further care, as do (10) carpenters, painters and sculptors, while some only tend and provide, like cowherds and shepherds. Therefore we also in our account of creation should make plain that things come to be well, but in that of providence we should show that they receive the necessary care after coming to be.

So how is man always born from man and ox (15) from ox, and each from its own seed and not another's, if there is no providence? For if one were to say that the thing goes on in sequence as at the first birth, that would be to say that providence at all events co-exists with the creation. For the fact that the created continues in sequence shows that providence was established together with creation: for to providence belongs the conduct of things (20) after creation. So he who said that would say nothing more than that the Creator of what is and He who provides for it are one and the same.

But who would not wonder at the work when he sees how the forms of men differ in so many thousands of ways and are nowhere exactly alike? But he who works out the explanation will find that the continual difference in form of individuals (25) is providential. For consider, if all had preserved the same characteristics without variation, what a confusion of affairs there would have been. What ignorance and obscurity would have taken hold of the man who did not recognise his own or distinguished the stranger, whether enemy or bad, from the friendly and the good. **[124]** All things would indeed have been one, as Anaxagoras said:[999] for if that were so nothing would have prevented copulation with sisters and mothers, nor open robbery and other crimes, if only one escaped immediately; for if seen one would not be recognised later. There would be no law or society established (5) nor would fathers and sons recognise each other nor would anything else human survive. For man would be blind to man and sight would afford him little; for he would recognise nothing other than age and size. Providence became the cause of such great goods for us by varying the form of men

---

998 Or possibly, with one MS, 'that have come to be'; cf. 'after coming to be' at 123.14, and below, n.1029. Telfer (1955, 428 n.3) suggests that the distinction between creation and providence may derive from Origen's lost commentary on Genesis.

999 Anaxagoras, fr.1, 'all things were together'.

always and everywhere and (10) never failing to do this,[1000] which is the surest sign that there is also a special providence for individuals. For each person is recognised even by the formation of his looks and his voice, even if that is not exactly preserved, on the grounds that his form is sufficient.[1001] For providence added this for us as an extra, as well as (15) the difference of colour, in order that the weakness of human nature might be assisted in many ways.

I believe that even the majority of animals that have the same form according to species, like crows and rooks, have certain differences in appearance by which they recognise each other as mates. In any case crows and rooks often gather together in large flocks but separate into (20) pairs as each male and female recognises its mate. How would they recognise each other if each did not have some individual stamp which is not easy for us to recognise, but is naturally and easily seen by members of its species? Also the tokens, the prophetic utterances, the omens and the divine portents (this is addressed to the pagans) preserve according to their own theory, as they themselves say, the outcomes **[125]** of their revelations, note them down as prophecies, and confirm the truth of the predicted outcomes.[1002]

But it is clear both from these points and from what will be said next that providence exists. So let us say what providence is. Providence, then, is (5) care for things by God. It is also defined as follows: providence is the wish of God by which all things receive a suitable way of life. But if providence is the wish of God there is every necessity that things should happen according to right reason, in the best way, most divinely and in the only way that they could be well, so that they could not be better arranged.[1003] (10) It is also necessary that the same being should be the maker and guardian of things. For it is neither sensible nor fitting that one should make and another tend things that come to be. For such an arrangement is always seen to be weak. A considerable indication of what has been said is present also in living things: for every parent also cares for the upbringing of its offspring, but man, in so far as he is able, provides also (15) for all other things that affect [his offspring's] life. Those which do not provide fail to do so through weakness.

1000 Literally 'omitting no time of doing this'; we follow the interpretation of the phrase adopted by both Burgundio and Telfer.
1001 'even if ... sufficient' is deleted by Morani, as absent in the Armenian version.
1002 This sentence is deleted by Morani as absent in the Armenian version.
1003 Verbeke and Moncho (1975, lxxiii) point out that this must exclude human actions themselves – if, we may add, Nemesius is to be consistent. See Introduction, 4.c–d.

So it has been proved that God is the source of providence and that providence is his wish.

SECTION 43

ABOUT WHAT MATTERS THERE IS PROVIDENCE

Divine providence extends to what happens to individual human beings, even though we cannot fully understand its workings.

It has been said that there is providence and what it is: it remains to say (20) about what matters there is providence, whether it is over universal matters, or particular matters, or over both universal and particular. Plato, then, holds that providence governs both the universal and the particular, and he divides his account of providence into three.[1004] [According to him] the

---

[1004] This Middle-Platonist account of three providences is also found, with variations in the details, in pseudo-Plutarch, *On Fate* 572f–574d, especially 572f–573a: 'the highest and primary providence is the thought of the first god, which is also a will that produces all things well; it is in accordance with this that, in the first place, each of the divine things is entirely ordered in the best and fairest manner. The second [providence] is that of the secondary gods who travel in the heaven; it is in accordance with this that mortal things come to be in an ordered fashion, and all the things that relate to the permanence and preservation of each kind. And one would be right to describe as third the providence and forethought of all the *daimones* who are stationed in the region of the earth and are guardians and watchers over human affairs'; and in Apuleius, *On Plato* 1.12, 'the primary providence is that of the highest and most supreme of all gods, who not only set in order the gods who dwell in heaven, whom he spread through all the parts of the universe for [its] safeguarding and glory, but also through nature brought into life within time those mortal creatures who surpass the other terrestrial creatures in wisdom [i.e. human beings]; and after establishing [his] laws he handed over to the other gods the arranging and safeguarding of the things which must happen day by day. From here the gods took over the governing of secondary providence, and maintain it so strenuously that all things, even those which are displayed on high to mortals [i.e. the movements of the heavens] preserve unchanged the condition of the Father's ordinance. But the *daimones*, whom we can call Genii and Household gods, [Plato] considers to be the servants of the gods and guardians and interpreters for men, if they require anything from the gods.' As Boys-Stones (2007) points out, Nemesius is alone in explicitly referring to three types of providence as such; Apuleius does not explicitly refer to the activity of the *daimones* as providence at all, and pseudo-Plutarch rather more cautiously says that 'one would be right to describe as third the providence of the *daimones*'. The Middle-Platonist account of providence ultimately rests on interpretation of the *Timaeus* (42de). Cf. Dillon (1996) 323–26, Bergjan (2002) 308–10, Sharples (2003), and Introduction 5.c.

first providence is that of the first god, and his providence [126] is primarily for the forms, next for the world universally, for example the heavens and the stars, and for all things universal, i.e. genera, substance, quantity, quality and other such things,[1005] and the species subordinate to them. But the secondary gods, (5) those that circle round the heaven, [according to Plato] watch over the coming-to-be of individual animals and plants and everything which comes to be and passes away. Aristotle too ascribes the coming-to-be of these to the sun and the circle of the zodiac.[1006] Plato declares that the third type of providence is over the conduct and end of actions and the ordering of goods (10) in living which are called natural and material and instrumental and their opposites. He says that certain appointed spirits around the earth oversee this providence and are guardians of human actions. The existence of the second and third providences is said to derive from the first, since potentially everything is controlled by the first god who appoints both the second and the (15) third sources of providence. It is worthy of praise that he refers all to God and says that all providence depends upon his wish; but not also his saying that the second providence is those that circle round the earth; for this is not providence, but fate and necessity.[1007] For it is necessary

---

1005 These are the Aristotelian categories as supreme genera. It is to be noted that they are contrasted with the Platonic Forms (the latter being transcendent and immaterial, the former enmattered?). Nemesius' list of objects of primary providence is at first sight strange. Apuleius follows the *Timaeus* (39–42) in referring to the highest god's setting in order the other gods and the rational parts of mortal souls; pseudo-Plutarch refers simply to 'divine things'. However, Nemesius' list *would* be highly appropriate as a list of the things of which a divine intellect might be aware – which may be an indication of its possible origin.

1006 Aristotle, *On Coming To Be and Perishing* 2.10 336a32ff.; *Physics* 2.2 194b13; *Metaphysics* Λ5 1071a15. [Plutarch], *On Fate* 9 572f–573a says of secondary providence that 'it is in accordance with this that mortal things come to be in an ordered fashion, and all the things that relate to the permanence and preservation of each kind'. Plutarch himself, at the end of *On the Generation of Soul in the Timaeus* (1030c), stresses the role of the heavens in the preservation of things that come to be, rather than the educational value of observation of the heavens for human souls emphasised by Plato (*Timaeus* 47a–c).

1007 Again Nemesius contrasts providence on the one hand with fate and necessity on the other. See the Introduction. The issue was already debated among the Platonists, for pseudo-Plutarch, *On Fate* 574cd considers whether secondary providence is co-ordinate with fate or subordinate to it. See Mansfeld (1999) 140–41, 143–44. For providence as superior to fate cf. Proclus, *On Providence and Fate and What Depends on Us* II.3.4–13 and II.4.3–10, pp.28–29 in Isaac (1979), with Steel (2005) 292–93; Boethius, *Consolation of Philosophy* 4.6.7–17; Sorabji (2004) vol. 2 89–92. (Sorabji indeed contrasts Nemesius' view with that of the Neoplatonists in allowing human action to be subject to providence but not to fate; the difference may rather lie in Nemesius' non-Platonic conception of human freedom, cf. above, Introduction 4.c. and n.82.)

that events should occur according to the relative position[1008] of these, and it cannot (20) be otherwise. But it has been shown long ago that nothing providential is subject to necessity.[1009] The Stoic philosophers, who give prominence to fate and freedom, leave no room for providence;[1010] but in truth they also abolish freedom, as was demonstrated earlier.[1011]

[**127**] Democritus, Heraclitus[1012] and Epicurus deny that there is providence, whether universal or special. Epicurus, at any rate, said: 'The blessed and the imperishable neither itself engages in affairs nor provides them for another, so that it is affected neither by anger nor by joy; all such things are a kind of (5) weakness.[1013] Anger is foreign to the gods;[1014] for anger is because of what is against the will, but nothing is against a god's will.' So these philosophers follow their own basic principles: for since they believe that this universe was formed of its own accord, they reasonably say that everything is without providence; for who would watch over that which had no creator?[1015] For it is plainly necessary that what originally came to be of its own accord[1016] will carry on (10) of its own accord. One must, then, reject their primary dogma: for if this is eliminated what has been said is satisfactory to prove that there is providence. So let us reserve for its proper places[1017] the refutation of these philosophers, and proceed to the view of Aristotle and the others who deny that there is a providence for particulars.

(15) Aristotle maintains that particular affairs are controlled by nature alone, as he hinted in Book 7 of the *Nicomachean Ethics*:[1018] for nature is

---

1008 *skhesis*, the technical term for an astrological configuration.
1009 See above, nn.919, 932, 941, and the Introduction, 4.d.
1010 This is Nemesius' judgement, one the Stoics themselves would have emphatically rejected; see above, n.932.
1011 Above, section 35.
1012 Siclari (1974, 291 n.119) and Morani suggest that this is a reference to Heraclitus fr.30, which, however, denies divine *creation* of the world – in the sense that it had no beginning in time – rather than divine *providence*.
1013 Epicurus, *Principal Doctrine* 1. Morani deletes 'Epicurus, at any rate ... against a god's will' as absent in the Armenian version.
1014 Cf. Lucretius 1.49.
1015 Bergjan (2002, 120 n.61) cites numerous parallels for this argument.
1016 *automaton*, the term used by Aristotle (*Physics* 2.6) for what is a result of mere chance.
1017 None of these philosophers is mentioned again. See the Introduction, part 2.
1018 The Greek text refers to '*Nicomachean Ethics* zeta'. Greek Z is the sixth letter of the alphabet, but as a numeral indicates 7 (and was so understood here by Burgundio). At *Nicomachean Ethics* 7.13 1153b25ff. Aristotle, discussing the claim that all creatures naturally pursue pleasure, says 'since neither their nature nor their best disposition either is or seems the

divine and, being present in everything that comes to be, it naturally prompts the choice of the advantageous and avoidance of the harmful. For, as has been said,[1019] each animal selects the food (20) suited to it and searches for the advantageous, and naturally knows the remedies of its ills.

Euripides[1020] and Menander[1021] in some places say that the intellect in each individual watches over him, but none of the gods. But intellect is concerned only with what is up to us, whether in action, in skill, or in contemplation, but providence **[128]** is concerned with what is not up to us.[1022] For it decides on our being rich or not and being healthy or not, while intelligence can bring about neither of these, and nor can nature, as Aristotle believes [it can].[1023] For the workings of nature are plain to see. What has intelligence or nature to do with a murderer sometimes receiving retribution, sometimes escaping? – unless someone were to say that (5) the sphere of intelligence and nature belongs to providence, the second[1024] to fate. But if what is in the sphere of intelligence and nature is providential,

---

same, they do not all pursue the same pleasure, but they do all pursue pleasure. But perhaps they do indeed pursue not the pleasure they think or would say [that they do], but the same one; for all things by nature possess something divine.' This seems closer to what Nemesius says here than does *Nicomachean Ethics* 6.13 1144b4ff., 'each *character* seems to belong to everyone in a way by nature', suggested by Verbeke and Moncho (1975) lxxiv n.51, and by Morani. Cf. Sharples (1983), 144–45 and nn. Bergjan (2002) 257 and n.172 compares Atticus' presentation of Aristotle; cf. n.1027 below.

1019 Above, section 1, 8.1–2; Basil the Great, *Homilies on the Six Days [of Creation]* 9, *PG* 29b 193ab, 'if in our account we go through how much untaught and natural care for their lives is present in these irrational animals'.

1020 Euripides fr.1018 Nauck^2, 'the mind in each of us is god'.

1021 Menander fr. 749 Koerte, 'the mind in each of us is god'; cf. frr. 13 ('for the good, mind is always god') and 64 ('the mind that will speak is god') Koerte, and *Arbitration (Epitrepontes)* 736–40 Koerte, 'you will say "So the gods have no thought for us". They have given each man his character (*tropos*) as a guardian ... this is god for us, the cause of each person's faring well or badly.' Cf. Sharples (1983) 145 and nn.

1022 In restricting providence to what is not in our power Nemesius risks both restricting God's power and adopting a Pelagian view of human action. See the Introduction, 3.b. and 4.c–d.

1023 Alexander of Aphrodisias, *On Fate* 6 (cf. *Supplement to On the Soul [mantissa]* 25) argues, probably taking over an earlier Peripatetic theory, and presenting his view as Aristotle's, that an individual's nature determines their actions, lives and deaths for the most part, though in the context, especially in *On Fate*, of arguing that this is not inevitable and that our nature can be overcome. He does not explicitly mention nature making us rich or healthy, but he does refer to the circumstances (by implication, unfavourable ones) to which our natural way of life may lead us. Bergjan (2002, 277–78) compares Nemesius' objections here to Eusebius' discussion in *Preparation for the Gospel* 6.6.

1024 I.e., such things as whether a murderer escapes or is punished.

and what follows on that is fated, what is up to us is abolished.[1025] But that is not the case; for it was proved that what is in the sphere of intelligence, both practical and theoretical, is up to us.[1026] Also not all that is providential is natural, even if natural events occur (10) providentially.[1027] For many works of providence are not the works of nature, as was shown in the case of murder.[1028] For nature is part of providence, not providence itself.

So those men ascribe providence for particulars to nature and intelligence, but the rest say that God is concerned with the preservation of what exists, so that nothing that has come to be[1029] should fail, and that providence is concerned with this alone. But, they say, (15) particular matters carry on as it may happen,[1030] and that is why many injustices, many murders and, in a word, all wrong-doing is endemic in men. Some of them happen to escape justice, some also are punished, and neither what is in accord with right reason nor the lawful invariably comes about. But how could one say that the supervisor is a god (20) where neither law nor reason rules?

1025 The argument assumes, as above, that providence and what is up to us cannot both be present in the same event.

1026 Above, section 40.

1027 If, following Aristotle, we regard what is natural as happening usually, this suggests that providence for Nemesius includes both the usual and the unusual. See the Introduction, 4.d. Atticus the Middle Platonist had criticised Aristotle for rejecting the Platonic world-soul governing the whole world and holding in the sublunary region nature is the cause for things *other* than human affairs: '[Aristotle says] that nature is not soul, and that the things in the region of the earth are managed by nature alone. For for each thing there are different causes. Of the heavenly things which are always in the same state and condition he supposes that fate is the cause; of the things beneath the moon, nature; of human affairs wisdom and forethought and soul, providing elegance in such divisions, but failing to see what is necessary' (Atticus, fr.8.2 des Places).

1028 Above, section 42.

1029 Reference to the preservation of species (cf. below, n.1038) might seem to require the present tense, 'nothing that comes to be', and that is in fact the reading of one MS. But in a Christian context the past tense of the majority of MSS is appropriate; the species came to be in the initial creation.

1030 The doctrine that providence is not concerned with particulars is found both in the general form that it is not concerned with details (attributed to the Stoics by Cicero, *On the Nature of the Gods* 2.167) and in the specific form that providence is concerned with universals rather than particulars – the distinctive view of Alexander of Aphrodisias: below, n.1038. The reference above to 'the rest' might suggest that Nemesius is here considering a popular view (so Telfer [1955] 437 n.5); that is no doubt true, but in doing so he appears to draw on a specific pagan philosophical tradition. See Sharples (2003) 151–52, and below, n.1032. Bergjan (2002, 257–58) regards this as a second *Peripatetic* view distinguished by Nemesius from that attributed to Aristotle at 127.15 above – which goes beyond what Nemesius explicitly says – and presents it as Alexander's without any hesitation.

For it happens that the good are most of all unjustly treated and humiliated and encompassed by many evils, while the wicked and violent grow in power, in wealth, in positions of command and the other worldly goods. But those who say these things seem to me to be ignorant of many other (25) insights[1031] about providence, but especially the immortality of the soul. For they suppose it to be mortal and circumscribe man's lot by this life. Next, they have warped judgments about what things **[129]** are good.[1032] For they think that those who are surrounded with wealth and give themselves airs because of their reputation and pride themselves on other material goods are happy and blessed. But they hold the goods of the soul to be of no account, though they greatly exceed bodily and external goods: for the goods (5) of the superior are superior. However, the virtues surpass wealth, health and the rest by as much as the soul surpasses the body. Consequently both on their own and with the other goods the virtues make people blessed, with the others in an indefinite sense, on their own and in themselves in a defined one: for some things are conceived in a defined way, such as two cubits long, others in an (10) indefinite one, such as a heap. For if you take away even a couple of hundredweight from a heap what is left is still a heap, and if you take away the bodily and external goods from blessedness in an indefinite sense and leave only the virtues, still in this situation blessedness remains. For virtue even on its own is sufficient for happiness.[1033] So every good person is blessed and every bad person is wretched, even if (15) he has all together what are called the goods of fortune. But the majority are ignorant of this and consider that only those with bodily well-being and wealth are blessed. Accordingly they blame providence, which [in fact] controls our affairs, judging not only from the apparent facts but also according to its own pre-existing knowledge. For God knows that it benefits him who is now worthy and good to be poor, and (20) that wealth, if it has come, destroys his judgment, so He keeps him in poverty to his benefit; and He knows that often the wealthy person would be more harsh if he were short of money,

---

1031 Literally 'theorems' (*theoremata*).

1032 Denial of the immortality of the soul and attaching undue importance to external goods are charges made against Aristotle, and in the former case against Alexander too, by both pagan and Christian authors; see Sharples (1983) 151 and notes there. Verbeke and Moncho (1975, lxxvi) describe Nemesius' own view here as Stoic; but it is also at home in Platonism (see Dillon [1996] 251–52 and 299).

1033 Nemesius' position here on the much-debated question of the relation between virtue and happiness appears to be a variation on the view of Antiochus of Ascalon (1st century BCE) that virtue on its own is sufficient for happiness, but the addition of material goods increases the happiness. On the whole ancient debate cf. Annas (1993) 364–425.

since he would attempt robberies or murders or some other greater wrongs, so He allows him to accumulate wealth.[1034]

Surely also poverty has often been to our advantage, as has the burial of our children and the flight of our (25) servants. For the preservation of worthless children or servants who became robbers would be more bitter than their loss. For we know nothing of the future and look only to the present, so that we judge wrongly what happens; but to God the future also is [130] as the present.[1035] But this has been said to those who condemn [providence], to whom it would be fitting to quote the scriptures: 'Shall the clay say to him that fashioneth it?'[1036] For how is a man not to be shunned when he makes laws contrary to God and instructs against the works of providence but does not even dare to speak (5) against human law-making?

But let us set aside such falsehoods, or rather impieties, and show how they wrongly state that, while universal and generic matters are subject to providence, particular matters are not governed by providence. For one could state only these three explanations why there should not be particular providence: either God is ignorant that it is good to watch over these things as well, (10) or he does not wish to, or he cannot.[1037] But ignorance and lack of understanding are something most foreign to the blessed being; for it itself is understanding and wisdom and knowledge. How could that of which not even a well-thinking man would be ignorant escape God's notice, that when all particular things are destroyed the universals will also be destroyed? For the universals consist entirely of particulars. (15) Surely the species are equal to all the particulars together, convert with them, perish together with them and are preserved together with them; but nothing prevents all individuals from perishing if they receive no care from above. So when they perish all the universals will be destroyed. But if they will say that His providence is for this alone, that all the particular things should not perish in order that (20) the species might be preserved,[1038] they fail to notice that

---

1034 Similar arguments justifying providence are found in Boethius, *Consolation of Philosophy* 4.5.35ff., especially 45; cf. also below, section 43 134.4ff.

1035 Cf. Sharples (1991) 229 and references there.

1036 Isaiah 29:16, 45:9; Romans 9:20.

1037 This set of possibilities goes back ultimately to the argument of Plato, *Laws* 10 900d–903a. For the setting out of the three possibilities in the way they are presented here, cf. Simplicius, *On Epictetus' Manual* 379.462ff. Hadot, and Maimonides, *Guide of the Perplexed* 3.16. See Sharples (2003) 118–21, and above, Introduction 5.d.

1038 That providence is concerned with the preservation of species is the distinctive position of Alexander of Aphrodisias, for example in his treatise *On Providence* which survives only in Arabic translation; see especially *On Providence* 89.5 Ruland, 'Socrates exists only in order

they are saying that there is a particular providence; for, as they themselves say, it is by His providence over these that He preserves the genera and the species.

But they say that he is not ignorant, but is unwilling **[131]** to exercise providence. But unwillingness arises from two causes, either from slackness or because of unsuitability. Who if not mad would accuse God of slackness? For again, slackness arises from two causes, pleasure and cowardice: for we are either slack as slaves to some pleasure or we hold back (5) through fear. But it is not lawful to think either of these of God. But if they declined to accuse God of slackness they might say that it was not fitting for God. For they would say that it was unworthy of such blessedness to descend to the cheap and trivial[1039] and, as it were, to be defiled by contact with material affairs and absurdities of choice, and for this reason He is unwilling. [But if so] they do not see that they are attaching to God two (10) of the worst emotions, disdain and fear of pollution. For it is either from disdain that the Creator neglects the control and management of particulars, which is a very extraordinary thing to say, or else to avoid pollution, as they themselves say. But if, while the sun's rays have the natur[al power] to draw up all liquids, they do not say that the sun and its rays are polluted when they shine (15) on mud, but remain immaculate and pure, in what way do they think that God is defiled by contact with earthly affairs?[1040] Such opinions are not

---

that Man should exist, and Xanthus, Achilles' horse, in order that Horse should exist'; Sharples (2003) 122–23. As an Aristotelian Alexander is also committed to the view that universals exist only in particulars (130.14 above), which Nemesius may be turning against him here, though without naming him. See also Alexander, *Quaestio* 2.21 68.5–11.

1039 A point which was repeatedly made by Alexander; see Sharples (2003) 117 and n.31.

1040 Cf. Theodoret, *On Providence*, PG 83 748.52ff. Migne, 'for if nothing can pollute the Sun, which is a body – for it is visible, and admits of dissolution – when it passes by dead bodies, and evil-smelling slime, and many other things that give off an evil odour, much more than the Sun can nothing of this sort defile the Creator, the Craftsman of all things, who is incorporeal and invisible and unalterable and always the same'. The idea that sunlight exemplifies the divine which cannot be polluted goes back at least to Euripides, *Heracles* 1231–32. It is also used by Neoplatonists. Cf. Julian, *Oration* 4 (*Hymn to King Sun*) 140d, 'the greatest proof of this is that not even the light, which most of all comes down to earth from there, is mixed with anything or admits any dirt and pollution, but it remains in all things in every way unpolluted and undefiled and unaffected'; Synesius, letter 57 in *Epistolographi Graeci*, 669.4–5 Hercher = letter 41, 51.304–05 Garzya, 'the sun's ray, even if it encounters mud, remains pure and undefiled'. Siclari observes (1974, 288 n.114) that Nemesius is turning the pagans' arguments against themselves; that is true, but he is following other pagans, and specifically Platonists, in the way he does so. See also above, n.390.

those of men who know the nature of God. The divine is such that it is free from harm,[1041] corruption and pollution and beyond all alteration. For defilement and all such states are the result of being changed. How is it not (20) utterly absurd to portray the master of any skill of any sort, especially a physician, as caring for the whole[1042] while leaving no particular, even the smallest, uncrafted and untended, since he knows that the part contributes to the whole, yet to portray God the creator as more ignorant than craftsmen?

Does he then wish to but cannot? How is it not altogether incongruous (25) to say that God is weak and unable to do good? In any case there are two ways in which one might say that God was unable to exercise providence over individuals, either by himself not being of a nature to do so or by particulars being unreceptive of providence. [132] But even they agree that it is in his nature to exercise providence, in that they say he does so universally, and also, while the inferior are not able to attain to what is above them, the sustaining power of the stronger extends down even to the last and unperceived. For all (5) things depend upon the divine will, and they draw thence their continuance and preservation. That the existence of individuals who form a plurality is receptive of providence is clear from the animals that are controlled by certain governance and leaderships, of which there are many types. For both bees and ants and the majority of creatures that flock together are subject to leaders, which (10) they follow obediently. But one may recognise this best by looking at the social organisation of men: for it is clearly receptive of administration and care by lawgivers and rulers. But how would what is receptive of these be unreceptive of the providence of the Creator?

No mean indication of there being also a providence over particulars is the naturally ingrained (15) knowledge of it in men. For in the grip of necessity we immediately take refuge with the divine and with prayers, as if nature led us untaught to its aid. But nature would not have led us untaught to what was not of a nature to happen; for also in sudden disturbances and fears we involuntarily call upon God (20) without even thinking. But everything that follows something naturally provides a strong proof which admits of no denial.

How then were those of this opinion led to give such an account? First by believing that the soul suffered dissolution together with the body; secondly by not being able to find the rationale of particular providence. But that the

---

1041 Literally, 'cannot be touched'.
1042 Literally, 'for the universal(s)'. This argument (but not this terminology) is already present in Plato, *Laws* 10 902d–903a.

soul is not mortal (25]) and that human affairs do not end together with this life is shown by the transmigrations of souls accepted by the wisest of the pagans, the so-called stations allotted to souls for the life of each and the punishments of souls which they suffer in accordance with themselves.[1043] These [views], even if defective in some **[133]** other way, still agree that the soul exists after this life and undergoes justice for its sins. But even if the rationale of particular providence is incomprehensible for us, as it indeed is according to the saying 'How unsearchable are your judgments, and your ways past finding out',[1044] (5) still one need not say on that account that there is no providence: for one would not say that there is no sea or sand because we do not know the measure of the sea nor the number of the grains of sand. On this basis, they would say that there were no men or other animals since they do not know the number of men and other animals. For individuals are innumerable for us, and what are innumerable are also (10) unknown to us. And what is universal can often be comprehended in an account while what is particular cannot.

Each person is liable to difference in two ways, one in relation to another person, the other in relation to himself; for the alteration and change in each person even internally each day is great, both in way of life and in his occupations, needs, desires and their (15) consequences. For this creature is quick-changing in his needs and easily influenced by his circumstances. So it is necessary also that the providence suitable for each should be different, varied, and divided over many and extended to match the incomprehension of the multitude, if it is to be present to help each person on each occasion and appropriate to him. The differences between (20) particulars are innumerable, and so the accounts of the providence suitable to each are innumerable; but if they are innumerable, they are unknowable by us.

However, one must not make one's own ignorance into an abolition of the guardianship of the world; for the things that you believe to be not well are judged by the creator to be reasonable, while you who are ignorant of the causes say that these things occur unreasonably. For what we suffer (25) in the case of other unknowns, that we suffer in the case of the works of providence. For **[134]** we comprehend its works by imagination of a sort, and that dim,[1045] getting certain images amid shadows of its works conjecturally from events. We say that some things come about through the consent of

---

1043 That is, the punishments are according to the previous life of each soul and the state in which it is as a result: compare Plato, *Laws* 10 904c.
1044 Romans 11:33.
1045 Cf., with Koch (1921) 48, I Corinthians 13:12.

God,[1046] but there are many forms of consent. For He often consents that the righteous person should fall into (5) troubles, in order that he may exhibit his hidden virtue to others, as in the case of Job. At other times He consents that something absurd should be done in order that through the action that seems absurd something great and wonderful should be achieved, as was the salvation of man through the Cross. In another way He consents that even a saintly man should suffer evil, as in the case of Paul, lest (10) through his good conscience and the power given to him he should fall into boastfulness.[1047] Someone is left in trouble at the right time for the improvement of another, in order that, seeing his fate, others might be instructed, as in the case of Lazarus and the rich man.[1048] For when we see others suffering we are naturally humbled, as Menander well said: 'Fearing the divine because of your trouble'.[1049] Someone is left in trouble (15) also for the glory of another and not through his fault or that of his parents, like the man blind from birth for the glory of the Son of Man.[1050] Again, someone is allowed to suffer to encourage another, in order that the suffering should be unhesitatingly accepted by others through the increased glory of him who suffered, in the hope of glory to come and desire of the good things awaited, as in the case of martyrs and those who (20) have sacrificed themselves for their country or their kindred or their masters. But if someone should think it unreasonable that the saintly person should suffer ill for the improvement of another, **[135]** let him learn that this life is a trial and a race for virtue; thus the greater the labours, so much greater are the crowns; for the recompense for the trials is according to the measure of endurance. That is why Paul was allowed to suffer a myriad tribulations,[1051] in order that he should win a greater and perfect crown (5) of victory.[1052] For all the works of providence come to be well and as is proper.

That God manages all things well and as is proper, and in the only

---

1046 Verbeke and Moncho (1975, lxxvii–lxxviii) connect this with Nemesius' emphasis on human autonomy, saying that some things are 'only tolerated' by God, not brought about by him.

1047 II Corinthians 12.7: 'And lest I should be exalted above measure, through the abundance of the revelations there was given to me a thorn in the flesh.' Telfer (1955, 448 nn.2–3) well points out that this example, and the preceding sentence too, are not such as to be directed to non-Christians; see the Introduction, 3.a.

1048 Luke 16:19–31.
1049 Menander, fr.719 Koerte.
1050 John 9:3.
1051 II Corinthians 7:4, 11:23–27; Telfer (1955) 449 n.8.
1052 II Timothy 4:7–8; Telfer (1955) 449 n.8.

possible way, can be most correctly seen by anyone who uses these two marks which are accepted by all; He is good and He alone is wise; so because He is good He reasonably exercises providence, and because He is wise He watches over (10) things wisely and as is best. For if He does not exercise providence He is not good, and if He does not do so well He is not wise. So one should attend to these marks and in no way condemn the works of providence nor blaspheme, but accept everything unquestioningly, admire all things, and be persuaded that all things happen well and fittingly, even if they appear unjust to the majority, in order that we may not (15) heap upon ourselves much blame for ignorance, in addition to blasphemy.

When we say that all things happen well, it is obvious that we are not talking about the evil of men nor of deeds that are up to us and are brought about by us, but about those of providence which are not up to us. So how is it that saintly men suffer bitter deaths and unmerited slaughters? For if they do so (20) unjustly, why did not a just providence prevent the murder? But if justly, those who committed the murders are altogether blameless. – In reply we shall say both that the murderer murders unjustly and that the murdered is murdered either justly or expediently.[1053] Sometimes it will be justly, because of actions that are out of place but hidden **[136]** from us; it will be so expediently if providence is intercepting evil action by the murdered person in the future, and[1054] because it is well for him that his life should be terminated at this point, as in the cases of Socrates[1055] and the saints. But the murderer murdered unjustly: for he did not do it for this reason, nor was it permissible for him to do so, but he robbed (5) intentionally for gain. For the deed is up to us, but suffering it is not up to us, for example being murdered. But no death is evil, except when for wickedness, as is clear from the death of holy men. But the wicked person, even if he dies in bed suddenly and painlessly, has died badly, bearing his sin as an evil obsequy. However, the murderer murdered wrongly; for in the case of (10) those who are justly put to death, the slain has put himself into the province of the public executioners, and in the case of those killed expediently, into that of polluted assassins. The same applies to the case of those who kill their

---

1053 Cf. Plotinus, 3.2 [47] 13, and Euripides, *Electra* 1244.

1054 It is not clear whether Nemesius is presenting *two* reasons – averting an evil deed, and in general that it is best for a person's life to end at a certain time (in which case 'and' might rather be rendered by 'or') – or whether there is a single reason, that it is best for a person's – even Socrates' – life to end because of the crimes he would otherwise commit in the future. Telfer, taking the passage in the second way, compares (1955, 451 n.3) Wisdom 4:10–14.

1055 Compare Plato, *Apology* 38c, *Crito* 53d.

enemies or make them prisoners and work all manner of evil on prisoners. And the same applies to the avaricious and stealers of goods: for it is both likely that those who are deprived of them benefit from not possessing them, and also the avaricious are unjust; for they (15) stole through avarice and not for the benefit of others.[1056]

[1056] It is hard to believe that the work was intended to end so abruptly. See the Introduction, part 2.

BIBLIOGRAPHY

Abbamonte, G. (1995), 'Metodi esegetici nel commento in Aristotelis *Topica* di Alessandro di Afrodisia', *Seconda Miscellanea Filologica*, Università degli Studi di Salerno, Quaderni del dipartimento di scienze dell'antichità 17, Naples: Arte Tipografica, 249–66.
Accattino, P. and Donini, P. L. (1996), *Alessandro di Afrodisia: L'anima*, Rome and Bari: Laterza.
Ackrill, J. L. (1972–73), 'Aristotle's definitions of *psuche*', *Proceedings of the Aristotelian Society* 73: 110–33.
Alberti, A. and Sharples, R. W., eds (1999), *Aspasius: the earliest extant commentary on Aristotle's Ethics*, Berlin: de Gruyter.
Amand, D. (E. Amand de Mendieta) (1973), *Fatalisme et liberté dans l'antiquité grecque*, Université de Louvain, Recueil de travaux d histoire et de philologie, 3.19, 1945; reprinted Amsterdam: Hakkert, 1973. (References are to the reprint).
Annas, J. E. (1993), *The Morality of Happiness*, New York: Oxford University Press.
Armstrong, A. H., ed. (1966–88), *Plotinus*, Cambridge, MA: Harvard University Press (LCL).
Arnim, J. von (1887), 'Quelle der Ueberlieferung über Ammonius Sakkas', *Rheinisches Museum* 42: 276–85.
Arnold, J. (2000), 'Origen Ω 183', *Suda On-Line*, www.stoa.org/sol/
Austin, J. (1956), 'If's and can's', *Proceedings of the British Academy* 42: 109–32.
Barnes, J. (1999), 'An Introduction to Aspasius', in Alberti and Sharples, eds, 1–50.
Baumgarten, H. (1962), *Galen über die Stimme*, Göttingen: Vandenhoeck and Ruprecht.
Bäumker, C. (1877), *Des Aristoteles' Lehre von den äussern und innern Sinnesvermögen*, Leipzig.
Beare, J. (1906), *Greek Theories of Elementary Cognition from Alcmaeon to Aristotle*, Oxford: Clarendon Press.

Beatrice, P. F. (2005), 'L'union de l'âme et du corps. Némésius d'Émèse lecteur de Porphyre', in Boudon-Millot and Pouderon, eds, 253–85.
Bender, D. (1898), *Untersuchungen zu Nemesius von Emesa*, Leipzig.
Bergjan, S.-P. (2002), *Der fürsorgende Gott*, Berlin: de Gruyter.
Blumenthal, H. J. (1996), *Aristotle and Neoplatonism in Late Antiquity. Interpretations of the De anima*, London: Duckworth.
Bobzien, S. (1998a), *Determinism and Freedom in Stoic Philosophy*, Oxford: Clarendon Press.
—— (1998b), 'The inadvertent conception and late birth of the free-will problem', *Phronesis* 43: 133–75.
Boeft, J. den (1970), *Calcidius on Fate: his doctrine and sources*, Leiden: Brill.
Bonitz, H. (1870), *Index Aristotelicus*, Berlin: Reimer.
Boudon-Millot, V. (2005), 'De l'homme et du singe chez Galien et Némésius d'Émèse', in Boudon-Millot and Pouderon, eds, 73–87.
—— and Pouderon, B., eds (2005), *Les Pères de l'Église face à la science médicale de leur temps*, Paris: Duchesne.
Boulnois, M.-O. (2005), 'L'union de l'âme et du corps comme modèle christologique, de Némésius d'Émèse à la controverse nestorienne', in Boudon-Millot and Pouderon, eds, 451–75.
Boys-Stones, G. R. (2007), 'Middle Platonists on fate and human autonomy', in: R.W. Sharples and R. Sorabji, eds, *Greek and Roman philosophy, 100 BC to 200 AD*, BICS supplementary volume 94, vol. 2, 431–47.
Brain, P. (1986), *Galen on Bloodletting*, Cambridge: Cambridge University Press.
Brennan, T. (2001), 'Fate and free will in Stoicism: a discussion of Susanne Bobzien, *Determinism and Freedom in Stoic Philosophy*', *Oxford Studies in Ancient Philosophy* 21: 259–86.
—— (2005), *The Stoic Life: Emotions, Duties, and Fate*, Oxford: Clarendon Press.
Burkhard, C. (1910), 'Zur Kapitelfolge in Nemesius' Peri phuseôs anthrôpou', *Philologus* 69: 35–39.
—— (1917), *Nemesii Episcopi Premnon Physicon ... a N. Alfano ... translatus*, Leipzig: Teubner.
Caston, V. (1997), 'Epiphenomenalisms: Ancient and Modern', *Philosophical Review* 106: 309–63.
Chiaradonna, R. (2005), 'L'anima e la mistione Stoica. *Enn.* IV.7 [2],8^{2}', in R. Chiaradonna, ed., *Studi sull'anima in Plotino*, Naples: Bibliopolis, 129–47.

Cohen, S. Marc (1992), 'Hylomorphism and Functionalism', in M. C. Nussbaum and A. O. Rorty, eds, *Essays on Aristotle's De Anima*, Oxford: Clarendon Press, 57–73.
Debru, A. (1994), 'L'expérimentation chez Galien', *ANRW* II 37.2, 1718–56.
—— (1996), *Le corps respirant. La pensée physiologique chez Galien*, Leiden: Brill.
—— (2005), 'Christianisme et galénisme: le mouvement volontaire chez Némésius d'Émèse', in Boudon-Millot and Pouderon, eds, 89–103.
De Lacy, P. H. (1978–84), *Galenus: De placitis Hippocratis et Platonis*, CMG vol.5.4.1, part 1 (1978), part 2 (1980), part 3 (1984), Berlin: Akademie-Verlag.
Demont, P. (2005), 'On philosophy and humoural medicine', in P. J. van der Eijk, ed., *Hippocrates in Context*, Leiden: Brill, 271–86.
Diels, H. (1879), *Doxographi Graeci*, Berlin: Reimer.
Dillon, J. M. (1973), *Iamblichi Chalcidensis in Platoni dialogos commentariorum fragmenta*, Leiden: Brill.
—— (1996), *The Middle Platonists*, 2nd edn, London: Duckworth.
Dobler, E. (1950), *Nemesius von Emesa und die Psychologie des menschlichen Aktes bei Thomas von Aquin*, diss. Freiburg (Schweiz), Werthenstein: Verlag "Sendbote der Heiligen Familie".
—— (2001), *Falsche Väterzitate bei Thomas von Aquin: Gregorius, Bischof von Nyssa oder Nemesius, Bischof von Emesa? Untersuchungen über die Authentizität der Zitate Gregors von Nyssa in den gesamten Werken des Thomas von Aquin*, Freiburg (Schweiz): Universitätsverlag (Dokimion, 27).
—— (2002), *Indirekte Nemesiuszitate bei Thomas von Aquin. Johannes von Damaskus als Vermittler von Nemesiustexten*, Freiburg (Schweiz): Universitätsverlag (Dokimion, 28).
Donini, P. L. (1987), 'Il *De fato* di Alessandro di Afrodisia: questioni di coerenza', *ANRW* II.36.2: 1244–59.
Dörrie, H. (1959), *Porphyrios' 'Symmikta Zêtêmata'*, Munich: C.H. Beck.
Domański, B. (1900), *Die Psychologie des Nemesius*, Münster: Aschendorff.
Dragona-Monachou, M. (1973), 'Providence and fate in Stoicism and Prae-Neoplatonism', *Philosophia* (Athens) 3: 262–304.
Dräseke, J. (1886), 'Apollinarios in den Ausführungen des Nemesios', *Zeitschrift für wissenschaftliche Theologie* 29: 26–36.
—— (1892), *Apollinarios von Laodicea, Sein Leben und seine Schriften*, Leipzig: J. Hinrichs (Texte und Untersuchungen zur Geschichte der Altchristlichen Literatur, 7).

Dulk, W. J. den (1934), *Krasis. Bijdrage tot de Grieksche Lexicographie*, Leiden: Brill.
Edelstein, L. and Kidd, I. G. (1988–89), *Posidonius: The Fragments²/The Commentary*, Cambridge: Cambridge University Press.
Eijk, P. J. van der (1988), 'Origenes' Verteidigung des freien Willens in *De Oratione* 6, 1–2', *Vigilae Christianae* 42: 339–51.
—— (1999), *Ancient Histories of Medicine*, Leiden: Brill.
—— (2000–01), *Diocles of Carystus*, Leiden: Brill.
—— (2005a), *Philoponus. On Aristotle On the Soul 1.1–2*, London: Duckworth.
—— (2005b), *Medicine and Philosophy in Classical Antiquity. Doctors and Philosophers on Nature, Soul, Health and Disease*, Cambridge: Cambridge University Press.
—— (2006), *Philoponus. On Aristotle On the Soul 1.3–5*, London: Duckworth.
—— (forthcoming), 'Le rôle de la *krasis* physiologique dans le comportement humain selon Aristotle et son interprétation par Jean Philopon', in: V. Barras and T. Birchler, eds, *Mélange – Crases – Tempéraments. La chimie du vivant dans la médecine e la biologie anciennes* (in press).
Ellis, J. (1994), 'Alexander's defense of Aristotle's Categories', *Phronesis* 39: 69–89.
Emilsson, E. K. (1994), 'Platonic soul-body dualism in the early centuries of the Empire to Plotinus', *ANRW* 2.36.7: 5331–62.
Evangelides, M. (1882), *Zwei Kapitel aus einer Monographie über Nemesios und seine Quellen*, diss. Berlin.
Fazzo, S. and Zonta, M. (1998), *Alessandro d'Afrodisia, Sulla Provvidenza*, Milan: Rizzoli.
Ferro, A. (1925), 'La dottrina dell'anima di Nemesio di Emesa', *Ricerche Religiose* [Rome] 1: 227–38.
Findlay, J. N. (1982), 'Why Christians should be Platonists', in D. J. O'Meara, ed., *Neoplatonism and Christian Thought*, Albany, NY: SUNY Press, 223–31.
Fine, G. (1981), 'Aristotle on Determinism: a review of Richard Sorabji's *Necessity, Cause and Blame*', *Philos. Rev.* 90: 561–79.
Flashar, H. (1966), *Melancholie und Melancholiker in den medizinischen Theorien der Antike*, Berlin: de Gruyter.
Föllinger, S. (2006), 'Willensfreiheit und Determination bei Nemesios von Emesa', in: Barbara Feichtinger et al., eds, *Körper und Seele. Aspekte spätantiker Anthropologie*, Leipzig, 143–57.

Fortenbaugh, W. W. (1971), 'Aristotle: Animals, Emotion and Moral Virtue', *Arethusa* 4: 137–65.
Frede, D. (1984), 'Could Paris (son of Priam) have chosen otherwise?', *Oxford Studies in Ancient Philosophy* 2: 279–92.
Freudenthal, G. (1995), *Aristotle's Theory of Material Substance: Heat and Pneuma, Form and Soul*, Oxford: Clarendon Press.
Frings, H. J. (1959) *Medizin und Arzt bei den griechischen Kirchenvätern bis Chrysostomos*, diss. Bonn.
Furley, D. J. and J. S. Wilkie (1984), *Galen on Respiration and the Arteries*, Princeton, NJ: Princeton University Press.
Gallay, P., ed. (1967), *Saint Grégoire de Nazianze. Lettres*, vol. 2, Paris: Les Belles Lettres.
Garofalo, I. (1991), *Galeno: Procedimenti anatomici*, 3 vols., Milan: Biblioteca universale Rizzoli.
Gossel, W. (1908), *Quibus ex fontibus Ambrosius in describendo corpore humano hauserit*, diss. Leipzig
Gossen, J. (1907), *De Galeni libro,* qui sunopsis peri sphugmôn *inscribitur*, diss. Berlin
Gottschalk, H. B. (1987), 'Aristotelian philosophy in the Roman world', *ANRW* II.36.2, 1079–174.
Goulet, R., ed. (1994), *Dictionnaire des philosophes antiques*, vol. 2, Paris: Éditions du CNRS.
Gourinat, J.-B. (2005), 'Le traité de Chrysippe *Sur l'âme*', *Revue de Métaphysique et de Morale* 48: 557–77.
Gruber, J. (1978), *Kommentar zu Boethius* De Consolatione Philosophiae, Berlin: de Gruyter (Texte und Kommentare, 9).
Grunert, P. (2002), 'Die Bedeutung der Hirnkammer in der antiken Naturphilosophie und Medizin', *Antike Naturwissenschaft und ihre Rezeption* 12: 151–82.
Hahm, D. E. (1994), 'Self-Motion in Stoic Philosophy', in Mary Louise Gill and James G. Lennox, eds, *Self-Motion from Aristotle to Newton*, Princeton, NJ: Princeton University Press, 175–225.
Hankinson, R. J. (1991), 'Galen's anatomy of the soul', *Phronesis* 36: 197–233.
Harig, G. (1974), *Bestimmung der Intensität im medizinischen System Galens* (Schriften zur Geschichte und Kultur der Antike, 11), Berlin: Akademie-Verlag.
Harnack, A. von (1892), *Medizinisches aus der ältesten Kirchengeschichte*, Leipzig.

Harris, C. R. S. (1973), *The Heart and the Vascular System in Ancient Greek Medicine*, Oxford: Clarendon Press.

Holl, M. (1921), 'Über die sogenannten "Hörner" des Uterus', *Archiv für Geschichte der Medizin* 13: 107–15.

Holzinger, K. von (1887), *Nemesii Emeseni libri Peri phuseôs anthrôpou versio latina*, Leipzig: G. Freytag.

Ierodiakonou, K. (1995), 'Medicine as a Stochastic Art', in P. J. van der Eijk, H. F. J. Horstmanshoff and P. H. Schrijvers, eds, *Ancient Medicine in its Socio-cultural Context*, Amsterdam: Rodopi, vol. 2, 473–85.

Inwood, B. (1985), *Ethics and Human Action in Early Stoicism*, Oxford: Clarendon Press.

Isaac, D., ed. (1979), *Proclus: Trois études sur la providence 2, Providence, fatalité, liberté*, Paris: Les Belles Lettres.

Jaeger, W. W. (1914), *Nemesios von Emesa*, Berlin: Weidmann.

—— (1938), *Diokles von Karystos*, Berlin: de Gruyter.

Jouanna, J. (1996), *Hippocrate. Airs, Eaux, Lieux*, Paris: Les Belles Lettres.

Kallis, A. (1978), *Der Mensch im Kosmos: das Weltbild Nemesios' von Emesa*, Münster: Aschendorff (Münsterische Beiträge zur Theologie, 43).

Kapetanaki, S. and Sharples, R. W. (2006), *Pseudo-Aristoteles (Pseudo-Alexander), Supplementa Problematorum*, Berlin: De Gruyter (Peripatoi, 20).

Karamanolis, G. E. (2006), *Plato and Aristotle in Agreement? Platonists on Aristotle from Antiochus to Porphyry*, Oxford: Clarendon Press.

Klibansky, R., Panovsky, E. and Saxl, F. (1992), *Saturn und Melancholie*, Frankfurt: Suhrkamp.

Koch, H. A. (1921), *Quellenuntersuchungen zu Nemesius von Emesa*, Berlin: Weidmann.

Krause, H. (1904), *Studia neoplatonica: dissertatio inauguralis ...* , Leipzig: Oswald Schmidt.

Lammert, F. (1917), 'Ptolemaios *Peri kritêriou kai hêgemonikou* und die Stoa', *Wiener Studien* 39: 249–58.

—— (1941), 'Hellenistische Medizin bei Ptolemaios und Nemesios. Ein Beitrag zur Geschichte der christlichen Anthropologie', *Philologus* 94: 125–41.

—— (1953), 'Zur Lehre von den Grundeigenschaften bei Nemesios, c. 5', *Hermes* 81: 488–91.

Larrain, C. (1994), 'Galen, *De motibus dubiis*, die lateinische Übersetzung des Niccolò da Reggio', *Traditio* 49: 171–233.

—— (1996), 'Kommentar zu Galen *De motibus dubiis* in der mittelalterlichen lateinischen Übersetzung des Niccolò da Reggio', *Traditio* 51: 1–41.

Leemans, E.-A. (1937), 'Studie over den Wijsgeer Numenius van Apamea met uitgave der fragmenten', *Mémoires de l'académie royale de Belgique, classe des lettres et des sciences morales et politiques,* ser. 2, vol. 37, no. 2. [Also includes the fragments of Cronius.]

Leven, K-H. (1987), *Medizinisches bei Eusebios von Kaisareia*, Düsseldorf.

Leyacker, J. (1927), 'Zur Entstehung der Lehre von den Hirnventrikeln als Sitz psychischer Vermoegen', *Archiv für Geschichte der Medizin* 19: 253–86.

Lietzmann, H. (1904), *Apollinaris von Laodicea und seine Schule*, Tübingen: J.C.B. Mohr.

Loofs, F. (1905), *Nestoriana*, Halle: Max Miemeyer.

Lovejoy, A. O. (1936), *The Great Chain of Being*, Cambridge MA: Harvard University Press.

McDonough, J. A. (1987), *Gregory of Nyssa: Against Fate*, in *Gregorii Nysseni Opera* vol. 3.2, Leiden: Brill.

Mansfeld, J. (1990), 'Doxography and Dialectic. The Sitz im Leben of the "Placita"', *ANRW* II.36.4: 3056–229.

—— (1999), 'Alcinous on fate and providence', in J. J. Cleary, ed., *Traditions of Platonism: Essays in honour of John Dillon*, Aldershot: Ashgate, 139–50.

—— and Runia, D. T. (1996), *Aëtiana*, vol. 1, Leiden: Brill.

Matthaei, C.F. (1802), *Nemesius Emesenus. De natura hominis*, Halle.

Mercken, H. P. F. (1990), 'The Greek Commentators on Aristotle's Ethics', in R. Sorabji, ed., *Aristotle Transformed: The Ancient Commentators and their influence*, London: Duckworth, 407–43.

Sauvé Meyer, S. (1993), *Aristotle on moral responsibility*, Oxford: Blackwell.

—— (1998), 'Moral responsibility: Aristotle and after', in S. Everson, ed., *Ethics*, Cambridge: Cambridge University Press, 221–40.

Morani, M. (1981), *La tradizione manoscritta del "De natura hominis" di Nemesio*, Milan: Vita e Pensiero, 1981.

—— (1982a), *Nemesio di Emesa. La natura dell'uomo*, Salerno: Grafiche Moriniello. [We have not been able to see this book.]

—— (1982b), 'Note critiche e linguistiche al testo di Nemesio', *Classical Philology* 77: 35–42.

Morani, M. (1987), *Nemesius. De natura hominis*, Leipzig.

Moraux, P. (1963), 'Quinta essentia', *RE* 24.1, 1171–263.
—— (1984), *Der Aristotelismus bei den Griechen*, vol. 2, Berlin: de Gruyter.
Müller, I. von (1895), 'Über Galens Werk vom wissenschaftlichen Beweis', *Abhandlungen der koniglichen bayrischen Akademie der Wissenschaften*, Munich, I. Klasse, 20.2: 403–78.
Neuhäuser, J. (1878), *Aristoteles' Lehre von dem sinnlichen Erkenntnissvermögen und seinen Organen*, Leipzig.
Nickel, D. (1971), *Galen. Über die Anatomie der Gebärmutter*, Berlin.
—— (2001), *Galen. Über die Ausformung der Keimlinge*, Berlin.
Nicol, D. M. (1968), 'A paraphrase of the Nicomachean Ethics attributed to the Emperor John VI Cantacuzene', *Byzantinoslavica* 29: 1–16.
Nutton, V. (1984), 'From Galen to Alexander. Aspects of medicine and medical practice in late antiquity', *Dunbarton Oaks Papers* 38:1–14.
Nutton, V. (2004), *Ancient Medicine*, London.
O'Daly, G. J. P. (1987), *Augustine's Philosophy of Mind*, London: Duckworth.
Peck, A. L. (1942), *Aristotle. On the Generation of Animals*, Cambridge, MA, and London: Harvard University Press (LCL).
Pépin, J. (1964), 'Une nouvelle source de Saint Augustin: le zêtêma de Porphyre sur l'union de l'âme et du corps', *Revue des études anciennes* 66: 53–107.
Pigeaud, J. (1987), *Folies et cures de la folie chez les médecins de l'antiquité gréco-romaine: la manie*, Paris.
Pohlenz, M. (1941), 'Tierische und Menschliche Intelligenz bei Poseidonios', *Hermes* 76: 1–13.
Polites, N. G. (1979), *Pêgai kai periekhomenôn tôn peri heimarmenês kephalaiôn tou Nemesiou Emesês*, PhD dissertation, Athens.
Polito, R. (2006), 'Matter, medicine and the mind: Asclepiades vs. Epicurus', *Oxford Studies in Ancient Philosophy* 30: 285–335.
Quasten, J. (1960), *Patrology*, vol. 3, Utrecht: Spectrum, repr. 1975. (Nemesius is discussed at 351–55, with a bibliography.)
Rashed, M. (2004), 'Priorité de l'*eidos* ou du *genos* entre Andronicos et Alexandre: vestiges arabes et grecs inédits', *Arabic Sciences and Philosophy* 14: 9–63.
Raven, C. E. (1923), *Apollinarianism: an Essay on the Christology of the early Church*, Cambridge: Cambridge University Press.
Reydams-Schils, G. (2002), 'Calcidius Christianus? God, body and matter', in T. Kobusch and M. Erler, eds, *Metaphysik und Religion: zur Signatur des spätantiken Denkens*, Munich: K. G. Saur, 193–211.

—— (2006), 'Calcidius on the Human and the World Soul and Middle-Platonist Psychology', *Apeiron* 39: 179–200.
Rist, J. M. (1988), 'Pseudo-Ammonius and the soul/body problem in some Platonic texts of late antiquity', *American Journal of Philology* 109: 402–15.
Robinson, J. A. T. (1977), *On Being the Church in the World*, London: SCM Press, reprinted Oxford: Mowbray. (References are to the reprint.)
Rocca, J. (2003), *Galen on the Brain*, Leiden.
Ruland, H.-J. (1976), *Die arabischen Fassungen zweier Schriften des Alexander von Aphrodisias: Über die Vorsehung und über das liberum arbitrium*, diss. Saarbrücken.
Rüsche, F. (1930), *Blut, Leben, Seele*, Paderborn: F. Schöningh.
Schroeder, F. M. (1987), 'Ammonius Saccas', *ANRW* 2.36.1: 493–526.
Schoener, E. (1964), *Das Viererschema in der antiken Humoralpathologie*, Stuttgart: Steiner.
Schöne, H. (1920), 'Verschiedenes', *Rheinisches Museum* 73: 137–60 (esp. 156–58).
Schulze, C. and Ihm, S., eds (2002), *Ärztekunst und Gottvertrauen. Antike und mittelalterliche Schnittpunkte von Christentum und Medizin*, Hildesheim: Olms.
Schwyzer, H.-R. (1983), *Ammonios: der Lehrer Plotins*, Opladen: Westdeutscher Verlag.
Seel, G. (2000), *Ammonius and the Sea-Battle*, Berlin: de Gruyter.
Sharples, R. W. (1978), 'Alexander of Aphrodisias *De fato*: some parallels', *Classical Quarterly* n.s. 28: 243–66.
—— (1983), 'Nemesius of Emesa and some theories of divine providence', *Vigiliae Christianae* 37: 141–56.
—— (1984), 'Review of D. J. O' Meara, ed., *Neoplatonism and Christian Thought*', *Religious Studies* 20: 705–08.
—— (1985a), 'Ambiguity and opposition; Alexander of Aphrodisias, *Ethical Problem* 11', *Bulletin of the Institute of Classical Studies* 32: 109–16.
—— (1985b), 'Theophrastus on tastes and smells', in W. W. Fortenbaugh et al., eds, *Theophrastus of Eresos: on his life and work*, New Brunswick, NJ: Transaction (Rutgers Studies in Classical Humanities, 2), 183–204.
—— (1986), 'Soft determinism and freedom in early Stoicism', *Phronesis* 31: 266–79.
—— (1987a), 'Alexander of Aphrodisias: Scholasticism and Innovation', *ANRW* II.36.2: 1176–243.
—— (1987b), 'Could Alexander (follower of Aristotle) have done better?

BIBLIOGRAPHY   231

A response to Professor Frede and others', *Oxford Studies in Ancient Philosophy* 5: 197–216.
—— (1990), *Alexander of Aphrodisias: Ethical Problems*, London: Duckworth.
—— (1991), *Cicero* On Fate *and Boethius* Consolation of Philosophy *IV.5-7 and V*, Warminster: Aris and Phillips.
—— (1995), *Theophrastus of Eresus. Commentary vol. 5. Sources on Biology (human physiology, living creatures, botany: texts 328-435)*, Leiden: Brill.
—— (1996), *Stoics, Epicureans and Sceptics*, London: Routledge.
—— (1998), *Theophrastus of Eresus: Sources for his Life, Writings, Thought and Influence, Commentary volume 3.1, Sources on Physics*, Leiden: Brill.
—— (2001a), 'Schriften und Problemkomplexe zur Ethik' in P. Moraux, ed. J. Wiesner, *Der Aristotelismus bei den Griechen*, vol. 3 *Alexander von Aphrodisias*, Berlin: de Gruyter, 513–616.
—— (2001b), 'Dicaearchus on the soul and on divination', in W. W. Fortenbaugh and E. Schütrumpf, eds, *Dicaearchus of Messana*, New Brunswick, NJ: Transaction (Rutgers Studies in Classical Humanities, 10), 143–73.
—— (2002), 'Alexander of Aphrodisias and the end of Aristotelian Theology', in T. Kobusch and M. Erler, eds, *Metaphysik und Religion: zur Signatur des spätantiken Denkens*, Munich: K. G. Saur, 1–21.
—— (2003), 'Threefold providence: the history and background of a doctrine', in R. W. Sharples and A. D. R. Sheppard, eds, *Ancient Approaches to Plato's Timaeus* (*Bulletin of the Institute of Classical Studies* supplement 78), 107–27.
—— (2004), *Alexander of Aphrodisias: Supplement to* On the Soul, London: Duckworth.
—— (2005), 'Ducunt volentem fata, nolentem trahunt', in C. Natali and S. Maso, eds, *La Catena delle cause, Determinismo e antideterminismo nel pensiero antico e in quello contemporaneo*, Amsterdam: Hakkert, 197–214.
—— (2007a), 'Peripatetics on Soul and Intellect', in R. W. Sharples and R. Sorabji, eds, *Greek and Roman philosophy, 100 BC to 200 AD, BICS* supplementary volume 94, vol. 2, 607–20.
—— (2007b), 'The Stoic Background to the Middle Platonist discussion of Fate', in M. Bonazzi and C. Helmig, eds, *Platonic Stoicism – Stoic Platonism*, Leuven: Leuven University Press, 169–88.

Shields, C. (1993), 'The Homonymy of the Body in Aristotle', *Archiv für Geschichte der Philosophie* 75: 1–30.
Siclari, A. (1974), *L'antropologia di Nemesio di Emesa*, Padua: La Garangola.
Skard, E. (1936), 'Nemesiosstudien: 1, Nemesius und die *Genesisexegese* von Origen', *Symbolae Osloenses* 16: 23–43.
—— (1937), 'Nemesiosstudien: 2, Nemesios und Galenus', *Symbolae Osloenses* 17: 9–25.
—— (1938), 'Nemesiosstudien: 3, Nemesios und die Elementenlehre des Galenos', *Symbolae Osloenses* 18: 31–41.
—— (1939), 'Nemesiosstudien: 4, Nemesios und die Physiologie des Galenos', *Symbolae Osloenses* 19: 46–56.
—— (1940), 'Nemesios', *RE* Suppbd. 7: 562–66.
—— (1942), 'Nemesiosstudien: 5, Galens Lehre von Tierischer und Menschlicher Intelligenz', *Symbolae Osloenses* 22: 40–48.
Smets, A. and Esbroeck, M. van, eds (1970), *Basile de Césarée sur l'origine de l'homme*, Paris: Éditions du Cerf (Sources chrétiennes 160).
Solmsen, F. (1950), 'Tissues and the soul', *Philosophical Review* 59: 435–68.
—— (1957), 'The vital heat, the inborn pneuma and the *aether*', *Journal of Hellenic Studies* 77: 119–23
—— (1961), 'Greek philosophy and the discovery of the nerves', *Museum Helveticum* 18: 151–67 and 169–97.
Somfai, A. (2004), 'Calcidius' commentary on Plato's *Timaeus* and its place in the commentary tradition: the concept of *analogia* in text and diagrams', in P. Adamson et al., eds., *Philosophy, Science and Exegesis in Greek, Latin and Arabic commentaries*, vol.1 (*Bulletin of the Institute of Classical Studies* supplement 83.1) 203–20.
Sorabji, R. (1988), *Matter, Space and Motion*, London: Duckworth.
—— (1993), *Animal Minds and Human Morals*, London: Duckworth.
—— (2000), *Emotion and Peace of Mind*, Oxford: Clarendon Press.
—— (2003), 'The mind-body relation in the wake of Plato's *Timaeus*', in G. J. Reydams-Schils, ed., *Plato's* Timaeus *as Cultural Icon*, Notre Dame, IN: University of Notre Dame Press, 152–62.
—— (2004), *The Philosophy of the Commentators, 200-600 AD*, London: Duckworth.
Spanneut, M. (1957), *Le Stoïcisme des Pères de l'Eglise*, Paris.
Staden, H. von (1989), *Herophilus. The Art of Medicine in Early Alexandria*, Cambridge: Cambridge University Press.
—— (1992), 'Jaeger's "Skandalon der historischen Vernunft": Diocles,

Aristotle and Theophrastus', in W. M. Calder III, ed., *Werner Jaeger reconsidered*, Illinois Classical Studies suppl. vol. 3: 227–65.
Steel, C. (1978), *The Changing Self*, Leiden: Brill.
—— (2002), 'Neoplatonic versus Stoic causality: the case of the sustaining cause ("sunektikon")', *Quaestio* 2: 77–93.
—— (2005), 'The philosophical views of an engineer. Theodorus' arguments against free choice and Proclus' refutation', in M. Bonazzi and V. Celluprica, eds, *L'eredità Platonica. Studi sul Platonismo da Arcesilao a Proclo*, Naples: Bibliopolis, 275–310.
Streck, M. (2001), 'Aristotelische und neuplatonische Elemente in der Anthropologie des Nemesius von Emesa', *Studia Patristica* 34: 559–64.
—— (2005), *Das schönste Gut: der menschliche Wille nach Nemesius von Emesa und Gregor von Nyssa*, Göttingen: Vandenhoeck and Ruprecht.
Strohmaier, G. (2003), 'Der Kommentar des Johannes Grammatikos zu Galen, *De usu partium* (Buch 11), in einer unikalen Gothaer Handschrift', in G. Strohmaier, *Hellas im Islam. Beiträge zu Ikonographie, Wissenschaft und Religionsgeschichte*, Wiesbaden, 109–12.
Sudhoff, W. (1913), 'Die Lehre von den Hirnventrikeln in textlicher und graphischer Tradition des Altertums und Mittelalters', *Archiv für Geschichte der Medizin* 7: 149–205.
Telfer, W. (1955), *Cyril of Jerusalem and Nemesius of Emesa*, London: SCM Press.
Temkin, O. (1973), *Galenism. Rise and Decline of a Medical Philosophy*, Ithaca, NY, and London: Cornell University Press.
Theiler, W. (1946), 'Tacitus und die antike Schiksalslehre', in O. Gigon et al., eds, *Phyllobolia für P. von der Mühll*, Basel: Schwabe, 35–90, reprinted in W. Theiler, *Forschungen zum Neuplatonismus*, Berlin: de Gruyter, ch. 2.
—— (1966), 'Ammonios und Porphyrios', in *Entretiens Hardt* 12: *Porphyre*, Vandoeuvres-Genève, 87–123.
Thompson, D'Arcy W. (1947), *A Glossary of Greek Fishes*, London: Oxford University Press (St Andrews University Publications, 45).
Tieleman, T. L. (2003), *Chrysippus on Affections*, Leiden: Brill.
Todd, R. B. (1976), *Alexander of Aphrodisias on Stoic Physics*, Leiden: Brill.
—— (1977), 'Galenic medical ideas in the Greek Aristotelian commentators', *Symbolae Osloenses* 52: 117–34.
—— (1984), 'Philosophy and medicine in John Philoponus' commentary on Aristotle's *De anima*', *Dumbarton Oaks Papers* 38: 103–10

—— (1996), *Themistius: On Aristotle On the Soul*, London: Duckworth.
Tracy, T. J. (1969), *Physiological Theory and the Doctrine of the Mean in Plato and Aristotle*, The Hague/Paris: Mouton.
—— (1983), 'Heart and Soul in Aristotle', in J. Anton and A. Preus, eds, *Essays in Ancient Greek Philosophy*, vol. 2, Albany, NY: SUNY Press, 321–39.
Urmson, J. O. (1988), *Aristotle's Ethics*, Oxford: Blackwell.
Vander Waerdt, P. (1985), 'Peripatetic soul-division, Posidonius, and Middle Platonic moral psychology', *Greek, Roman and Byzantine Studies* 26: 373–94.
Verbeke, G. (1971), 'Filosofie en christendom in het mensbeeld van Nemesius van Emesa', *Mededelingen van de Koninklijke Vlaamse Academie voor Wetenschappen, Letteren en Schone Kunsten van België, Klasse der Leteren*, Brussels, Jaarg. 33 no. 1.
—— and J. R. Moncho, eds (1975), *Némésius d'Émèse, De natura hominis, traduction de Burgundio de Pise*, Leiden: Brill (Corpus Latinum commentariorum in Aristotelem Graecorum, Suppl. 1).
Wallace-Hadrill, D. S. (1968), *The Greek Patristic View of Nature*, Manchester: Manchester University Press.
Walzer, R. (1947), *Galen on Jews and Christians*, Oxford.
Weisser, U. (1979), *Buch über das Geheimnis der Schöpfung und die Darstellung der Natur (Buch der Ursachen) von Pseudo-Apollonios von Tyana*, Aleppo: Institute for the History of Arabic Science, University of Aleppo (Sources and studies in the history of Arabic-Islamic science. Natural sciences series, 1).
Westerink, L. G. (1964a), 'Philosophy and medicine in late antiquity', *Janus* 51: 169–77.
Waszink, J. H. (1947), *Quinti Septimi Florentis Tertulliani De Anima*, Amsterdam.
—— (1962), *Plato:Timaeus a Calcidio translatus*, London: Warburg Institute and Leiden: Brill (Plato Latinus, 4).
Whiting, J. (1992), 'Living Bodies', in M. C. Nussbaum and A. O. Rorty, eds, *Essays on Aristotle's De Anima*, Oxford: Clarendon Press, 75–91.
Wyller, E. A. (1969), 'Die Anthropologie des Nemesios von Emesa und die *Alicibiades I*-Tradition', *Symbolae Osloenses* 44: 126–45.
Zambon, M. (2002), *Porphyre et le moyen-Platonisme*, Paris: Vrin.
Zeller, E. (1903), *Die Philosophie der Griechen* vol. 3.2 (4th edn), Leipzig: Reisland.

INDEX OF PASSAGES CITED

Within entries, references to pages precede references to notes and are separated from each other with a semi-colon; single note references are preceded by 'n.', multiple note references in a single entry by 'nn.'.

AENEAS OF GAZA
Theophrastus 12.11–25 n. 357

AËTIUS/PSEUDO–PLUTARCH
Tenets
1.12.4 n. 477; 1.29.2, 4, 7 n. 949; 3.5 n. 539; 4.2–3 n. 252; 4.2.1 n. 258; 4.2.3 n. 259; 4.2.4 n. 328; 4.2.5 n. 260; 4.2.6 n. 261; 4.2.7 n. 262; 4.3.3 n. 253; 4.3.5 n. 256; 4.3.9 n. 255; 4.3.12 n. 257; 4.4 n. 636; 4.4.4 n. 624; 4.6.2 n. 322; 4.8 nn. 510–12; 4.12 nn. 498–99; 4.13 nn. 518, 520, 522–24; 4.21 n. 586; 4.21.1 n. 186; 5.1 n. 588

ALBINUS
Epitome of Platonic Doctrine
4.6, 4.8, 5.7 n. 603

ALCINOUS
Instruction Manual (Didascalicus)
17.4 nn. 132, 513; 26 nn. 929, 934, 940

ALEXANDER OF APHRODISIAS
Ethical Problems
5 (125.5–6, 126.3–5) n. 702; 6 (126.20–32), 7 (127.23–28, 127.34–128.2) n. 703; 7 (127.35–128.2) n. 702; 9 n. 149; 11 nn. 149, 887; 12 n. 149; 12 (132.19–20) n. 873; (133.1) n. 872; (133.9) n. 873; 13 (137.5–9) n. 702; 21 (412.1) n. 720; 29 n. 149; 29 (159.20–21) n. 888; (160.5ff.) 180; n. 909; (160.19–25) n. 903

On Aristotle On Sense Perception
28.2 n. 521

On Aristotle's Topics
43.26–28 n. 232; 236.10–16 n. 307

On Fate
6 n. 1023; 8 n. 952; 11 (178.8–15) n. 954; 12 (180.9) n. 903; 13 29; n. 921; (182.1) n. 923; 14 (184.15–20) n. 971; 17 (188.11–12) n. 925; 22 n. 922; 27 (198.12–20) n. 988; 31 n. 929; (201.28) n. 925

On Mixture
3 (216.14–217.2) n. 376; 4 (218.1–2, 8–9) n. 392; 10 (224.14) n. 267; 15 (231.22–232.6) n. 379; (232.2) n. 380

On Providence
6.22, 24.15 (Ruland) n. 183; 33.1–8, 87.5–91.4 n. 339; 89.5 n. 1038

On the Soul
15.5–8 n. 378; 81.13–83.2 n. 188; 98.22–24 n. 727

Quaestiones
1.8, 1.17 n. 263; 1.25 (41.11–19) n. 339; 1.26 n. 263; 2.19 (63.18–28)

n. 339; 2.21 (68.5–11) n. 1038; 2.23 n. 198
Supplement to On the Soul (mantissa)
1 (102.32–103.2) n. 321; (104.11–17) n. 320; 2 (*On Intellect*) (113.18–24) n. 405; 3 n. 263; (114.7ff.) n. 270; (114.24ff.) n. 266; (114.25ff.) n. 268; (115.33–34) n. 286; (115.33–116.1) n. 376; (116.5–13) n. 378; (116.10–13) n. 376; (117.1–9, 9–21, 21–30) n. 277; (117.32ff.) n. 272; 17 (150.19) n. 265; 20 (162.10–14) n. 307; 22 (169.33) n. 265; 23 n. 639; (172.16) n 265; 25 n. 1023

[ALEXANDER OF APHRODISIAS]
Medical Problems (Ideler)
1.16–17 n. 731; 2.60 n. 737
On Fevers
6.1–2 n. 731
Supplementary Problems (Kapetanaki and Sharples)
1.9 n. 753; 2.28 n. 785

ALEXANDER OF TRALLES
Therapeutics
vol.2 p.525.24 Puschmann n. 275

AMMONIUS
On Aristotle's On Interpretation (*CAG* 4.5)
130.27–128.10 n. 170; 148.11–15 n. 954

ANASTASIUS OF SINAI
Questions and Answers, in *PG* 89 n. 17

ANAXAGORAS
59B1 DK n. 999

ANAXARCHUS
72A1 DK n. 875

ANAXIMENES
13B2 DK n. 490

ANONYMOUS
On Aristotle's Nicomachean Ethics (*CAG* 20)
130.19 n. 645; 141.10–20 n. 887; 143.1ff. n. 874; 148.1 n. 894; 149.14ff. 180; n. 909; 149.22 n. 909; 149.33 n. 949; 153.15–17 n. 903; 155.19 n. 949; 156.6–7 n. 957; 171.23–28 n. 669; 177.30 n. 874; 199,15–23 n. 981; 199.17–23 nn. 85, 985; 204.7–9 n. 720; 206.1–2 n. 985; 248.25–26 n. 148

ANONYMUS LONDINIENSIS
I.29–II.6 n. 641; II.34–36 n. 642; XIV.19–20 n. 471

ANONYMUS PARISINUS
On Acute Diseases
1 n. 131; 10 n. 864

APOLLINARIS
fr.169 Lietzmann n. 185; fr.170 Lietzmann n. 343; fr.171 Dräseke n. 483

APPIAN
Mithridatica
537 n. 242

APULEIUS
On Plato
1.12 n. 1004

ARETAEUS OF CAPPADOCIA
Causes and Signs of Acute Diseases
1.5.1 n. 660

ARISTOTLE
Categories
5 4a10–11 n. 296; 8 11a15–19 n. 281

INDEX OF PASSAGES CITED

Eudemian Ethics
1.1 1214a15–21 n. 657; 2.1 1219b37 n.
628; 2.6 1223a2–9 nn. 79, 916; 2.7
1223a26 n. 895
Generation of Animals
2.3 736b27 n. 187; 3.11 762b26 n. 203
History of Animals
1.1 486a13ff. n. 431; 486a14 n. 422;
486b24–487a1 n. 445; 486b25 n.
444; 487a1–10 n. 422; 487b10 n.
201; 1.3 489a17–18 n. 546; 1.6
490b7 n. 420; 1.11 492a22 n. 578;
492a28 n. 578; 492b23 n. 283;
492b26 n. 568; 1.15 494b16 n. 558;
2.1 498a3–31 n. 810; 500a13–32
n. 445; 500a25 nn. 443–44; 2.14
505b12 n. 436; 2.15 505b27 n.
420; 506a20ff. n. 441; 2.16 506b26
n. 439; 2.17 508a25 n. 543; 4.8
533a14 n. 575; 5.13 544a31 n. 796;
5.16 548b10 n. 201; 549a8 n. 201;
6.1 558b12–13, 558b21 n. 796; 6.16
570a15 n. 203; 7.7 586a15 n. 784;
8.1 588a23 n. 361; 588b4ff n. 194;
588b20 n. 201; 9.1 608a17 n. 361;
10.3 635b19 n. 788
Metaphysics
Δ 21 1022b15–21 n. 641; Δ30
1025a15–19 n. 894; H1 1042a28
n. 263; Θ2 n. 985; Θ5 n. 971; Θ5
1071a15 n. 1006
Meteorology
2.4 359b30–360b27 n. 469; 3.6 378b1
n. 470; 4.5 382b2–5 n. 478; 4.11
389a29–31 n. 478
Nicomachean Ethics
1.1 1094a4 n. 636; 1.7 1098a4 n. 635;
1.9 1099b18–20 n. 657; 1.13 10;
n. 629; 1.13 1102a27ff. n. 629;
1102a33 n. 628; 1102b28ff. n.
629; 1102b29 nn. 628, 635; 2.1
1103a32–33 n. 955; 2.3 1104b15
n. 642; 2.5 1105b19–1106a12 n.

987; 1105b23 n. 642; 2.5 1106a2–4,
9–10 n. 983; 2.6 1106b24–28 n.
891; 3 26; 3.1 1110a2 n. 870;
1110a4–19, 1110b3–7 n. 877;
1110b9–15 n. 881; 1110b15–17
n. 873; 1110b18–24 n. 883;
1110b24–27 n. 884; 1110b31–32
n. 885; 1111a22–24 nn. 887, 888;
1111a24–b3 n. 891; 3.1–3 n. 871;
3.2 nn. 894–5; 3.2 1111b10–12
n. 895; 1111b13–16 n. 896;
1111b34–1112a1 n. 900; 1112a3–5
n. 899; 3.3 180; nn. 906, 909; 3.3
1112a21 n. 898; 1112a23–26 n. 950;
1112a31–33 n. 949; 1112b2–8 n.
911; 1112b21–23 n. 908; 1113a4–5
n. 902; 1113a10–11 n. 905;
3.4–5 30; 3.5 1113b6–11 n. 959;
1113b7–8 nn. 79, 916; 1113b26–29
n. 957; 1114a4–b25 n. 955; 3.10
1117b28 n. 664; 4.7 1127b14–15
nn. 981–2; 4.9 1128b29–30 n. 721;
5.1 1129a13–14 n. 985; 1129a14–15
n. 986; 6.2 1139a27–36 n. 695;
6.4 1140a10–16 n. 962; 6.5, 6.7 n.
973; 6.13 1144b4ff. n. 1018; 7 n.
663; 7.1–10 n. 896; 7.3 1147a25 n.
899; 7.5 n. 639; 7.7 1150b25 nn.
502, 659; 7.10 1152a17ff. n. 659;
7.11 1152b13 n. 681; 1152b17 n.
677; 7.12 1153a1 nn. 665, 671;
1153a13–15 n. 677; 1153a14–15 n.
688; 1153a22 n. 665; 7.13 1153b7,
9, 12, 13 n. 690; 1153b14–19 n.
689; 1153b16–17 n. 690; 7.13
1153b25ff. n. 1018; 1154a26ff.
n. 671; 1154a28–29 n. 704;
1154b3ff. n. 659; 1154b12 n. 662;
1154b15–17 n. 704; 1154b17–20
n. 678; 1154b24–26 n. 692; 8.2
1155b26 n. 656; 10 n. 663; 10.3
1173a30 n. 688; 1173a31–b7
n. 683; 1173b8–10 n. 671;

238   INDEX OF PASSAGES CITED

1173b12–13 n. 666; 1173b15–18
  n. 679; 10.4 1174a13–b14 n. 682;
  1174b21 n. 665; 1175a15 n. 695;
  10.5 1175b25ff. n. 693; 1176a1ff.
  n. 694; 1176a15ff. n. 696; 10.7
  1177b26 n. 188; 10.8 1178a9ff. n.
  670; 10.9 1179b20ff. n. 657
On Coming to Be and Perishing
  1.6 323a6–10, 2.2 329b24–27 n. 478;
  2.3–4 n. 456; 2.4 n. 469; 2.10
  336a32ff. n. 1006
On Divination in Sleep
  2 463b15–17 n. 502
On Dreams
  2 459a26 n. 550; 459b3–5 n. 509;
  459b15 n. 533; 459b18–22 n. 541;
  460b2–3 n. 592; 460b26–27 n. 541;
  3 461a22–23 n. 502; 461a26–b7 n.
  550; 461b21–2 n. 592
On the Generation of Animals
  1.2 716a7 n. 495; 1.18 724b23ff. n.
  431; 1.19 726b2–5 n. 425; 726b3ff.
  n. 426; 726b7 n. 785; 726b9–10 n.
  425; 726b31ff., 727a26ff. n. 426;
  727b32 n. 495; 1.20 n. 787; 1.20
  727b36ff. n. 788; 728a10 n. 784;
  728b33 n. 426; 729a11 n. 495; 2.1
  734b28 n. 434; 2.2–3 736a–737a
  n. 505; 2.3 737a27–28 n. 426; 2.4
  739b25 n. 426; 740a21 n. 425; 3.1
  749b15 n. 796; 4.5 774a2–3 n. 426;
  4.8 776b11–12 n. 426
On the Heaven
  1.2 268b14 n. 470; 269b4 n. 479; 1.3
  270a30 n. 470; 270b21 n. 479; 2.12
  292b3–8 n. 363; 3.2 300a20 n. 325
On Interpretation
  9 30; 13 23a15–16 n. 915
On Memory
  1 450a9 nn. 535, 554; 450a12–14 n.
  599; 450a23 n. 592; 450a24–25
  n. 599; 450a31 nn. 592, 596;
  450b11–18 n. 550; 450b21–451a2

  n. 592; 2 453a19 n. 502
On the Movement of Animals
  7 701b17–18 n. 509
On Philosophy
  fr.10 Rose n. 388
On the Parts of Animals
  1.1 641b6 n. 509; 2.1 647a3–5 n. 434;
  2.2 647b10ff. n. 431; 647b23 n.
  434; 648a5 n. 420; 2.3 650a25
  n. 747; 650a34–b13 n. 425; 2.10
  656b26–31 n. 565; 656b27ff. n.
  533; 656b32ff. n. 542; 657a2 n.
  543; 2.13 658b3–10 n. 867; 2.16
  660a1–2 n. 567; 2.17 660b6 n. 543;
  3.3 665a15 n. 847; 3.5 668a9–13 n.
  425; 3.6 669a3–7 n. 276; 669a13
  n. 839; 3.10 673a8 n. 228; 4.5
  678a33 n. 420; 4.10 686a1 n. 437;
  686a25–687b25 n. 442; 686a27 n.
  238; 687a2–23 n. 807; 688a18–b33
  n. 445; 689b19ff. n. 810; 4.11
  690b29–31 n. 567; 691a6–8 n. 543
On the Progression of Animals
  13 712a13ff. n. 810
On Sensation and Sensible Objects
  1 437a5ff. n. 533; 437a5–7 n.
  534; 437a8–9 nn. 535, 554; 3
  440b21–4 441a3 n. 558; 4 n. 572; 4
  440b30–441a2 n. 559; 442b4ff. nn.
  535, 554; 442b5 n. 555
On Sleep and Waking
  2 455a6–7 n. 546; 455a14ff. nn. 535,
  554; 455a20 n. 507; 455a23–32 n.
  546; 455a23–b2 n. 548
On the Soul
  1.1 403a30 n. 709; 403a31 n. 706; 1.2
  403b31–404a2 n. 256; 404b6 n. 188;
  405a8–13 n. 256; 405b5 n. 254; 1.3
  405b31–406a2 n. 322; 406a22–25 n.
  326; 1.4 408a30–34 n. 322; 408b32
  n. 328; 1.5 410b10–15 n. 266;
  411b28–29 n. 628; 2.1 412a6–11 n.
  312; 412a12 n. 470; 412a17–19 n.

312; 412a20 n. 470; 412a20–21 nn.
315, 320; 412a22–28 n. 313; 412a27
n. 261; 412a27–28 n. 315; 412a28 n.
470; 412b15–17 n. 320; 412b18–21
n. 314; 412b20 n. 314; 412b27–
413a3 n. 314; 413a3–7 n. 316;
2.2 413b4–10 n. 546; 413b12–13
n. 628; 2.2 413b24–27 n. 318;
414a14–19 n. 312; 414a20–21 n.
316; 2.3 414a31–32 n. 628; 414a33
n. 628; 414b2 n. 895; 415a3 n. 628;
2.4 415a17 n. 628; 415b18–19 n.
493; 415b24 n. 509; 2.5 416b34,
417b5ff., 418a1–3 n. 509; 2.6
418a10ff. nn. 535, 554; 2.7 n. 523;
418a29 nn. 533–34; 419a13–21 n.
523; 2.9 421a18–22 nn. 558–59;
421b22 n. 582; 2.10 422b8 n. 576;
422b10–14 n. 572; 2.11 422b22–23
n. 548; 423a26ff. n. 548; 423b28–29
n. 555; 3.1 425a14ff., 3.3 428b22
nn. 535, 554; 3.5 nn. 187, 188; 3.7
431a5 n. 509; 3.9 432a18–22 n. 633;
432a23ff. n. 632; 3.9–11 n. 633; 3.10
433a22–30 n. 633; 433a27 n. 656;
3.12 434b23 n. 546; 3.13 435a18–19
n. 549; 435a23 n. 555; 435a24–25 n.
547; 435b4, b13 n. 546
Physics
2.2 194b13 n. 1006; 2.5 196b33–197a5
n. 894; 2.5–6 n. 949; 2.6 n. 953;
2.8 198b36 n. 916; 4.4 212a6–6a n.
403; 8.4 255a5ff. n. 325; 8.5 n. 324;
8.6 259b16–20 n. 46
Politics
1.1 1253a2, 7 n. 225
Prior Analytics
1.13 32a18–29 n. 915; 32b5–18 n. 916
Rhetoric
1.10 1369b18ff. n. 656
Topics
3.1 116b18–22 n. 307; 3.6 120b3–6 n.
331; 5.2 130b8 n. 232

fragments
45 Rose³ n. 297

[ARISTOTLE]
Magna Moralia
1.12 1187b37 n. 895
On Breath
4 482b21 n. 839
Problems
3.9 872a18–26 n. 541; 11.49 904b17
n. 533; 12.12 907b9 n. 583; 30.1
953b38–39 n. 784
On the Universe
3 392b35 n. 479

ARISTOXENUS
fr. 42a.4 n. 721

ARIUS DIDYMUS
Fragments on physics 28 nn. 380, 392

ASPASIUS
On Aristotle's Nicomachean Ethics
3.24–27 n. 905; 35.17–20 n. 621;
42.13–20 n. 687; 42.27ff. n. 642;
44.21–24 n. 646; 45.16–22 n.
654; 45.13–14 n. 646; 61.5–6 n.
876; 65.33ff. n. 887; 67.21 n. 89;
71.16ff. 180; n. 909; 180; 71.31
n. 909; 72.19–73.5 n. 911; 75.9ff.
n. 903; 77.4–5 n. 957; 150.31 n.
690; 156.26 n. 704; 157.1 n. 704

ATHANASIUS
Life of St. Antony 14 n. 979

ATHENAEUS
12 513A n. 674

ATTICUS
fr.3 des Places n. 996; fr.7.42–53 des
Places n. 324; fr.8.2 des Places n.
1027

AUGUSTINE
City of God
10.30 n. 357; 11.11, 13, 12.1–9 n. 980;
22.30 n. 82
Letters
166, 551.7–12 n. 401
Literal Interpretation of Genesis
8.21 (p.261.8 Zyda) n. 397
On the Magnitude of the Soul
5.7 p.139.9 Hörmann n. 397
On the Two Souls
12.16 n. 345

BARDESANES
quoted by Eusebius, *Preparation for the Gospel* 6.10.1–10 (GCS 43.1 335.1–337.3 Mras) n. 363

BASIL THE GREAT
Homilies on the Psalms
14.6, *PG* 29 261C n. 225
Homilies on the Six Days [of Creation]
2.5 (*PG* 29 40A) n. 949; 9 (*PG* 29 192A) nn. 238, 251; 9 (*PG* 29 193AB) n. 1019
On the Origin of Man
2.7 p.244.14–20 Smets and Esbroeck (1970) n. 218
On the Structure of Man
2.3 (*PG* 30 45A) n. 218

BIBLE
Old Testament and Apocrypha
Daniel
6:19–24 n. 244
Deuteronomy
18:10–11 n. 589
Genesis
1:1 n. 482; 1:26 nn. 207, 234; 1:26–27 n. 247; 2:2 n. 340; 2:7 n. 334; 3:7 n. 217; 3:14 n. 220; 3:15 n. 243; 3:19 n. 211; 5:24 n. 944; 39:7–18 n. 878

Isaiah
8:19 n. 589; 29:16 n. 1036; 45:9 n. 1036
Jeremiah
10:23 n. 964
Job
1:5 n. 967; 38:30 n. 484; 41:23–24 n. 484
Joshua
10:12–14 n. 943
2 Kings
2:11 n. 944
Leviticus
19:26, 31 n. 589
Proverbs
12:10 n. 235
Psalms
49[48]:13=20 n. 212; 94[93]:11 n. 965
2 Samuel
11–12, 12:15–25 n. 344
Susanna [= Daniel 13]
19–23 n. 878
Wisdom
4:10–14 n. 1054

New Testament
Acts
28:3–6 n. 245
1 Corinthians
13.12 n. 1045; 14:15 n. 373; 15:47–49 n. 210; 15:48 n. 213
2 Corinthians
7:4, 11:23–27 n. 1051; 12.7 n. 1047
Hebrews
11:5 n. 944
John
5:17 n. 342; 9:3 n. 1050
Luke
16:19–31 n. 1048; 20:36 n. 947
Matthew
5:28 n. 966
2 Peter
2:4 n. 215

INDEX OF PASSAGES CITED

Romans
9:20 n. 1036; 11:33 n. 1044; 12:19 n.
718
2 Timothy
4:7–8 n. 1052

BOETHIUS
Consolation of Philosophy
4.5.35ff. n. 1034; 4.6.7–17 n. 1007;
4.6.15–17 n. 82; 5.1 n. 952;
5.2.9–10 n. 82; 5 metr.5 9–11 n. 238
*On Aristotle's On Interpretation,
second version*
193.23–198.3 n. 170; 195.10ff. n. 921;
217.17–218.25 n. 170; 220.10–15 n.
954; 223.15–226.25 n. 170

CAELIUS AURELIANUS
Acute Affections
1.8.53–56 n. 609; 2.30.161 n. 727

CALCIDIUS
On Plato's Timaeus
21 n. 475; 143 nn. 934, 939; 143–54
n. 934; 144–45 n. 935; 152 n. 934;
153 n. 929; 155 (189.16–190.5)
n. 915; 156 (190.8ff.) n. 916; 159
(192.17–19) n. 952; 173 nn. 181,
183; 176 n. 168; 214–35 n. 118;
219 nn. 105, 118; 220 nn. 272, 277;
221 n. 376; 227 nn. 270, 376; 231 n.
131; 276 n. 118; 300 n. 105

CEDRENUS
Compendium of Histories
vol.1 p.446.22–447.8 Bekker n. 879

CHRYSIPPUS
See *Stoicorum veterum fragmenta*

CICERO
On Divination
1.5 n. 588; 1.70 n. 388; 1.102 n. 588;
1.113 nn. 388, 588; 2.100 n. 388
On Fate
30 n. 929
On the Laws
1.26 n. 132
On the Nature of the Gods
2 21; 2.133 n. 237; 2.140 nn. 131, 132,
238; 2.148–59 n. 250; 2.152–53 n.
250; 2.167 n. 1030; fr.8 Pease n.
183
Tusculan Disputations
1.18–22 n. 116; 1.20 n. 131; 1.21 n.
369; 1.79 n. 278

CLEMENT OF ALEXANDRIA
Protreptic
10.100 p.72.28 n. 251
Miscellanies (Stromata)
6.16.4 n. 84; 7.16.102 n. 657

CONSTANTINE POPHYROGE-
NITUS
Excerpts on virtues and vices
vol.1 p.140.1–9 Buettner-Wobst and
Roos n. 879

CRONIUS
fr.12 Leemans (1937) n. 355

CYRIL OF ALEXANDRIA
Against Nestorius
2, prologue (*PG* 76 60D/*ACO* 1.1.6
p.33.2–6) n. 401
Letter to Acacius
15 (*PG* 77.193D/*ACO* 1.1.4 p.27.8 n.
401

DAVID
Preliminaries (Prolegomena), CAG 18.2
15.17–18 n. 231

DEMOCRITUS
68B34 DK n. 246

DIDYMUS CAECUS
On Psalm 30.5–6, 139.1–13 Gronewald
n. 185

DIOGENES LAËRTIUS
7.52 n. 511; 7.54 n. 603; 7.106 n. 657;
7.111 n. 646; 7.111–12 n. 698;
7.112–13 n. 719; 7.116 n. 676;
7.135 nn. 269, 280; 9.26–27 n. 874;
9.59 n. 875; 10.136 n. 676

EPICURUS
Fragments
Fr. 7 1.3 Arrighetti n. 676; fr. 318
  Usener n. 522
Letter to Herodotus
46 n. 522
Letter to Menoeceus
127ff. n. 669
Principal Doctrines
1 n. 1013; 3 n. 680; 29 n. 669

EPIPHANIUS
Panarion
haeresis 64.2.2–5 (*GCS* vol.2 p.
  404.4–12 Holl and Dummer) n. 879

ERASISTRATUS
Frs. 86–90 Garofalo n. 766

EROTIAN
Lexicon of Hippocratic Words
72.18–19 Nachmanson n. 471

ETYMOLOGICUM MAGNUM
s.v *splên* (724.17–18 Gaisford) n. 753

EURIPIDES
Electra
1244 n. 1053
Heracles
1231–32 n. 1040
fr.1018 Nauck² n. 1020

EUSEBIUS
Preparation for the Gospel
3.4.2 n. 924; 4.3.11 n. 925; 6.6 n. 1023;
  6.10.1–10 n. 363; 15.11.1 n. 324;
  15.17 n. 266

EUSTHATIUS
Commentary on the Iliad
1.401, 2.615, 3.618 n. 716; Vol. 4,113
  n. 706

GALEN
Art of Medicine
2.1 (1.310 K) n. 434; 10.5 (1.333 K) n.
  864; 12.6 (1.338 K) n. 638
Exhortation to study the Arts
9 (p.21.4–6 K) n. 191
On the Affected Parts
1.2 (8.26 K) n. 431; 1.6 (8.50–53 K)
  n. 614; (8.53–55 K) n. 617; 1.7
  (8.67 K) n. 107; 2.9 (8.113 K)
  n. 574; 3.8 (8.172 K) n. 839; 3.9
  (8.173 K) n. 506; 3.9–10 (8.182 K)
  n. 502; 3.12 (8.202 K) n. 779; 4.1–2
  (8.226–28 K) n. 610; 4.9 (8.266–68
  K) n. 614; (8.267 K) n. 617; 5.1
  (8.300–01 K) n. 827; 5.6 (8.339
  K) n. 727; 6.3 (8.395 K) n. 747;
  (8.396–98 K) n. 860; (8.401 K)
  n. 860
On Anatomical Procedures
1.3 (2.233 K) n. 804; 1.5 (2.246 K,
  2.489 K) n. 806; 8.2 (2.657 K) n.
  831; 9.2 (2.716 K) n. 432; 14.2
  (169–70 Simon) n. 804
On the Anatomy of the Uterus
3.1–3 (2.890K) n. 794
On the Anatomy of Veins and Arteries
1 (2.780 K) nn. 746, 748
On Black Bile
4 (5.117 K) n. 736; (5.119 K) n. 429;
  7 (5.135 K) n. 856; (5.139–40 K)
  n. 750

On the Causes of Diseases
3 (7.15–16 K) n. 771
On the Causes of Pulses
4 (9.157 K) n. 641; 1.5 (9.7 K) nn. 763, 771
On the Causes of Respiration
1 (4.465 K) n. 834; 2 (4.467 K) n. 615
On the Causes of Symptoms
1.6 (7.115 K) n. 575; 1.7 (7.137 K) n. 643; 2.2 (7.159 K) n. 649; 2.3 (7.168 K) n. 723
On the Composition of Drugs according to Places
4.1 (12.706 K) n. 779; 5.5 (12.871 K) n. 506; 10.2 (13.237 K) n. 753
On the Diagnosis of the Affections of the Soul
8 (5.41 K) nn. 164, 921
On Differences between Fevers
2.11 (7.374 K) n. 737; 2.14 (7.381 K) n. 732
On Differences between Pulses
4.2 (8.702 K) n. 760
On Differences between Symptoms
4 (7.63 K) n. 732
On Difficulty of Breathing
1.4 (7.761 K) n. 837; 1.9 (7.775 K) n. 822; 1.9 (7.787 K) n. 821; 1.11 (7.782 K) n. 838; 1.12 (7.790–91 K) n. 823; 1.18 (7.802 K) n. 838; 2.2 (7.827 K) n. 831; 3.6 (7.914 K) n. 823
On the Dissection of Veins and Arteries
9 (2.823 K) n. 779
On the Doctrines of Hippocrates and Plato
1.6 n. 798; 1.6.5–6 (5.185–86 K) nn. 544, 803; 1.9 (5.302–05 K) n. 804; 2.4.17 (5.230 K) nn. 131, 132, 513; 2.4.27 (5.233 K) n. 619; 2.4.42 (5.238 K) n. 803; 2.7.18 (5.271 K) n. 621; 2.8.4–5(5.273 K) n. 723; 2.8.6 (5.274 K) nn. 726, 730; 2.8.7–12 (5.274–275 K) n. 727; 2.8.11 (5.275 K) n. 729; 2.8.17 (5.276 K) n. 725; 2.8.18 (5.276 K) n. 730; 3.1.31 (5.292 K) n. 513; 3.7.23 (5.340 K) n. 621; 4.2.8 (5.367–68 K), 4.2.19 (5.370 K), 4.4.32 (5.389 K) n. 646; 4.7.40–41 (5.425–26 K) n. 621; 5.2.2 (5.432 K) n. 646; 5.2.33 (5.440 K) n. 307; 5.3 (5.446 K) n. 576; 5.3.7 (5.446 K) n. 527; 5.5.32 (5.466 K), 5.6.22 (5.473 K) n. 621; 5.6.38 (5. 476–77 K) n. 202; 6.1.2 (5.506 K) n. 766; 6.1.5–17 (5.506–09 K) n. 648; 6.1.15 (5.509 K) n. 731; 6.3.41 (5.532 K) n. 748; 6.4.1 (5.532 K) n. 757; 6.4.13–14 (5.536 K) n. 754; 6.8 n. 732; 6.8.27 (5.570 K) n. 751; 6.8.36 (5.572–73 K) n. 768; 6.8.37 (5.573 K) n. 760; 6.8.38–39 (5.573 K) n. 770; 6.8.41 (5.473–74 K) n. 760; 6.8.72 (5.581 K) n. 513; 7 n. 518; 7.3.26–29 (5.608 K) n. 836; 7.5.2–7 (5.618–19 K) n. 525; 7.5.4 (5.618 K), 7.5.6 (5.619 K) n. 527; 7.5.13 (5.621 K) n. 552; 7.5.13–14 (5.621 K) n. 551; 7.5.16 (5.622 K) n. 563; 7.5.32 (5.625 K) n. 525; 7.5.33 (5.625 K) n. 534; 7.5.33–39 (5.625–26 K) n. 535; 7.5.33–37 (6.525–26 K) n. 525; 7.5.40 (5.626–27 K) n. 521; 7.5.40 (5.627 K) n. 533; 7.5.40–41 (5.627 K) n. 527; 7.5.45 (5.628 K) n. 580; 7.5–6 n. 507; 7.5–7 n. 518; 7.6.23–4 (5.633–34 K) n. 556; 7.6.24 (5.634 K) n. 536; 7.6.25 (5.634 K) n. 572; 7.6.30–31 (5.636 K) n. 509; 7.7.1 (5.637 K) n. 530; 7.7.19 (5.642 K) n. 525; 7.7.22 (5.643 K) n. 523; 7.6.27 (5.635–36 K) n. 508; 8 n. 766; 8.1.27 (5.656 K) nn. 746, 749; 8.4 n. 417; 8.4.2–3 (5.671–72

K) n. 431; 8.4.4 (5.672 K) n. 429;
8.4.21–22 (5.676 K) n. 421; 8.4.22
(5.676 K) n. 423; 8.6.41 (5.698
K) n. 423; 8.8.7 (5.709 K) n. 771;
8.8.11 (5.709–10 K) n. 803; 9 n.
766; 9.8.19–21 (5.789 K) n. 816;
9.9.7 (5.793 K) n. 766
*On the Elements according to
Hippocrates*
2.9–3.64 n. 485; 2.18 (1.419 K) nn.
486, 643; 2.43 (1.424 K) n. 643;
2.52 (1.426 K), 3.32 (1.432 K) n.
486; 4.2 (1.442 K) n. 467; (1.442–43
K) n. 468; (1.443 K) n. 466; 4.6
(1.444 K) n. 488; 5.14 (1.452 K)
n. 471; 5.21 (1.454 K) n. 455; 5.25
(1.455 K) n. 471; 5.28 (1.455 K),
5.31 (1.456 K) n. 448; 6.29 (1.465
K) n. 422; (1.466 K) n. 431; 6.35
(1.468 K) n. 452; 6.39 (1.470 K)
n. 451; 6.40 (1.470 K) n. 452; 7.3
(1.473 K) n. 459 ; 8.11 (1.479 K) nn.
422, 435; 8.11–15 (1.479–80 K) n.
431; 8.12 (1.479–80 K) n. 423; 8.13
(1.480 K) n. 451; 9.13 (1.484 K) n.
460; 10.3 (1.492 K) n. 422; 10.3–6
(1.492–93 K) n. 421; 10.7 (1.493 K)
n. 418; 11.1 (1.494 K) n. 429; 11.3
(1.494 K) n. 427; 11.16–19 (1.498
K) n. 428; 13.9 (1.503 K) n. 429;
14.1 (1.506 K) n. 427
On the Formation of the Foetus
3.26 (4.672 K) n. 513; 5.18 (4.685–86
K) n. 737
On Hippocrates' Aphorisms
1.2 (17B.359 K) n. 725; 4.21 (17B.682
K) n. 753; 6.2 (18A.10 K) n. 736
On Hippocrates' Epidemics I
1.2.80 (17A.187 K) n. 619; 2 n. 727
On Hippocrates' Epidemics III
1.17 (17A.558 K) n. 732
On Hippocrates' Epidemics VI
1.3 (17A.821 K) n. 731; 4.26 (17B.210
K) nn. 641, 676; 5.1 (17B.228 and
233 K) n. 732; 5.5 (17B.247 K)
n. 803; (17B.253 K) n. 771; 5.9
(17B.258 K) n. 757; 5.22 (17B.283
K) n. 779; 5.26–27 (17B.284 K) n.
790
On Hippocrates' On the Nature of Man
1, prooemium (15.7 K) n. 435; 1.3
(15.28–29 K) n. 468; 1.7 (15.40 K)
n. 572; 1.18 (15.58 K) n. 448; 2.6
(15.143 K) n. 749; 5.8 (8.358 K)
n. 732
On Hippocrates' On Nutriment
1 (15.226 K) n. 421
On Hippocrates' Prognostic
3.35 (18B.286 K) n. 727
On Hippocrates' Prorrheticon
2.4 (16.598 K) n. 731; 3.8 (16.728 K)
n. 746
On the Method of Healing
4.7 (10.297 K) n. 741; 6.4 (10.408–09
K) n. 804; 7.13 (10.527 K) n. 757;
9.15 (10.650.7–9 K) n. 223; 10.4
(10.681 K) n. 740; 11.16 (10.796 K)
n. 753; 12.8 (10.865 K) n. 424; 13.1
(10.874.1–4 K) nn. 122, 222
On Mixtures
1.8 (1.563–65 K) n. 561; (1. 567 K)
n. 562; 1.9 (1.570 K) n. 638; 2.5
(2.614–21 K) n. 866; 3.1 (1.654 K)
n. 732
On the Movement of Muscles
1.1 (4.369–73 K) n. 803; (4.372 K)
n. 830; (4.373 K) n. 805; 1.1–2
(4.367–76 K) n. 804; 2.5 (4.440 K)
n. 798; (4.443 K) n. 819; 2.6 (4.446
K) nn. 827–28; (4.448 K) n. 819;
2.8 (4.454–58 K) n. 814
On the Natural Faculties
1.5, 1.6 n. 732; 1.6 (2.12 K) n. 555;
1.6–7 n. 766; 1.8, 1.10–12 n. 732;
1.16 (2.65 K) n. 859; 1.17 (2.70 K)
n. 736; 2.2 (2.78 K) n. 854; 2.6 (2.98

INDEX OF PASSAGES CITED   245

K) n. 736; 2.8 (2.118 K) n. 855;
2.9 (2.132 K) n. 753; (2.132–34 K)
nn. 857–58; (2.135 K) n. 753; 2.12
(2.185–86 K) n. 754; 3.4 (2.155 K)
n. 744; (2.156 K) nn. 737, 743; 3.6
(2.160 K) n. 756; 3.8 (2.177 K) n.
732; 3.9 (2.178 K) n. 733; 3.13 n. 732
On my own Opinions
15.2 (116.20–118.5 Nutton = *On the Substance of the Natural Faculties* 4.762–63 K) n. 298
On Plethos
10.19–22 (7.566–67 K) n. 429
On Prediction from Pulses
2.1 (9.272 K), 3.7 (9.384 K) n. 771;
4.12 (9.424 K) n. 731
On the Preservation of Health
6.14 (6.444 K) n. 727
On the Properties of Foods
1.1.9 (6.459 K) n. 725; 1.1 (6.467 K) n. 854
On Semen
1.7.4 (4.536 K) n. 790; 1.7.15–19 (4.538–39 K), 1.10 n. 795;
1.12.3–12 (4.555–57 K) n. 776;
1.12.15 (4.557 K) n. 777; 1.14.6–10 (4.562–63 K) n. 776; 1.14.8–10 (4.563 K) n. 780; 1.14–16 n. 782;
1.15.8–10 (4.565 K) n. 780; 1.15.11 (4.565 K) n. 783; 1.15.65–74 (4.578–80 K) n. 780; 1.16.23 (4.586–87 K) n. 785; 1.16.25 (4.587 K) n. 783; 1.16.25 (4.586–87 K) n. 785; 1.16.5 (4.582 K) n. 783; 1.17.5 (4.590 K) n. 778; 2 n. 786; 2.1 n. 789; 2.1.5 (4.594 K) n. 794; 2.2.2 (4.610 K), 2.2.22 (4.615 K) n. 791;
2.3.4–5 (4.616 K) n. 790; 2.4 n. 789; 2.4.24 (4.624 K) n. 791; 2.4.33 (4.625 K) n. 792; 2.6.3 (4.643 K) n. 790; 2.6.15 (4.648 K) n. 861
On Simple Medicines
1.5 (11.390 K), 1.8 (11.394 K) n. 573;

1.37 (11.445 K), 1.38–39 (11.450–54 K) n. 572; 4.7 (11.639–40 K) n. 574;
4.15 (11.670–71 K) n. 431; 4.22 (11.699 K) n. 582; 6.1 (11.791.17 K), 9 (12.160 K) n. 303; 11.1.2 (12.328 K) n. 471
On Temperaments
1.8 (1.559.4–9 K) n. 302
On Tremor, Palpitation, Convulsion and Rigor
5 (7.594 K) n. 649; 5 (7.597 K) n. 424;
5 (7.598 K) n. 649; 5 (7.606 K) n. 494
On Unstable Imbalance
2 (7.735 K) n. 433
On the Usefulness of the Parts
1.1 (2.3–9 K) nn. 121, 367; 1.2 (3.1 K) n. 493; 1.3 (3.5–7 K) n. 807; 1.7 (3.14–15 K) n. 865; 1.13 (3.37 K) n. 862; 1.16 n. 766; 1.17 (3.47ff. K) n. 804; 1.22 (80.13–15 K) nn. 121, 368; 2.15 (3.145 K) n. 442; 3.1 (3.173 K) n. 810; 3.3 (3.179 K) n. 864; (3.179–85 K) n. 810; 3.4 (3.184 K) n. 809; 3.9 (3.211 K) n. 861; 3.10 (3.233 K) n. 445; (3. 241 K) n. 246;
(3.242 K) n. 442; 4.1–4 (3.266–72 K) n. 743; 4.1–6 n. 732; 4.1 n. 745;
4.1 (3.267 K) n. 741; 4.2 (3.270 K) n. 753; 4.2 (3.267 K) n. 738; 4.3 (3.269 K) n. 751; 4.4 (3.271–72 K) n. 858; 4.6 (3.273–74 K) n. 752;
4.7 (3.275 K) n. 740; 4.12 (3.298 K) n. 751; 4.12 (3.300 K) n. 763;
4.13 (3.303 K) nn. 751, 763, 854;
(3.306 K) n. 751; (3.307 K) n. 854;
4.15 (3.316ff. K) n. 753; (3.316 K) n. 857; 4.19 (3.324–25 K) n. 814;
5.3 (3.349 K) n. 854; 5.4 (3.353–54 K) n. 854; (3.355 K) n. 725; (3.356 K, 3.360 K) n. 854; (3.361 K); 5.5 (3.366 K) n. 859; 5.6 (3.370 K) nn. 858–59; 5.10 (3.380 K) n. 224; 5.12

(3.387–88 K) n. 854; 6.2 (3.411 K) n. 843; 6.4 (3.422 K) n. 816; 6.9 (3.442 K) n. 843; 6.10 (3.450–52 K), 6.17 (3.496–98 K) n. 770; 7.1 (3.516 K) n. 843; 7.1–2 n. 838; 7.3 (3.518 K) n. 848; (3.521 K) n. 841; 7.3–5 (3.523–28 K) n. 840; 7.5 n. 614; 7.5 (3.525 K) n. 843; 7.7 (3.532 K) n. 742; (3.535 K) n. 849; 7.8 (3.538 K) n. 760; (3.539–40 K) n. 846; 7.9 (3.545 K) nn. 771, 773; 7.11 n. 614; 7.11 (3.551 K) n. 848; 7.13 n. 168; 7.14 (3.578 K) n. 805; 7.17 n. 616; 7.20 (3.595–96 K) n. 615; 7.21 (3.601 K) n. 851; 7.22 (3.602 K) n. 443; 8.1 (3.609–10 K) n. 438; 8.2 (3.614 K) nn. 132, 513; 8.3 (3.623 K) n. 577; 8.4 (3.626 K) n. 438; 8.7 (3.652–53 K) n. 850; 8.10 (3.663 K) n. 544; (3.663–64 K) n. 545; (3.663 K) n. 542; 9.4 (3.700 K) n. 780; 9.8 (3.714 K) n. 542; 9.11 (3.724 K), 9.14 (3.741–43 K) n. 815; 9.16 (3.747 K) n. 569; 10.1 (3.759 K) n. 542; 10.12 n. 521; 11.4 (3.855 K) n. 739; 11.10 (3.881 K) nn. 542–43; 11.14 (3.899–901 K) n. 867; 12.3 (4.9–11 K) n. 804; 12.10 (4.41 K) n. 864; 13.5 (4.98–101 K) n. 817; 14.6 (4.161 K) n. 442; 14.7 n. 795; 14.7 (4.170–71 K) n. 860; 14.10 n. 786; 14.11 (4.190 K) n. 783; (4.193 K) n. 794; 14.13 (4.201 K) n. 755; (4.202 K) n. 860; 15.6 n. 766; 15.6 (4.241–42 K) n. 853; 16.2 (4.266 K) n. 748; (4.268 K) n. 547; (4.270 K) n. 563; (4.271 K) nn. 549, 577; 16.3 (4.273 K) n. 535; (4.275 K) n. 569; (4.276 K) n. 815; 16.4 (4.282–83 K) nn. 617, 619; 16.6 (4.295 K) n. 578; 16.12 (4.321 K) n. 860

On the Usefulness of Respiration
3.8 (4.491 K) n. 826; (4.491–92 K)
n. 825; 5 (4.501–11 K) n. 544; 5.8 (4.510 K) n. 825

On Venesection
23 (11.313 K) n. 779

Synopsis on Pulses
9 (9.459 K) n. 771; 21 (9.492K) n. 121

That the Faculties of the Soul follow the Mixtures of the Body (Quod animi mores)
3 (4.773 K) n. 298; (4.775.18–776.3 K) n. 301; 6 (4.789–91 K) n. 969

To Glauco on the Method of Healing
2.12 (11.139 K) n. 753

To Patrophilus on the Establishment of the Medical Art
8 (1.252 K) n. 460

[GALEN]
Historia philosopha
DG p. 636 n. 498

Introduction or Physician
9 (14.695 K) n. 448; 13 (14.735 K) n. 727

Medical Definitions
27 (19.355.7–8 K) n. 231

On Diagnosis and Treatment of Kidney Affections
6 (19.688 K) n. 448

On Incorporeal Qualities
3 (19.471.15–472.5 K) n. 280

On Remedies that are Easily Obtained
1.1 (14.313 K) n. 131

GEORGIUS MONACHUS (GEORGIUS HAMARTOLUS)
Chronicle
2 (p.457.20–458.7 de Boor) n. 879

GREGORY OF NAZIANZUS
Letters
198–201 Gallay n. 5
Poems to Other Persons
7 (*PG* 37 1551–1577) n. 5

INDEX OF PASSAGES CITED

GREGORY OF NYSSA
Against Fate
48.5–9 McDonough (1987) n. 927
Catchetical Oration
6 n. 230
Controversy (Antirrheticus) against Apollinarius
209.1, 211.26, 213.7, 213.21–25, 214.19–21 Mueller n. 185
On the Creation of Man
2 (*PG* 44.132–33) n. 207; 7 (*PG* 44 141A) n. 221; 8 (*PG* 44 144B) n. 238; (*PG* 44 144D) n. 237; 12 (*PG* 44 156C) n. 132; (*PG* 44 156D) n. 513; 38 (*PG* 44 229bc, 235b) n. 31
Oration 2 on the words "Let us make man"
PG 44 284b n. 218

[GREGORY OF NYSSA]
On the Soul
PG 45 128–221 n. 12

GREGORY THE GREAT
Homilies on the Gospels
29 (*PL* 76 1214C) n. 191

[HELIODORUS]
On Aristotle's Nicomachean Ethics
42.18 n. 877

HERACLITUS
22B30 DK n. 1012
22B118 DK n. 491

HERMOGENES
On Invention (Rhetores Graeci vol. 7.2 Walz)
p.756.12–13, p.760.9 n. 886
On Styles (De ideis), Rhet. Gr. vol.7.2 Walz)
p.920.14 n. 886

HERODOTUS
2.68.3 n. 283

HEROPHILUS
T 101–03, 105, 189–90 von Staden n. 783
T 191.16–19 von Staden n. 785

HIPPASUS OF CROTON
18A7 DK n. 492

HIPPOCRATES
Airs, Waters, Places
22.3 (2.78 L) n. 779
Epidemics
2.2.1 (5.84 L) n. 728; 6.5.15 (5.320 L) n. 779
On Fleshes
16 (8.604 L) n. 850
On Generation
2 (7.472 L) n. 779
6 n. 786
On Humours
11 (5.490 L) n. 748
On the Nature of Man
2 (6.34–36 L) n. 486; (6.36 L) n. 487
On Places in Man
2 (6.278 L) n. 850
Prorrheticon
1.72 (5.528 L) n. 727

[HIPPOCRATES]
Letters
23 (9.934.9 Littré) n. 131

HOMER
Iliad
15.362ff. n. 337; 18.108–10 n. 660

IAMBLICHUS
Life of Pythagoras
36.267 (p.145.15 Dübner) n. 262
On the Mysteries

fr.4 Dillon (1973) n. 288
cited by Stobaeus 1.49.32, p.363.20
Wachsmuth n. 263

JULIAN THE EMPEROR
Against the Christians
171.14–172.1 Neumann n. 483
Orations
4 140d n. 1040; 6 183b n. 189

LEO
Synopsis on the Nature of Man
68 n. 753

LUCRETIUS
On the Nature of Things
1.49 n. 1014; 4.353–55 n. 538; 4.387 n. 541; 4.436–42 n. 539

MAIMONIDES
Guide of the Perplexed
3.16 n. 1037

MANILIUS
Astronomicon
4.12–22, 4.106–18 n. 917

MELETIUS
On the Nature of Man
20 n. 753

MENANDER
Arbitration (Epitrepontes)
736–40 Koerte n. 1021
Fragments (Koerte)
13, 64 n. 1021; 719 n. 1049; 749 n. 1021

MICHAEL GLYCAS
Annals (*PG* 128) n. 20

NEMESIUS
On the Nature of Man
[excluding references in footnotes attached to the specific passages themselves]
1 3, 21; n. 372; 1, 2.13–4.24 n. 122; 4.19 n. 240; 5.4–8 21; 5.19ff. n. 412; 6.5 n. 104; 6.6 n. 481; 6.6–10 n. 37; 6.14–16 n. 980; 6.18–20 n. 37; 7.8–9 n. 36; 7.12–14 n. 416; 7.12–9.22, 9.2–3 n. 122; 9.22–10.21 6; 9.22ff. n. 412; 10.11 n. 36; 10.14–19 n. 980; 11.15 nn. 104, 214, 481; 13.10–15.3 n. 250; 13.12 22; 13.19 21 n. 304, 2 5, 8, 19–21, 32; n. 114; 2, 17.4–5 85 n. 411; 17.10 n. 592; 17.17 n. 108; 20.17 n. 113; 21.5–6 n. 666; 21.6–22.3 n. 277; 21.19–22 nn. 407, 666; 22.3–17 n. 277; 22.10–17 n. 377; 22.24–23.6 n. 336; 23.24ff. 21; 23.25 nn. 69, 724; 24.1ff n. 70; 24.15 n. 65; 24.20–21 n. 66; 26.22–27.11 n. 410; 28.4ff. n. 412; 28.7–9 n. 27; 30.18–32.19 6; 30.22 n. 48; 31.23–32.13 n. 472; 32.12 n. 48; 32.20–33.19 6; n. 114; 34.15–17 n. 167; 35.11–37.9 20; 36.16–21 n. 204; 36.26–37.1 n. 971; 37.4–9 21; 37.10 n. 64; 37.12 n. 67; 37.12–16, 17–19 n. 121; 2–3 3–4; 3 5, 8, 32; n. 360; 3, 39.6 n. 375; 41.14–42.11 6; 43.6–8 n. 390; 44.15–16 6; 44.19–21 6; n. 49; 44.20 n. 592; 4–28 3; 4, 45.2 n. 418; 45.12 n. 417; 5 n. 222; 5, 47.6 n. 462; 47.24 n. 453; 49.1–5 n. 453; 53.7 n. 214; 54.24 n. 611; 55.1 n. 51; 6 9; 6–11 n. 623; 6, 56.2–4 n. 54; 55.13 n. 497; 55.24 n. 611; 56.2 nn. 607, 611; 56.2–4 n. 623; 56.3 nn. 590, 798; 56.5 nn. 667, 800, 812; 56.5ff. n. 496; 56.5–21 n. 575; 56.12 n. 581; 57.3 n. 571; 57.4–5 n. 510; 57.7–15 n. 60; 57.8 22; nn.

INDEX OF PASSAGES CITED

132, 812; 57.8–10 n. 53; 57.9 n.
592; 57.11 n. 584; 7, 57.20 n. 524;
58.14–59.13 n. 518; 58.15 n. 68;
59.7–10 nn. 54, 623; 59.13–18 n.
518; 59.18–19 n. 564; 7–11 10; 8,
63.7 n. 550; 63.7–8 n. 577; 63.17
n. 560; 64.2 nn. 544, 607; 64.10
nn. 590, 798; 64.13–15 n. 550;
64.15 n. 570; 65.7–8 n. 566; 65.17
n. 611; 65.24 nn. 54, 611, 623; 9,
66.7 nn. 54, 611, 623; 66.9 n. 553;
10, 67.7 nn. 54, 611, 623; 12 9;
nn. 248, 623, 630; 12, 68.4 n. 611;
68.9 n. 892; 68.9–10 n. 613; 68.11
nn. 104, 105, 214, 611; 68.11–13
nn. 55, 623; 68.12 nn. 606–7, 798;
13 9, 25; n. 623; 13, 68.15–16 n.
605; 68.22 n. 584; 69.15–16 313;
69.17–71.4 n. 504; 69.18 nn. 607,
611; 69.18–20 n. 623; 69.20 n. 798;
69.25–70.10 n. 550; 70.13ff n. 72;
14 10; n. 630; 14, 71.6–7 n. 622;
71.6ff. n. 812; 71.7 n. 799; 71.11
n. 587; 15, 72.4 n. 799; 72.9–17
n. 57; 72.10 n. 812; 72.17–18 n.
58; 72.18–19 n. 632; 72.19–20 10;
15–25 3 n. 9; 16–21 11; 16, 73.8
n. 621; 73.9ff. n. 626; 73.11–12 n.
652; 73.20ff. n. 621; 74.1–2 n. 650;
74.2–3 nn. 621, 650; 75.1 n. 648;
75.2 n. 644; 17, 75.9 10; 75.12 n.
655; 75.19–20 n. 653; 18, 76.8 n.
703; 76.13 nn. 800, 812; 77.3–4 nn.
700–01; 77.11–14 n. 701; 77.11–19
n. 700; 77.20ff. n. 668; 78.3–5 n.
671; 79.16 5; 19 n. 979; 20, 81.3
n. 660; 21, 82.7 nn. 69, 556; 22 n.
621; 22, 82.20–22 n. 801; 82.21–22
n. 61; 82.22 nn. 517, 798; 23 nn.
219, 623; 23, 83.7–9 n. 773; 83.9 n.
772; 83.12 nn. 772, 824; 83.12–14
n. 733; 83.15ff. n. 802; 84.11–12
n. 737; 84.23 n. 892; 23–25 11, 29;

n. 869; 24, 85.5 n. 784; 85.6–11 n.
852; 85.15 n. 824; 85.18–20 n. 766;
85.19 nn. 735, 824; 85.21 n. 824;
25 nn. 623, 626; 25, 85.23–24 nn.
666, 758; 85.23ff. n. 626; 86.1ff.
n. 802; 86.9–10 n. 144; 86.22ff n.
74; 26 nn. 869, 963; 26, 87.18 n.
811; 87.18–19 n. 892; 87.20 n. 812;
87.20ff. n. 634; 87.21–22 n. 812;
87.23 n. 893; 27 nn. 625, 634, 758;
27, 88.1, 88.3, 88.22 n. 892; 88.25
n. 62; 88.25–6 n. 828; 89.5–7 n.
550; 27–28 n. 869; 28, 89.19 n. 758;
89.22 n. 893; 90.12 n. 62; 91.22 n.
818; 92.2–7 n. 737; 95.18 n. 592;
29 169 n. 871; 29–43 3; 30 29; nn.
151, 870; 30, 95.10 n. 892; 95.17
n. 992; 30–34 26, 28–31; nn. 145,
174, 871; 31, 96.25 n. 893; 97.12 n.
892; 32, 98.10–14 n. 869; 98.12–14
n. 893; 99.5 n. 892; 34 29–30; n.
161; 34, 102.12 n. 151; 103.2–5 n.
961; 103.10ff. 27; 103.11 n. 984;
103.11–12 n. 157; 34–38 31; 34–39
28; 35 29; 35, 104.13–105.5 n. 91;
35–38 n. 162; 36 n. 161; 37 28;
37, 108.13–18 n. 90; 38 27–30;
nn. 167, 353; 38, 110.13–111.13
n. 90; 110.21–111.13 nn. 88, 92;
111.14–112.6 n. 89; 39 28, 39;
39, 113.17 28; 39–41 30–31; nn.
145, 162, 174, 893; 40 n. 1026;
40, 115.17–21 n. 34; 116.3–6 n.
90; 116.4 n. 989; 41 n. 174; 41,
117.7–8 n. 365; 117.9–10 n. 975;
118.4–8 16; 118.13–15 n. 980;
119.4ff. 15; 119.16–17 nn. 85, 982;
120.25–121.9 n. 102; 41–43 n.
237; 42 3; n. 1028; 42, 120.21–23
n. 28; 121.10 n. 214; 125.1 n. 604;
42–43 31; 43 3, 8, 27; n. 351; 43,
126.17–21 n. 88; 128.8–11 n. 102;
131.12–16 n. 47; 136.9–16 n. 95

NESTORIUS
fr.201–202, pp. 66, 162, 219–220 Loofs
  (1905) n. 414

NUMENIUS
fr.4a des Places n. 266; fr.4b des Places
  n. 265

OLYMPIODORUS
On Plato's Phaedo
78.15ff., 20–24, 27 Norvin n. 288

ORIBASIUS
Books to Eunapius
Proem, 1.5 n. 64
Medical Collections, Books of Uncertain Order
8 n. 732; 62.5, 21–23, 50 n. 614

ORIGEN
Against Celsus
2.20 n. 929; 3.41 n. 392; 4.74 n.
  233; 4.74–78 n. 237; 4.87 n. 363;
  5.20–23 n. 947; 7.5 p.156.22 n. 415
Homily on Exodus
8.4 n. 249
Homilies on Genesis
1.12 nn. 233–34; 1.15 n. 209
On John
10.51 n. 249; 20.24.208 n. 592
On Principles
2.6.6 n. 392; 2.8 n. 415; 3.1.4 n. 882
Selected Comments on the Psalms
vol. 12, p. 1272.16–17 n. 592

ORION
Etymologicum s.v. *splên* (143.27–28
  Sturz) n. 753

OVID
Metamorphoses
1.84–86 n. 238

PALLADAS
Anth. Pal. 10.45 n. 251

PANAETIUS
fr. 86 van Straaten n. 626

PHILO OF ALEXANDRIA
Allegory of the Laws
2.22–23 n. 196
On the Confusion of Tongues
186 n. 380; 187 n. 471
On the Creation of the World
77 n. 216; 77 ff. n. 207; 82 n. 246; 135
  nn. 193, 214
On Dreams
1.32 n. 131
On the Eternity of the World
42 p.86.1 n. 337
On the Special Laws
3.111 nn. 132, 513; 4.92 n. 131; 4.93,
  123 nn. 132, 513

PHILODEMUS
Papyri from Herculaneum
1005, col. V 8–13 (p. 173 Angeli) n.
  471

PHILOPONUS
On Aristotle's On the Soul
3.24ff., 5.17–19 n. 603; 9.3–10.9 n.
  254; 10.9–11 n. 263; 12.26–30 n.
  268; 50.16–55.5 n. 284; 50.25–52.3
  n. 309; 52.26–53.8 n. 263; 89.18–20
  n. 274; 142.6–15 n. 291; 142.15–22
  n. 292; 142.22–26 n. 294;
  142.26–33 n. 295; 142.33–143.1 n.
  297; 144.22–25 n. 297; 145.1–5 n.
  307; 155.20–30 n. 607; 183.30–34
  n. 309; 274.8–10 n. 77

PHOTIUS
Library
249 440a33 n. 246

# INDEX OF PASSAGES CITED

PLATO
Alcibiades I
129e n. 189
Apology
38c n. 1055
Axiochus
365e n. 189
Cratylus
403b n. 382
Crito
53d n. 1055
Gorgias
523cd n. 382
Laws
7 791a2 n. 395; 10 17, 31–32; 10 886a n. 991; 900d–903a n. 1037; 902d–903a n. 1042; 904c n. 1043
Meno
70a n. 657; 81c ff. n. 603
Phaedo
62b n. 189; 78–79 n. 370; 78b ff n. 288; 79b–80b n. 260; 79c n. 381; 80a n. 288; 81e–82a n. 354; 86b n. 290; 91e–92e n. 291; 92e–93a n. 292; 93ae n. 294; 93e–94a n. 295; 94bc n. 304; 94be n. 292; 102e–103a, 103d n. 384; 105e–107a n. 385; 106ce n. 371; 115ce n. 189
Phaedrus
245e nn. 260, 324; 248c n. 934
Philebus
33e n. 601; 34a nn. 512, 593; 36c–42c n. 672; 39b n. 594; 46ab n. 685; 51b–52b n. 674; 53c ff. n. 677
Republic
2 364 17; 5 469d n. 189; 477c nn. 157, 914; 6 511de n. 598; 7 534a n. 598; 9 572a n. 388; 10 27; 10 617e n. 939; 620a n. 354; 620c n. 382
Theaetetus
161d n. 594; 179c n. 594; 186cd n. 556; 191d nn. 593, 596–7;192a n. 596

Timaeus
31b n. 480; 31b–32c n. 461; 31c n. 206; 32b n. 476; 32b ff. n. 456; 34b ff. nn. 347, 348; 35b–36b n. 260; 36e n. 348; 39–42 n. 1004; 41–43 n. 351; 41ab n. 48; 41de n. 934; 41e n. 352; 42de 27; n. 1004; 43a n. 395; 43ab n. 219; 43c n. 512; 44a n. 395; 45b–46c n. 524; 46a n. 512; 47a–c n. 1006; 49b ff. n. 468; 55d n. 473; 55e ff. n. 473; 56d ff. n. 474; 63e–64a n. 557; 65d–66c n. 572; 67b n. 576; 70a n. 131; 70b nn. 132, 513, 638; 70bc n. 717; 70c, 70d, 71d n. 638; 86–87 n. 969; 86b, 86b–87b n. 657; 86cd, 86d n. 661; 86de n. 658; 86e, 87b n. 657; 87b, 87d n. 662; 88b n. 657; 89a nn. 657, 662; 90a 22; nn. 238, 251; 91e–92a 22; n. 238

PLOTINUS
1.1 [53] 3.1–3 n. 184; 4.14–16 n. 391; 8 n. 184; 11.8–15 n. 357; 3.1 [3] 2.25–36 n. 920; 5, 7 n. 920; 7.14ff. n. 921; 9.5, 10.4 n. 82; 3.2 [47] 4.11 n. 350; 10 n. 82; 13 n. 1053; 3.4 [15] 3 n. 209; 3.6 [26] 4 nn. 642, 648; 1–4 n. 284; 4.1 [2] 1.32, 62 n. 346; 4.3 [27] 22.1–9 n. 391; 22.7–10 n. 398; 24.11–13 n. 350; 30 n. 500; 4.4 [28] 27.9–11 n. 350; 4.7 [2] n. 116; 4.7 [2] 1.5–6 n. 184; 8^2 n. 376; 12.12–13,17–19 n. 288; 5.3 [49] 13 n. 500; 6.7 [38] 11.24–30 n. 350

PLUTARCH
The Cleverness of Animals
973a n. 612
On Garrulousness
509e–510a n. 993
On the Generation of Soul in the Timaeus
1030c n. 1006

On the Impossibility of Living Pleasantly according to Epicurus
1092d n. 676
On Moral Virtue
441bc n. 621
On Stoic Self-Contradictions
1053d n. 278
That a Philosopher ought to converse especially with Men in Power
777c n. 612

[PLUTARCH]
Epitome of Physical Opinions
5.5 n. 786; 5.5.1 n. 787 and see AËTIUS
On Fate
568c–570e, 570a n. 934; 570f, 571a n. 913; 571bc n. 915; 571cd n. 916; 572c n. 952; 572f–573a nn. 1004, 1006; 572f–574d n. 1004; 574cd n. 1007

PORPHYRY
Introduction (Isagôgê)
20.11–12, 19–22 n. 228
Letter to Anebo
24.1, 25.3–7 Sodano n. 924
Miscellaneous Investigations
2 85
On Abstinence
2.37 n. 269; 3.3 n. 612; 3.4.2 n. 205
Sentences
3 n. 401; 14 n. 370; 16 n. 531; 27 nn. 393, 402; 31 nn. 393, 398; 35 n. 40; 41 n. 531
To Gaurus
11.2 (p. 48 Kalbfleisch) n. 531
Fragments (Smith)
247 n. 324; 264 n. 531; 439 n. 324

POSIDONIUS
F33 Edelstein–Kidd n. 621

PRISCIAN OF LYDIA
Answers to Chosroes

42.15, 16–17 n. 372; 44.15–28 n. 376; 44.17–20 n. 286; 46.4ff. n. 297; 46.25 n. 370; 50.25–28 nn. 372, 376; 50.25–52.7 n. 372; 50.28–51.4 n. 374; 51.4–9 n. 378; 51.9–18 n. 383; 51.13 n. 399; 51.18 n. 386; 51.25–26 n. 389; 51.33–52.5 n. 392; 52.7 n. 397; 52.13–16 n. 386

PROCLUS
On Providence and Fate and What Depends on Us
II.3.4–13 n. 1007; II.3.13–19 n. 82; II.4.3–10 n. 1007; II.4.10–19 n. 82

PSELLUS
Short Works on the Soul
28.4 n. 675

PTOLEMY
Tetrabiblos
1.3.4 n. 917

PTOLEMY THE GRAMMARIAN
Differences between Words
p.395.10 n. 721

PYTHAGORAS, LIFE OF
quoted by Photius, Library 249 440a33 n. 246

RUFUS OF EPHESUS
On Melancholy
fr. 127 Daremberg–Ruelle n. 502

SALLUST
Catiline
1 n. 238

SCHOLIA
on Aristophanes' Frogs 844 n. 713
on Sophocles' Ajax 41a.2 n. 716

INDEX OF PASSAGES CITED 253

SENECA
Letters
41.5 n. 391; 92.30 n. 238; 94.56 n. 238
On the happy life
15.7 n. 82
Questions concerning Nature
2.21 n. 465; 2.36f. n. 924

SEXTUS EMPIRICUS
Against the Professors (Against the Mathematicians)
7.208 n. 538; 7.241, 246 n. 501; 7.300 n. 582; 7.384 n. 675; 8.275 n. 612; 9.20–22 n. 388
Outlines of Pyrrhonism
1.65 n. 586; 1.65ff. n. 612; 3.10ff. n. 183; 3.131 n. 403

SIMPLICIUS
On Aristotle's Categories
78.4ff. n. 263; 271.21 n. 280; 214.24 n. 195
On Aristotle's Physics
580.3 n. 403
On Epictetus' Manual
379.462ff. Hadot n. 1037

SORANUS
Matters Related to Women
1.14 n. 794

STOBAEUS
Selections (Anthology)
1.17 n. 380; 1.19 n. 631; 1.49 n. 354; 1.49.34 n. 624; 2.6.166 nn. 654, 656; 2.7.1c n. 713; 2.7.10 nn. 698, 719; 2.7.10c n. 714

STOICORUM VETERUM FRAGMENTA
1.143 n. 624; 1.176 n. 932; 1.285–87 n. 657; 2.47 n. 380; 2.54 n. 498; 2.135 n. 612; 2.201 n. 915; 2.382–83 n.

280; 2.391 n. 195; 2.418 n. 478; 2.442 n. 267; 2.444 n. 266; 2.458 n. 196; 2.471 n. 392; 2.471.25 n. 657; 2.472.15 n. 471; 2.473 nn. 376, 392; 2.482, 485, 487–88 n. 280; 2.499 n. 889; 2.528 n. 932; 2.625 n. 945; 2.790 n. 285; 2.806 n. 278; 2.827a n. 624; 2.836 n. 186; 2.886 n. 657; 2.913, 937 n. 932; 2.934 n. 675; 2.939 nn. 925, 929; 2.956–57 n. 929; 2.988 n. 882; 3.229 n. 662; 3.416, 23 n. 722; 3.434 n. 676; 3.471 n. 307

STRATO
fr. 128–29 Wehrli n. 505

SUDA
s.v. 'Origenes' (vol.3 p.622.8–18 Adler), s.v. *parakhratai* (vol.4 p.46.3–6 Adler) n. 879

SYNESIUS
Letter 57 in *Epistolographi Graeci*, p.669.4–5 Hercher = letter 41, p.51.304–05 Garzya n. 1040

TACITUS
Annals
6.22 n. 920

TATIAN
Oration to the Greeks
9 p.10.7–10 Schwartz n. 82

TERTULLIAN
Apology
50 n. 874
On the Soul
5.4–6 n. 277; 6.1 n. 270; 6.6 nn. 271, 277; 14.2 n. 626

THALES
11A11 DK n. 489

THEMISTIUS
On Aristotle's On the Soul
16.19ff. nn. 324, 326; 46.12 n. 321
On Aristotle's Physics
118.8 n. 403

THEODORE OF MOPSUESTIA
Letter to Domnus
PG 66 1013a n. 414
On the Incarnation
PG 66 973c, 992c n. 414

THEODORET
On Providence
2, *PG* 83 p.581 nn. 181, 183; 3, *PG* 83 p.597 n. 238; 4, *PG* 83 p.613 n. 221; 5, *PG* 83 p.641 nn. 244, 245; 10, *PG* 83 p.748 n. 1040
On Jeremiah
10:24–25 (*PG* 81 572.10–14 Migne) n. 964
Remedy for Greek Attitudes
3.48.3 n. 621; 5.17 n. 328; 5.18 nn. 112, 253; 6.57 nn. 939, 940

THEOPHILUS
Against Autolycus
2.27 n. 214

THEOPHRASTUS
On the Causes of Plants
6.1, 6.4 n. 572
On Fire
11, 23 n. 826

THUCYDIDES
2.49.3 n. 729

XENOCRATES
frr. 203–4 Isnardi–Parente n. 271

XENOPHON
Memorabilia
1.4.11 n. 238

Zeno of Citium
See *Stoicorum veterum fragmenta*

ZENO OF ELEA
29A8, 29A19 DK n. 874

GENERAL INDEX

Within entries, references to pages precede references to notes and are separated from each other with a semi-colon; single note references are preceded by 'n. ', multiple note references in a single entry by 'nn. '.

Abammon n. 924
abdomen 145, 147, 162; mouth of 143
abyss (in Bible) 98
Achilles n. 1038
acropolis, head as 22
action, actions, acts 168–69, 182, 195–99, 201, 210, 212, 220; nn. 870, 962, 989, 1003, 1007, 1022–23
activity (*energeia*) 131, 138, 190; nn. 261, 934
actuality 53, 64–66, 68, 94; nn. 261, 313, 320
Adrasteia n. 934
Adrastus of Aphrodisias 26
adultery, adulterers 71, 199; n. 934
advantageous 212
advice 197
Aëtius (doxographer) 19–20; nn. 118, 252, 254
Aëtius of Amida 25
affection (*pathos*) 11, 45, 58, 103, 112, 129–32 *and see* emotions, feelings; of the body 134
affective part of the soul 10, 125, 127–31
age 62
agent 174–76
air 43, 52, 56, 82, 88, 92–99, 102, 105, 108, 163; nn. 254, 256, 392, 416
airiness 88

Alcmaeon n. 258
Alexander of Aphrodisias 14, 26, 29–32; nn. 401, 457, 916, 921, 959, 1030, 1032, 1039; works, *On Fate* 30; *On Providence* n. 177; *On the Soul* n. 171; *Supplement to On the Soul* (*mantissa*) 20;
Alexandria 83; n. 879
Alfanus 4
allegory n. 588
alteration, faculty of 145; sensation a process of 102
Ambrose 12; nn. 77, 137
Ammonias (son of Hermias) 30
Ammonius (Saccas) 18, 54, 80; nn. 265, 372, 390
Anastasius of Sinai 4
Anaxagoras nn. 422, 949
Anaxarchus 170; nn. 151, 874
Anaximenes 99
Andronicus 27; nn. 646, 697
angels 41, 44–46, 50, 202; nn. 191, 215, 977, 980
anger 131, 141, 172–73, 175–77, 200, 211; nn. 192, 660, 881, 891, 895
anguish (*agônia*) 142
animal, animals 8, 16, 20–21, 35, 37–39, 41–43, 45–49, 52, 55, 62, 72–76, 157, 167, 175–78, 195, 198, 200, 206, 208, 210, 217–18; nn.

191, 234, 236–37, 357, 359–60,
363, 903, 962, 1019
anonymous commentary on
   Nicomachean Ethics 2–5 26; n. 148
Antiochus of Ascalon n. 1033
Antisthenes nn. 674, 874
ants 56, 217; n. 220
ape 75–76; n. 364
Apollinaris 2, 6–7, 14, 35, 70, 98; nn.
   185, 187, 336, 373, 392
Apollo 197; n. 929
Apollodorus n. 269
Apollonius of Tyana, pseudo-, *Book
   on the Secrets of Nature and the
   Hidden Causes of Things* n. 22
apparition (*phantasma*) 100
appetite 48, 128, 176, 178–79, 185; nn.
   895, 903, 905
appetitive part of the soul 10
apple 108
Apuleius 31; n. 1005
Aquinas, Thomas n. 14
Arabic version 2, 4
archangels n. 980
Arian heresy n. 332
Aristippus n. 677
Aristo n. 864
Aristophanes of Byzantium n. 446
Aristotle, Aristotelian(s), Aristotelianism 1, 5, 8, 10, 11, 14–15,
   17, 19, 23, 25, 26, 28, 30, 36, 39,
   52–53, 64, 67, 69, 88, 95, 97, 105,
   126–27, 128, 138, 155, 210–12;
   nn. 50, 82, 117, 145, 157, 162, 174,
   187–89, 236, 258, 263, 311, 313,
   319–20, 325, 410–11, 416, 417,
   422, 433, 427, 446, 505, 584, 587,
   591, 592, 621–22, 633, 659, 722,
   949, 970, 977, 981, 1005, 1018,
   1023, 1027, 1032, 1038; Aristotle,
   works: *Eudemus* n. 297; *History of
   Animals* 91; *Meteorology* n. 417;
   Nicomachean Ethics 10, 26; nn.

146, 627; *On Coming to Be and
   Perishing* n. 417; *On the Parts of
   Animals* 9; n. 417; *On the Soul*
   10–11; nn. 10, 627; *Parva Naturalia*
   10–11
Arius (Christian heretic) n. 145
Arius Didymus 20; n. 277
Armenian version vii, 2, 4; nn. 271,
   333, 362, 901, 1001–02, 1013
Arnobius n. 45
arteries 89, 146, 150–53
artery, pulmonary 164
arts n. 911 *and see* crafts, skills
asceticism 7, 979, n. 670
Asclepiades, on respiration n. 831
Aspasius, *On Aristotle's Nicomachean
   Ethics* 26, n. 646
assassin 220
assent 117,185, 191
asses 73
astringency, perception of 115
astrology, nativity-casters 16, 186; nn.
   91, 161, 168, 917–18, 920, 1008
Athenaeus, of Naucratis n. 446
Atomists n. 485
atoms 52
Atropos n. 934
attachment 59, 79
Atticus (the Platonist) 17; nn. 97, 148,
   319, 1018
attraction, faculty of 145
attunement 53, 60–61, 64, 76; nn. 262,
   308 *and see* harmony, temperament
Augustine 12, 15
autonomous, autonomy 6–7, 14, 16,
   194–95, 198–202, 204; nn. 930,
   948, 964, 1046 *and see* freedom
avaricious 221
avoidance 117,169, 212
awareness of self 42; sensory 112

Babylon 204
badness 60, 66, 69, 199

GENERAL INDEX

balance, of qualities in body 43, 44, n. 222 *and see* temperament
Basil, medical knowledge of 12
Bathsheba n. 344
beard 180–81
beasts of burden 46, 49; wild beasts 43–44, 49
beauty 63, 66; nn. 307, 323
bees 56, 217
beetles 43
beginning 200
belief 177–78; n. 899
benevolence, of God n. 180
bile 56, 64, 141, 145; nn. 273, 660; black 87–89, 166; n. 737; yellow 87–90, 143, 165; nn. 660, 737; bitter 133
birds 40, 43, 49, 90; n. 240
birth 70–71, 195, 201, 207
bitterness, perception of 115
bivalves 38–39
bladder 90, 147
blame 169, 171–73, 175, 184, 197; n. 934
blasphemy 220
blending n. 298 *and see* mixture
blessed, blessedness 202, 214
blind 219
blood 52, 55–56, 80, 87–90, 141, 149, 153, 166; nn. 272, 768
bloodless animals 56
bluntness 96–97; perception of 107, 112
boasting, boastfulness 219; nn. 981–982
body, bodies, bodily 1, 5, 7–9, 12, 15, 18–20, 32, 35–37, 40–42, 44–46, 50–51, 53–55, 57–60, 62–70, 71–72, 74–86, 99, 178, 184, 199–200, 205–06, 214, 217; nn. 31, 112, 114, 184–85, 187, 189, 193, 214, 227, 234, 248, 263, 266, 268–69, 277–79, 286, 288, 298, 315–316, 318–319, 324, 332–333, 336, 351, 372, 376, 378, 392, 394, 398, 406–07, 410, 412–413, 415, 969, 1040; bodily goods 214; bodily pleasure 135–37
Boethius 30
Boethus n. 263
bone(s) 38, 89, 111, 165, 167; n. 307
boundary 8, 37, 40–41; n. 193
brain 25, 56, 89, 106, 112, 115, 118, 151, 158, 161, 165; n. 852; cavities of 10, 110–12, 116, 121, 122, 160; frontal cavities of 101; damage to 122
breasts 91, 153
breath, breathing 37, 42, 51, 55–56, 63, 66, 146, 183; nn. 253, 272; vital 151–52 *and see* pneuma
breathing 158, 162
bronchial tube 164
building n. 955
bulk 83; n. 402
Burgundio of Pisa 4; nn. 353, 661

Calcidius, *On Plato's Timaeus* 29–30; n. 949
Cappadocia 2
cardiocentrism n. 722
Carneades n. 918
carnivores 47
carotid arteries 154
carpenters 207
cartilage 89, 116, 143
cartaliginous part of windpipe 124, 164
cartilaginous fish 56
categories n. 1005
cattle 39–40, 49
cause(s) 185–86, 189–91, 195, 198, 218; nn. 949, 952, 954, 962, 1027; efficient n. 832; final n. 832; material n. 832
cavities of brain 10, 25, 101, 110, 116, 118, 121, 160

258 GENERAL INDEX

cavity, left c. of heart 150
cerebellum 121–22
cerebral cavities 25
Chalcedon, Council of n. 4
chance 30, 180–81, 198, 200; nn. 162, 894, 949, 952, 1016 *and see* luck
change, changeable 200–03, 218; n. 977
channels, invisible in the body 146
character 64, 196; n. 1021
charity 206
chest 90
children 74, 175–76, 199, 215; nn. 278–79
chill, in fear 143
choice(s), choose, choosing 15, 26, 28, 93, 118, 157, 169–71, 175–79, 187–90, 192, 195, 197, 199–203, 212; nn. 85, 871, 885, 894–95, 897, 902–03, 927, 942, 949, 971, 981, 983
chorus-men 79
Christ 50, 84, 194; nn. 185, 408, 413 *and see* Son of Man
Christianity, Christian(s) 1–3, 5–7, 77, 194, 204; nn. 151, 918, 947, 962, 977, 979, 990, 1029, 1032
Christology 6; nn. 401, 406, 410
Chrysippus 20, 29, 57, 59, 185; nn. 277–78, 307, 498, 621, 646, 798, 921–22
Church 7
Cicero nn. 587, 588
circumstance(s) 171, 173–74, 218
city 44
Cleanthes 20, 57; nn. 277, 666
Clement of Alexandria 12; n. 151
clothing 43–44
Clotho n. 934
co–fated events n. 929
coherence 43; n. 222
cold 92–93, 53, 63; nn. 302, 307
coldness, perception of 115

colon 162
colour 107, 206, 208
combined (*sumpeplegmenos*), functions 11
coming to be 95, 200, 210; n. 1006 *and see* generation
command 214
common sensibles n. 535
community 44; n. 224
compatibilism, of responsibility and determinism 14, 183; nn. 81, 920, 934
compilation 17
completeness of treatise 3–4
complexion 63
composite, composition 178; nn. 288, 372, 903
compulsion 169
concepts 118; n. 280; natural 121
concurrence n. 952
condition 191–92; conditional fate 27, 192; nn. 81, 929, 934, 936
cone, optic 105
conflagration 193
conscience 219
consent 86, 218–19; nn. 413–14
consequence(s), outcomes 187–89, 192; nn. 934, 936, 968
Constantinople, first Council of n. 185
consternation (*ekplêxis*) 142
constitution 200
contemplation, contemplatives 41, 64, 134, 135, 136, 137, 139, 140, 202, 212; nn. 42, 313
contingency 15, 182–84, 186, 192–93, 195; nn. 162, 913, 915–15
contraries 93, 96
contraries 63 *and see* opposites
co-operation 44
copulation 156, 207
corals 38
corporeal 72
corpse 55

GENERAL INDEX

corruption 217
counterfactual 14
country 219
cowards 64
cowherds 207
crab 56, 90; n. 275
craft(s), craftsman 44, 50, 198, 207, 217; nn. 961–62 *and see* art, skill
Craftsman (divine) 13, 75; n. 1040 *and see* Demiurge
Cratippus nn. 388, 587, 588
crayfish 56, 90
creation 3, 16, 69–70, 75, 98, 202, 206–07; nn. 332, 336, 977, 997–98, 1012, 1029
creator, maker 37–38, 40, 93, 94, 98, 110, 113, 159, 160, 165, 168, 184, 192, 208, 211, 217–18; nn. 237, 1040
Cretans 197
Critias 52; nn. 254, 274
crocodile 58
Cronius 73
crops 47–48, 50; n. 237
cross, the 219
crown, of victory 219
crows 40, 208
cube 96
cure 133–34; pleasure as 135, 136
cuttlefish 56; n. 275
Cyril of Alexandria 6; n. 174
Cyzicus n. 332

daimones n. 980 *and see* demons
Daniel 49
date of treatise 2
dates 115
David 71; n. 344
days 205
dead bodies n. 1040
death(s) 37, 41, 45, 59, 220; nn. 214, 229, 1023
decay 195

decision 185
deer 47, 90
defined 214
deliberation, deliberative 118, 176–83, 196–97, 201; nn. 871, 898, 903, 905–06, 909, 911, 954, 961
Demiurge 73; n. 351 *and see* Craftsman
Democritus 3, 11, 51–52, 155, 211; nn. 254, 520, 522
demons 44, 46 *and see daimones*
density 96–97
depending on us n. 934 *and see* up to us
desertion n. 934
desire(s) 37, 62, 129, 132, 175, 177, 189–90, 200; nn. 192, 202, 881, 891, 895; part of the soul 10, 128, 132–34
despondency n. 661
determinism 14, 29; nn. 81, 161–162, 918, 920–22, 934
diagonal 180
diaphragm 162; n. 813
Dicaearchus nn. 258, 262, 324, 369, 388, 587, 588
diet n. 657
difference 207, 218
digestion 11, 165–66, 175; nn. 223, 869
Dinarchus 53, 59; nn. 258, 262, 592
Diocles of Carystus n. 505
Diogenes of Apollonia 11
Diomedes n. 874
Dionysius 170; n. 874
disabled 204
discursive reasoning 83
disease 63–64; nn. 307, 657
disharmony n. 297
disposition(s) 57, 74–75, 138, 196, 200, 203–04; nn. 981–82, 1018
dissolution n. 1040
distress 132, 136, 140, 169, 171–73, 175
divination 118

divine 206, 217; n. 1018 *and see* God, god(s); divine intellect nn. 318, 405
dogs 113
doves 47, 157
doxography 89; nn. 252, 488, 518
dreams 81, 118, 124, 153, 206; n. 248
drink 43–44, 173
drought 180–81
drugs 134; nn. 303, 657; fourfold (*tetrapharmakos*) 95
dry 53, 63, 92–93, 199; nn. 302, 307
dualism, of soul and body n. 50
ductus deferens n. 783

eagle(s) 47, 56; n. 363
ears 110, 116, 146; veins behind 154, n. 144
earth, earthy 40, 43, 50, 72, 88, 92–99, 102, 179, 202, 210; nn. 220, 416, 934, 1004, 1027, 1040
education n. 657
eels n. 203
Egypt, Egyptians 186, 204; n. 924
elements 37, 42–43, 53, 61, 67, 71–72, 78, 87–88, 91–99; nn. 298, 325
Elijah 193; n. 944
embryo 156
embryology n. 543
embryonic development n. 853
Emesa 2
emotion(s) 11, 49, 172, 175; n. 192 *and see* affections, feelings
Empedocles nn. 416, 734, 520
encouragement 197
end 177, 182
endurance 219
enemies 180, 207, 221
enjoyment 49, 172
enkranis 121
Enoch n. 944
ensiform 145
envy (*phthonos*) 140
Epictetus nn. 97, 930

Epicurus 3, 51, 105, 137, 211; n. 520
epididymis n. 780
epigastric muscles n. 813
epiphanies, divine 206
equal possibility 182–83, 197–98; n. 912
equilibrium 43
Erasistratus 11, 24; nn. 428, 505, 731, 766, 798
error, sensory 113
eternal, eternity 178, 180, 185, 192, 198; n. 898
Ethiopians 171; n. 879
Eunomians 85; n. 411
Eunomius 2, 6, 14, 69; nn. 2, 4, 48, 145, 336, 410
Euripides 212
Eusebius 12, 13; n. 492
evacuation 42
evil(s) 41, 132, 140, 184, 195, 200–03, 214, 219–20; n. 1054; evildoers 206
excellence 138
excretion 146, 160, 165
executioner 220
exercise 134
expiation 186, 187
external goods 214; n. 1032
eyes 64–65, 105, 106, 146; nn. 314, 410

face n. 307
faculties, of soul 99
fall nn. 415, 980; Fall, the 8, 42, 45; nn. 218, 230
Fallopian tubes n. 794
farming 46, 49
fat 38, 90; perception of 112
fate, fated 3, 15–16, 27, 29–30, 73, 183–92, 194, 197, 204, 210–13; nn. 9–10, 81–82, 167–68, 893, 924, 926–27, 929, 932–34, 949, 964, 991, 1007, 1027
fathers 207

GENERAL INDEX 261

fault 219
fear(s) 58, 142, 217, 219; of God, 206
feeding 43
feelings 57 *and see* affections, emotions
feet 159, 161
female 157
fertility nn. 144, 779
fetal membrane 156
fibres 89, 90, 159
figs 115
figures (geometrical) 58
filter-paper n. 379
final cause n. 832
fingers 74, 113, 167
fire 43, 52, 63, 82, 88, 92–99, 185–86; nn. 416, 254, 256, 392
fish 43, 47, 56, 90
fitness n. 307
flame n. 392
flavour 102, 115
flesh 43, 63, 80, 89, 90, 159, 167
flocks 217
Flood, the n. 218
flux 42
flying 197
fodder 46
food 41–44, 46–47, 56, 80, 147, 175, 212; food-chain 47–48
foolish 189
foot 90
force 169–70, 172, 174; forced movement 67
forecasting, foretelling 50; n. 388
foreknowledge 17, 29, 206
forethought n. 1027
forgetting 120–21
form(s) 64–66, 68, 72, 210; nn. 261, 263, 311, 313; Platonic Forms, 3, 121; n. 1005
fortuitous goods 199
fourfold drug (*tetrapharmakos*) 95
free, freedom, free will 183–85, 211;

nn. 10, 82, 93, 161, 365, 921, 964, 1007
friendly 207
fruits 42–43, 47
future 215; n. 1054

Galen 1, 5, 8, 10, 11, 12, 13–4, 20–21, 23–25, 61, 76, 105, 143; nn. 77, 113, 122, 206, 226, 233, 298–300, 303, 305, 367, 417, 422, 433, 446, 457, 493, 518, 532, 543, 607, 722, 731, 786, 830; works, *On Demonstration* 12, 24, 143; nn. 299, 499, 518; *On Semen* 13; nn. 140, 776, 782; *On the Doctrines of Hippocrates and Plato* 10, 12; n. 417; *On the Natural Faculties* 13; nn. 140, 419, 732; *On the Usefulness of the Parts* 9, 12; nn. 77, 136, 137, 140, 732, 994; *On the Usefulness of Respiration* 13; n. 140; *On the Voice* n. 614; *That the Faculties of the Soul Follow the Mixtures of the Body* 12, 21; nn. 300, 659, 969; *On Mixtures* 12; nn. 222, 417, 456; *On Simple Medicines* 12; *On the Elements according to Hippocrates* 13; nn. 222, 417, 447, 456; *On the Affected Parts* 13; *On the Movement of the Muscles* 13; *On Hippocrates' On the Nature of Man* nn. 417, 419; *On Hippocrates' On Nutriment* n. 421
gall bladder n. 737
garment 80
genera, generic 193, 210; n. 1005
generation 37, 145, 153 *and see* coming-to-be
generative faculty of the soul 126
Genesis, book of 21; nn. 10, 336
Genii n. 1004
geometricians 104
Georgian version 2, 4

Gibeon n. 943
giving 198
glands 89, 167
glass, vision through 108
glory 219
glottis 125
goats 43, 47, 168
God 16, 31, 40–41, 45, 50, 68, 71, 74, 83–85, 98, 136, 139, 140, 180, 184, 187, 192–95, 199, 201–06, 208–10, 213–15, 217–20; nn. 81, 180, 214–15, 336, 345, 401, 414, 909, 949, 1046; in Plato 97
god(s) 186–87, 191–93, 197, 210–13; nn. 191, 232, 351, 398, 934, 1004–05, 1020–21
gold 56
good 60–61, 66, 69, 132, 140, 199, 214, 220; good works 206
goods 37, 41, 210, 214, 221
governance 217
grace 7, 42, 45, 86; n. 37
greedy 73
Gregory of Nazianzus 2
Gregory of Nyssa 2, 4, 12; n. 37; *On the Creation of Man* n. 10
grey hair 180–81, 183; n. 909
grief (*akhthos*) 140
grievance (*mênis*) 141
growth 37, 66, 72, 158, 175, 195
grubs n. 220
guardians 210, 218; nn. 1004, 1021
gullet 147
gymnastics n. 911

habit(s) 15, 57, 133, 175, 204
hail 180–182
hair 38, 43, 89, 111, 167, *and see* grey hair
hand 74, 90, 113, 159, 161; nn. 250, 307
happiness 138, 214; n. 1033
hare(s) 43, 47, 75

harmful 212
harmonic 52; n. 260
harmony nn. 262, 307 *and see* attunement
harshness, perception of 115
hate 169, 175
head 90, 154; as acropolis 22; head to heels, structure of medical discussions n. 131
healing n. 223
health, healthy 63–64, 66, 137, 177, 199, 212, 214; n. 307
heap 214
hearing 9, 102, 108, 114, 116, 139
heart 23, 56, 129, 131, 141, 146, 150; n. 852
heartbeat n. 731
heat 63; innate n. 761; natural 163
heaven(s), heavenly 40–41, 48, 50–51, 67, 72; nn. 168, 210, 251, 934, 1004, 1006, 1027; heavenly beings, bodies 71; n. 950
heaviness 67
Hebrews 18, 41, 46, 98, 118; nn. 118, 214, 233; *and see* Jews
Helen n. 929
hens 157
Heliodorus, on Aristotle's *Nicomachean Ethics* 27
Heraclitus 3, 52, 99, 211; n. 1012
Herophilus nn. 766, 831
hesitation (*oknos*) 142
heterogeneous parts 12, 88–90
Hipparchus of Nicaea 104
Hipparchus of Pontus 99
Hippasus of Croton n. 492
Hippo 52
Hippocrates, 24, 61, 88, 98, 145; nn. 424, 427, 609
Hippocratic writings: *Epidemics* 2; n. 727; *On the Nature of Man* 11; n. 417; *On Fleshes* 11; *On Places in Man* 11

GENERAL INDEX

hips 159
holy men 220
homogeneous parts 12, 56, 88–90
horns 111; of the uterus 156
horses 39, 167; n. 1038
hot 53, 92–93; nn. 302, 957
house, housing 43–44
household gods n. 1004
human beings, as distinct from animals: 90, 98–99, 110, 113, 116, 139, 157, 159, 167, 168
humours 12, n. 273; theory of four 87–88
hungry 197; n. 957

Iamblichus 6, 8, 19–20, 73; nn. 110, 184, 357, 360, 924
Ibycus 205
icosahedron 96
ignorance 69, 133, 169, 172–74, 215, 218, 220; nn. 885, 890
illness, mental n. 657
ill-temper 64
illumination n. 401
illusion, sensory 109, 113
images 100, 218
imagination 9–10, 25, 66, 100–03, 121, 218; n. 318
imitative birds 49
immaterial 202; nn. 383, 977
immortal, immortality 5, 8, 41–42, 44–46, 50, 72, 77, 80, 177, 214; nn. 193, 214, 227, 288, 319, 351, 371, 1032
imperishability n. 371
impossible 182, 183; n. 915
imprints (*tupoi*) 120
impulse 37, 117, 153, 170, 175, 185–186, 191, 199; nn. 873, 903, 960; movement according to 9, 11, 103, 128, 158
inanimate 37–38, 47, 62, 71–72, 186, 195

incarnation 5, 32, 78, 204; nn. 230, 392, 407–08, 410
inclination 40; nn. 210, 214
incorporeal 37, 55, 57–59, 66, 69, 76, 82, 86, 202; nn. 266, 280, 383, 392, 401, 1040
individual(s) 17, 208–10, 214–15, 217–18; n. 168, 1023 *and see* particulars
initiating cause n. 871
injustice 206, 213
innate ideas n. 599
innumerable 218
inquiry 179
insects 56; n. 274
insensitive 38
instrument (*organon*) 9, 76, 80, 138; n. 410; body as i. for soul 99; instrumental goods 199, 210
insubstantial 59
intellect, intellectual 35–37, 40, 45–46, 78, 83, 197, 201, 212; nn. 184–88, 318, 373, 400, 1005
intelligence 212–213; nn. 807, 903
intelligible 21, 35, 40, 63, 68–69, 72, 80–82, 84; nn. 260, 388
intentional, intended 168–71, 173–76, 197, 200, 220; nn. 868–69, 891, 894
intercostal muscles 124
intestines 56, 147, 162
intuition 120
invisible n. 1040
involuntary 29; n. 868
Iohannes Cono 4
iron 38, 62, 79; nn. 198, 392
irrational 40; n. 1019
Italy n. 993

jaw 58
jellyfish n. 199
Jewish exegesis n. 588
Jews 204; n. 990 *and see* Hebrews
Job 98, 199, 219

John of Damascus, *On the Orthodox Faith* 4
Joseph 171; nn. 871, 878
joy 136, 211
judgement 67, 117, 191, 199; n. 964
juice, transformation of food into (*khulôsis*) 148
just, justice 45, 213, 218, 220
juxtaposition 79–80; nn. 286, 379, 383

kakhexia n. 657
kardia 145
khorion n. 793
khulôsis 148
kidneys 56, 147, 166
killing 204
kindred 219
kinds, natural nn. 1004, 1006
knees 159
knowledge 45–46, 64, 69, 215; nn. 232, 313; tree of knowledge, 42

Lacedaemonians 197
Lachesis n. 934
Laius n. 929
Laodicea 35; n. 2
Laplace n. 922
lark (bird) 43
larynx 124; n. 843
Latin version 2, 4; n. 362
laughter 45
law(s), lawful 184, 190–91, 193, 197, 207, 213, 215; nn. 922, 934, 936, 1004
lawgivers 217
Lazarus 219
leaders 217
lean, perception of 112
learning 44, 46, 60, 74, 196, 204; n. 955
legs 159
lewdness 64, 155
licentious, licentiousness 172, 203

life 53, 65, 66, 72, 80, 81; nn. 191, 350, 1023, 1054; way of life 62, 208
ligament 89, 90, 111, 158
ligature of windpipe 164
light 102, 105; light analogy 5, 8, 18, 71–72, 82; nn. 392, 394, 401, 1040
lightness 67
limbs 63, 90; n. 307
line 59; n. 280
lion 47, 49, 62, 73, 168; n. 354
liquid, perception of 112; quality of 88
liver 56, 129, 147–49, 162, 164, 166; n. 852
lobsters 56; n. 275
localisation of cognitive functions 25; in the brain n. 607
locomotive part of the soul 10
love, divine 204
Lucian 12
luck 194–95; n. 949 *and see* chance
Lucretius 11
lung 56, 90, 124, 164; n. 307
lust 199
luxuriousness 199–200
lying 198, 203; n. 981
lyre, lyre-playing 60, 64, 186; n. 955

magnet 38; nn. 197–98
maker *see* creator
mania 101, n. 657
Manichaeans 6, 53, 71; nn. 114, 264, 345
marrow 89
martyrs, martyrdom 172, 219
masters 219
material goods 210; n. 1033
mathematics 179
matter, material 54–55, 64, 66, 71, 98, 100, 200–02; nn. 268, 314, 345
Maximus Confessor 4; n. 18
mean 175; doctrine of n. 702
meat 42; n. 218

GENERAL INDEX

medicine 3, 23, 43–44, 49, 63, 181; n. 911
meeting 176; n. 894
melancholics 101, n. 657, n. 659
Meletius 4
membranes 89; cerebral 89
memory 9–10, 25, 107, 113, 118–23; n. 514
Menander 212
mental illness n. 657
mercy, merciful 45
metals n. 303
meteorological phenomena n. 915
Michael Glycas 4
microcosm 50; n. 246
Middle Platonism, Middle Platonists 6, 15, 17, 19–20, 27, 30–31; nn. 81, 114, 161, 277, 350, 376, 913, 916, 929, 932, 934, 936, 1004, 1027
milk 153
mind nn. 214, 398, 1020–21
mirrors 109
Mithridates n. 242
mixed actions 170; nn. 870, 876–77
mixed faculties 162
mixture 12, 13, 14, 61–64, 76, 79–80, 82, 84; nn. 302, 372, 376, 378–79, 383, 408, 659 *and see* blending
modesty (*aidôs*) 142
moist 52–53, 63; nn. 302, 307
money, money-making 214; n. 911
monism 98
monkeys n. 240
monsters, sea- 50
moon 67, 193
mortal 8, 41, 44, 46, 50, 61, 69, 193, 218; nn. 193, 214, 333, 351, 1004, 1006
Moses 40, 69–70, 98
most part, for 180–81, 183; nn. 909, 916
mother 199, 207
motion, movement, moving 37, 55, 66–68, 185, 197–98; nn. 323–24, 950; perception of 107; quality of 96–97
mouth 125, 146, 147, 152, 165
movement 151; according to impulse 9, 103, 158
mud n. 1040
murder, murderer 205–06, 212–13, 215, 220; n. 1024
muscles 114, 158, 161, 163, n. 814
musician 64

nails 89, 111, 167
natural endowment n. 657
nature, natural (*phusikos*) 75–76, 86, 180–81, 185–86, 194–95, 197–98, 200, 203–04, 211–13, 217; nn. 102, 413, 909, 954, 956, 988, 1018–19, 1027; natural condition n. 223; natural goods 210; natural motions, movement 67; n. 325; nature does not make jumps nn. 194, 241; functions 11, 131; vs. vital (*zôtikos*) n. 731; vs. psychic 11; nn. 759, 103, 163; vs. psychic and vital 157
navigation 181; n. 911
Nearchus n. 874
necessary, necessity, necessitation 16–17, 180, 182, 185–87, 189, 192–95, 198, 200, 210–11, 217; nn. 915, 919, 922, 927, 932, 934, 949, 964, 968, 991, 1007
neck n. 307
needs 45
Nemesis 190; n. 934
Neoplatonism, Neoplatonists 5–6, 14; nn. 50, 127, 187, 232, 277, 350, 916, 970, 977, 1007, 1040
Neopythagorean 18
nerve 10, 38, 89, 90, 101, 114, 115, 158; n. 223; returning 124; sensory 110, 160; soft 116; optic 106, 112, 151–52
Nestorius 6; nn. 4, 401, 414

266 GENERAL INDEX

Nicander n. 727
Nicasius Ellebodius 4
Nicocreon 170
nights 205
Nilus Doxopatres 4
non-being n. 345
non-Christians n. 1047
non-rational 48–50, 69, 73–76, 176–77, 186, 195
non-rational part of soul 11, 127, 150
nose 110, 125, 152, 165; runny 102
nostrils 116, 146
not intentional 172–73
nourishment 55, 66, 72, 158
number 52, 58, 68–69, 107, 113; n. 260
Numenius 18, 54; nn. 105, 265–66, 319, 355, 588, 631
nutrition 11, 145; four faculties of 145
nutritive part of the soul 10, 125, 127
nymphs 46; n. 232

observation n. 1006
octahedron 96
odour n. 1040
Oedipus n. 929
offspring 208
oil 43
oiliness, perception of 115
old, growing n. 915
Olympiodorus 27
omens 208
omnipotence 17; n. 180
omniscience n. 180
opinion 67
opposite, opposites 60, 66, 93, 96, 182–83, 199, 203; nn. 296–97, 887, 915, 959, 971, 981
opsis n. 519
optics n. 519
oracles 192
order 16–17, 205; nn. 991, 1004, 1006
ordering, organisation of Nemesius' material 20, 32

organic, different name for heterogeneous 90
organs 85–86
Oribasius 24, 25; nn. 614, 776
Origen (the pagan Neoplatonist) 18
Origen (the Christian) 1–2, 6, 9, 12, 18, 21, 86, 119, 171; nn. 4, 105, 207, 214, 230, 233, 237, 245, 360, 413, 588, 589, 592, 871, 879, 998; *Commentary on Genesis* [not extant] 18; nn. 214, 237, 998
origin, of action 169, 172, 174–75, 195, 197; n. 881
outcomes *see* consequences
oxen 43, 46, 207
oysters 43

paganism, pagan(s) 1, 5, 7, 17, 31, 85, 188, 205, 208, 218; nn. 918, 947, 979, 1030, 1032, 1040
pain 44, 59, 98, 129; nn. 223, 957
painters 109, 207
palate 115, 125
palpitation 131
Panaetius 9, 10, 126–27; n. 278
papyrus 80, n. 378
pardon 44–45, 169; n. 227
parents 57, 200, 208, 219; nn. 278–79, 336
Paris n. 929
part 217
particular 31, 57, 173–75, 178, 199, 209, 211, 213, 215, 217–18; nn. 899, 1030, 1038
partridge 43, 47, 56
passages (*poroi*) 89
Paul 40, 49, 219
pebbles 79
Pelagian, Pelagianism 7; nn. 38, 1022
penis n. 783
perceptible, perceptual 35, 37, 72
perfection 42
Peripatetic(s) 31; nn. 161–62, 684, 735,

GENERAL INDEX

915–16, 1023, 1030
perishing 95
permanence 205; nn. 1004, 1006
persuasion n. 957
perverted 206
pharynx n. 843
Philo of Alexandria 18, 21; nn. 105, 118, 214, 233, 588, 589, 731; works, *On the Creation of the World* 18; *On Dreams* n. 589
Philopator 29–30, 185–86; n. 165
Philoponus 12, 13; nn. 492, 592
phlebotomy 89
phlegm 56, 87–89
phrenitis 122; nn. 607, 609
physical training 181
physicians 145, 217
physiology, elementary n. 417; Galenic 10
piety 37, 41, 50, 184
pigeon 43
pigs 47; n. 793
pipe 186
pity (*eleos*) 140, 169
place 72, 82–84; n. 404; perception of 107, 112
placenta n. 793
plan 178
planets 193
plants 37–39, 42, 47, 72–73, 148, 184, 195, 198, 200, 210; nn. 202, 236, 962
Plato, Platonism, Platonists 1, 3, 5–9, 10, 16–17, 20, 25, 27–28, 31, 35, 52, 57, 60–61, 69, 72–74, 77, 80, 95–97, 103, 105, 117, 120, 136, 190, 192–93, 209–10; nn. 82, 154, 161–62, 192, 202, 258, 263, 298, 324, 333, 336, 400, 416, 584, 592, 636, 657, 881, 915, 929, 932–33, 952, 968, 1005, 1007, 1027, 1032, 1040, *and see* Middle Platonism, Neoplatonism; Plato, works:

Phaedo 8; *Timaeus* 13; nn. 105, 208, 417; *Philebus* n. 673
pleasure 40, 45, 132, 134–39, 169, 175, 196; nn. 955, 1018
plenitude, principle of n. 241
Plotinus 7, 18, 35, 54, 80; nn. 184, 345, 592
Plutarch 12, 19, n. 457; pseudo-Plutarch 19, 27–28, 31; nn. 252, 254, 949
pneuma 24; nn. 266, 350, 760, 784; intellective 103; optic 105; psychic 10, 101, 112, 118, 121, 163; nn. 544, 731, 776, 798; vital n. 731 *and see* breath
pneumatic 150
point n. 280
pointless n. 954
poisons, poisoning 49; n. 869
pollution 8, 217; n. 1040
poor 199
Porphyry 1, 6, 18–20, 24, 29–30, 73, 84–85, 106; nn. 105, 110, 113–14, 167–68, 184, 284, 297, 305, 324, 326, 345, 347, 353–54, 357, 372, 376, 390, 488, 518, 592
portents 208
Posidonius 10, 21–23, 24; nn. 127, 134, 202, 206, 280, 363, 621
Posidonius of Byzantium 25, n. 607
possible, possibility 27, 182; nn. 157, 913, 915
potency, potentiality 15, 64, 66, 94; n. 971
poverty 200, 214–15; n. 897
power 85, 182, 199, 203–4, 214, 217, 219; nn. 157, 902, 913, 981, 1022
practical 201–02, 213; practical wisdom *see* sagacity
practice 196; 203
praise 169, 171, 175, 184, 197; n. 934
Praxagoras, on veins and arteries n. 766
prayer 16–17, 51, 184, 186–87, 192, 206, 217; nn. 924, 927, 942

precincts 206
predictions 206
pregnancy 157
preservation 213, 217; preservation of kinds, species 215; nn. 1004, 1006, 1029, 1038
prevention 182; n. 915
principle (*arkhê*) 92; n. 962 *and see* origin
Priscian of Lydia 18
prisoners 221
Proclus 30
Prodicus 11
production 198; productive cause 170
prohêgoumenos n. 937
prophecy, prophets 186, 192, 204, 206, 208; nn. 248, 925
proportion n. 307
prostitute 172
proud 73
providence 3, 8, 16–17, 27, 31–32, 50, 70–71, 93, 184, 191–92, 195, 199–200, 204–20; nn. 9–10, 102, 151, 168, 181, 237, 919, 932, 968, 991, 996, 998, 1004–07, 1012, 1022, 1025, 1030, 1034
prudence *see* sagacity
psychic (*psukhikos*), functions 11
psychic vs. natural n. 759
psychic, vs. natural and vital 157
pulsation 11, 131, 145, 150, 158
pulse lore 24
pungency, perception of 115
punishment 76, 169, 184, 213, 218; nn. 1024, 1043
purification, of blood 166
putrefaction 70
pyramid, shape of 96
Pythagoras, Pythagorean 16, 52, 54, 68, 118; nn. 258, 329, 588, 946; *and see* Neopythagorean

quality elementary 12, 54–55, 58–59, 61–64, 68–69, 76–77, 92–3, 210; nn. 222, 263, 277, 280, 297, 311
quantity 54–55, 58, 68, 77, 210
Quellenforschung 23; n. 417

race, for virtue 219
rain 48, 180–81, 183; n. 915
raisins 115
rarity 96–97
ratio 58
rational, rationality, rational soul 10, 16, 35, 37–41, 44–46, 48–50, 61, 65, 72–74, 126, 127, 200–02; nn. 191, 318, 971, 1005
ray, visual 104, 106
reason 9–10, 22, 37, 40, 45, 64, 67, 76, 103, 142, 175, 189, 198, 201; nn. 186, 192–93, 202, 304, 318, 365, 971, 979 *and see* right reason; immanent and expressed 10, 123–25, n. 584; disturbance of 121–22; capable of being obedient to n. 621
recognition 207–08
recollection 60, 120; n. 336
recreation 49
recurrence, eternal 16, 193; n. 947
Reggio di Calabria n. 993
regime 200, n. 657, n. 659
regress arguments n. 268
regret 136, 173
reincarnation 72
rejoicing 198
relation 6, 83–84; nn. 401, 406
remedies 49, 206, 212; n. 363
repentance 6, 44–45; n. 230
reporting, of sensations to brain 112, 115
reproduction 11, n. 495; theory of 24
reproductive part of the soul n. 621
reputation 214
resemblance n. 278
residues, in body n. 813

GENERAL INDEX

resistance n. 269
resourcefulness 75
respiration 11, 161–64
responsibility 7, 14, 16, 29–30, 192; nn. 37, 81 *and see* depending on us, up to us
rest, perception of 107
restorative pleasure n. 671; 137
resurrection 70, 194
retention, faculty of 145
retribution 205, 212
reverence 206
reward 206
rhetoricians 173
rheum 146
rich 177, 182, 199, 212, 219; n. 1023
right and left 161
right reason 208, 213
righteous, righteousness 199, 219
rising (of heavenly bodies) 180; n. 915
robbery 207, 215, 220
Rome 83
rooks 208
roughness, perception of 107, 112
rule, rulers 199, 217
ruling part of the soul 115, 126, n. 722

sacrifice 186, 199; n. 359
sadness n. 661
sagacity 201; n. 973
sailing, sailors 170, 192
saints, saintly 219–20
saltiness, perception of 115
salvation 7, 219; nn. 37, 229
sand 218
Satan 6; nn. 230, 980
sausage-like membrane 156
scales 43
scholastic nn. 871, 906, 913
sciences 44–46, 50, 118, 179–81; n. 911
scriptures 193, 198, 205, 207, 215
scrotum 154
Scythians 180; n. 910

sea 50, 193, 218; sea creatures 56; n. 274; sea-anemones n. 199
seasons 48, 62, 205
seaweed 47
seed 43, 88, 153, 165, 207
selection 176, 178
self n. 80; self-awareness 42; self-changing 68; self-control 177, 189–90, 196; nn. 896, 955; self-indulgence 73; self-motion, self-moving 52, 66–68; nn. 260, 324–25, 889
sensation, senses, sensitivity, sensible objects 9–10, 22, 37–39, 44, 72, 85, 102, 111–12, 151; nn. 132, 191, 196, 223, 318, 410, 412, 812
sense organs 10, 90, 102, 110
sensitive part of the soul 10, 126
separation 59, 62, 145
serpent n. 220
servants 215
service to gods 187
setting (of heavenly bodies) 180; n. 915
sexual activity 133, 134, 135, 153, 166; nn. 495, 790
sexual desire 153; nn. 621, 661
shame, shameful 58, 142, 171
shape 64; n. 280; perception of 107, 112
sharpness 96–97; perception of 107, 112, 115
sheep 43, 47, 62, 168
shelled animals 90
shellfish 56
shells 39, 43; n. 200
shelter 46
shepherds 207
shipwreck 192
shock (*akhos*) 140
sight 65–66, 102, 104–09, 139; nn. 314, 410
silver 56
similarity 57–58; nn. 278–79

GENERAL INDEX

sin 41, 45, 49, 72, 199, 205, 218, 220; nn. 215, 415
sinews 63; n. 307
sinewy fibres 159
sisters 207
size, perception of 107
skills 45–46, 74–75, 118, 180–81, 187, 195, 212, 217; n. 363; *and see* art, craft
skin 43, 114, 146, 167
slackening 62
sleep 64, 81, 162; nn. 386, 388, 587, 830
smell 9, 102, 108, 114, 116–17, 139, 165
smoky element, in digestion 152
smoothness, perception of 107, 112
snake 43, 90, 110; n. 363
society 207
Socrates 193, 220; nn. 1038, 1054
Socratic paradox n. 82
solid, quality of 88
Solomon 71; n. 344
solstices 180
Son of Man 219
sons 207
sooty element, in digestion 152
Soranus 20; n. 277
soul 1, 5–9, 16, 18–20, 23, 31–32, 35–37, 41–42, 44–45, 48, 51–86, 178, 184, 197–98, 200, 214, 217; nn. 31, 113–14, 117–18, 184–85, 187, 189, 191, 202, 227, 234, 252–54, 260, 263, 266, 270, 272, 277–79, 286, 288, 297–98, 304, 307, 313, 315–16, 318–20, 324, 332–33, 336, 345, 350–51, 357, 360, 369, 372, 376, 378, 383, 392, 394, 398, 400, 404, 406–07, 410, 412–13, 934, 940, 1005–06, 1027, 1032, 1043; soul of universe/ world-soul 52, 71–73, 190–91; nn. 208, 269, 934, 1027; as opposed to nature 11; coming into being of 95; division of 125; faculties of 9–12, 99
soul, of the (*psukhikos*) 159–61
sound 102, 116; production of n. 614
sources, Nemesius' n. 457; Nemesius' use of n. 663
species 208, 210, 215; n. 1029
speech 40, 158, 164, 124–25, 126; nn. 612, 812
spermatic duct n. 780
spinal cord 158, 160, 161, 167
spirit 6, 37, 50, 129, 132, 210; nn. 185, 373, 980
spirit(ed part of soul) 10, 48, 128, 167; n. 202
spleen 149, 162, 166
sponge 39; n. 201; oiled sponge 80; nn. 378–79
spongiform bone 165
spontaneity 194–95; n. 949
squid 56
stars 48, 50, 183–84, 186–87, 192–93, 205, 210; n. 927
state, *hexis* n. 350
stationariness 96–97
stealers 221
sternum 145
Stobaeus, John 19; nn. 252, 254, 258, 261
stochastic arts, skills 181; n. 911
Stoics, Stoicism 10, 11, 16, 20, 28–29, 51, 54, 69, 97, 100, 183, 185, 187, 189, 193, 211; nn. 82, 114, 186, 195, 236–37, 266, 269, 277, 280, 350, 392, 457, 503, 511, 586, 603, 620, 634, 654, 656, 657, 675, 676, 698, 719, 722, 723, 873, 889, 915, 922–23, 929–30, 932–33, 938, 946, 949, 978, 1010, 1030, 1032
stomach 56, 147
stone 62, 184; n. 350
storm 170

GENERAL INDEX   271

stranger 207
Strato 11
strength 63, 199; n. 307
structure of Nemesius' treatise 3
studies 55
sublunary n. 1027
substance 52–54, 60, 68–69, 71–72, 76–78, 85–86, 182, 190, 210; nn. 260, 263, 277, 296–97, 345, 934
substrate 60–62, 64–65, 77; nn. 288, 297
suffering 219
sulphur 94
sun 8, 67, 81–82, 179, 193, 210; nn. 392, 394, 1040; sunrise 180; n. 954; sunset 180; n. 915
supervenience 112
surface n. 280
Susanna 171, 205; nn. 871, 878
sweat 146
sweetness, perception of 115
swimmers (kind of fish) 90
symmetry 63
sympathy 40
Syria 2
Syriac version 2, 4
systematisation n. 949
systolic movement n. 771

tangible objects 112
taste 9, 102, 108, 114–15, 139, 165
taste-qualities 115
teaching, taught 203–04
tears 146
teeth 125, 180
teleology 9, 13, 165–66; nn. 543, 807
telos 138
temperament 21, 199–200; nn. 419, 969
temperate 203
tendon 90, 159
tension 62
terror (*kataplêxis*) 142
Tertullian 20; n. 45

testicles 154, 166; n. 776
tetrapharmakos n. 471
Thales 52, 99; n. 258
Theodore of Mopsuestia 2, 6; nn. 2, 4, 38, 413–14
Theodoret 19; n. 237; *Remedy for Greek Attitudes* 19; nn. 252, 254
Theodorus of Asine 73; n. 356
Theodotus n. 372
Theodotus of Byzantium n. 77
Theophrastus 26; n. 949
theoretical 201, 213
thirsty 197
thorax 124, 161, 163
thought 74, 103, 107; discursive 117; location of 25; role in perception 113
three-dimensional 55; n. 269
throat 164
throwing goods overboard 170
Thucydides 145
thunderbolt 94
toleration n. 1046
tongue 110, 115, 125, 147, 165
tool 37
tooth 89
top-skin 90
tortoises 43
touch 9, 39, 43, 102, 108–11, 114, 139
trachea n. 829
training 204; n. 657
transmigration 8, 19–21, 73–74, 218; nn. 357, 359–60
transparent, in vision 108
treachery n. 934
treasure 176, 180, 195; nn. 868, 894, 952
trees 38
trial 219
triangle, equilateral 96; scalene 96
tripartition of contingent n. 916
trouble 219
true 178; truth about future 30

ugliness n. 307
unalterable, unchangeable nn. 979, 1040
uncompounded 81–82, 84, 86; nn. 386, 389
unconfused 80
uncorrupted n. 389
understanding 75, 103, 179
unification, union 78–81, 84–86; nn. 195, 372, 378, 383, 389, 392, 413–14
unintentional 29, 168, 170–75; nn. 868–71, 885
universal 31, 57, 173, 178, 193, 199, 209–10, 215, 218; nn. 1030, 1038, 1042; universal soul 71
Universe 69–70, 91, 97, 193, 206, 211; nn. 991, 1004
unjust 214, 220–21
unmoved 66–68; n. 324
unnatural 131
unwilling n. 868
up to us 175–82, 184–89, 192, 194, 196–98, 200–01, 203, 212–13, 220; nn. 893, 910, 912, 916, 926, 948–949, 959, 962, 1025 *and see* depending on us, responsibility
upright posture of man 22; n. 238
Uriah 71; n. 344
urinary bladder n. 737
urination 90
urine 146
usefulness, of respiration 163; Galenic term (*khreia*) n. 833
usual nn. 916, 1027 *and see* most part
uvula 125

Valla, Giorgio 4
vapour 52, 102, 116
varicose bundle 154
varicose helper 155
vegetative part of the soul 125, 127
vein 90; hollow 148; pulmonary 164

veins 89, 147, 150–52, 153
venesection 89
ventricle, left of heart n. 768 *see also* cavity
vertebrae 161
vessel 82, behind ear n. 144
vice 16, 203
Vindicianus 11
vindictiveness (*kotos*) 141
violent 214
viper 49
Virgin Mary n. 414
virtue, virtuous 16, 28, 41, 45, 50, 74, 118, 175, 192, 196, 198, 200, 203, 206, 214, 219; n. 1033
visible 21, 40, 69; n. 1040; objects 105–06
vision 9, 104–09; primacy of n. 575
vital (*zôtikos*), functions 11, 150; (*zôtikos*) vs. natural (*phusikos*) n. 731, vs. psychic, and natural 157
voice 39–40, 116, 124, 208
voluntary 3, 14–16, 26; n. 868
vomiting 146
votive offerings 206

waking 64
walking 183, 185
warm 63; n. 307
wasps 56
water 43, 52, 56, 71, 88, 92–99, 184; nn. 378–379, 416, 88; perception of 115; vision through 108
wax, of ears 146
weakness 63; n. 307
wealth 200, 214–15; n. 897
wet 92–93
wetness, perception of 115
whelp 65
whiteness 59
wicked, wickedness 173, 198, 200, 214, 217, 220; n. 885
wilderness 204

will 15–16, 211; will of God, 192, 193, 217
willingly n. 894
windpipe 124, n. 829
wine 43, 79; nn. 378–79
wineskin 82
wings 43
wise, wisdom 201, 215, 220; nn. 1004, 1027
wish 177; nn. 895, 897; of God, 208–10
wolf 47, 73, 75; n. 354
womb 100, 165
women 155–56
wood 62, 79
Word (= Christ) 84, n. 414

world 180, 210; n. 1027
worms 39; n. 203
wrath (*orgê*) 141
writing 50
wrong-doing 213

Xenocrates 55, 68; nn. 258, 271, 329

year 180, 205

Zeno (of Elea) 170; nn. 151, 874
Zeno the Stoic 9, 11, 126; nn. 272, 657, 698, 731
Zeus 197
zodiac 210
zoophytes 39; n. 202